# TEXAS SCIENCE FUSION

fusion [FYOO • zhuhn] a combination of two or more things that releases energy

**This Write-In Student Edition belongs to**

______________________________

**Teacher/Room**

______________________________

# Consulting Authors

**Michael A. DiSpezio**
*Global Educator*
North Falmouth, Massachusetts

**Marjorie Frank**
*Science Writer and Content-Area Reading Specialist*
Brooklyn, New York

**Michael Heithaus**
*Executive Director, School of Environment, Arts, and Society*
*Associate Professor, Department of Biological Sciences*
Florida International University
North Miami, Florida

**Donna Ogle**
*Professor of Reading and Language*
National-Louis University
Chicago, Illinois

**Front Cover:** *crab* ©Mark Webb/Alamy; *geyser* ©Frans Lanting/Corbis; *frog* ©DLILLC/Corbis; *flask* ©Gregor Schuster/Getty Images; *rowers* ©Stockbyte/Getty Images.

**Back Cover:** *gecko* ©Pete Orelup/Getty Images; *bike* ©Jerome Prevost/TempSport/Corbis; *computer* ©Michael Melford/Getty Images; *landscape* ©Rod McLean/Alamy.



Printed in the U.S.A.

ISBN 978-0-544-02551-6

15 16 0607 23 22

4500860071 BCDEFG

# Program Advisors

**Paul D. Asimow**
*Professor of Geology and Geochemistry*
California Institute of Technology
Pasadena, California

**Bobby Jeanpierre**
*Associate Professor of Science Education*
University of Central Florida
Orlando, Florida

**Gerald H. Krockover**
*Professor Emeritus of Earth, Atmospheric, and Planetary Science Education*
Purdue University
West Lafayette, Indiana

**Rose Pringle**
*Associate Professor School of Teaching and Learning*
College of Education
University of Florida
Gainesville, Florida

**Carolyn Staudt**
*Curriculum Designer for Technology*
KidSolve, Inc.
The Concord Consortium
Concord, Massachusetts

**Larry Stookey**
*Science Department*
Antigo High School
Antigo, Wisconsin

**Carol J. Valenta**
*Associate Director of the Museum and Senior Vice President*
Saint Louis Science Center
St. Louis, Missouri

**Barry A. Van Deman**
*President and CEO*
Museum of Life and Science
Durham, North Carolina

# Texas Reviewers

**Max Ceballos**
*District Science Specialist*
Edinburg, Texas

**Tamara L. Cryar**
*Cook Elementary*
Austin, Texas

**Heather Domjan**
*University of Houston*
Houston, Texas

**Ashley D. Golden**
*Washington Elementary*
Big Spring, Texas

**Linda Churchwell Halliman**
*Cornelius Elementary School*
Houston, Texas

**Ellen Lyon**
*Hays Consolidated ISD*
Kyle, Texas

**Stephanie McNeil**
*Bastian Elementary*
Houston, Texas

**Sue Mendoza**
*District Science Coach*
El Paso ISD
El Paso, Texas

**Christine L. Morgan**
*Emerson Elementary*
Midland, Texas

**Genaro Ovalle III**
*Elementary Science Dean*
Laredo ISD
Laredo, Texas

**Hilda Quintanar**
*Science Coach*
El Paso ISD
El Paso, Texas

# Power up with Texas Science Fusion!

Grade 5

Your program fuses . . .

e-Learning & Virtual Labs

Labs & Explorations

Write-In Student Edition

. . . to generate new energy for today's science learner— you.

S.T.E.M.

Engineering & Technology

STEM activities throughout the program!

# Write-In Student Edition

Be an active reader and make this book your own!

Write your ideas, answer questions, make notes, and record activity results right on these pages.

Learn science concepts and skills by interacting with every page.

# e-Learning & Virtual Labs

Digital lessons and virtual labs provide e-learning options for every lesson of *ScienceFusion*.

On your own or with a group, explore science concepts in a digital world.

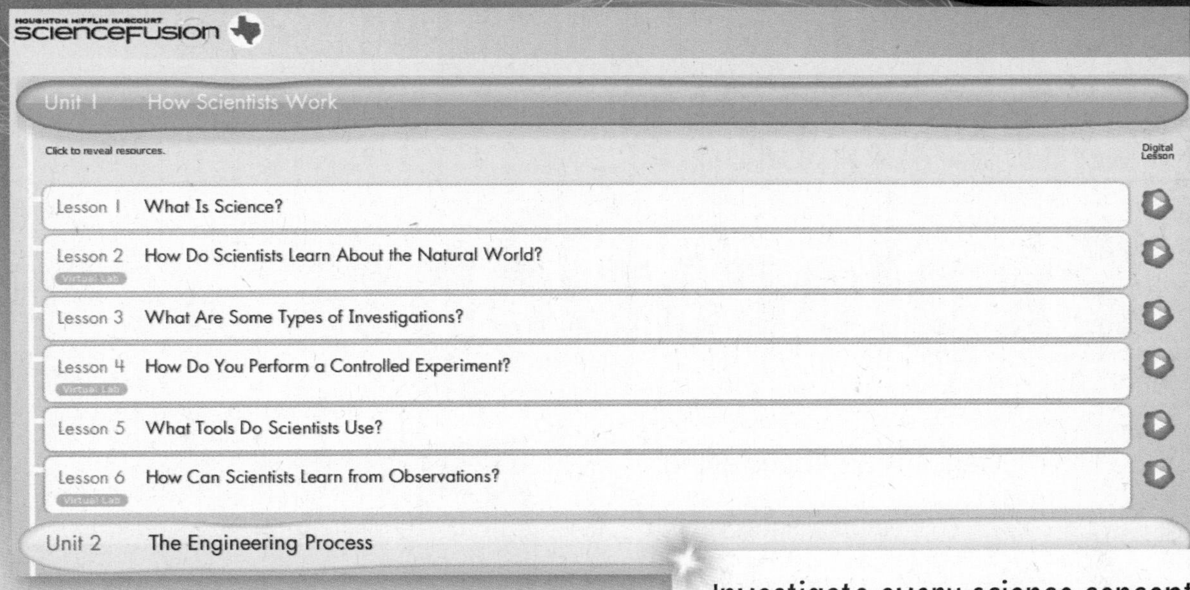


Investigate every science concept with multiple virtual labs in every unit.

## Continue your science explorations with these online tools:

- ScienceSaurus
- NSTA SciLinks
- Video-based Projects
- People in Science
- Media Gallery
- Vocabulary Cards

## Science Readers for Texas with complete AUDIO!

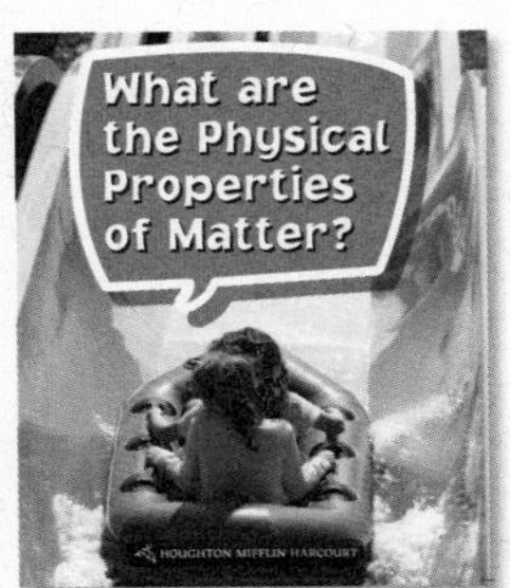

# Labs & Explorations

Science is all about doing.

## How Does Drought Affect Plants?

A drought happens when a place gets much less rainfall than normal. What happens to plants when their environment changes and they do not get the usual amount of water?

**Materials**
5 plastic cups
black marker
125 seeds
potting soil
water
measuring cup

1. Label the cups *A through E.*
2. Fill each cup with moist potting soil. Plant 25 seeds in each cup.
3. Water the cups according to the following schedule:
   - Cup A—50 mL of water each day
   - Cup B—25 mL of water each day
   - Cup C—50 mL of water every other day
   - Cup D—50 mL of water once a week
   - Cup E—no water
4. Make a hypothesis about how the seeds in the different cups will grow
5. Place the cups on a sunny windowsill. Observe the cups for two weeks.

30

Exciting investigations for every lesson.

Ask questions and test your ideas.

Draw conclusions and share what you learn.

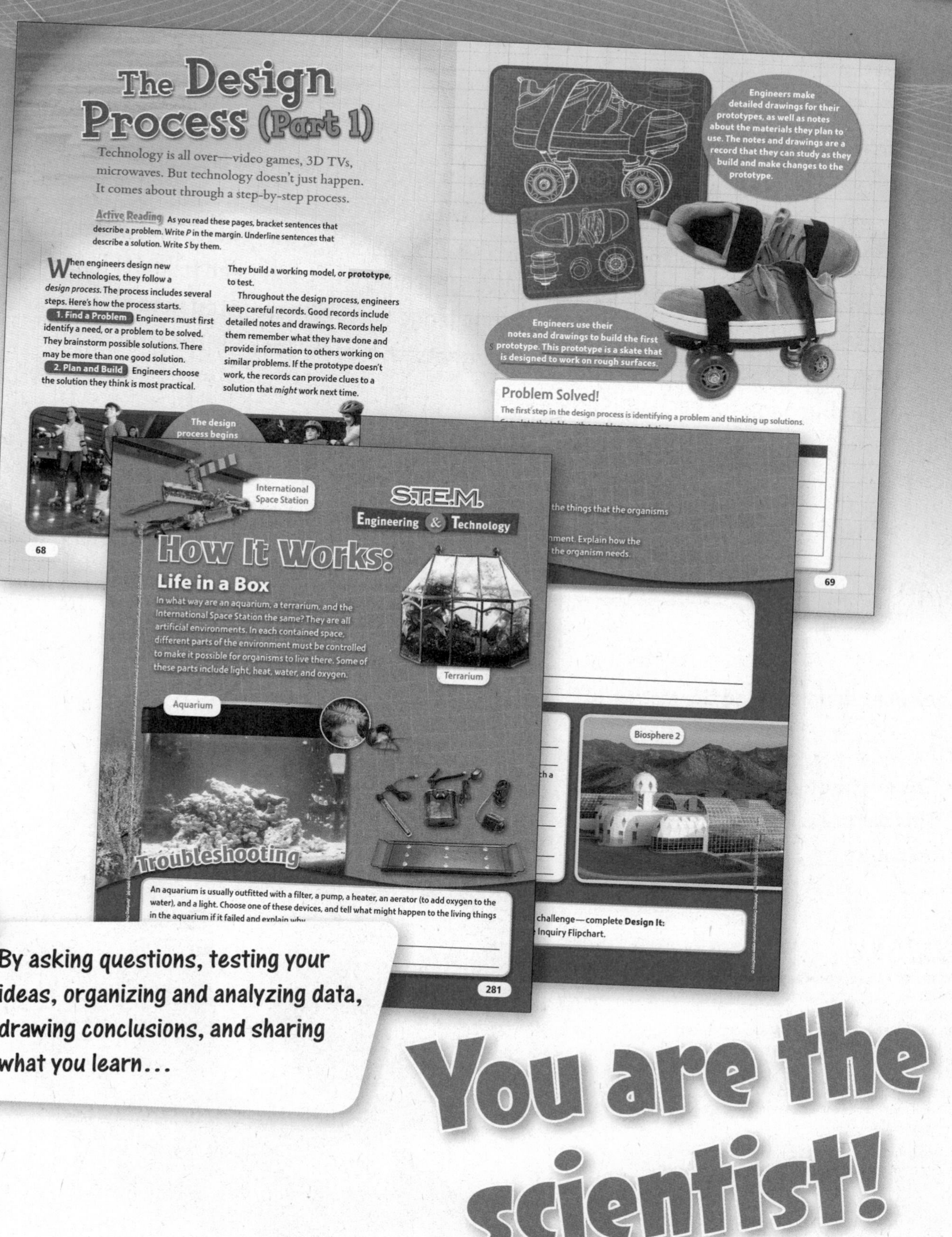

# The Design Process (Part 1)

Technology is all over—video games, 3D TVs, microwaves. But technology doesn't just happen. It comes about through a step-by-step process.

Active Reading As you read these pages, bracket sentences that describe a problem. Write *P* in the margin. Underline sentences that describe a solution. Write *S* by them.

When engineers design new technologies, they follow a *design process*. The process includes several steps. Here's how the process starts.

**1. Find a Problem** Engineers must first identify a need, or a problem to be solved. They brainstorm possible solutions. There may be more than one good solution.

**2. Plan and Build** Engineers choose the solution they think is most practical. They build a working model, or **prototype**, to test.

Throughout the design process, engineers keep careful records. Good records include detailed notes and drawings. Records help them remember what they have done and provide information to others working on similar problems. If the prototype doesn't work, the records can provide clues to a solution that *might* work next time.

The design process begins

68

Engineers make detailed drawings for their prototypes, as well as notes about the materials they plan to use. The notes and drawings are a record that they can study as they build and make changes to the prototype.

Engineers use their notes and drawings to build the first prototype. This prototype is a skate that is designed to work on rough surfaces.

Problem Solved!

The first step in the design process is identifying a problem and thinking up solutions.

69

International Space Station

S.T.E.M. Engineering & Technology

How It Works: Life in a Box

In what way are an aquarium, a terrarium, and the International Space Station the same? They are all artificial environments. In each contained space, different parts of the environment must be controlled to make it possible for organisms to live there. Some of these parts include light, heat, water, and oxygen.

Terrarium

Aquarium

Troubleshooting

An aquarium is usually outfitted with a filter, a pump, a heater, an aerator (to add oxygen to the water), and a light. Choose one of these devices, and tell what might happen to the living things in the aquarium if it failed and explain why.

281

Biosphere 2

challenge—complete **Design It:** Inquiry Flipchart.

By asking questions, testing your ideas, organizing and analyzing data, drawing conclusions, and sharing what you learn...

# You are the scientist!

# Texas Essential Knowledge and Skills

Dear Students and Family Members,

The *ScienceFusion* Student Edition, Inquiry Flipchart, and Digital Curriculum provide a full year of interactive experiences built around the Texas Essential Knowledge and Skills for Science. As you read, experiment, and interact with print and digital content, you will be learning what you need to know for this school year. The Texas Essential Knowledge and Skills are listed here for you. You will also see them referenced throughout this book. Look for them on the opening pages of each unit and lesson.

Have a great school year!

Sincerely,
The HMH *ScienceFusion* Team

Look in each unit to find the picture.

Check it out: Unit 1
This picture is found on page _____.

TEKS 5.1

**Scientific investigation and reasoning.** The student conducts classroom and outdoor investigations following home and school safety procedures and environmentally appropriate and ethical practices. The student is expected to:

**A** demonstrate safe practices and the use of safety equipment as described in the Texas Safety Standards during classroom and outdoor investigations; and

**B** make informed choices in the conservation, disposal, and recycling of materials.

Answer Key: page 51

**Check it out:** Unit 1
This picture is found on page _____.

**Check it out:** Unit 2
This picture is found on page _____.

**Check it out:** Unit 1
This picture is found on page _____.

**TEKS 5.2**

**Scientific investigation and reasoning.** The student uses scientific methods during laboratory and outdoor investigations. The student is expected to:

**A** describe, plan, and implement simple experimental investigations testing one variable;

**B** ask well-defined questions, formulate testable hypotheses, and select and use appropriate equipment and technology;

**C** collect information by detailed observations and accurate measuring;

**D** analyze and interpret information to construct reasonable explanations from direct (observable) and indirect (inferred) evidence;

**E** demonstrate that repeated investigations may increase the reliability of results;

**F** communicate valid conclusions in both written and verbal forms; and

**G** construct appropriate simple graphs, tables, maps, and charts using technology, including computers, to organize, examine, and evaluate information.

**TEKS 5.3**

**Scientific investigation and reasoning.** The student uses critical thinking and scientific problem solving to make informed decisions. The student is expected to:

**A** in all fields of science, analyze, evaluate, and critique scientific explanations by using empirical evidence, logical reasoning, and experimental and observational testing, including examining all sides of scientific evidence of those scientific explanations, so as to encourage critical thinking by the student;

**B** evaluate the accuracy of the information related to promotional materials for products and services such as nutritional labels;

**C** draw or develop a model that represents how something works or looks that cannot be seen such as how a soda dispensing machine works; and

**D** connect grade-level appropriate science concepts with the history of science, science careers, and contributions of scientists.

**TEKS 5.4**

**Science investigation and reasoning.** The student knows how to use a variety of tools and methods to conduct science inquiry. The student is expected to:

**A** collect, record, and analyze information using tools, including calculators, microscopes, cameras, computers, hand lenses, metric rulers, Celsius thermometers, prisms, mirrors, pan balances, triple beam balances, spring scales, graduated cylinders, beakers, hot plates, meter sticks, magnets, collecting nets, and notebooks; timing devices, including clocks and stopwatches; and materials to support observations of habitats or organisms such as terrariums and aquariums; and

**B** use safety equipment, including safety goggles and gloves.



Answer Key: page 10, page 93, page 43

Check it out: Unit 3
This picture is found
on page ____.

Check it out: Unit 5
This picture is found
on page ____.

Check it out: Unit 7
This picture is found
on page ____.

**TEKS 5.5**

**Matter and energy.** The student knows that matter has measurable physical properties and those properties determine how matter is classified, changed, and used. The student is expected to:

**A** classify matter based on physical properties, including mass, magnetism, physical state (solid, liquid, and gas), relative density (sinking and floating), solubility in water, and the ability to conduct or insulate thermal energy or electric energy;

**B** identify the boiling and freezing/melting points of water on the Celsius scale;

**C** demonstrate that some mixtures maintain physical properties of their ingredients such as iron filings and sand; and

**D** identify changes that can occur in the physical properties of the ingredients of solutions such as dissolving salt in water or adding lemon juice to water.

**TEKS 5.6**

**Force, motion, and energy.** The student knows that energy occurs in many forms and can be observed in cycles, patterns, and systems. The student is expected to:

**A** explore the uses of energy, including mechanical, light, thermal, electrical, and sound energy;

**B** demonstrate that the flow of electricity in circuits requires a complete path through which an electric current can pass and can produce light, heat, and sound;

**C** demonstrate that light travels in a straight line until it strikes an object or travels through one medium to another and demonstrate that light can be reflected such as the use of mirrors or other shiny surfaces and refracted such as the appearance of an object when observed through water; and

**D** design an experiment that tests the effect of force on an object.

**TEKS 5.7**

**Earth and space.** The student knows Earth's surface is constantly changing and consists of useful resources. The student is expected to:

**A** explore the processes that led to the formation of sedimentary rocks and fossil fuels;

**B** recognize how landforms such as deltas, canyons, and sand dunes are the result of changes to Earth's surface by wind, water, and ice;

**C** identify alternative energy resources such as wind, solar, hydroelectric, geothermal, and biofuels; and

**D** identify fossils as evidence of past living organisms and the nature of the environments at the time using models.





Answer key: page 119, page 211, page 322

**Check it out:** Unit 9
This picture is found on page _____.

**Check it out:** Unit 11
This picture is found on page _____.

**Check it out:** Unit 12
This picture is found on page _____.

## TEKS 5.8

**Earth and space.** The student knows that there are recognizable patterns in the natural world and among the Sun, Earth, and Moon systems. The student is expected to:

**A** differentiate between weather and climate;

**B** explain how the Sun and the ocean interact in the water cycle;

**C** demonstrate that Earth rotates on its axis once approximately every 24 hours causing the day/night cycle and the apparent movement of the Sun across the sky; and

**D** identify and compare the physical characteristics of the Sun, Earth, and Moon.

## TEKS 5.9

**Organisms and environments.** The student knows that there are relationships, systems, and cycles within environments. The student is expected to:

**A** observe the way organisms live and survive in their ecosystem by interacting with the living and non-living elements;

**B** describe how the flow of energy derived from the Sun, used by producers to create their own food, is transferred through a food chain and food web to consumers and decomposers;

**C** predict the effects of changes in ecosystems caused by living organisms, including humans, such as the overpopulation of grazers or the building of highways; and

**D** identify the significance of the carbon dioxide-oxygen cycle to the survival of plants and animals.

## TEKS 5.10

**Organisms and environments.** The student knows that organisms undergo similar life processes and have structures that help them survive within their environments. The student is expected to:

**A** compare the structures and functions of different species that help them live and survive such as hooves on prairie animals or webbed feet in aquatic animals;

**B** differentiate between inherited traits of plants and animals such as spines on a cactus or shape of a beak and learned behaviors such as an animal learning tricks or a child riding a bicycle; and

**C** describe the differences between complete and incomplete metamorphosis of insects.



Answer Key: page 419, page 466, page 532

# Contents

Levels of Inquiry Key ■ DIRECTED ■ GUIDED ■ INDEPENDENT

EARTH SCIENCE

LIFE SCIENCE

# Safety in Science

**Indoors** Doing science is a lot of fun. But, a science lab can be a dangerous place. Falls, cuts, and burns can happen easily. When you are doing a science investigation, you need to be safe. Know the safety rules and listen to your teacher.

Adult scientists have to follow lab safety rules, too.

## Pay attention to these safety rules.

1. **Think ahead.** Study the investigation steps so you know what to expect. If you have any questions, ask your teacher. Be sure you understand all caution statements and safety reminders.
2. **Be neat and clean.** Keep your work area clean. If you have long hair, pull it back so it doesn't get in the way. Roll or push up long sleeves to keep them away from your activity.
3. **Oops!** If you spill or break something, or get cut, tell your teacher right away.
4. **Watch your eyes.** Wear safety goggles anytime you are directed to do so. If you get anything in your eyes, tell your teacher right away.
5. **Yuck!** Never eat or drink anything during a science activity.
6. **Don't get shocked.** Be careful if an electric appliance is used. Be sure that electric cords are in a safe place where you can't trip over them. Never use the cord to pull a plug from an outlet.
7. **Keep it clean.** Always clean up when you have finished. Put everything away and wipe your work area. Wash your hands.
8. **Play it safe.** Always know where to find safety equipment, such as fire extinguishers. Know how to use the safety equipment around you.

## Outdoors

Lots of science research happens outdoors. It's fun to explore the wild! But, you need to be careful. The weather, the land, and the living things can surprise you.

This scientist has to protect his eyes.

### Follow these safety rules when you're doing science outdoors.

1. **Think ahead.** Study the investigation steps so you know what to expect. If you have any questions, ask your teacher. Be sure you understand all caution statements and safety reminders.
2. **Dress right.** Wear appropriate clothes and shoes for the outdoors. Cover up and wear sunscreen and sunglasses for sun safety.
3. **Clean up the area.** Follow your teacher's instructions for when and how to throw away waste.
4. **Oops!** Tell your teacher right away if you break something or get hurt.
5. **Watch your eyes.** Wear safety goggles when directed to do so. If you get anything in your eyes, tell your teacher right away.
6. **Yuck!** Never taste anything outdoors.
7. **Stay with your group.** Work in the area as directed by your teacher. Stay on marked trails.
8. **"Wilderness" doesn't mean go wild.** Never engage in horseplay, games, or pranks.
9. **Always walk.** No running!
10. **Play it safe.** Know where safety equipment can be found and how to use it. Know how to get help.
11. **Clean up.** Wash your hands with soap and water when you come back indoors.

UNIT 1

# How Scientists Work

## Big Idea

Scientists answer questions by careful observations and investigations.

**TEKS** 5.2A, 5.2B, 5.2C, 5.2D, 5.2E, 5.2F, 5.2G, 5.3A, 5.3C, 5.3D, 5.4A, 5.4B

## I Wonder Why

**Why do some scientists work outdoors and others work inside a laboratory?**

*Turn the page to find out.*

**Here's Why** Scientists work to answer questions. Some questions can be answered with outdoor investigations. Other questions require tools in a lab.

In this unit, you will explore the Big Idea, the Essential Questions, and the Investigations on the Inquiry Flipchart.

Levels of Inquiry Key ■ DIRECTED ■ GUIDED ■ INDEPENDENT

**Big Idea** Scientists answer questions by careful observations and investigations.

## Essential Questions



**Science Notebook**

Before you begin each lesson, be sure to write your thoughts about the Essential Question.

**TEKS** **5.2A** describe...simple experimental investigations... **5.2C** collect information by detailed observations and accurate measuring **5.2D** analyze and interpret information to construct reasonable explanations from direct (observable) and indirect (inferred) evidence **5.2E** demonstrate that repeated investigations may increase the reliability of results

Lesson 1

Essential Question

# What Is Science?

## Engage Your Brain!

Find one answer to the following question in this lesson and write it here.

What are some science skills you could use when studying fish in an aquarium?

______________________________

______________________________

______________________________

## Active Reading

### Lesson Vocabulary

List the terms. As you learn about each one, make notes in the Interactive Glossary.

______________________________

______________________________

______________________________

______________________________

### Use Headings

Active readers preview headings and use them to pose questions that set purposes for reading. Reading with a purpose helps active readers focus on understanding what they read in order to fulfill the purpose.

# What All Scientists Do

Digging up fossils. Peering through telescopes. Mixing chemicals in a lab. Using computers to make weather predictions. These are only a few of the things scientists do.

**Active Reading** As you read these two pages, turn the heading into a question in your mind, and underline sentences that answer the question.

Does solving puzzles and searching for buried treasures sound like fun? If so, you might like being a paleontologist. Paleontologists are scientists who study the history of life on Earth. Like all scientists, they try to explain how and why things in the natural world happen. They answer questions by doing investigations. An **investigation** is a procedure carried out to carefully observe, study, or test something in order to learn more about it.

In addition to knowing a lot about living things of the past, paleontologists have to use many skills. In fact, all scientists use these skills. All scientists **observe**, or use their five senses to collect information. And all scientists **compare**, finding ways objects and events are similar and different.

### Observe

**Write one observation you could make about the fossil.**

_______________________________

_______________________________

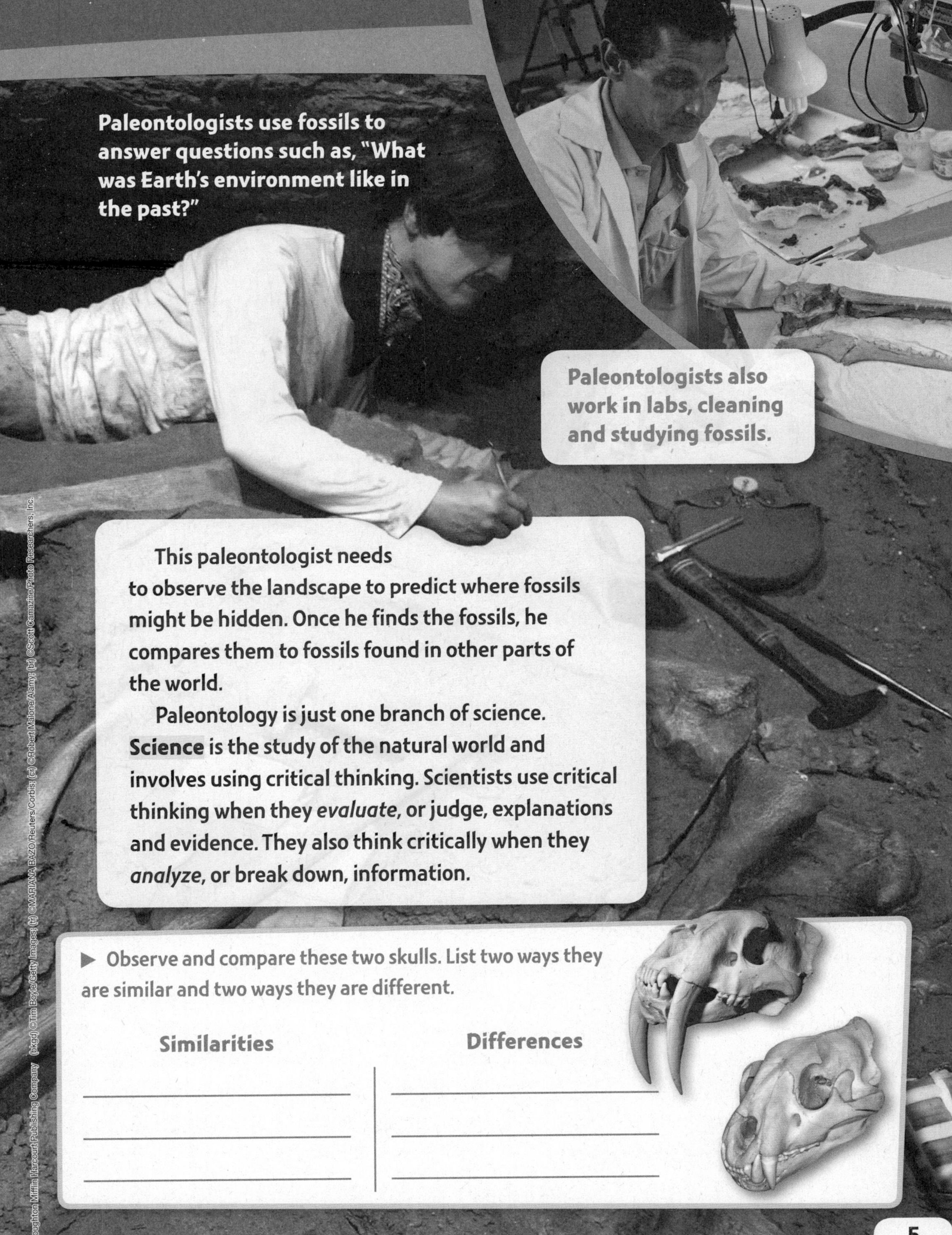

Paleontologists use fossils to answer questions such as, "What was Earth's environment like in the past?"

Paleontologists also work in labs, cleaning and studying fossils.

This paleontologist needs to observe the landscape to predict where fossils might be hidden. Once he finds the fossils, he compares them to fossils found in other parts of the world.

Paleontology is just one branch of science. **Science** is the study of the natural world and involves using critical thinking. Scientists use critical thinking when they *evaluate*, or judge, explanations and evidence. They also think critically when they *analyze*, or break down, information.

▶ Observe and compare these two skulls. List two ways they are similar and two ways they are different.

| Similarities | Differences |
|---|---|
| ______________ | ______________ |
| ______________ | ______________ |
| ______________ | ______________ |

# Prove It!

# Rotten Meat turns into Maggots!

In the 1600s, keeping meat fresh wasn't easy. Meat quickly spoiled and filled with worm-like maggots. Where did they come from?

**Active Reading** On these pages, circle examples of evidence.

▶ Draw a large *X* through the explanation that was shown *not* to be true.

Information collected during a scientific investigation is called **evidence.** Evidence helps support conclusions, such as dinosaurs lived on Earth. Some evidence is direct, such as seeing a fossil dinosaur skull. Direct evidence is also called *empirical evidence.* Another kind of evidence is indirect, or inferred evidence, such as finding a dinosaur's fossil footprint.

Travel back in time to the 1660s. Most scientists explain that flies and maggots come from rotting food. As evidence they show how a dead animal's body soon becomes loaded with maggots.

But Dr. Francesco Redi, an Italian scientist, is not convinced. Redi examines all sides of the scientific evidence supporting the current explanation to develop his *critique,* or review of the facts. He then proposes an alternative explanation: Living things must come from other living things. He **plans and conducts investigations** to gather evidence. Redi traps maggots inside jars with pieces of meat. He watches the

The meat in the open jar soon became "wormy," while the meat in the sealed jar did not.

Redi placed fresh meat in two jars. He covered one jar and left the other jar uncovered.

maggots turn into adult flies. He observes adult flies laying eggs and more maggots coming out of these eggs.

Redi then sets up an experiment. He places meat in several jars. Some jars are sealed, others are not. Redi observes that only the meat in jars he left open have maggots.

Redi repeats his experiments many times. He tries dead fish, frogs, and snakes. All the evidence supports his idea: Living insects can only come from other living insects.

▶ Fill in the blanks in this sequence graphic organizer.

Use critical thinking to develop ________________.

↓

Plan and conduct ________________.

↓

Use ________________ to explain observations.

Maggots Hatch from eggs that flies lay.

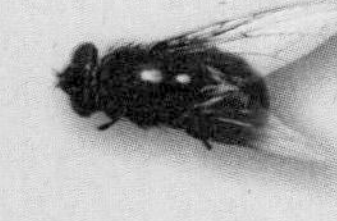

# A Sticky Trap

Humans are too big to get stuck in a spider's web. But there are some sticky traps you need to avoid when thinking like a scientist.

**Active Reading** As you read these two pages, turn the main heading into a question in your mind. Then underline sentences that answer the question.

► Look at the words in the spider web below. Star the things you *should* use to draw conclusions properly. Cross out the others.

Opinions

Favorites

Observations

Logical reasoning

Inferences

Evidence

Feelings

## How to Draw Conclusions

Scientists **draw conclusions** from the results of their investigations. Any conclusion must be backed up with evidence. Other scientists evaluate the conclusion based on how much evidence is given. They also evaluate how well the evidence supports the conclusion.

Don't jump to conclusions too quickly. That's a sticky trap in science! As Dr. Redi did, repeat your investigations. Think about what you can **infer** from your observations. And then—only then—draw your conclusions.

Suppose you spend a week observing spiders. You might conclude that all spiders build webs to catch their food. This may be true of the spiders you observed, but it's not true of all spiders. Some spiders, such as wolf spiders, hunt for their prey instead.

| | |
|---|---|
| **Observation**<br>Information collected by using the senses | The insect is stuck in the spider web. |
| **Inference**<br>An idea or a conclusion based on an observation | A spider is going to use the bug for food later. |
| **Opinion**<br>A personal belief that does not need proof | Spiders are really gross! |

## Logical Reasoning

Personal feelings and opinions should not affect how you do investigations. Nor should they affect your conclusions. An **opinion** is a belief or judgment. It doesn't have to be backed up with evidence.

Doing science is about using *logical reasoning* to evaluate evidence and to draw conclusions. When you reason logically, you use things that you know to be true or false to draw conclusions. For example, knowing that some spiders are venomous justifies concluding that people should be careful when handling spiders.

▶ Write one observation, one inference, and one opinion about what you see in the photo.

| | |
|---|---|
| **Observation** | |
| **Inference** | |
| **Opinion** | |

# Knowledge Grows

How is a man investigating electricity and wires more than 350 years ago connected to the latest video game release?

Stephen Gray, a scientist born in 1666, was working at home when he discovered that electrical energy could move along a short metal wire. Gray carried his materials to friends' homes. He showed them how the materials worked and, together, they made the wire longer and longer.

Today there are so many ways for scientists to **communicate**, or share, the results of investigations. When scientists communicate clearly, others can repeat their investigations. They can compare their results with those of others. They can expand on one another's ideas. In these ways, scientific knowledge grows.

## Communicate

List several ways you can communicate.

_______________

_______________

_______________

_______________

1729 Stephen Gray shows that electrical energy can be carried through a wire.

1882 Thomas Edison opens the first electricity generating station.

Knowledge grows when it is communicated. Each science discovery leads to new questions. More is learned and new things are invented.

The first video game was invented in 1958. The inventor was a scientist named William Higinbotham. The reason? To make Visitor's Day at his lab more interesting for the public! Hundreds of people lined up to play the game.

Take a look at the timeline. The science behind Higinbotham's game goes back hundreds of years or more.

1947 The transistor, needed to make radios and computers, is invented.

1953 The first computer is sold.

1958 William Higinbotham invents the first video game.

1967 First handheld calculator invented.

The first arcade games were not very complex.

1971 First coin-operated arcade video games in use.

1972 The first home video game systems are sold.

1977 The first handheld video games are sold.

2009 Scientists use super-fast video game cards inside computers to investigate the structure of molecules.

The video games of today are fast, complex, and interactive.

# Meet Scientists

There are more people working as scientists today than ever before in history. Yet, there are plenty of unanswered questions left for you to answer!

**Active Reading** As you read these two pages, underline what each type of scientist studies.

## Astronomer

Astronomers ask questions about how the universe works. Because novas, black holes, and galaxies are so far away, they use time/space relationships to investigate them. For example, astronomers measure space distances in units called light-years. That's how far light can travel in one Earth year.

## Do the Math!

### Use Fractions

Earth and Mars travel around the sun. Each time Earth makes one complete trip, Mars makes about $\frac{1}{2}$ of its trip.

1. How many trips does Earth make around the sun in the time it takes Mars to make one trip?

_______________

2. In the drawing below, put an *X* where Mars will be after Earth completes five trips around the sun.

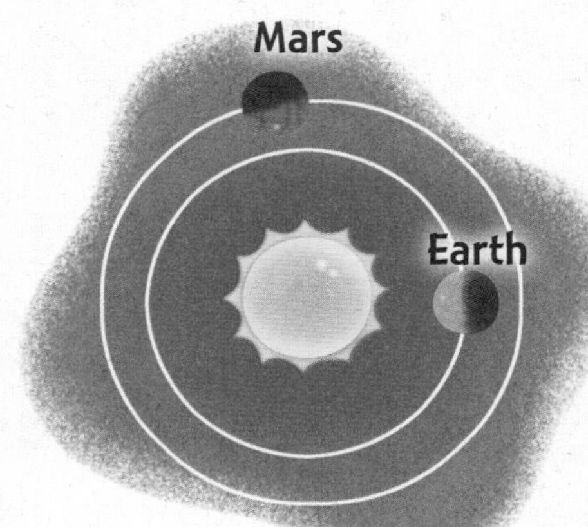


You don't have to be a pro to do astronomy. People have discovered many comets and exploding stars using telescopes in their back yards!

## Order

When you **order**, you place objects or events one after another in the correct sequence. Write the numbers *1, 2, 3,* and *4* to show the order of the images below.

_____ _____ _____ _____

## Botanist

Botanists investigate questions about plants. For example, some botanists study how environmental conditions affect a plant's life cycle.

## Taxonomist

Taxonomists are scientists who identify types of living things and classify them by how they are related. When you classify, you organize objects or events into categories based on specific characteristics.

## Classify

Look at the butterflies on this page. What are some ways you could classify them?

_______________

_______________

_______________

When you're done, use the answer key to check and revise your work.

**Read the summary, and fill in the missing words.**

The goal of a scientist is to understand the natural world. To do this, a scientist plans and conducts 1. ____________________.

Scientists use the 2. ____________________ they gather to draw 3. ____________________.

A good scientist does not let his or her personal beliefs, or 4. ____________________, influence their study.

There are many important skills that scientists use. For example, when scientists use 5. ____________________, they use things they know to be true and false to draw conclusions.

**Read each of the statements below. Write the science skill that each student used.**

6. Angela made a list of how the two planets were alike.

____________________

7. Krystal sorted the rocks into five groups based on their color.

____________________

8. Robbie explained the results of his investigation to his classmates.

____________________

9. Dmitri noted how the feathers looked and felt.

____________________

10. Juan organized the steps of the process from first to last.

____________________

Answer Key: 1. investigations 2. evidence 3. conclusions 4. opinions 5. logical reasoning 6. compare 7. classify 8. communicate 9. observe 10. order

# Brain Check

Lesson 1

Name ____________________

## Word Play

1 Complete the crossword puzzle. If you need help, use the terms in the yellow box.

**Across**

1. The study of the natural world through investigation
5. Collecting information by using the senses
6. An idea or a conclusion based on an observation
7. Facts and information collected over time
8. To put things into groups
9. A belief or a judgment

**Down**

2. The sharing of information
3. The observations and information that support a conclusion
4. The process of studying or testing something to learn more about it
5. To arrange things by when they happened or by their size

| | | | | |
|---|---|---|---|---|
| classify | communication | evidence* | inference | investigation* |
| knowledge | observing | opinion* | order | science* |

* Key Lesson Vocabulary

# Apply Concepts

2 Compare these two birds. List how they look similar and different.

Similarities:

______________________

______________________

Differences:

______________________

______________________

3 Suppose someone tells you they saw a bird never before seen in your state. What kinds of evidence would you ask for?

______________________

______________________

______________________

4 Many types of germs live in soil. How should this affect the way you conduct a soil sample investigation?

______________________

______________________

______________________

5 One morning you see an outdoor garbage can tipped over. Plastic bags are torn open. What could you infer?

______________________

______________________

______________________

**Take It Home!**

How can you communicate with people around the world, collect real data, and help answer a question? Research citizen science projects online. Choose an interesting project. Participate with your family.

Inquiry Flipchart page 4

**TEKS** **5.2C** collect information by detailed observations and accurate measuring **5.2D** analyze and interpret information to construct reasonable explanations from direct (observable) and indirect (inferred) evidence **5.2F** communicate valid conclusions in both written and verbal forms

Name ______________________________

Essential Question

# How Do Scientists Learn About the Natural World?

## Set a Purpose

What will you learn from this investigation?

______________________________

______________________________

______________________________

______________________________

______________________________

## Think About the Procedure

How did you choose what predictions to write on your origami predictor?

______________________________

______________________________

______________________________

______________________________

## Record Your Data

In the table below, record your results.

| Date | Origami Prediction | Weather Service Prediction | Actual Weather |
|---|---|---|---|
| | | | |
| | | | |
| | | | |
| | | | |
| | | | |
| | | | |
| | | | |

## Draw Conclusions

Use logical reasoning. Of the two kinds of weather predictions, which one was more likely to be correct? Explain.

## Analyze and Extend

1. Why was repeating this investigation over several days better than doing it for just one day?

2. How do you think the weather service makes its predictions?

3. Why is it important that scientists make good weather predictions?

4. The line graph shows average October air temperatures in Houston, TX. Can you predict the air temperature in Houston next October? If so, how?

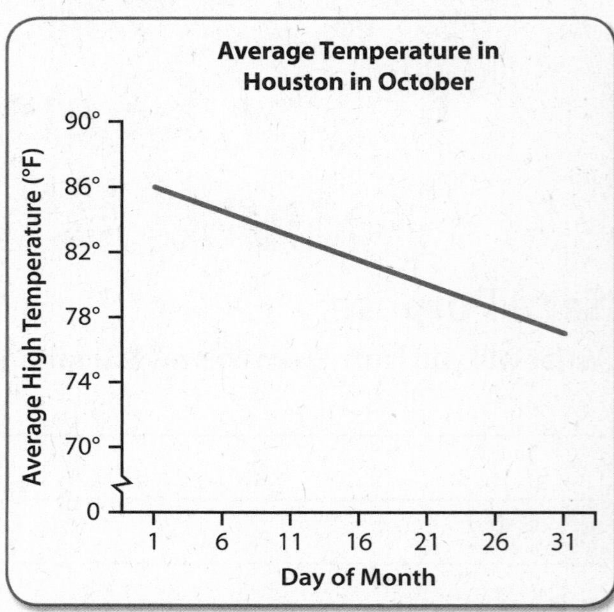


5. What else would you like to find out about how scientists make predictions? Write each idea as a question.

## Directions

1. Carefully tear this page out of your book.
2. Cut out the square below. You will use it to make your origami weather predictor.
3. On each set of lines, write a weather prediction.
4. Follow the instructions on the back of this page to fold and use your origami weather predictor.

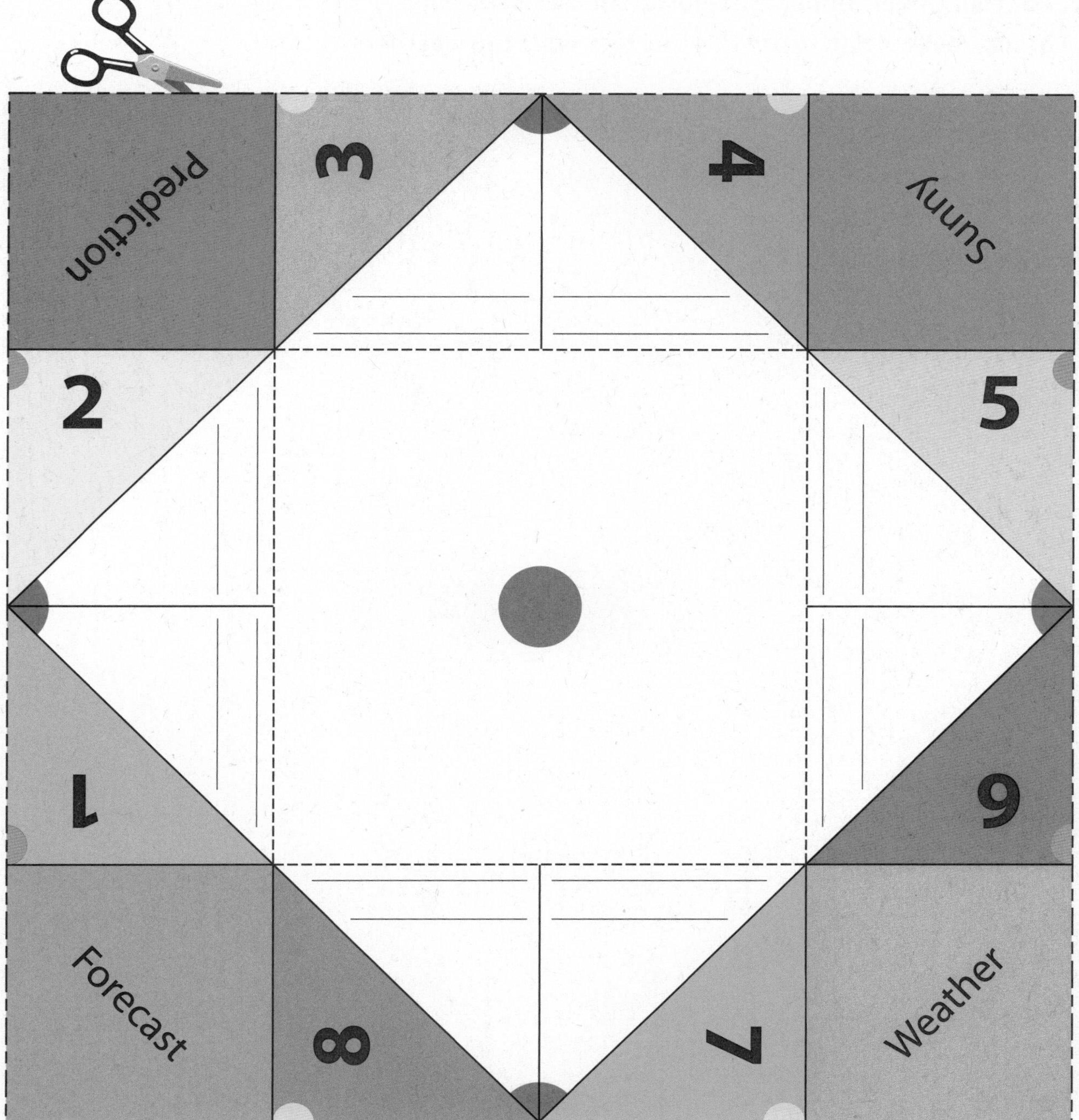

## Directions (continued)

5. Fold the blue dots into the blue circle. Turn the paper over, and fold the green dots into the green circle.
6. Fold the paper in half so that the yellow dots touch each other. Make a crease, and unfold the paper. Fold it in half again so that the pink dots touch each other.
7. Put your fingers under the colorful squares. With your group, make a plan to use this tool to predict the weather.

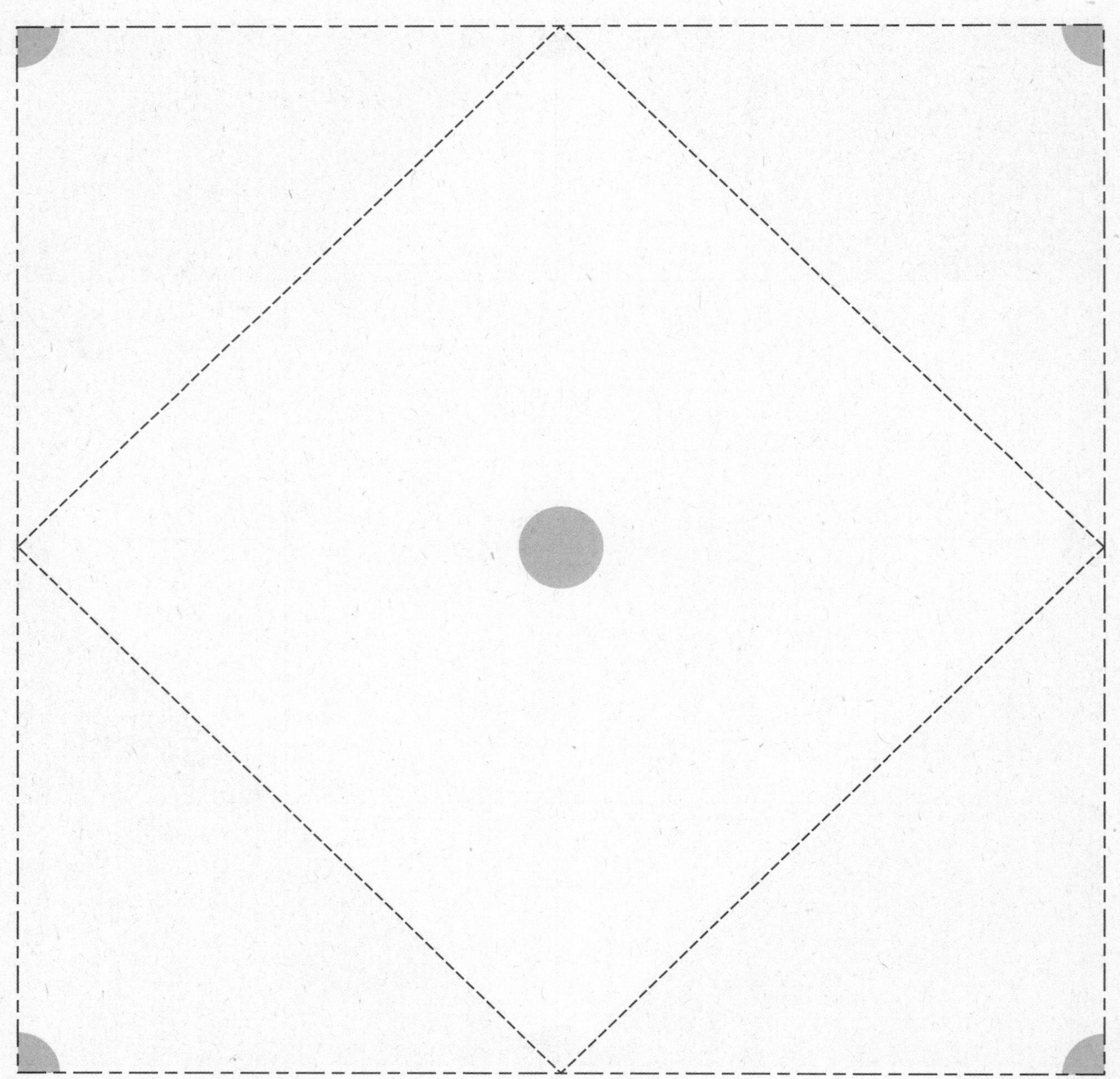

**TEKS** **5.2A** describe, plan, and implement simple experimental investigations...**5.2B** ask well-defined questions, formulate testable hypotheses... **5.2D** analyze and interpret information to construct reasonable explanations from...evidence **5.2G** construct appropiate simple graphs...using technology, including computers, to organize...information **5.3C** draw or develop a model...

Essential Question

# What Are Some Types of Investigations?

## Engage Your Brain!

Find one answer to the following question in this lesson and write it here.

What did this scientist do prior to starting her experiment with plants?

______________________

______________________

______________________

______________________

## Active Reading

### Lesson Vocabulary

List the terms. As you learn about each one, make notes in the Interactive Glossary.

______________________

______________________

______________________

______________________

### Main Ideas

The main idea of a paragraph is the most important idea. The main idea may be stated in the first sentence, or it may be stated elsewhere. Active readers look for main ideas by asking themselves, What is this paragraph mostly about?

# A Process for Science

Testing bridge models, mapping a storm's path, searching the sky for distant planets—each of these investigations uses scientific methods.

**Active Reading** As you read these two pages, draw a line under each main idea.

How does the shape of the room affect the sound of a voice?

How does having a cold affect a person's singing?

Can a human voice shatter glass?

How high a note can a singer sing?

## Start with a Question

People often ask questions about things they notice. Scientists also ask questions about things they observe. But scientists ask well-defined questions, which are testable questions that can be answered by investigations. A scientific investigation always begins with a question.

## Plan an Investigation

Once a scientist has a testable question, it is time to plan an investigation. **Scientific methods** are ways that scientists perform investigations. There are many ways that scientists investigate the world. But all scientific methods use logic and reasoning.

► Suppose you've just heard an opera singer warm up her voice. Write your own science question about the sounds a singer makes.

_______________________________________

_______________________________________

## Experimental Testing

In an experiment, scientists control all the conditions of the investigation. They study what happens to a group of samples that differ in only one factor or condition.

## Observational Testing

Scientists use observational testing to analyze, evaluate, and critique scientific explanations.

## Using Models

Scientists use models when they cannot experiment on the real thing. Models help scientists investigate things that are large (like a planet), expensive (like a bridge), or uncontrollable (like the weather).

## Investigations Differ

The method a scientist uses depends on the question he or she is investigating. An **experiment** is an investigation in which all of the conditions are controlled. Models are used to represent real objects or processes. Scientists conduct observational testing to study processes in nature that they can observe but can't control.

## Drawing Conclusions

Whatever scientific methods are used, scientists will have results they can use to draw conclusions. The conclusions may answer the question they asked before they began. They may point to other questions and many more ideas for investigations.

► Write the type of investigation you should use to answer the following questions.

**How do different bridge designs react to strong winds?**

___________________________

**How fast does the wind blow where a bridge will be built?**

___________________________

**Which type of paint works best to keep a bridge from rusting?**

___________________________

# Explosive Observations

How does a hurricane affect animals? How do whales raise their young? Repeated observations can help answer questions such as these.

**Active Reading** As you read these two pages, place a star next to three examples of repeated observation.

Some science questions can only be answered by making repeated observations. This is because some things are just too big, too far away, or too uncontrollable for experiments.

In Yellowstone National Park, for example, heated water shoots out of holes in the ground. This is called a geyser. Old Faithful is a famous geyser that erupts about every hour. Observations of the geyser collected over many years can be used to predict when the next eruption will occur. A prediction is a statement, based on information, about a future event.

Old Faithful

## Analyze, Evaluate, and Critique

The time until Old Faithful's next eruption is affected by how long the previous eruption lasted. The data in the table are the result of observational testing. Do the data support the statement above? Explain.

_______________________________________________

| Length of Eruption (min) | 1.5 | 2 | 2.5 | 3 | 3.5 | 4 | 4.5 |
|---|---|---|---|---|---|---|---|
| Eruption Interval (min) | 50 | 57 | 65 | 71 | 76 | 82 | 89 |

The first observation of a whale is often its spout.

Scientists have many questions about whales—the largest mammals on Earth. How long do whales live? How do they communicate? How do they care for their young? How far can they travel in a year? These questions can be answered with repeated observation.

For example, the tail flukes of whales are different from one whale to another. Scientists take photos of the flukes and use them to identify individual whales. Once they know which whale is which, they can recognize them each time they are seen in the ocean.

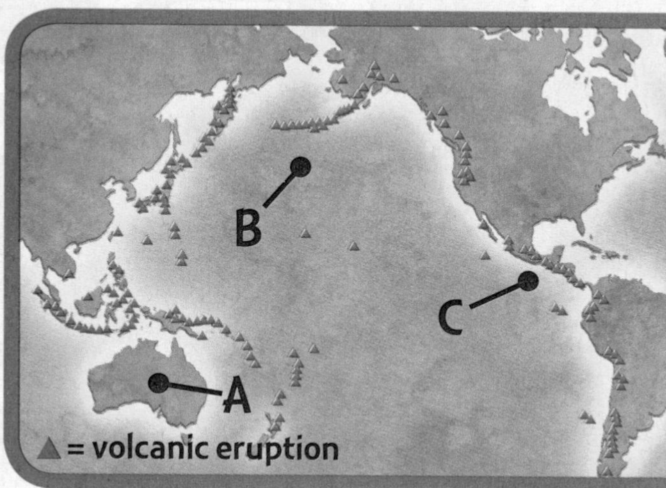


## Predict

Scientists have observed and recorded volcanic eruptions for hundreds of years. The map to the left shows that data. Which location—A, B, or C— is most likely to have a volcanic eruption? _____

Why do you think scientists call this region the "Ring of Fire"?

_______________

_______________

# Super Models

How does a bat fly? How might Saturn's rings look close up? How does a heart work? These are some science questions that can be answered with models.

**Active Reading** Circle different types of models that are described on these two pages.

Complex models can be made on a computer. This model shows where the most damage would occur if an earthquake were to strike.

## When Modeling Is Needed

When scientists can't experiment with the real thing, they use models. Models are used to represent how something works or looks that can't be seen. They are also used to investigate things with many hidden parts, such as an ant colony. The closer a model represents the real thing, the more useful it is. Models are changed with new discoveries. Scientists draw conclusions and make predictions by studying their models.

## Types of Models

Models are made in different ways. One way is to build a physical model. An earthquake shake table with model buildings on it is a physical model. Another way is to program computer simulation models. Scientists can speed up time in computer models so that they can see what might happen long in the future. Drawing diagrams and flow charts is a third way to make models. These two-dimensional models can be used to show how ideas are related.

Earthquakes are difficult to predict, and they can cause damage. New structures are designed to prevent damage.

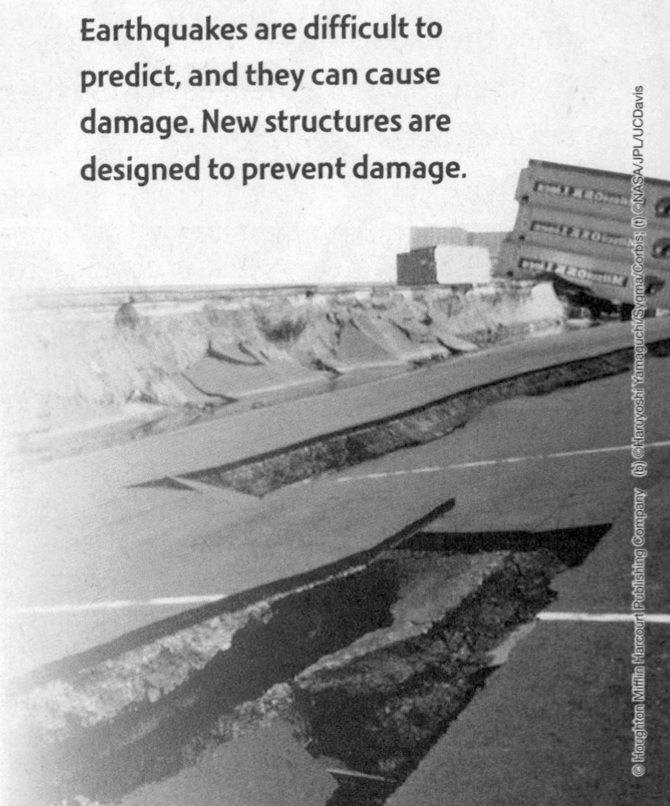

Scientists build "shake tables" that model the motion of real earthquakes. This photo shows two types of houses being tested. Which house seems to be safer in an earthquake?

## Use Models

How is an earthquake model made of gelatin like a real earthquake? How is it unlike a real earthquake?

Alike: ______________________________________

______________________________________

Different: ______________________________________

______________________________________

You can model the effects of an earthquake, using gelatin for the ground and buildings made of blocks.

# How to Excel *in* Experimentation

You're enjoying a frozen juice pop. The heat of your tongue melts the pop. As you slurp the liquid, you think about how different substances freeze.

I know that water freezes at 0 degrees Celsius. How does adding other substances to water affect the temperature at which it freezes?

**Active Reading** As you read the next four pages, circle lesson vocabulary each time it is used.

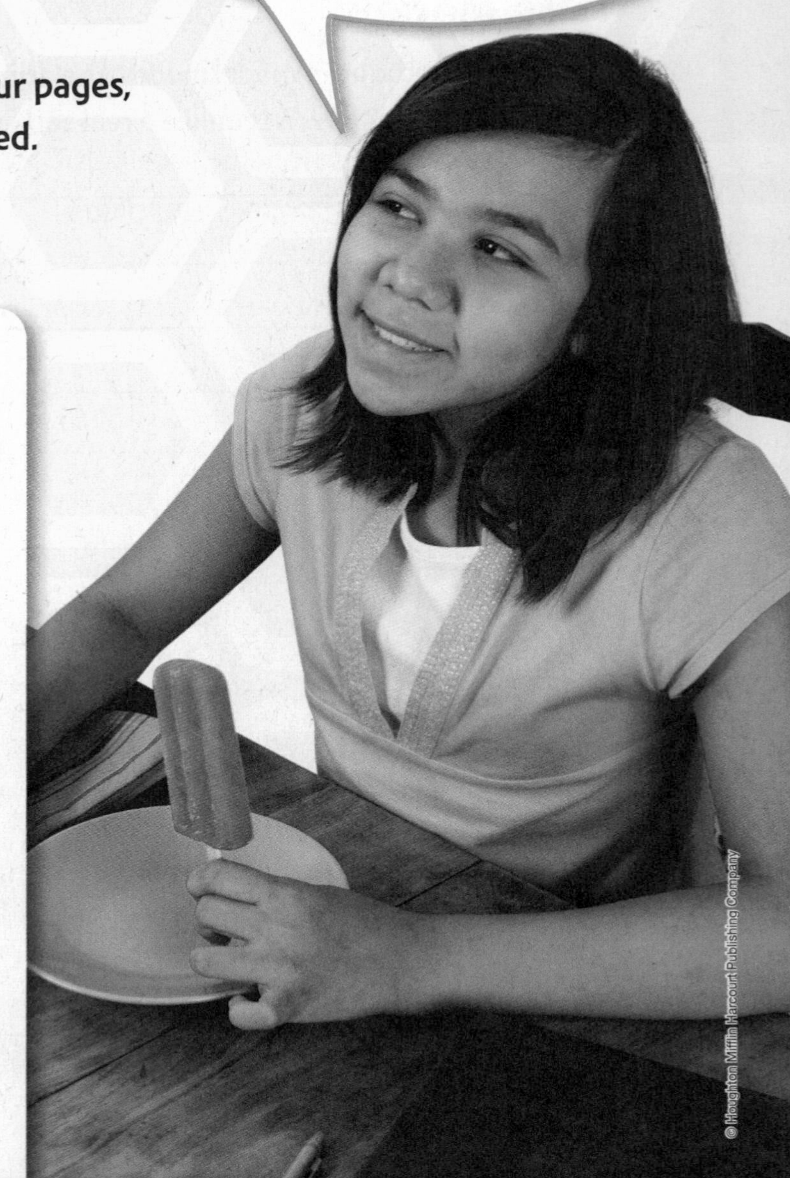

## Ask Questions

You know a freezer is cold enough to freeze water. You also know that juice is mostly water. You ask "Does adding substances to water affect its freezing point?"

Many science questions, including this one, can be answered by doing experiments. An **experiment** is a procedure used to test a hypothesis. It's a good idea to make some observations before stating a hypothesis. For example, you might put a small amount of orange juice in a freezer. Then you'd check it every few minutes to look for changes.

## Hypothesize

A *hypothesis* is a statement that can be tested and will explain what can happen in an investigation. In the case of the freezing question, you think about what you already know. You can also talk to other people. And you can do research such as asking an expert.

You find out that the freezing point and melting point of a material should be the same temperature. An expert suggests that it is better to measure the melting point than the freezing point.

## Design an Experiment

A well-designed experiment has two or more setups. This allows you to compare results among them. For the freezing/melting experiment, each setup will be a cup of liquid.

A **variable** is any condition in an experiment that can be changed. In most experiments, there are many, many variables to consider. The trick is to keep all variables the same in each setup, except one. That one variable is the one you will test.

Among the setups should be one called the control. The **control** is the setup to which you will compare all the others.

You've decided to dissolve different substances in water and freeze them. Then you plan to take them out of the freezer and use a thermometer to check their temperatures as they melt.

### Hypothesize

Fill in the blank in the hypothesis. Any substance dissolved in water will ____________________ the temperature at which the mixture freezes and melts.

### Identify and Control Variables

When you identify and control variables, you determine which conditions should stay the same and which one should be changed. Circle the variable that will be tested. Underline the variables that will remain the same.

- the kinds of cups
- the amount of water
- the material that is dissolved in the water
- the temperature of the freezer
- the types of thermometers
- the amount of time you leave the cups in the freezer

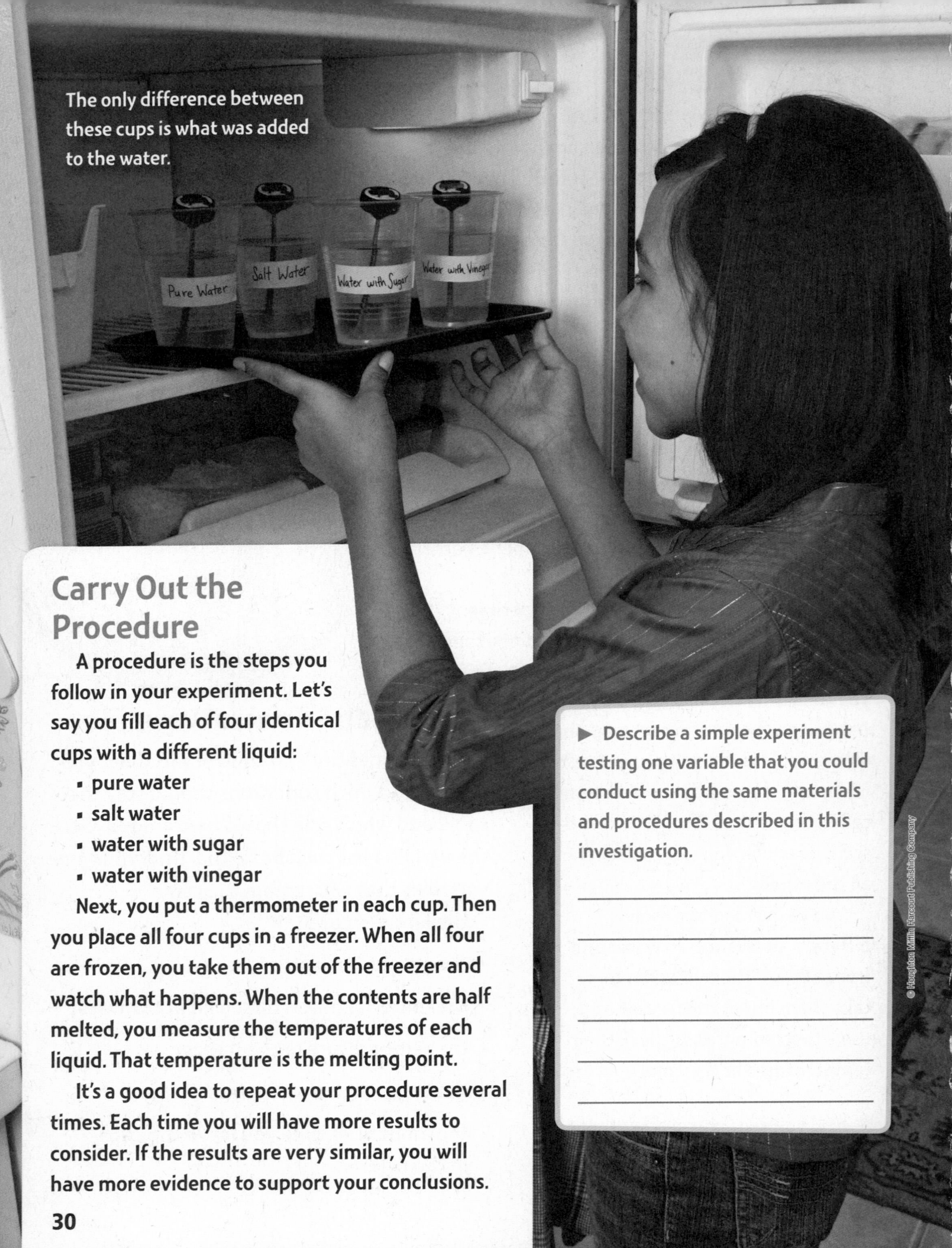


The only difference between these cups is what was added to the water.

## Carry Out the Procedure

A procedure is the steps you follow in your experiment. Let's say you fill each of four identical cups with a different liquid:

- pure water
- salt water
- water with sugar
- water with vinegar

Next, you put a thermometer in each cup. Then you place all four cups in a freezer. When all four are frozen, you take them out of the freezer and watch what happens. When the contents are half melted, you measure the temperatures of each liquid. That temperature is the melting point.

It's a good idea to repeat your procedure several times. Each time you will have more results to consider. If the results are very similar, you will have more evidence to support your conclusions.

▶ Describe a simple experiment testing one variable that you could conduct using the same materials and procedures described in this investigation.

______

______

______

______

______

______

## Record and Analyze Data

You could write down your observations as sentences. Or you could make a table to fill in. No matter how you do it, make sure you record correctly. Check twice or have a team member check.

Once the experiment is completed and the data recorded, you can analyze your results. If your data is in the form of numbers, math skills will come in handy. For example, in the data table below, you'll need to know how to write, read, and compare decimals.

| Melting Point Experiment | |
|---|---|
| Substance | Melting Point (°C) |
| Pure water | 0.0 |
| Salt water | −3.7 |
| Sugar water | −1.8 |
| Vinegar water | −1.1 |

## Draw Conclusions and Evaluate the Hypothesis

You draw conclusions based on your results. Remember that all conclusions must be supported with evidence. The more evidence you have, the stronger your conclusion. What conclusion can you draw based on this experiment?

Once you've reached a conclusion, look at your hypothesis. Decide if the hypothesis is supported or not. If not, try rethinking your hypothesis. Then design a new experiment to test it. That's what scientists do—build on what they learn.

### Experiment!

Ask a well-defined question you could answer using experimental testing.

______________________________

______________________________

______________________________

Plan, describe, and implement an experiment that tests the effect of only one variable.

Why It Matters

# Special Delivery: Data Displays

Once you've completed a science investigation, you'll want to share it. What's the best way to communicate the data you collected?

**As part of their investigations, scientists collect, record, and interpret data. They use technology, including computers, to construct graphs, tables, maps, and charts. These kinds of displays help scientists organize, examine, and evaluate lots of information. Some kinds of displays are more suited to certain kinds of data than others.**

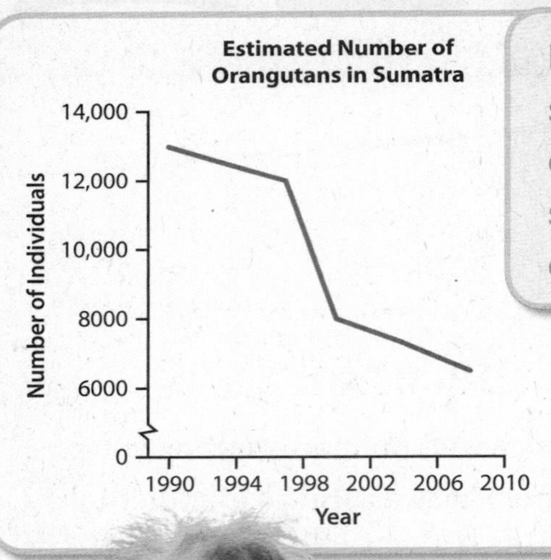


Line graphs are suited to show change over time, especially small changes, such as the amount you grow each year.

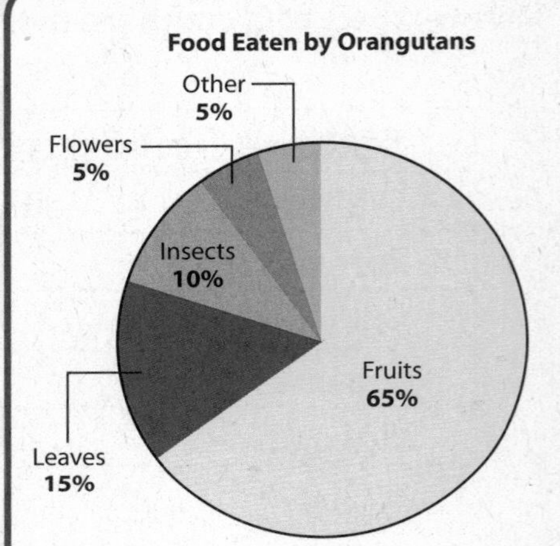


Circle graphs are suited to comparing parts to the whole. If you want to show fractions or percents, use a circle graph.

Diagrams are suited to show data that do not include numbers. This diagram shows how an orangutan uses a tool to eat seeds in fruit.

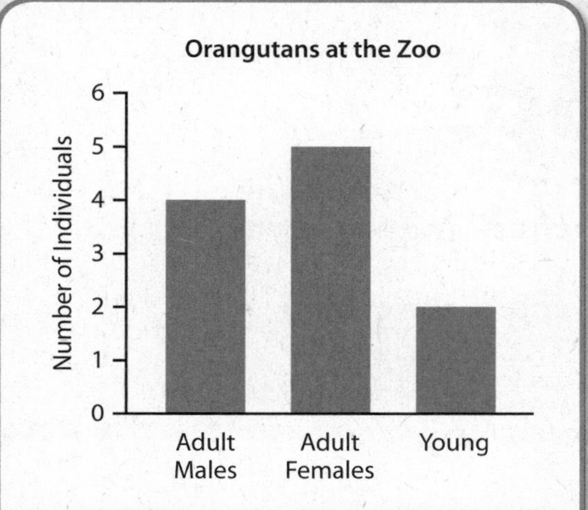


Bar graphs are suited to compare things or groups of things. When your data are in categories, use a bar graph.

# Do the Math!

## Construct a Bar Graph

Use technology to construct a bar graph using the data in the table. Decide whether you want the bars to be vertical or horizontal. Carefully label the intervals on each axis. Draw the bars. Then title and label all the parts of your graph. Attach your graph in the space below.

| Number of Orangutans Counted | |
|---|---|
| Day | Number |
| Monday | 7 |
| Tuesday | 13 |
| Wednesday | 10 |
| Thursday | 2 |
| Friday | 6 |

**When you're done, use the answer key to check and revise your work.**

**The outline below is a summary of the lesson. Complete the outline. When you are done, check and revise your work.**

## Summarize

I. Scientific Methods
   A. All start with a question
   B. Investigations differ
      1. experiments
      2. (1) ____________________
      3. (2) ____________________
   C. All have results from which to (3) ____________________

II. Observational Testing
   A. Some things are just too big, too far away, or too uncontrollable for experiments
   B. Examples
      1. volcanoes
      2. (4) ____________________

III. Using Models
   A. Needed to understand systems that have many hidden parts
   B. Types of models
      1. diagrams and flow charts
      2. (5) ____________________
      3. (6) ____________________

IV. Experiments
   A. Ask well-defined questions
   B. Hypothesize
   C. (7) ____________________
   D. Carry out the procedure
   E. (8) ____________________
   F. Draw conclusions

V. Organizing and Displaying Data
   A. Data displays help communicate
   B. Kinds of data displays
      1. circle graphs
      2. (9) ____________________
      3. (10) ____________________
      4. (11) ____________________

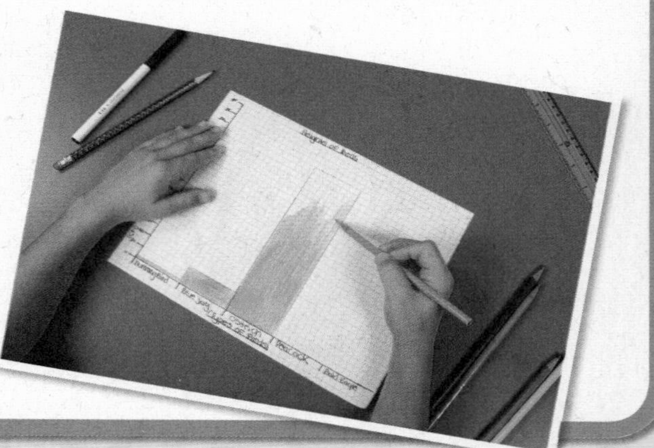

Answer Key: 1. models 2. observational testing 3. draw conclusions 4. geysers or whales 5. computer simulation models 6. physical models 7. Design an experiment 8. Record and analyze data 9. line graphs 10. bar graphs 11. diagrams

Name ____________________

# Word Play

**1** Read each clue. Then find and circle the term in the word search puzzle.

**Clues**

1. All the ways scientists do investigations: _ _ _ _ _ _ _ _ _ _ _ _ _ _ _ _ _ _ _
2. These show how something works that can't be seen: _ _ _ _ _ _
3. The part of an experiment used to compare all the other groups: _ _ _ _ _ _ _
4. What scientists do that is the basis for their investigations: _ _ _   _ _ _ _ _ _ _ _ _ _ _ _
5. Any condition in an experiment that can be changed: _ _ _ _ _ _ _ _
6. A type of graph suited to show change over time: _ _ _ _   _ _ _ _ _
7. A statement that can be tested and that explains what you think will happen in an experiment: _ _ _ _ _ _ _ _ _ _
8. The steps you follow in your experiment: _ _ _ _ _ _ _ _ _
9. To use patterns in observations to say what may happen next: _ _ _ _ _ _ _
10. An investigation that is controlled: _ _ _ _ _ _ _ _ _ _

| | | | | | | | | | | | | | | | | |
|---|---|---|---|---|---|---|---|---|---|---|---|---|---|---|---|---|
| R | T | A | S | N | O | I | T | S | E | U | Q | K | S | A | R | S |
| C | O | L | L | E | C | T | D | A | T | A | R | S | A | T | S | I |
| S | C | I | E | N | T | I | F | I | C | M | E | T | H | O | D | S |
| B | B | N | Z | X | E | J | E | O | E | S | T | S | A | U | Y | E |
| A | Z | E | Y | N | P | I | D | D | V | U | L | O | T | Q | S | H |
| R | F | G | L | A | C | E | A | A | U | F | Q | E | A | T | V | T |
| G | W | R | A | M | D | N | R | E | P | L | P | T | D | V | L | O |
| R | C | A | N | C | I | I | R | I | W | N | C | I | D | O | D | P |
| A | E | P | A | C | A | D | G | R | M | I | U | N | R | A | M | Y |
| P | I | H | A | B | G | K | N | I | D | E | P | T | O | B | Z | H |
| H | N | K | L | Y | R | H | L | E | A | H | N | Y | C | C | U | A |
| R | Y | E | W | D | A | X | R | V | M | O | A | T | E | N | R | A |
| A | N | G | L | B | M | P | R | O | C | E | D | U | R | E | Y | D |

**CHALLENGE:** How many other important words from this lesson can you find in the word search? Write them below.

____________________

____________________

____________________

____________________

____________________

____________________

# Apply Concepts

2 For each question, state which kind of investigation works best: observational testing, using models, or experimental testing. Then explain how you would do the investigation.

What kinds of birds visit a feeder at different times of the year?

Does hot water or cold water boil faster?

What are the parts of an elevator and how does it work?

How does the length of a kite's tail affect the way it flies?

3 Ryan hypothesizes that darker colors heat up faster. He places a thermometer inside a red wool sock, a green cotton glove, and a black nylon hat. What's wrong with his procedure?

Use scientific methods to help your family enjoy a healthy snack. Design an experiment to find out whether coating apple slices in lemon juice can stop them from turning brown. Perform your experiment.

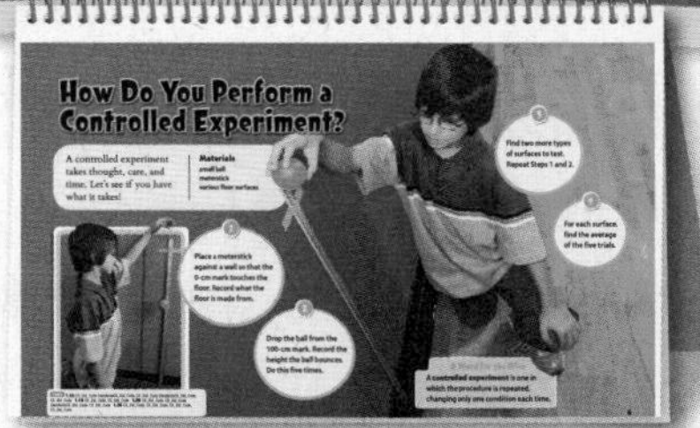

Inquiry Flipchart page 6

**TEKS** **5.2D** analyze and interpret information to construct reasonable explanations from... evidence **5.2E** demonstrate that repeated investigations may increase the reliability of results **5.2F** communicate valid conclusions in both written and verbal forms **5.4A** collect, record, and analyze information using tools, including...meter sticks...and notebooks...

Name ______________________________

Essential Question

# How Do You Perform a Controlled Experiment?

## Set a Purpose

**What will you learn from this experiment?**

______________________________

______________________________

______________________________

______________________________

______________________________

______________________________

______________________________

## Think About the Procedure

**What is the tested variable in this experiment?**

______________________________

**Each time you try the same test, it is called a trial. Why is it important to do repeated trials of this experiment?**

______________________________

______________________________

______________________________

## Record Your Data

**In the table below, record your results.**

| Surface Material | Height Ball Bounced | | | | | |
|---|---|---|---|---|---|---|
| | Trial 1 | Trial 2 | Trial 3 | Trial 4 | Trial 5 | Average |
| | | | | | | |
| | | | | | | |
| | | | | | | |
| | | | | | | |

## Draw Conclusions

Based on the empirical evidence from your experiment, what can you conclude?

## Analyze and Extend

1. Analyze and interpret information using direct (observable) evidence. Think about the materials the ball bounced on. What was it about them that affected the height of the bounce?

2. Analyze and interpret information using indirect (inferred) evidence. Tennis is played on three types of surfaces: grass, packed clay, and hard courts. Hard courts are often made from asphalt, the black road surface material. How do these surfaces compare to the surfaces that you tested? How would they affect the bounce of your ball?

3. **REVIEW** Suppose your data are different from other groups. How could you demonstrate that the data you obtained are reliable?

4. **REVIEW** Ask a well-defined question about how a ball bounces. Remember, a well-defined question is specific and testable.

.1A demonstrate safe practices and the use of safety equipment as described... well-defined questions, formulate testable hypotheses, and select and use appropriate and technology **5.4A** collect, record, and analyze information using tools...

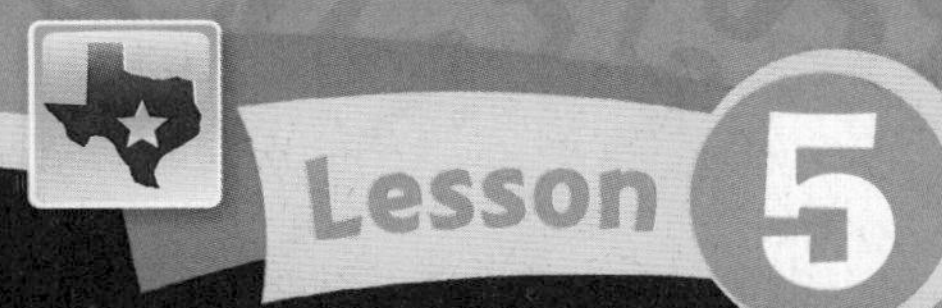


ntial Question

# What Are Some Science Tools?

## Engage Your Brain!

Find the answer to the following question in this lesson and write it here.

This scientific equipment is filled with liquids. What tools can scientists use to measure the volume of a liquid?

______________________________

______________________________

______________________________

## Active Reading

### Lesson Vocabulary

the terms. As you learn about each one, ke notes in the Interactive Glossary.

______________________________

______________________________

______________________________

______________________________

### Compare and Contrast

Many ideas in this lesson are connected because they explain comparisons and contrasts—how things are alike and different. Active readers stay focused on comparisons and contrasts when they ask themselves, How are these things alike? How are they different?

uiry Flipchart p. 7 — Making Measurements/Get Detailed
pp. 8–11 — Science Tools Activities

# Field Trips

If you like school field trips, you might want to become a field scientist. Field scientists travel around the world studying science in the wild. They pack their tools and take them along.

**Active Reading** As you read these two pages, box the names of all the science tools.

Field scientists go "on location" to investigate the natural world. Their investigations are often in the form of repeated observations. They use observational testing to evaluate scientific explantions. Choosing appropriate tools and technology to extend their senses is often their first step.

## Collecting Net

What kinds of animals swim near the shore of a pond? A scientist might use a collecting net and an observation pan to answer this question. By carefully pulling the net through the water, they can catch small animals without harming them.

## Hand Lens

How does an ant move? How does it use its mouthparts? A hand lens might help answer these questions. Hold the hand lens near your eye. Then move your other hand to bring the object into view. Move the object back and forth until it is in sharp focus.

# Do the Math!

## Estimate by Sampling

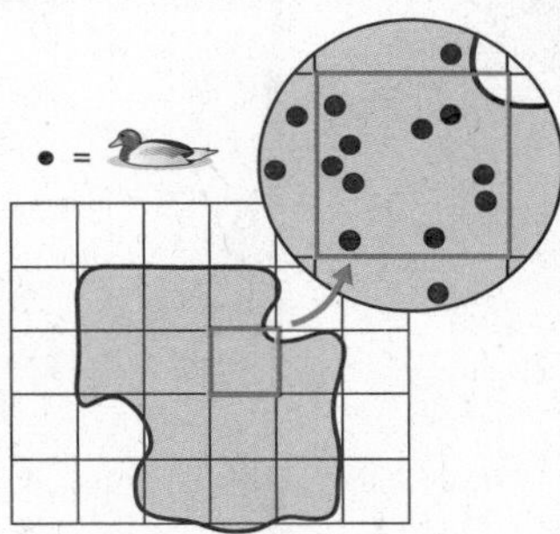

Scientists photograph ducks from a plane and then draw a grid over the photo. How many ducks do you estimate are on the whole lake?

_______________

Why might your estimate differ from the actual number of ducks?

_______________

_______________

_______________

## Cameras

What do lionfish eat? How do they catch their food? To investigate, a scientist might use an underwater video camera. Cameras help scientists record events.

# Into the Lab

What's living in a drop of pond water? Lots of tiny critters! Some behave like animals. Others are like plants. All are too small to be seen with only a hand lens.

**Active Reading** As you read these two pages, draw lines connecting the pairs of tools being compared to each other.

Science tools can be heavy and expensive. If you want to observe the tiniest pond life, you'll need science tools that are too big or too delicate to be carried into the field. For example, scientists use computers to record and analyze data, construct models, and communicate with other scientists.

## Use Numbers

Some tools help scientists count things. Some scientists estimate, while others perform complex mathematical calculations. All scientists must be comfortable **using numbers**.

▶ To find the magnification of a light microscope, multiply the power of the eyepiece lens by the power of the objective lens. The letter *X* stands for how many times bigger objects appear.

| Eyepiece Magnification | Objective Magnification | Total Magnification |
|---|---|---|
| 10X | 40X | |
| 15X | 60X | |
| 8X | 100X | |

## Light Microscope

The tiny living things in pond water are **microscopic**, or too small to see with just your eyes. A light microscope magnifies things, or makes them look bigger. The object to be viewed is placed on a clear slide. Light passes through the object and two lenses. You look through the eyepiece and turn knobs to focus an image.

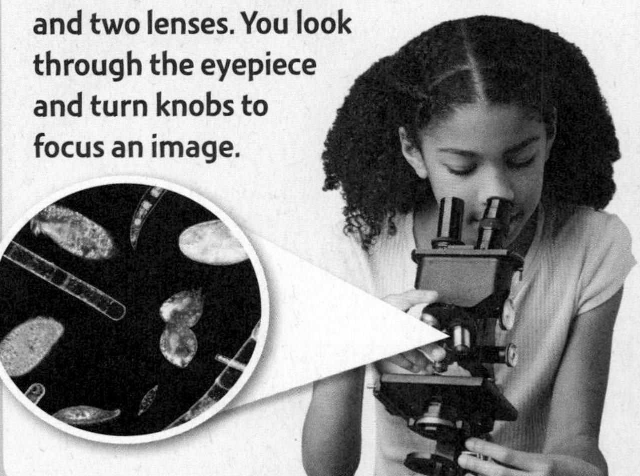

## Dropper

A dropper is a tube with a rubber bulb on one end. Squeeze the bulb and then dip the tip into a liquid. Release the bulb, and the liquid will be sucked up the tube. When you slowly squeeze the bulb, the liquid drops out.

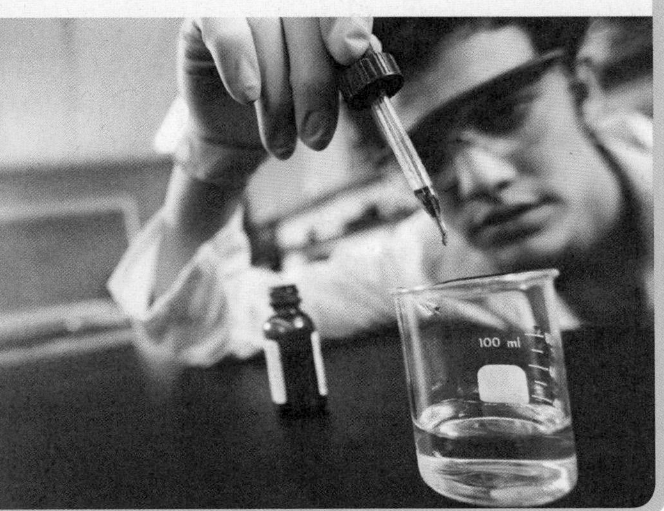


## Electron Microscope

Light microscopes have been around for 500 years. But technology, or people's use of tools, has improved. Today a scanning electron microscope (SEM) can magnify an object up to one million times. The SEM shoots a beam of electrons at the object. An image of the surface of the object appears on a computer screen.

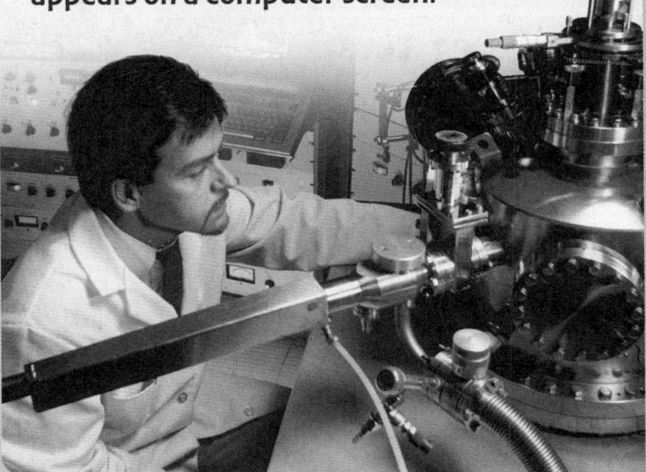

## Pipette

A pipette is a tool like a dropper, but it's more exact. It is used to add or remove very small amounts of liquids. Pipettes often have marks on the side to measure volume. One kind of pipette makes drops so tiny that they can only be seen with a scanning electron microscope!

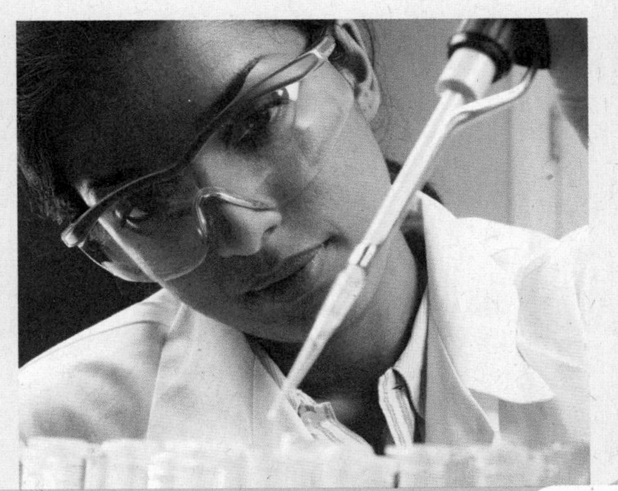

# Measuring Up

What do a digit, a palm, a hand, a dram, a peck, a rod, and a stone have in common? They all are, or were at one time, units of measurement!

**Active Reading** As you read the next four pages, circle all the units of measurement.

When you **measure**, you make observations involving numbers and units. Today most countries use the International System (SI) units in daily life. If you were to visit these countries, you'd purchase fruit or cheese by the *kilogram*. In the United States, most everyday measurements use units from the time when English colonists lived in America.

However, scientists around the world—including those in the United States—use the SI, or metric system.

The metric system is based on multiples of 10. In the metric system, base units are divided into smaller units using prefixes such as *milli-*, *centi-*, and *deci-*. Base units are changed to bigger units using prefixes such as *deca-* and *kilo-*.

## Measuring Length

Length is the distance between two points. The base metric unit of length is the *meter*. Rulers, metersticks, and tape measures are tools used to measure length.

A caliper can be used to measure the distance between the two sides of an object.

## Measuring Time

Time describes how long events take. The base unit of time is the second. Larger units are the minute, the hour, and the day. Smaller units include the millisecond and microsecond. Clocks, stopwatches, timers, and calendars are some of the tools used to measure time.

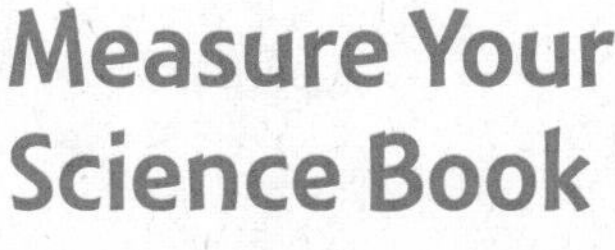

### Measure Your Science Book

Use a metric ruler and units to measure the length, width, and thickness of your science book.

Length: ____________________

Width: ____________________

Thickness: ____________________

## Measuring Temperature

Temperature describes how hot something is. Thermometers are used to measure temperature. Scientists measure temperature in degrees Celsius. So do most other people around the world. In the United States, degrees Fahrenheit are often used to report the weather, to measure body temperatures, and in cooking.

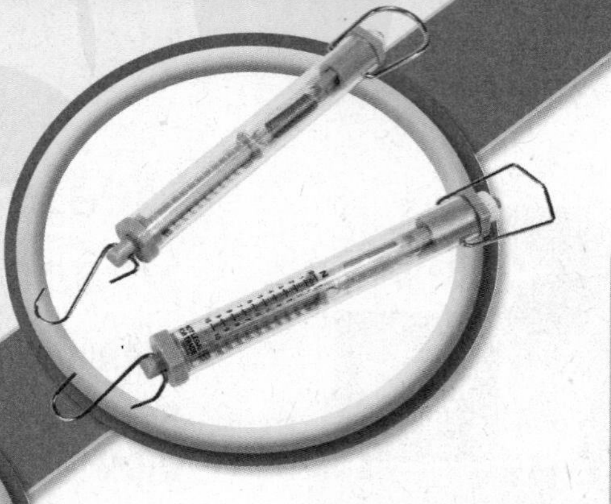

With this balance, you can directly compare the masses of two objects. Put one object in each pan. The pan that sinks lower contains the greater mass.

## Pan Balance

A **balance** is a tool used to measure mass. *Mass* is the amount of matter in an object. The base unit of mass is the kilogram. One kilogram equals 1,000 grams.

To measure in grams, place an object in one pan.

Add gram masses to the other pan until the two pans are balanced. Then add the values of the gram masses to find the total mass.

Always carry a balance by holding its base.

This pan balance has drawers where the masses are stored.

## Three Beams

A triple-beam balance measures mass more exactly than the pan balance. It has one pan and three beams. To find the number of grams, move the sliders until the beam balances.

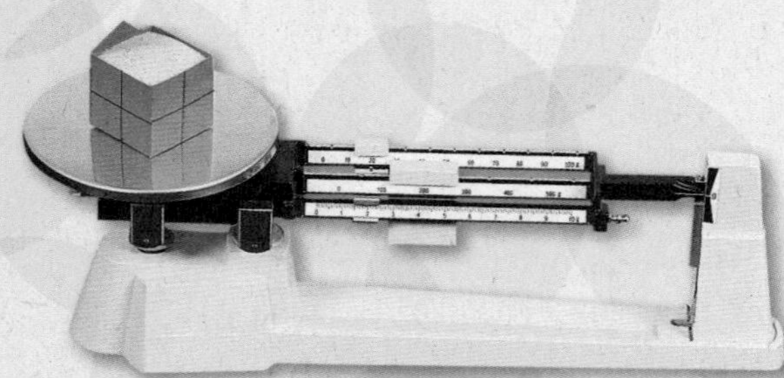

## Digital Mass

An electronic balance calculates the mass of an object for you. It displays an object's mass on a screen.

## How Strong?

A **spring scale** is a tool used to measure force. Force is a push or a pull. When an object hangs down from the scale, the force of gravity, or weight, is measured. When the spring scale is used to pull an object, it measures the force needed to move the object. Either way, the base unit is called a newton.

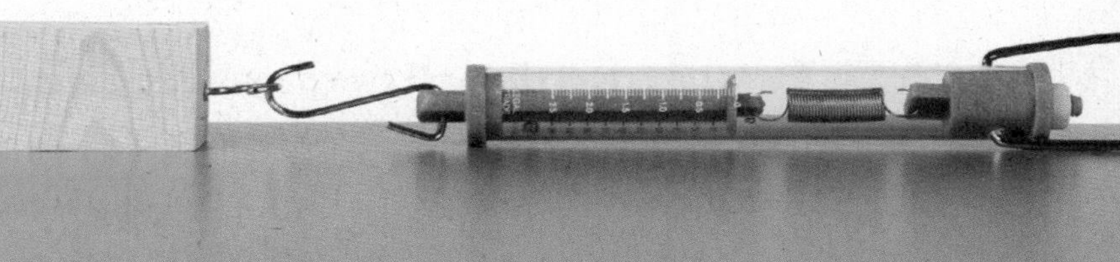

▶ **Draw lines to match the tools to what they measure and the units.**

| Tool | What It Measures | Units |
|---|---|---|
| 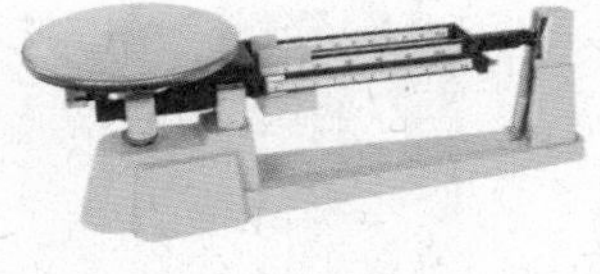 | ▪ force ▪ | ▪ seconds, minutes, hours, days, years, etc. |
| 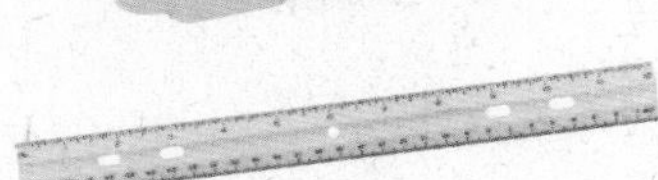 | ▪ temperature ▪ | ▪ grams, milligrams, kilograms, etc. |
|  | ▪ length ▪ | ▪ newtons |
| 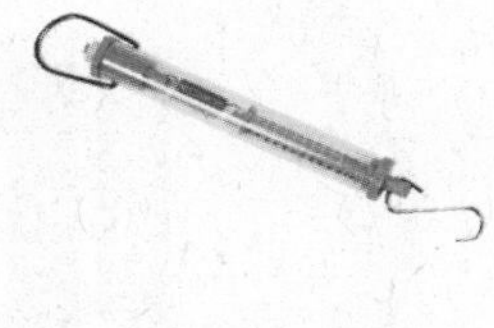 | ▪ mass ▪ | ▪ degrees Celsius, degrees Fahrenheit |
| 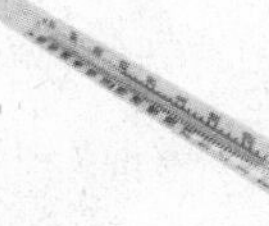 | ▪ time ▪ | ▪ meters, kilometers, millimeters, etc. |

# More Measuring

It's a hot day and you're thirsty. Would you prefer 1,000 milliliters or 1,000 cubic centimeters of lemonade? Not sure? Read on!

**Active Reading** **As you read the next two pages, circle important words that are defined, and underline their definitions.**

## Units of Volume

**Volume is the amount of space a solid, liquid, or gas takes up. There are two base metric units for measuring volume. A *cubic meter* is one meter long, one meter high, and one meter wide. The *liter* is the base unit often used for measuring the volume of liquids. You're probably familiar with liters because many drinks are sold in 1-liter or 2-liter bottles. These two metric units of volume are closely related. There are 1,000 liters (L) in one cubic meter ($m^3$).**

► **One cubic centimeter ($cm^3$) is equal to 1 milliliter (mL). Both are equal to about 20 drops from a dropper. Which is greater—1,000 mL or 1,000 $cm^3$?**

_______________________________

1 cm

1 cm

1 cm

## Finding Volume

You can find the volume of a rectangular prism by multiplying length times width times height. To find the volume of a liquid, use a measuring cup, beaker, or graduated cylinder. Use water to find the volume of an irregular solid. Put water in a graduated cylinder. Note the volume. Then drop the object in and note the new volume. Subtract the two numbers to find the volume of the object.

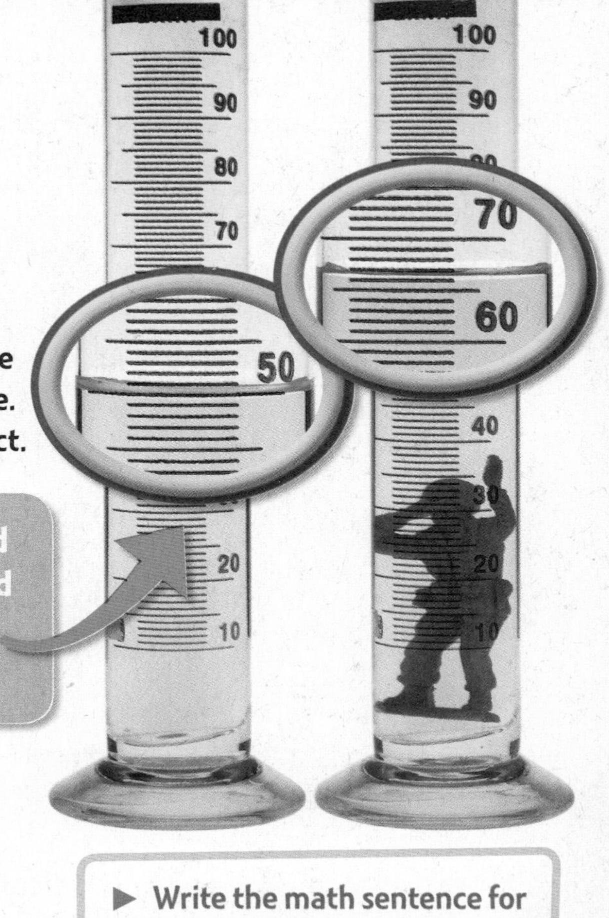


The surface of a liquid in a graduated cylinder is curved. This curve is called a *meniscus*. Always measure volume at the bottom of the meniscus.

▶ Write the math sentence for finding the volume of the toy.

_______________

## Accurate Measurements

When a measurement is close to the true size, it is **accurate**. Try to measure as accurately as you can with the tools you have. Make sure a tool is not broken and that you know how to use it properly. Also pay attention to the units on the tools you use. Accurate measurements are important when doing science investigations, when baking, and when taking medicines.

Follow these tips to improve your accuracy:

- ✓ Handle each tool properly.
- ✓ Use each tool the same way every time. For example, read the measurement at eye level.
- ✓ Measure to the smallest place value the tool allows.
- ✓ Measure twice.
- ✓ Record your measurements carefully, including the units.

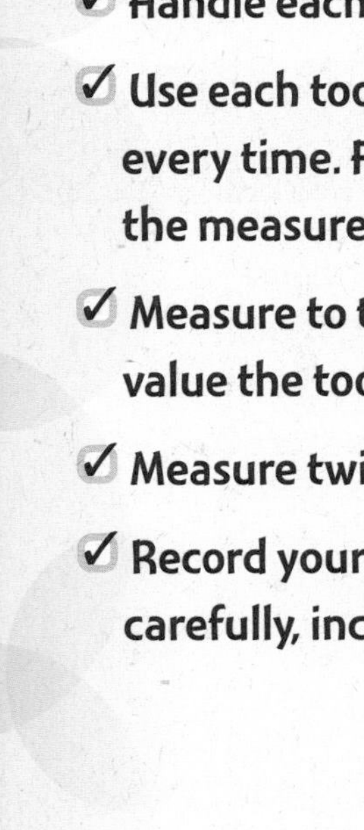

# Computing Information

Out in the field or in the lab, you may measure properties of objects or count how often something happens. What modern tools can help organize and make sense of all these data? Let's find out.

**Active Reading** As you read these two pages, circle the main idea in each section.

Calculators and computers are tools that can help you make sense of data. You can use these computing tools to make precise calculations. You can also use them to record, organize, and communicate information. Computers can be used to make bar, line, or circle graphs to display numerical data. This makes patterns and trends in the data easier to recognize.

## Computers

Computers are used to record and organize information during indoor and outdoor investigations. Scientists and engineers can use computers to:

- analyze their data;
- write up their results; and
- share the results of their investigations with others.

# Probes

A *digital probe* is an electronic tool used to make observations, or measurements. Some digital probes can do more than one thing. The probe shown here measures temperature. The data it collects can be downloaded into a computer to make a graph. Other kinds of probes can measure the amount of oxygen dissolved in a stream or the current in an electric circuit.

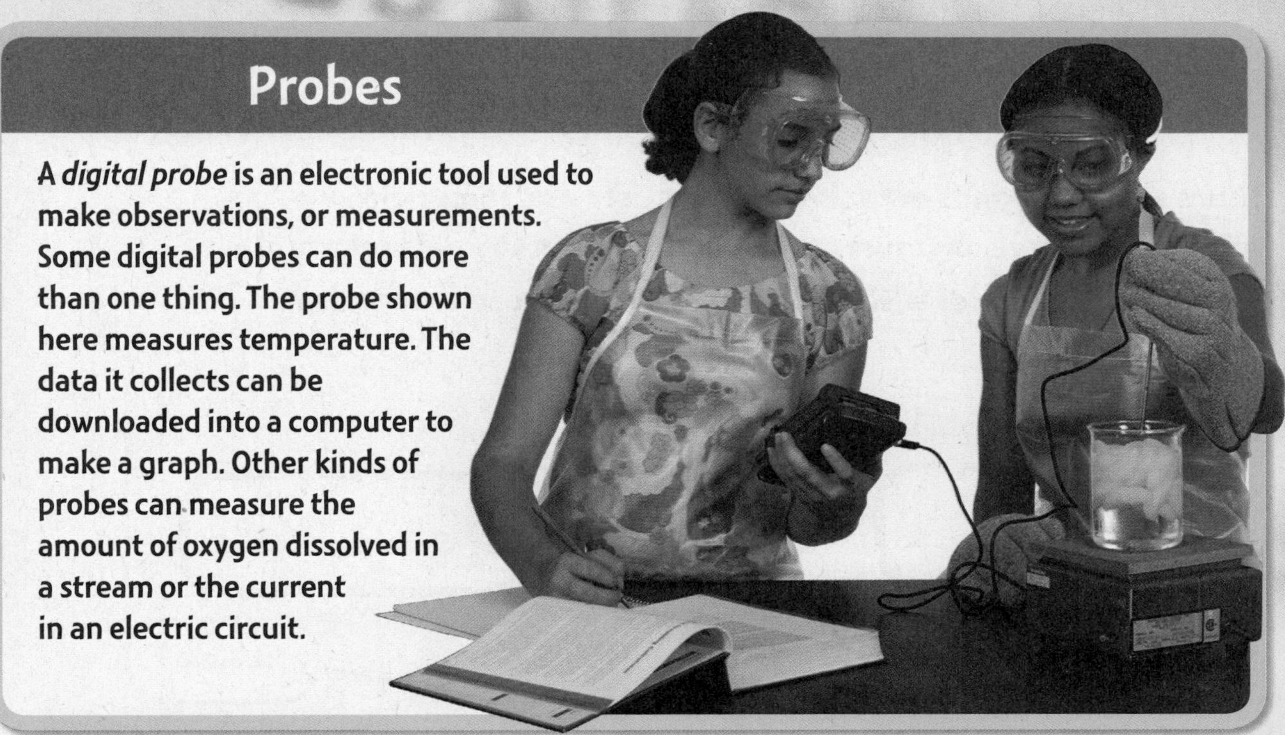

Data from outdoor investigations can be quickly shared with others using portable computers.

## Analyze Data

The table shows data collected by a temperature probe placed in an oven. Use a computer to plot the data on a graph. Then write a conclusion about what is happening in the oven.

| Time (min) | 0 | 5 | 10 | 15 | 20 |
|---|---|---|---|---|---|
| Temp. °C | 25 | 65 | 175 | 175 | 175 |

_______________

_______________

_______________

_______________

**When you're done, use the answer key to check and revise your work.**

**There are many kinds of tools that scientists use. Tools help scientists observe, measure, and study things in the natural world. Fill in the blank boxes with examples of tools that scientists use.**

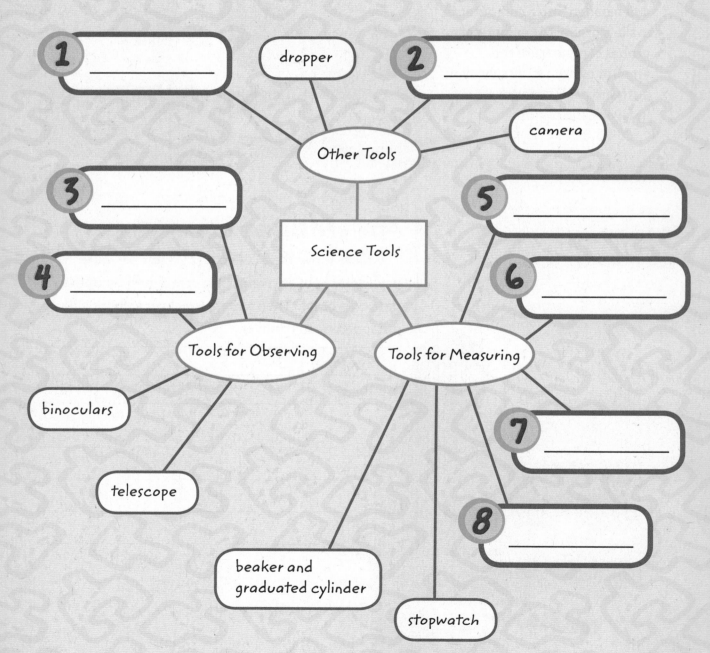

Science Tools

- Other Tools
  - 1 ___________
  - dropper
  - 2 ___________
  - camera
- Tools for Observing
  - 3 ___________
  - 4 ___________
  - binoculars
  - telescope
- Tools for Measuring
  - 5 ___________
  - 6 ___________
  - 7 ___________
  - 8 ___________
  - beaker and graduated cylinder
  - stopwatch

Answer Key: 1 and 2—computer or collecting net; 3 and 4—microscope or hand lens; 5, 6, 7, and 8—thermometer, balance, spring scale, and ruler or meterstick

Name ____________________

# Word Play

**1** Put the scrambled letters in order to spell a science term.

| | Scrambled | Answer | Clue |
|---|---|---|---|
| 1. | treem | ◯ _ _ ◯ _ | A metric unit of length |
| 2. | amrg | _ _ ◯ _ | A metric unit of mass |
| 3. | rdsgeee seCisul | _ _ _ _ _ _ ◯<br>_ _ _ _ _ ◯ _ | A metric unit for temperature |
| 4. | taceurca | _ _ _ _ ◯ _ _ ◯ | A measurement close to the true size |
| 5. | townne | _ _ _ ◯ _ _ | A unit used to measure force |
| 6. | trile | _ _ _ _ ◯ | A metric unit of volume |
| 7. | inpsrg casel | _ _ _ _ _ _<br>_ _ _ _ ◯ | A tool used to measure force |
| 8. | nap cablane | _ ◯ _<br>_ _ _ _ _ _ _ | A tool used to measure mass |
| 9. | dceson | ◯ _ _ _ _ _ | A metric unit of time |
| 10. | veumol | _ _ _ ◯ _ _ | The amount of space a solid, liquid, or gas takes up |
| 11. | tagurdade lycnidre | _ ◯ _ _ _ _ _ _ _<br>_ _ _ _ _ _ ◯ _ | A tool used to measure volume |

**Riddle:** Place the circled letters in order to solve the riddle below.

Why did the captain ask for a balance?

He wanted to _ _ _ _ _ _ _

the mass of the _ _ _ _ _ _ _ _.

# Apply Concepts

2 Tell how you use one or more of these tools to investigate each question.

How are two fossil teeth similar and different?

_______________

_______________

_______________

Which kinds of butterflies are found in a field?

_______________

_______________

_______________

What do scientists already know about the bottom of the ocean?

_______________

_______________

_______________

Does the mass of a ball affect how far it rolls?

_______________

_______________

_______________

3 Identify what each tool measures and the metric units it uses.

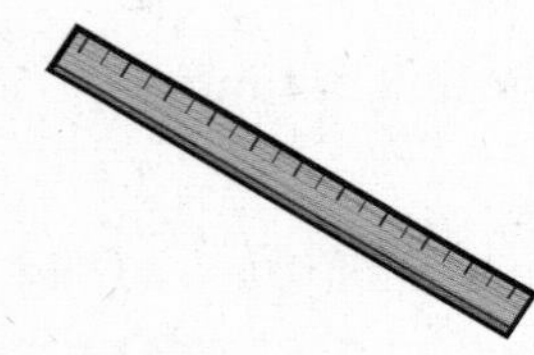

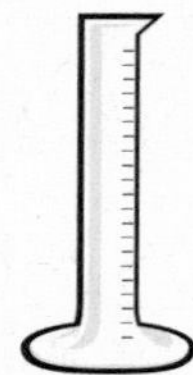

_______________ _______________ _______________

_______________ _______________ _______________

At your school or public library, find a book about how scientists work or the tools they use. Read and discuss the book with your family. Prepare a brief summary to present to your classmates.

Inquiry Flipchart page 12

**TEKS** **5.1A** demonstrate safe practices and the use of safety equipment... **5.2A** describe and implement... experimental investigations... **5.2B** Ask well-defined questions, formulate testable hypotheses... **5.2C** collect information by detailed observations and accurate measuring **5.2D** analyze and interpret information to construct reasonable explanations from... evidence **5.4A** collect, record, and analyze information using tools, including... pan balances... graduated cylinders, beakers... **5.4B** use safety equipment, including safety goggles and gloves

Name ______________________________

Essential Question

# How Can Scientists Learn from Observations?

## Set a Purpose

What will you learn from this investigation?

______________________________

______________________________

______________________________

______________________________

______________________________

## Think About the Procedure

What planning must I do before this investigation?

______________________________

______________________________

______________________________

What is a safety tool used in this investigation? What is a safety practice?

______________________________

______________________________

What properties of objects are measured in this investigation? What tools are used to measure them?

______________________________

______________________________

______________________________

______________________________

______________________________

## Record Your Data

In the space below, record your results.

Soil Sample: ______________

My Observations:

Amount of water held by 100 mL of soil: ______________

Mass Before Drying: ______________

Mass After Drying: ______________

## Draw Conclusions

Compare your data with the data from other groups. What can you conclude?

## Analyze and Extend

1. Few plants can survive in sandy soil. Use empirical evidence and logical reasoning to identify a characteristic of sandy soil.

2. Why would a farmer want to know about the soil on his or her farm?

3. How was this investigation different from a controlled experiment?

4. Why was it important to know the mass of the soil before it was dried for one week?

5. What else would you like to find out about different types of soils?

# Ask a Zoologist

wombat

**Q.** Do all zoologists work in a zoo?

**A.** Some, but not all, zoologists work in zoos. Zoologists are scientists who study animals. The word "zoo" comes from the Latin word for animal.

**Q.** Do zoologists get to play with animals?

**A.** No. Most zoologists study wild animals in their habitats. They try to observe animals without disturbing them.

**Q.** Do zoologists get to have wild animals as pets?

**A.** Wild animals do not make good pets. Zoologists do not take wild animals home. Pets such as cats and dogs have grown used to living with people. Wild animals have not.

## Now It's Your Turn!

What question would you ask a zoologist?

_______________

_______________

_______________

_______________

Wombats live in Tasmania and southeastern Australia.

# Animals That Start with "K"

Some zoologists study animal behavior, or how animals act. A zoologist spotted some interesting behaviors in Australia and wrote these journal entries. Match the sentences with the pictures by entering the day of the journal entry near the picture it describes.

**Day 1** This afternoon we saw an adult koala carrying a young koala on its back.

**Day 2** Today our team saw a kangaroo. It had a joey (a young kangaroo) in its pouch.

**Day 3** Our team saw a kangaroo hopping quickly. We measured its speed—nearly 24 kilometers per hour!

**Day 4** This morning we saw a koala. It was eating leaves from a eucalyptus tree.

**Day 5** We saw two kangaroos boxing with each other.

# Unit 1 Review

Name ______________________

## Vocabulary Review

Use the terms in the box to complete the sentences.

| balance<br>control<br>evidence<br>experiment<br>spring scale<br>variable |
|---|

TEKS 5.2A

1. An investigation in which all conditions are controlled is a(n) ______________________.

TEKS 5.2B, 5.4A

2. Jane wants to measure the mass of a rock. The tool she should use is a(n) ______________________.

TEKS 5.2A

3. Any condition in an experiment that can be changed is a(n) ______________________.

TEKS 5.2A

4. The information that scientists gather during an investigation is called ______________________.

TEKS 5.2A

5. The setup or condition to which you compare all the others in an experiment is the ______________________.

TEKS 5.2A, 5.2B, 5.4A

6. Jaime wants to find out how much force it takes to pull a toy car up a ramp. The tool he should use is a(n) ______________________.

## Science Concepts

Fill in the letter of the choice that best answers the question.

TEKS 5.2B

7. Which of the following is the best testable hypothesis related to friction?

   Ⓐ You can use a spring scale to measure friction.

   Ⓑ Many different objects can produce friction.

   Ⓒ Friction increases as the roughness of the surface increases.

   Ⓓ Friction is caused by the attraction between particles.

TEKS 5.2C, 5.4A

8. Students look out the window for 5 minutes. In their notebooks, they record the number, type, and color of the vehicles that pass. What are students doing?

   Ⓐ concluding

   Ⓑ observing

   Ⓒ hypothesizing

   Ⓓ experimenting

Analyze and evaluate the information below to answer questions 9 and 10.

Abe built this setup to investigate how far a toy car would travel after it left the ramp. He used a meterstick to measure distance.

| Number of Books | Distance Traveled (m) |
|---|---|
| 2 | 1.50 |
| 4 | 2.50 |
| 6 | 3.75 |

TEKS 5.2D, 5.4A

9. Which is a conclusion that Abe can draw?

Ⓐ The toy car would have traveled farther if Abe had used a different ramp.

Ⓑ Adding two books to the height doubled the distance the car traveled.

Ⓒ A toy car will travel 6 meters if there are 8 books under the end of the ramp.

Ⓓ The greater the number of books under the ramp, the farther the car traveled.

TEKS 5.2E

10. How could Abe increase the reliability of his results?

Ⓐ Do the same experiment with different cars.

Ⓑ Do the experiment more times at each height.

Ⓒ Do the same experiment with different ramps.

Ⓓ Do the experiment on a different surface.

Use the following information to answer questions 11 and 12.

Jen wants to find out how the temperature of water affects the amount of sugar it can dissolve. She places 100 mL of water at 25 °C, 50 °C, and 75 °C into three containers. Jen adds measured masses of sugar to each container until no more will dissolve. She records all her data in a notebook.

TEKS 5.2A, 5.2B

11. Which of the following tools will Jen use in her experiment?

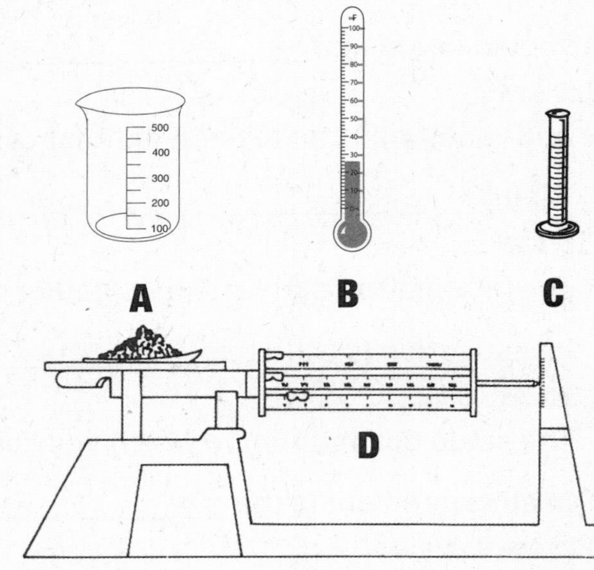


Ⓐ Only A and C

Ⓑ Only B and D

Ⓒ A, B, and C

Ⓓ A, B, C, and D

TEKS 5.2C

12. Which would be the best way for Jen to record her observations and data?

Ⓐ in a table

Ⓑ as a line graph

Ⓒ as a circle graph

Ⓓ in a Venn diagram

Name ______________________________

TEKS 5.2A, 5.3A

**13.** **Lena adds 5 g of fertilizer and 1 cup of water to Plant A and places it in the shade. She adds no fertilizer and 1 cup of water to Plant B and places it in the sun. She measures and records the growth of the two plants every other day for 10 days. Which of the following best describes Lena's experimental design?**

Ⓐ It is a well designed experiment to test the effect of fertilizer on plant growth.

Ⓑ It is a well designed experiment to test the effect of sunshine on plant growth.

Ⓒ It is a poorly designed experiment because she only measured the growth for 10 days.

Ⓓ It is a poorly designed experiment because it has no control and too many tested variables.

TEKS 5.2D, 5.3A

**14.** **Which is the best explanation for the observation that clothes hung in the sun dry faster than those hung in the shade?**

Ⓐ Sunshine causes air to flow around the clothes, carrying the water away.

Ⓑ Air in the shade is more humid than air in the sun, so water can't change to a gas as quickly.

Ⓒ More energy strikes the clothes in the sun, so water changes to a gas more quickly.

Ⓓ The light from the sun works with the heat to make the clothes dry faster.

TEKS 5.2D, 5.3A

**15.** **The table below shows the results of an experiment designed to study how exercise affects heart rate.**

| Time | Person A Heart Rate (beats/min) | Person B Heart Rate (beats/min) | Person C Heart Rate (beats/min) |
|---|---|---|---|
| Before exercise | 75 | 62 | 70 |
| After exercise | 120 | 110 | 130 |

**Which of the following statements is the best conclusion for this experiment?**

Ⓐ Heart rate is not affected by exercise.

Ⓑ Heart rate is increased by exercise.

Ⓒ Exercise triples a person's heart rate.

Ⓓ Exercise decreases a person's heart rate.

TEKS 5.2B, 5.4A

**16.** **Fahim wants to know more about how birds protect their nests. Which equipment should Fahim choose for his experiment?**

Ⓐ a recorder and a collecting net

Ⓑ a camera and a notebook

Ⓒ a hand lens and a stopwatch

Ⓓ a calculator and a clock

## Apply Inquiry and Review the Big Idea

Write the answers to these questions.

TEKS 5.2D, 5.2G

17. Maria counts the number of people who attend several basketball games. She uses a computer to create the bar graph.

    How many more people did Maria observe at Game 2 than at Game 1?

    ______________________________

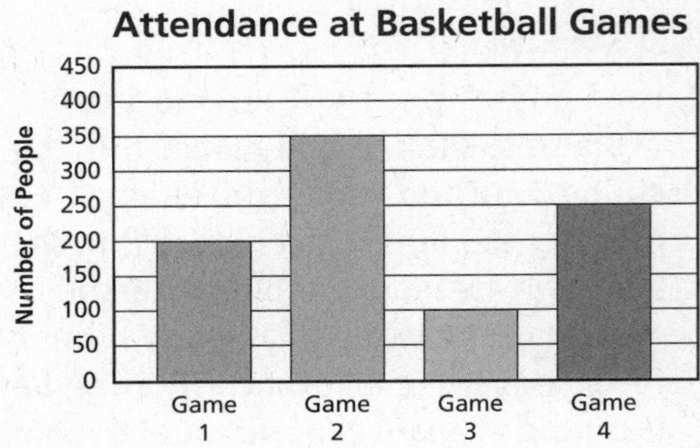


TEKS 5.2A, 5.2B, 5.2C

18. Keisha observes that sliced apples turn brown when exposed to air. She thinks that pouring a liquid, such as water, ginger ale, or lemon juice, over the apple slices will keep them from turning brown. What is Keisha's hypothesis? How could she set up a controlled experiment to test it? What variables will she control? How would she know if her hypothesis is correct?

    ______________________________

    ______________________________

    ______________________________

    ______________________________

TEKS 5.2D, 5.2F, 5.3C

19. Draw a diagram to show why a pot of boiling water left for too long over a stove dries up. Use your diagram to explain the process.

    ______________________________

    ______________________________

TEKS 5.2B, 5.2C,5.4A

20. Tia is observing a worm she found on a branch. What tools might Tia use to make observations about the worm?

    ______________________________

    ______________________________

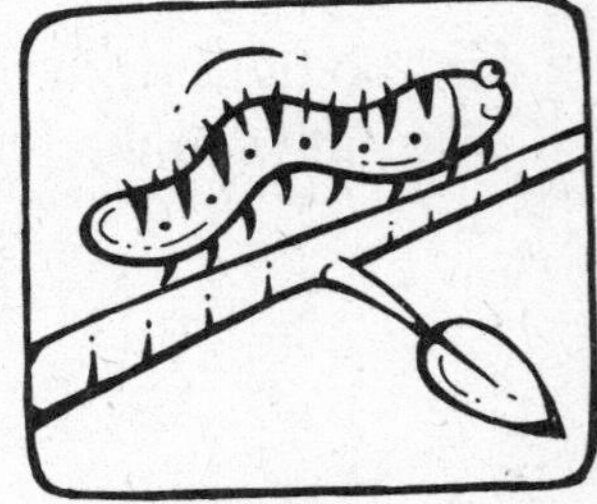

UNIT 2

# The Engineering Process

## Big Idea

Technology is all around us. Engineers apply their knowledge of science to design solutions to practical problems.

**TEKS** 5.2B, 5.2C, 5.2D, 5.2F, 5.2G, 5.3A, 5.3B, 5.3D, 5.4A

## I Wonder Why

Mixers, rollers, cutters, tumblers, and hoppers, all run by electricity! I wonder why it takes so many machines to make a gumball?

**Here's Why** Food processing relies on technology. Machines produce treats that always have the same taste, color, smell, and size. When a gumball pops out of the dispenser, you know exactly what you're getting!

In this unit, you will explore the Big Idea, the Essential Questions, and the Investigations on the Inquiry Flipchart.

Levels of Inquiry Key ■ DIRECTED ■ GUIDED ■ INDEPENDENT

**Big Idea** Technology is all around us. Engineers apply their knowledge of science to design solutions to practical problems.

## Essential Questions



**Science Notebook**

Before you begin each lesson, be sure to write your thoughts about the Essential Question.

**TEKS** **5.2D** analyze and interpret information to construct reasonable explanations from... evidence **5.2G** construct appropriate simple...charts using technology, including computers... to organize, examine and evaluate information **5.3D** connect grade-level appropriate science concepts with the history of science, science careers, and contributions of scientists

Lesson 1

Essential Question

# What Is the Design Process?

## Engage Your Brain!

Find the answer to the following question in this lesson and record it here.

What are the steps for designing technology such as the robot arm you see here?

______________________________

______________________________

______________________________

______________________________

______________________________

______________________________

## Active Reading

### Lesson Vocabulary

List the terms. As you learn about each one, make notes in the Interactive Glossary.

______________ ______________

______________ ______________

### Problem–Solution

Ideas in this lesson may be connected by a problem–solution relationship. Active readers mark a problem with a *P* to help them stay focused on the way information is organized. When multiple solutions are described, they mark each solution with an *S*.



Inquiry Flipchart p. 13 — Technology in Our Lives / Invent Your Own Technology

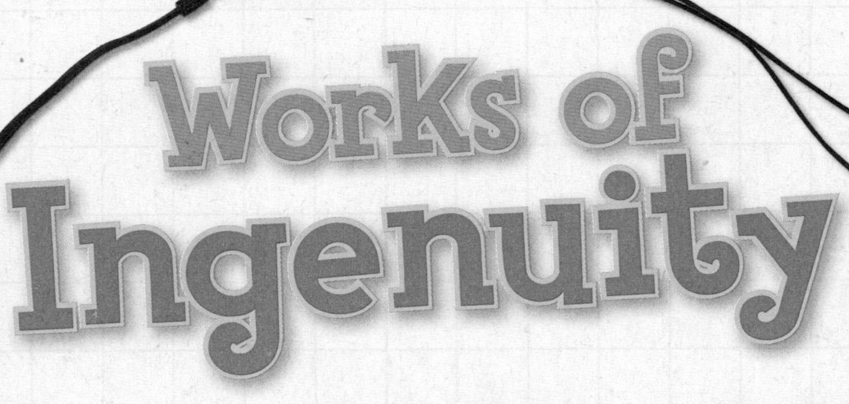

# Works of Ingenuity

Did you brush your teeth this morning? Did you run water from a faucet? Did you ride to school in a car or bus? If you did any of those things, you used a product of engineering.

**Active Reading** As you read these pages, underline the names of engineered devices.

Engineered devices, such as computers, help us solve many problems. Engineers use computers and hand-drawn diagrams to plan their designs.

Engineers are problem solvers. They invent or improve products that help us meet our needs. Engineers use their knowledge of science and mathematics to find solutions to everyday problems. This process is called **engineering**.

From the start of each day, we use the products of engineering. Engineered devices are found all around us. They include simple tools and complex machines.

Engineers work in many fields. Some design and test new kinds of materials. Some work in factories or on farms. Others work in medical laboratories. Engineers also design the engines that may one day fly people to Mars!

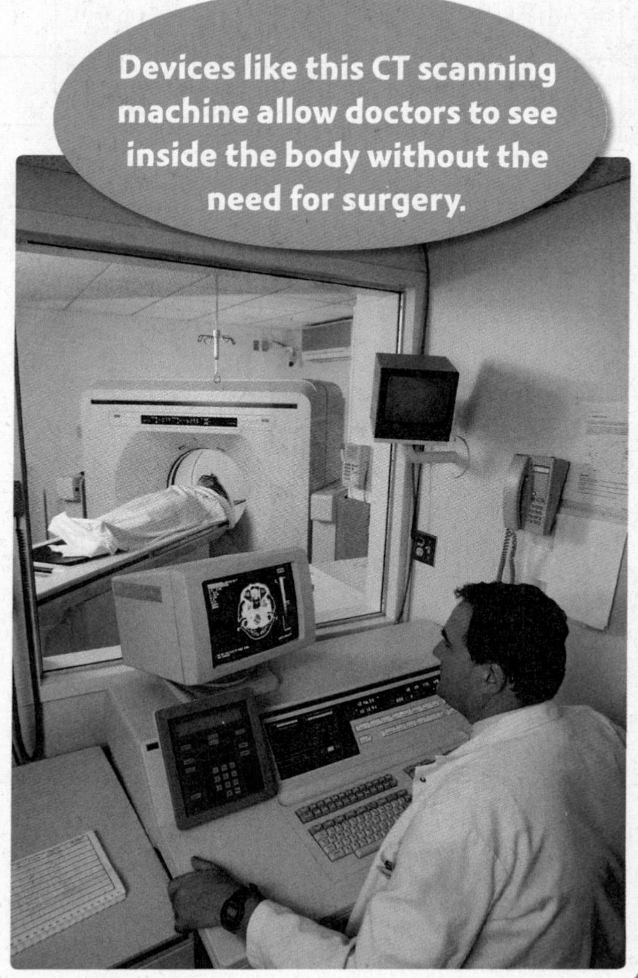

Devices like this CT scanning machine allow doctors to see inside the body without the need for surgery.

Sometimes engineers design devices with one purpose in mind—fun!

## Engineering Diary

In the space below, draw or use computers to construct a chart listing some of the engineered devices you use every day. Explain the need that each device meets.

# The Right Tool for the Right Job

When you see or hear the word *technology*, you may think of things such as flat screen TVs, computers, and cell phones. But technology includes more than just modern inventions.

**Active Reading** As you read these two pages, underline sentences that describe how technology affects our lives.

Stone tools, the wheel, and candles were invented a long time ago. They are examples of technology. **Technology** is any device that people use to meet their needs and solve practical problems.

Technology plays an important role in improving our lives. Tools and machines make our work easier or faster. Medicines help us restore our health and live longer. Satellites help us predict weather and communicate.

Technology changes as people's knowledge increases and they find better ways to meet their needs. For example, as people's knowledge of materials increased, stone tools gave way to metal tools. As people learned more about electricity, washboards and hand-cranked washing machines gave way to electric washers.

Centuries ago, many people washed their clothes on rocks in a river. The invention of the washboard allowed people to wash their clothes at home.

Over the past 150 years, engineers have improved washing machines. Even today, new washers are being designed to work faster and more efficiently.
The washboard helped make washing clothes easier, but it was still hard work. In the 1800s, engineers designed machines that could be filled with water and had a hand-cranked wringer. The wringer made getting the water out of clothes easier.

## Use Inferred Evidence

Look at the washboard. They were made of a wooden frame and a corrugated, or wavy, metal body. What technologies must have been developed before washboards were invented?

# The Design Process (Part 1)

Technology is all over—video games, 3D TVs, microwaves. But technology doesn't just happen. It comes about through a step-by-step process.

**Active Reading** As you read these pages, bracket sentences that describe a problem. Write *P* in the margin. Underline sentences that describe a solution. Write *S* by them.

When engineers design new technologies, they follow a *design process.* The process includes several steps. Here's how the process starts.

**1. Find a Problem** Engineers must first identify a need, or a problem to be solved. They brainstorm possible solutions. There may be more than one good solution.

**2. Plan and Build** Engineers choose the solution they think is most practical. They build a working model, or **prototype**, to test.

Throughout the design process, engineers keep careful records. Good records include detailed notes and drawings. Records help them remember what they have done and provide information to others working on similar problems. If the prototype doesn't work, the records can provide clues to a solution that *might* work next time.

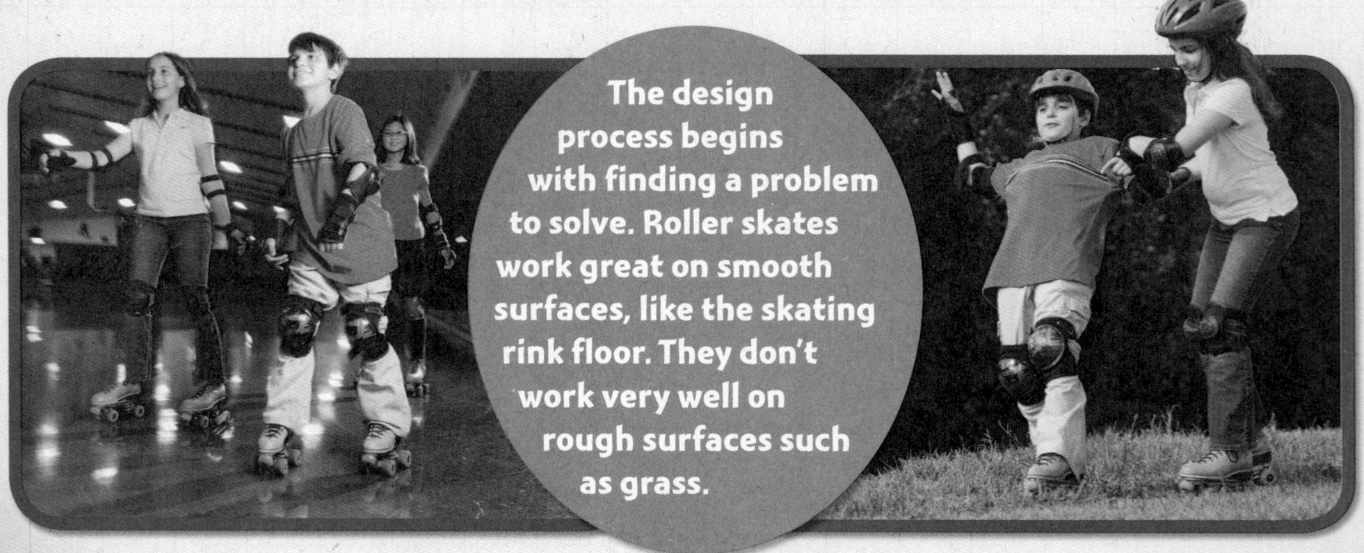

The design process begins with finding a problem to solve. Roller skates work great on smooth surfaces, like the skating rink floor. They don't work very well on rough surfaces such as grass.

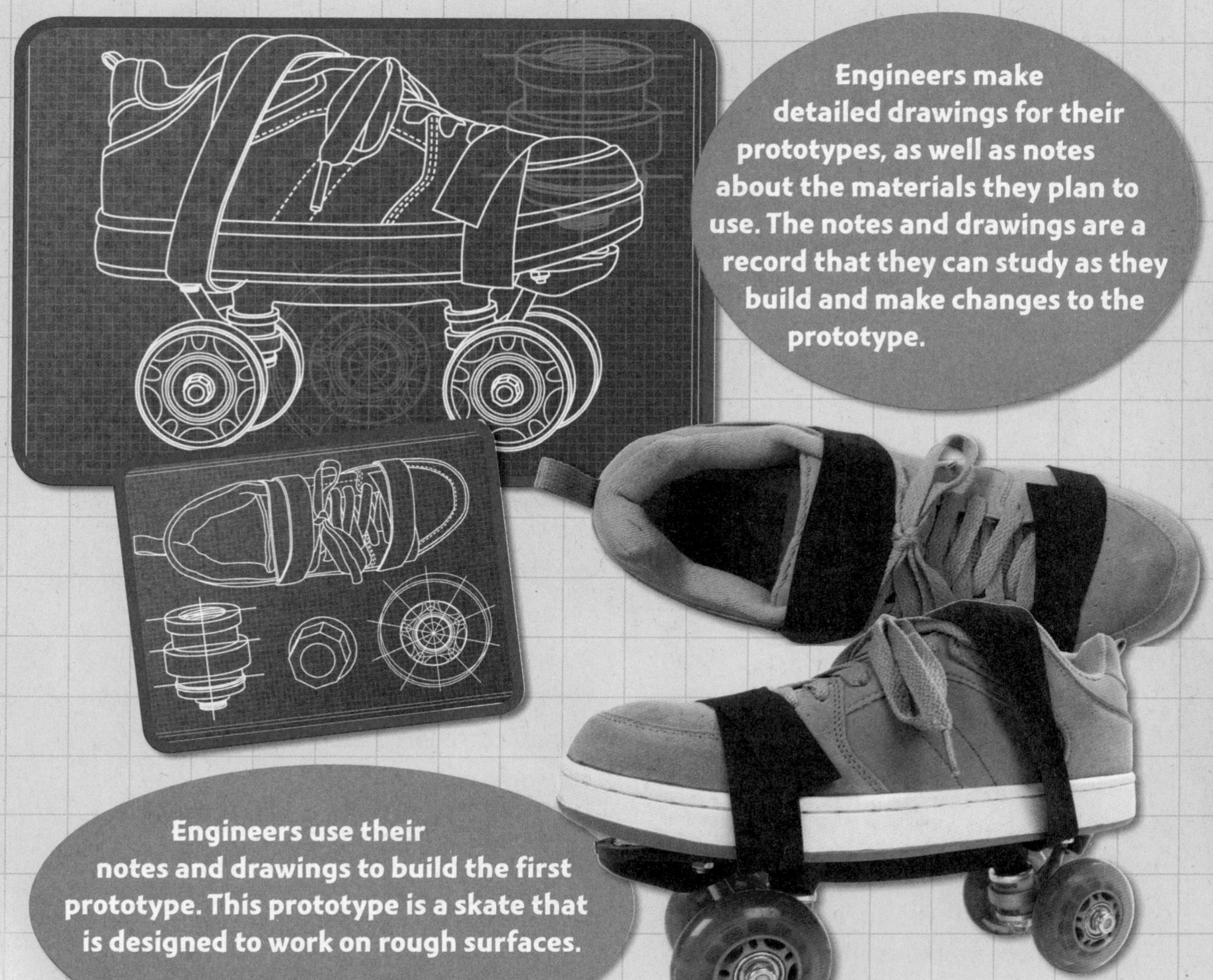
Engineers make detailed drawings for their prototypes, as well as notes about the materials they plan to use. The notes and drawings are a record that they can study as they build and make changes to the prototype.
Engineers use their notes and drawings to build the first prototype. This prototype is a skate that is designed to work on rough surfaces.

## Problem Solved!

The first step in the design process is identifying a problem and thinking up solutions. Complete the chart with a problem or a solution.

| Problem | Solution |
|---|---|
| Cord for the computer mouse keeps getting tangled | |
| | Watch face that lights up |
| | Hand-held electronic reader |
| Injuries in car crashes | |

# The Design Process (Part 2)

Do you get nervous when you hear the word *test*? A test is a useful way to decide both if you understand science and if a prototype works.

**Active Reading** As you read these two pages, draw boxes around clue words that signal a sequence or order.

The skate designers are steadily working through the steps of the design process. They have found a problem and built a prototype. What's next?

**3. Test and Improve** After engineers build a prototype, they test it. **Criteria** are standards that help engineers measure how well their design is doing its job. The tests gather data based on the criteria. The data often reveal areas that need improvement.

**4. Redesign** After testing, engineers may decide that they need to adjust the design. A new design will require a new prototype and more testing.

A prototype is usually tested and redesigned many times before a product is made on a large scale and sold to consumers.

**5. Communicate** Finally, engineers communicate their results orally and in written reports.

Engineers use criteria to test a prototype. They may gather data on how fast someone can skate on a rough surface or the number of times the person falls. Speed and safety are two criteria in the test you see here.

The design is modified if it doesn't meet all criteria. An unsafe design will be reworked even if the design meets all other criteria. The engineers focus on improvements. They revise their drawings and keep notes on design changes.

This is the redesigned skate. It has larger wheels that work better on rough surfaces. The skater can skate faster for longer distances without falling.

## Do the Math!

### Solve a Problem

Engineers tested a wheel that was 100 mm in diameter. Then they tested a wheel that was 0.15 larger.

Convert 0.15 to a fraction.

_______________________________

What is the size of the larger wheel?

_______________________________

# If At First You Don't Succeed...

Suppose Thomas Edison asked himself, "How many times must I make a new prototype?" What do you think his answer was?

Many things affect how long it takes to reach the final product for new technology. The kinds of materials needed, the cost, the time it takes to produce each prototype, and safety are just some of the criteria engineers consider.

Thomas Edison tried 1,000 times to develop a light bulb that didn't burn out quickly. It took him nearly two years to develop a bulb that met the criterion of being long-lasting.

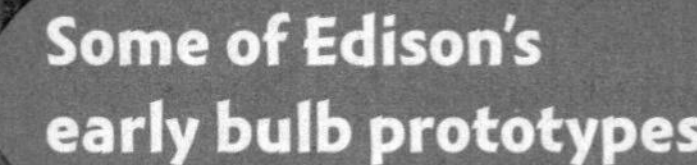

Some of Edison's early bulb prototypes

Cars must pass crash tests before they can be sold to the public.

Cars of the future may look different or run on fuels different from those of today. Years of testing and redesign occur before a new car is brought to market.

Finding materials that work well affects the design process. Edison found that the materials used to make light bulbs must stand up to heat.

Some technologies cost a lot of money to develop. For example, prototypes for many electronic devices are expensive to build. The cost of building the prototype, in turn, affects the cost of the final product.

It may take many years to develop new cars, because they must undergo safety and environmental testing. Environmental laws limit the pollutants that a car may release and determine the gas mileage it must get.

## Criteria Match Up

Draw a line from the technology to criteria that must be considered during the design process.

| **Technology** | **Must Be Considered** |
|---|---|
| Hydrogen car | Lightweight, sturdy |
| Laptop computer | Finding fuel |
| Bicycle | Portable, long battery life |

When you're done, use the answer key to check and revise your work.

**In the blanks, write the word that makes the sentence correct.**

| engineering | technology |
|---|---|

1. The things that engineers design to meet human needs are ________________
2. ________________ is the process of designing and testing new technologies.
3. Toothbrushes, washing machines, and computers are examples of ________________
4. ________________ uses math and science to test devices and designs.

## Summarize

**Fill in the missing words to explain how engineers conduct the design process. Use the words in the box if you need help.**

| communicating | engineering | keep good records |
|---|---|---|
| needs | problem | prototype |

5. ________________ is the use of science and math to solve everyday problems. Engineers invent and improve things that meet human 6. ________________ . The design process that engineers follow includes finding a 7. ________________ , building and testing a 8. ________________ , and 9. ________________ results. During each step of the design process, engineers 10. ________________ .

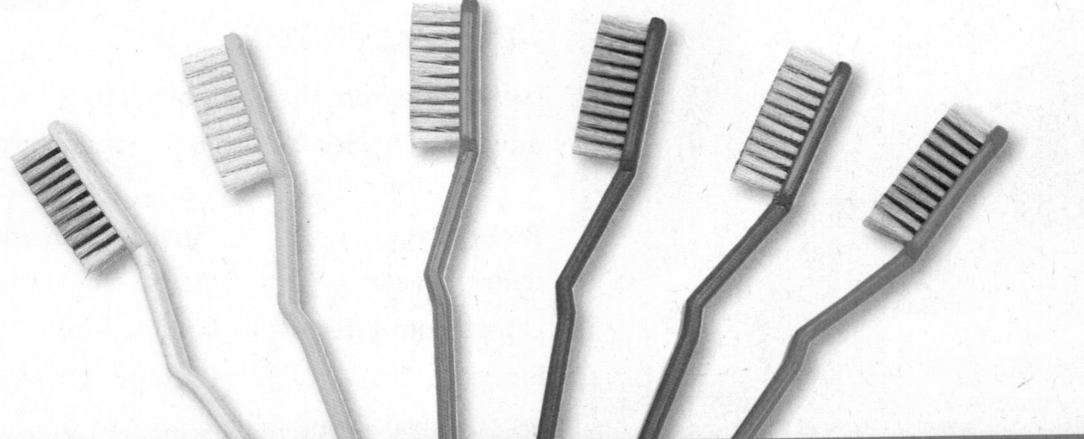



Answer Key: 1. technology 2. Engineering 3. technology 4. Engineering 5. Engineering 6. needs 7. problem 8. prototype 9. communicating 10. keep good records

# Brain Check

Lesson 1

Name ______________________________

## Word Play

**1** **Beside each sentence, write *T* if the sentence is mostly about using technology. Write *E* if the sentence is mostly about the engineering design process.**

_____ 1. Sarah sent a text message to Sam on her cell phone.

_____ 2. The nurse used a digital thermometer to measure the patient's temperature.

_____ 3. Henry tested three brands of blender. He wanted to see which one made the creamiest smoothies.

_____ 4. Workers at the factory use machines to bottle spring water.

_____ 5. Jessica invented a better mousetrap. She patented her invention.

_____ 6. Eli used math to figure out how much weight a bridge could hold.

_____ 7. The nurse is using a new x-ray machine.

_____ 8. Mayling is designing a refrigerator that uses less electricity.

_____ 9. Guillermo's new snowblower makes snow removal faster and easier.

_____ 10. Laptop computers are designed to be smaller, lighter, and easier to carry.

# Apply Concepts

**2** Match the picture of the technology to the need it fulfills. Draw a line from the picture to the matching need.

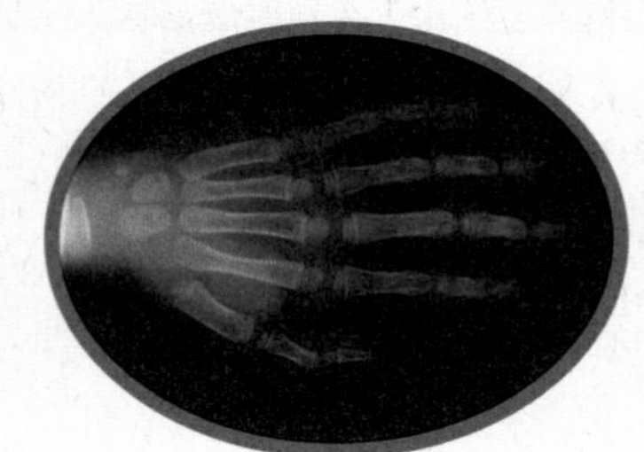

go to school

get up on time

see clearly

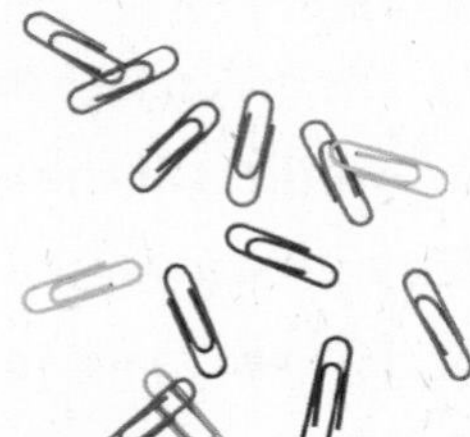

make a cake

fix a broken bone

keep papers together

**3** Write the missing words in the sentences below. Use the word box if you need help.

| brainstormed | good records | problem | prototype |
|---|---|---|---|

Jeremy had a ________________ that he wanted to solve—his go-cart was too slow. Jeremy and his friend Todd ________________ ideas to make it faster. Together, they designed a ________________ and tested it. They kept ________________ that showed that the go-cart really was faster.

Name ____________________



4 Circle the words or phrases that are criteria for designing skates that will be safe. Cross out those that are *not* criteria for safety.

roll smoothly | brake easily | come in different styles
fit snugly | come in different colors | sturdy

5 Look at the flow chart showing the steps of the design process. Then read the list of steps for designing a thermos. These steps are not in order. Write the letter of each step in the appropriate box of the flow chart.

**The Design Process**

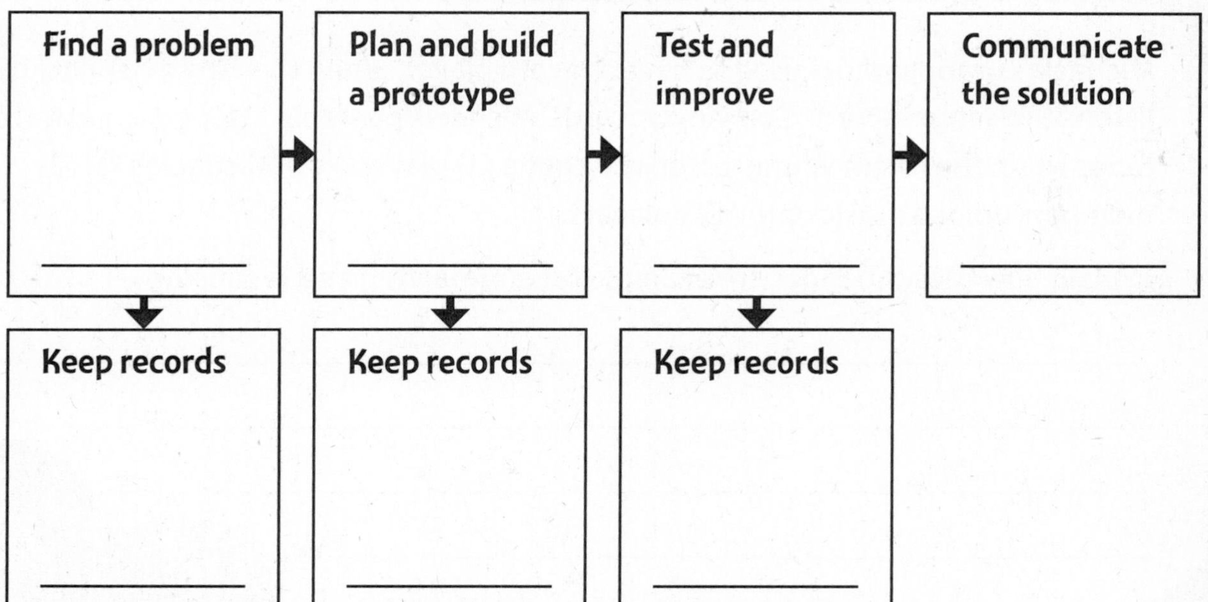


**Steps for Designing a Thermos**

**A** Keep data tables.

**B** Write a report

**C** Write down ideas.

**D** Make drawings.

**E** Measure the temperature inside the container.

**F** Keep hot things hot and cold things cold.

**G** Use insulating materials to make a container.

6 Sylvia is an engineer. Her friend Martin is an artist who paints with oil paints. Martin tells Sylvia that cleaning oil paint out of brushes takes a lot of time. It's messy, too. Write three or more sentences explaining what Sylvia would do to engineer a solution to Martin's problem.

7 Michaela's grandparents used to have a record player. When they were her age, they listened to songs recorded on vinyl records. Michaela's parents listened to cassette tapes when they were young. Later, they got a CD player. Now, Michaela's family members upload music onto MP3 players.

Explain how these changes are examples of engineering and technology.

**Take It Home!**

Ask an older person about a technology that has changed since he or she was young. Discuss how engineering has changed that technology over the years.

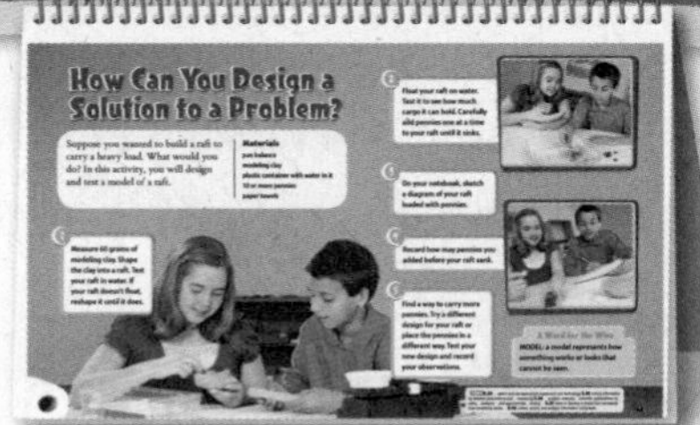

Inquiry Flipchart page 14

**TEKS 5.2A** describe, plan, and implement simple experimental investigations...**5.2D** analyze... information from...indirect (inferred) evidence **5.2G** construct...charts using technology **5.4A** collect... information using...pan balances

Name ______________________________

Essential Question

# How Can You Design a Solution to a Problem?

## Set a Purpose

**What is the purpose of this investigation?**

______________________________

______________________________

## State Your Hypothesis

**Sketch a raft with pennies on it to show what you think will be the best design. Write a brief description of your raft's key features.**

______________________________

______________________________

______________________________

## Think About the Procedure

**What variables can affect the results of this investigation?**

______________________________

______________________________

______________________________

______________________________

## Record Your Data

**In the space below, construct a chart to organize, evaluate, and examine information. Include information about each raft design and its performance.**

| | | |
|---|---|---|
| | | |
| | | |
| | | |

## Draw Conclusions

**Why did some of your model rafts work better than others?**

## Analyze and Extend

1. **Based on evidence from your investigation, sketch a raft design you think would NOT float. Explain why.**

2. **Mary and Sarah built identical raft models. Mary's raft sank after adding only 6 pennies. Sarah's raft held 12 pennies before it sank. Infer a possible reason for the difference.**

3. **Scientists often build and test models to solve problems. Based on this investigation, explain what are the advantages of solving problems in that way.**

4. **REVIEW Formulate another testable hypothesis related to how you can build a raft to carry a heavy load.**

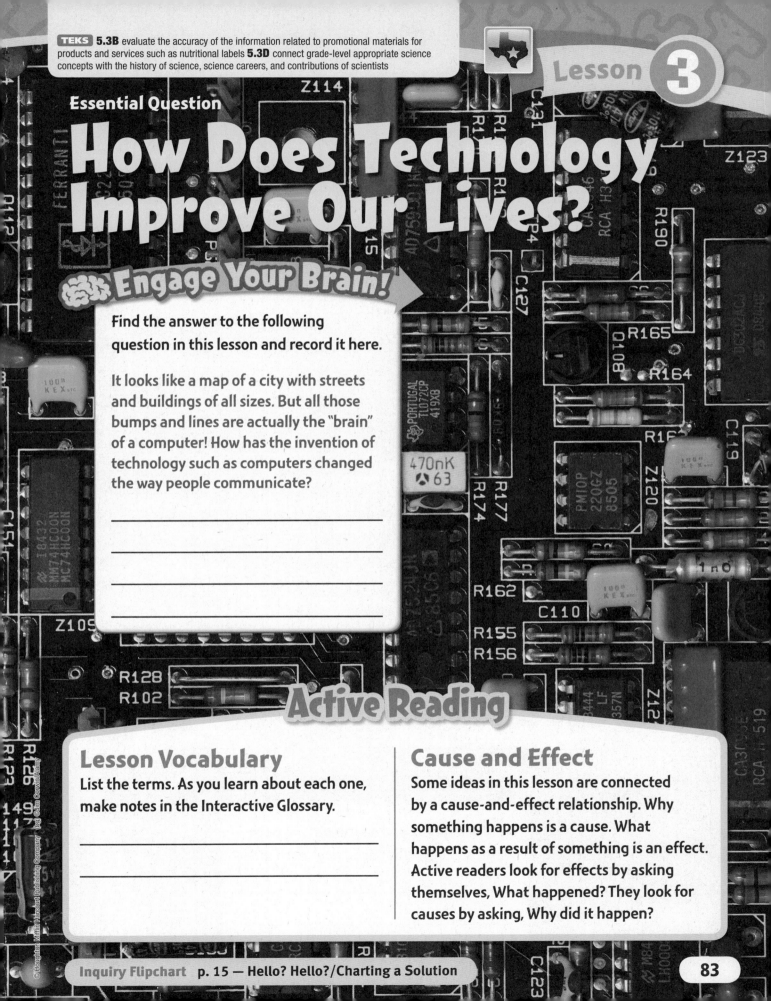

TEKS 5.3B evaluate the accuracy of the information related to promotional materials for products and services such as nutritional labels 5.3D connect grade-level appropriate science concepts with the history of science, science careers, and contributions of scientists

Lesson 3

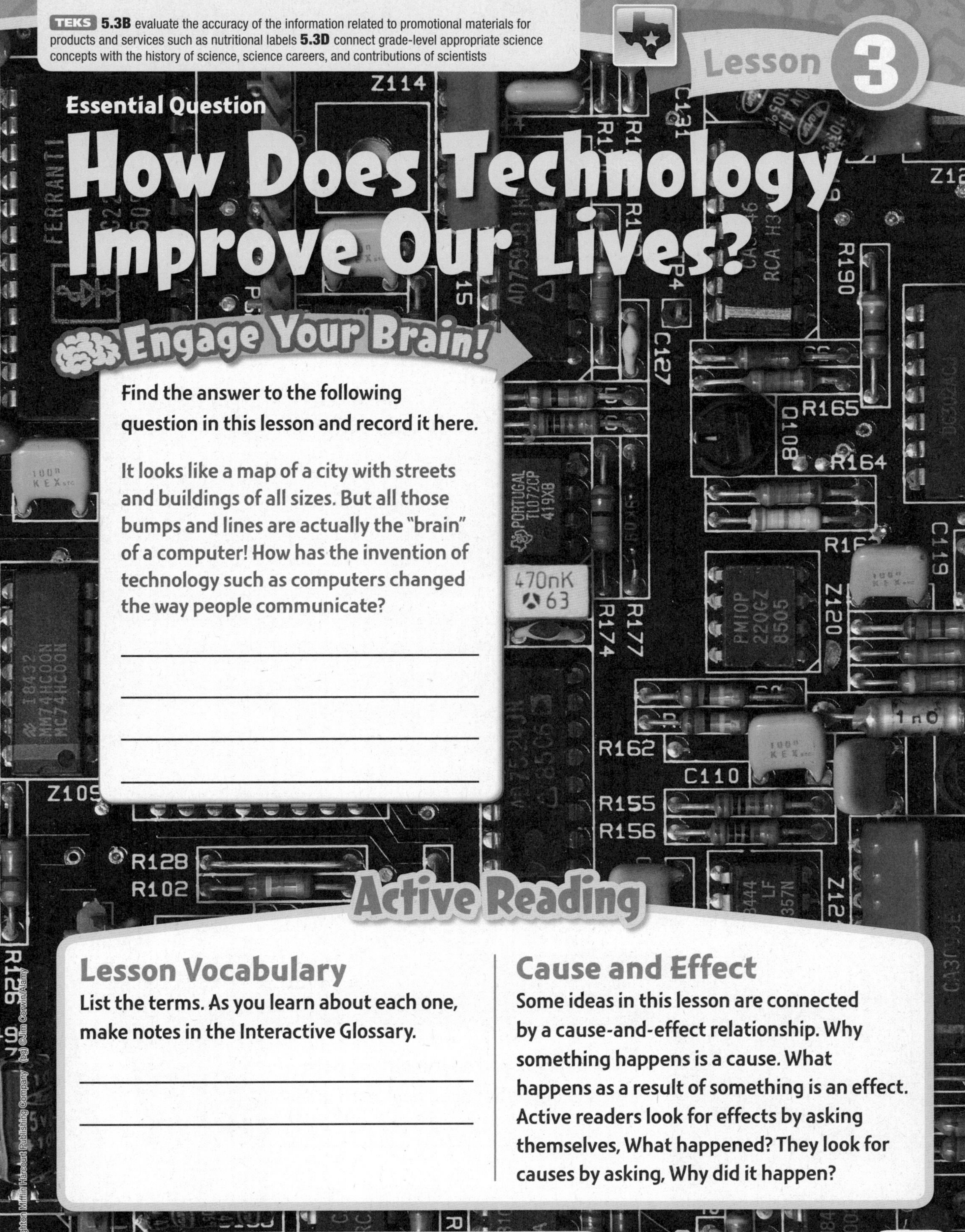

Essential Question

# How Does Technology Improve Our Lives?

## Engage Your Brain!

**Find the answer to the following question in this lesson and record it here.**

It looks like a map of a city with streets and buildings of all sizes. But all those bumps and lines are actually the "brain" of a computer! How has the invention of technology such as computers changed the way people communicate?

______________________________

______________________________

______________________________

______________________________

## Active Reading

### Lesson Vocabulary

List the terms. As you learn about each one, make notes in the Interactive Glossary.

______________________________

______________________________

### Cause and Effect

Some ideas in this lesson are connected by a cause-and-effect relationship. Why something happens is a cause. What happens as a result of something is an effect. Active readers look for effects by asking themselves, What happened? They look for causes by asking, Why did it happen?



Inquiry Flipchart p. 15 — Hello? Hello?/Charting a Solution

# The Technology Zone

Pick up your pencil and look at it carefully. You are holding technology in your hand.

**Active Reading** As you read these two pages, draw boxes around the names of two things that are being compared.

Most of the things you use every day are *technology*. Pencils, bikes, light bulbs, even the clothes you wear are technology. Cooking food uses technology. What makes something a technology is not how modern it is. Technology doesn't need to be complex or require electricity to operate.

What technology must do is meet a human need. A pencil lets you write your thoughts or work math problems. Think about what needs are being met as you read about the technologies on these two pages. How would you meet those needs without these items?

► Bike helmets and doorknobs are both technology. What need does each meet?

_______________________________________________

_______________________________________________

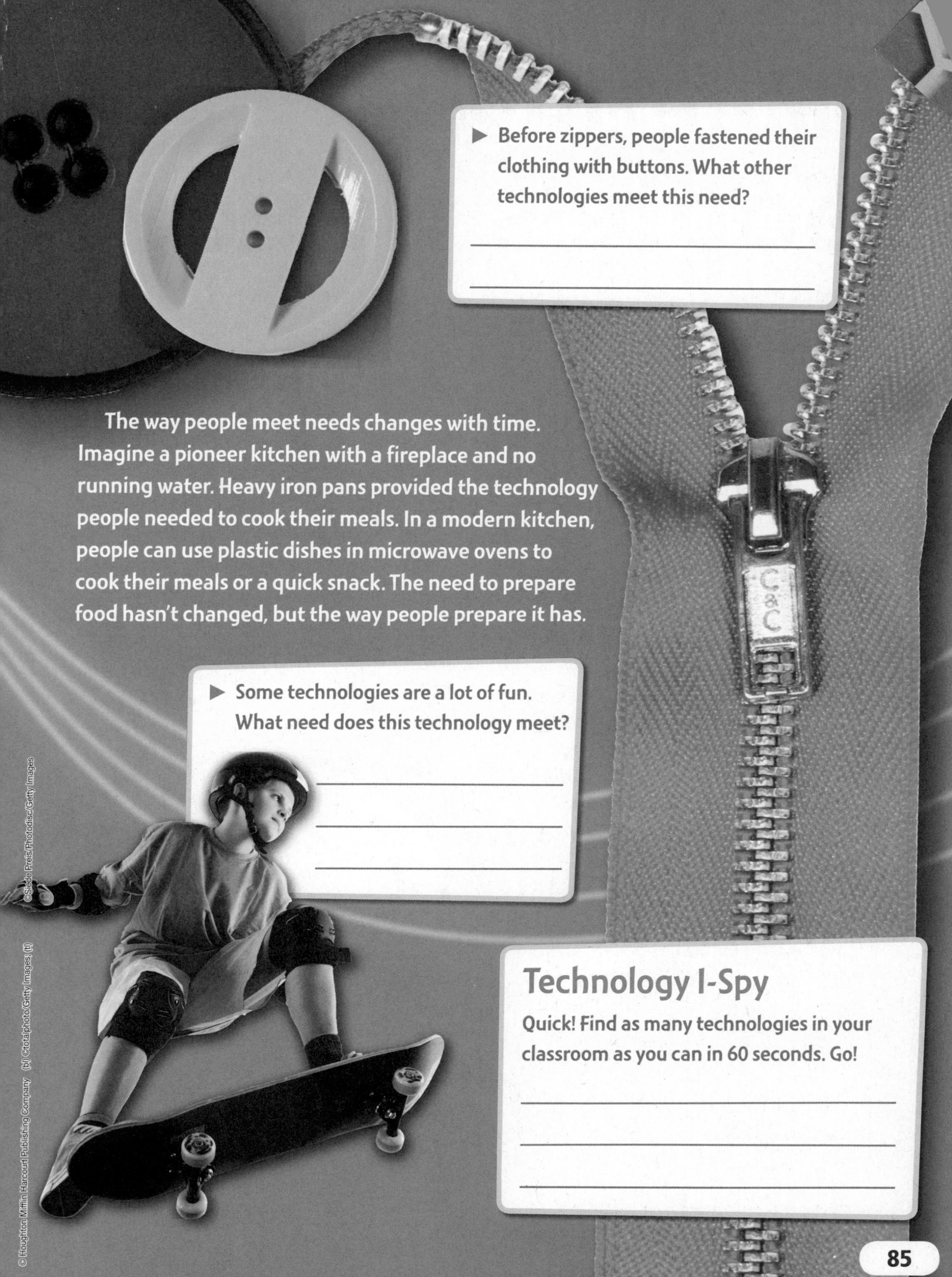


▶ Before zippers, people fastened their clothing with buttons. What other technologies meet this need?

The way people meet needs changes with time. Imagine a pioneer kitchen with a fireplace and no running water. Heavy iron pans provided the technology people needed to cook their meals. In a modern kitchen, people can use plastic dishes in microwave ovens to cook their meals or a quick snack. The need to prepare food hasn't changed, but the way people prepare it has.

▶ Some technologies are a lot of fun. What need does this technology meet?

## Technology I-Spy

Quick! Find as many technologies in your classroom as you can in 60 seconds. Go!

# Meeting People's Needs

It's 1860. You want to contact a distant friend. Today, you might send a text message. What about then?

**Active Reading** As you read these two pages, draw one line under a cause. Draw two lines under its effect.

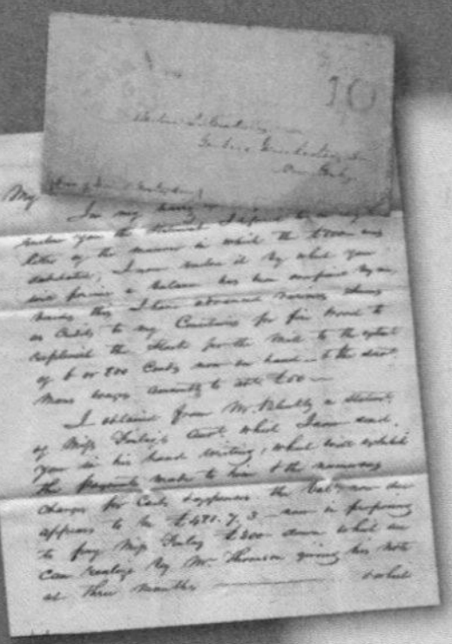

**1858**

**In the early 1800s, long-distance mail was carried by horseback riders, steamboats, and stagecoaches. A stagecoach took 25 days to carry a letter 3,000 km (1,700 mi) from St. Louis to San Francisco.**

**1869**

**When the transcontinental railroad opened, the time it took to move a letter across the country was cut down to a week or less.**

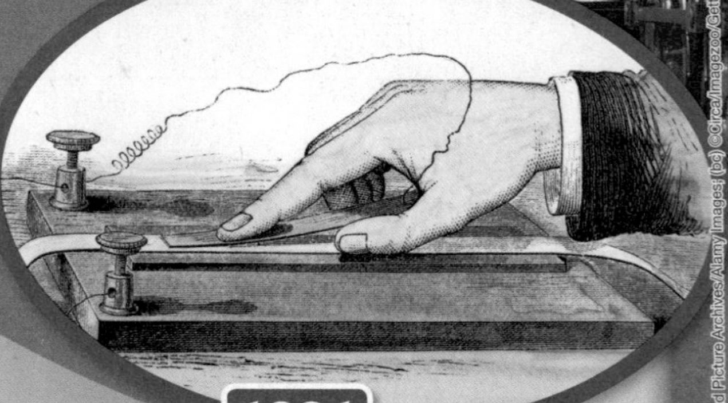

**1881**

**The time it took to send a message across the country was reduced to minutes with the invention of the telegraph.**

In the early 1800s, communicating with someone far away might take weeks or months. Sometimes such communications were not possible at all. As people began to move westward across the growing United States, the need for reliable communication increased. The timeline on these pages shows ways technology changed in response to this need.

The time it took to communicate with someone across the country decreased as new technologies developed. What once took weeks, then days, then minutes now happens almost instantly! Today, people text back and forth almost as fast as they can talk in person. E-mails can be sent to many people at one time. New technologies for communicating seem to develop faster and faster. What could be next?

**1915**

**Cross-country telephone service began in the United States.**

**1993**

**The first smartphone was developed.**

## Do the Math!

### Solve a Problem

Suppose you send two text messages per minute. How many text messages could you send in the time it took to carry a letter by stagecoach from St. Louis to San Francisco in 1858?

___

___

___

# Technology Risks and Benefits

A cell phone lets you communicate from almost anywhere. What happens when the phone dies or a newer, better model comes out?

**Active Reading** As you read these two pages, **underline** the things that are being contrasted.

Technology can have both positive and negative effects. Positive effects are called *benefits*. Benefits are the ways that a technology fills a need. For example, a cell phone lets friends and family communicate with you wherever you are. It might let you surf the Internet or download useful applications, too.

Negative effects are called *risks*. Cell phone technology changes fast, and some people switch to new models after just a few months. More resources are used up, and the old phones sometimes end up in a landfill. This risk is environmental.

No matter what the technology, there are both risks and benefits. Think about how each technology described here impacts your life. Are the benefits worth the risks?

### Computers

| BENEFITS | RISKS |
| --- | --- |
| Computers let you communicate with friends and family. They let you surf the Internet for information that can help with homework, and they let you play games. | Computer technology changes quickly, and many computers end up in landfills. Computers are expensive, and using the Internet can expose you to sites that are unsafe. |

## Automobiles

| BENEFITS | RISKS |
| --- | --- |
| Cars allow personal freedom by letting you go almost anywhere. They carry heavy items that you could not move on your own. | Cars use gasoline that is made from a limited resource—oil. They cause air pollution, and they can be dangerous if not driven properly. |

## MP3 Players

| BENEFITS | RISKS |
| --- | --- |
| MP3 players let you download and listen to your favorite music without disturbing others. | Turning up the volume can damage your hearing. You may not be able to download some songs. |

## Risks Versus Benefits

New technologies are being invented every day. One relatively new kind is digital print materials. List some benefits and risks associated with this new technology.

| BENEFITS | RISKS |
| --- | --- |
| ______________________ | ______________________ |
| ______________________ | ______________________ |
| ______________________ | ______________________ |

# Smart Choices

There are many new products and services today. How do you decide which ones to choose?

**Active Reading** As you read these two pages, underline types of information you can use to make smart choices.

Many more products and services come to market as new technologies develop. Companies with similar products or services compete against one another. Each claims that its product or service is best. Companies use *promotional materials*, such as the ones shown below, to catch your interest. But are the claims true? Before buying, smart shoppers clearly identify their own needs and wants. Then they evaluate the accuracy of the claims. Smart shoppers compare prices and features between similar products or services. They weigh the pros and cons of a product before buying.

These promotional materials make claims about the benefits of renting or buying computer games. How do you decide which one is best for you?

GAMES R US
Don't Pay More for New Games When You Could Rent for Less!
When you subscribe to our service, you could rent up to SIX Brand-New games for just $20 each!
So, why wait? Act Now!
Just pay an annual membership and renewal fee of $120 and start renting!

GAMEGARAGE
Buy It Now! Keep It Forever!
New bestsellers starting at $40!
Used classics as low as $15!
Build your collection!
Play over and over with your friends!
Preorder the hottest upcoming titles!

Promotional labels on products in the grocery store also try to catch your eye. These products may make claims about being healthful, having great taste, or being low in fat. Evaluating product claims may be a challenge. Luckily, there is a *nutritional label* on each. It tells you about a product's essential ingredients. Nutritional labels are designed to help you compare foods so that you can make healthful food choices.

Fresh fruits and vegetables are healthful. Yet processed, prepackaged, ready-to-eat foods may seem more convenient if you're on the go. Look at nutritional labels to decide which is best for you.

**Nutrition Facts**

Serving Size 1 strip (14g)

| Servings per Container | 10 |
|---|---|
| **Amount per Serving** | |
| **Calories** | 60 |
| Calories from Fat | 9 |
| | **% Daily Value*** |
| **Total Fat** 1g | **1%** |
| Saturated Fat 0g | **0%** |
| Trans Fat 0g | |
| **Cholesterol** 0mg | **0%** |
| **Sodium** 55mg | **2%** |
| **Total Carbohydrate** 12g | **4%** |
| Sugars 8g | |
| **Protein** 0g | |
| Vitamin C | 10% |

Not a significant source of dietary fiber, vitamin A, calcium, and iron.

*Percent Daily Values are based on a 2,000 calorie diet.

Ingredients: Apples from Concentrate, Corn Syrup, Dried Corn Syrup, Sugar, Partially Hydrogenated Cottonseed Oil. Contains 2% or less of: Citric Acid, Sodium Citrate, Acetylated Monoglycerides, Fruit Pectin, Dextrose, Malic Acid, Vitamin C (ascorbic Acid), Natural Flavor, Color (red 40, yellows 5 & 6, blue 1).

## Make a Choice!

Look at the three apple products on this page. Read the claims. Weigh the pros and cons. Which one will you choose? Explain why you made your decision.

______________________________

______________________________

______________________________

# Living Technology

The many branches of science are often connected. Engineered devices are sometimes used on living things. This connects engineering and biology.

This plant cleans wastewater to make it safe to return to the environment.

Engineers who work with living things are called bioengineers. When bioengineers apply the engineering design process to living things, they are practicing **bioengineering**.

A bioengineer may design a fish farm to raise large numbers of fish for food or other uses.

An important part of bioengineering has to do with the environment. Bioengineers design tools to prevent or clean up pollution, for example. Any product used to benefit organisms or their environment is an example of **biotechnology**.

Bioengineering also deals with health and nutrition. For instance, plants can be engineered to grow faster or larger to feed more people. Food for livestock may be engineered to make the animals healthier.

Bioengineers also design biotechnology that helps detect or treat diseases. For example, scanners in hospitals can look inside the body. They let doctors see a diseased or damaged organ. Other devices help surgeons perform operations.

Some bioengineers design devices that replace human body parts. Artificial legs help people who have lost their own. Artificial skin helps people with burns. Bioengineers have even developed artificial hearts.

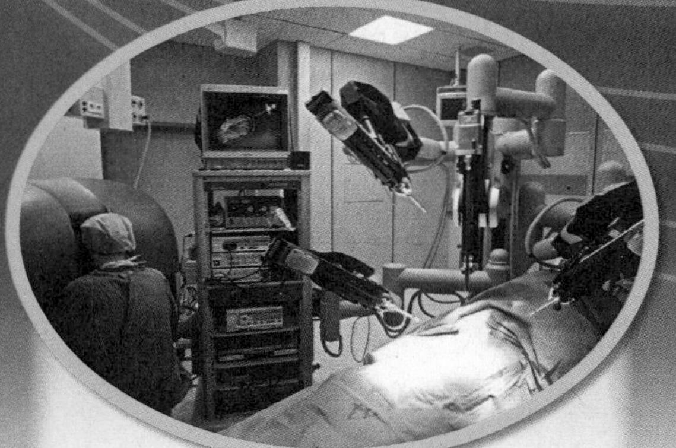

**Surgeons today can use computer-assisted machines in delicate operations.**

**This artificial heart may not look like a real human heart, but it works nearly the same.**



## Bioengineering and Human Needs

Identify the human need met by each of these biotechnologies.

| **Biotechnology** | **Need** |
|---|---|
| Water treatment plant | |
| Fish farm | |
| Robotic surgery | |
| Artificial heart | |

When you're done, use the answer key to check and revise your work.

## Summarize

**Fill in the missing words to explain how technology improves our lives. Use the words in the box if you need help.**

| | | |
|---|---|---|
| benefits | bioengineering | risks |
| promotional materials | need | technology |

Technology may be simple or complex, but all technology meets a 1. ___________________. 2. ___________________ changes as the needs of people change. Technology may have both a positive and a negative effect on people. Positive effects are called 3. ___________________. Negative effects are called 4. ___________________. 5. ___________________ make claims about products, but smart shoppers should always evaluate the accuracy of the claims. The application of the engineering design process to living things is 6. ___________________.

**Draw a line from the picture to the statement that best summarizes what the picture shows.**

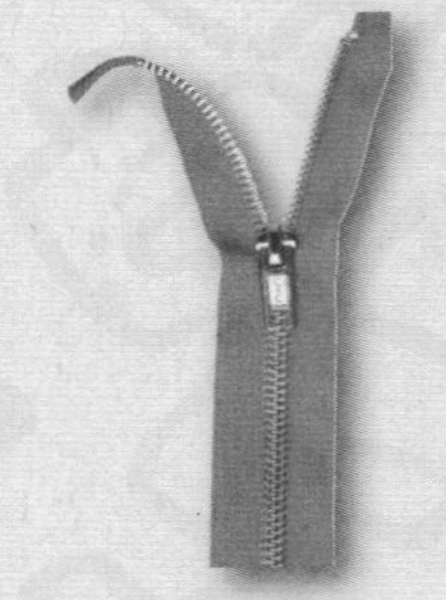

7. Bioengineering may develop technologies that protect the environment, improve nutrition, or replace body parts.

8. A benefit of packaged food is convenience. A risk is an increase in the amount of trash.

9. Even a simple fastener is technology because it meets a human need.

10. Communication technology has changed greatly over time.

Answer Key: 1. need 2. Technology 3. benefits 4. risks 5. promotional materials 6. bioengineering 7. line to artificial heart 8. line to dried apples 9. line to zipper 10. line to smartphone

# Brain Check



Name ________________________

## Word Play

1 Use the words in the box below to help you unscramble the highlighted words in each statement. Then, write the unscrambled word on the line.

One irsk of using a computer is being exposed to unsafe Internet sites.

________________________

A fish farm is an example of hetooblyincgo.

________________________

otyleonchg is anything that meets a need or solves a problem.

________________________

Engineers work with living organisms in the process of nnneeeiiiggbor.

________________________

mintroooalpaalsiremt make claims about products.

________________________

| benefit | bioengineering* | biotechnology* |
|---|---|---|
| risk | promotional materials | technology |

* Key Lesson Vocabulary

# Apply Concepts

**2** Describe how changes in transportation have affected communication over long distances. Give an example.

______________________________________________

______________________________________________

**3** Name two benefits and two risks for each of these technologies.

**4** Evaluate the accuracy of the label on this product. Explain if the label is accurate, or if it isn't.

______________________________

______________________________

______________________________

______________________________

With a family member, identify five examples of technology in your home. Explain to the family member what needs are met by each of the technologies. Try to identify the risks and benefits of each one.

# 10 THINGS YOU SHOULD KNOW ABOUT Prosthetic Designers

1. Prosthetic designers help people who are missing a body part, such as a hand, arm, or leg.
2. The people they help may have lost a body part from an injury or a disease. Or it may have been missing from birth.
3. Prosthetic designers create the prosthesis that replaces the missing body part.
4. To design a prosthesis, prosthetic designers need to study how the human body moves.
5. A prosthetic designer looks for new ways to improve how a prosthesis is made.
6. They use both computers and traditional tools including drills.
7. A prosthesis is made to meet the needs of each user.
8. A person may need a special prosthesis to swim, run, bike, or golf.
9. A prosthesis is designed to move easily, naturally, and under the wearer's control.
10. Prosthetic designers can change people's lives!

# Designing Sports Prostheses

**For each image, write the number of the design criteria that meet each person's needs.**

1. It should allow the leg to bend forward and the knee to lock.
2. It should fit comfortably at the knee and allow the ankle to rotate.
3. It should be lightweight, flexible, and resist high-force impacts.
4. It should be lightweight and able to rotate 180°.
5. It should be waterproof and allow the ankle to lock.
6. It should have attachments for gripping different objects.
7. It should be able to rotate 90° and have good traction.

Inquiry Flipchart page 16

TEKS **5.2B**...select and use appropriate equipment and technology **5.2C** collect information by detailed observations and accurate measuring **5.2F** communicate valid conclusions in both written and verbal forms

Name ____________________

Essential Question

# How Can You Use Engineering to Solve a Problem?

## Set a Purpose

**What problem are you trying to solve?**

____________________

____________________

**How would a jar opener be useful?**

____________________

____________________

____________________

## Think About the Procedure

**What is a prototype?**

____________________

**Describe two ideas for your prototype.**

____________________

____________________

____________________

____________________

____________________

## Record Your Data

**Draw a detailed plan for your jar opener. Label the materials. Describe how it will work. Then build and test your prototype.**

____________________

____________________

____________________

## Draw Conclusions

What criteria did you use to test your prototype?

Based on the tested criteria, write a valid conclusion about the results of your investigation. Then, communicate your conclusion in verbal form to your class.

Describe how you tested your prototype. Record any data you collected.

## Analyze and Extend

1. Did your prototype need improvements? Describe them.

2. Summarize how you designed and tested your jar opener.

3. Describe another jar opener design that is possible using the materials provided.

4. Think of other designs you might make if you had different materials. How would that design work?

# Unit 2 Review

Name ______________________

## Vocabulary Review

Use the terms in the box to complete the sentences.

| |
|---|
| bioengineering |
| biotechnology |
| criteria |
| engineer |
| prototype |
| technology |

TEKS 5.3D

1. People who use scientific knowledge to solve practical problems are producing ______________.

TEKS 5.3D

2. A person who uses science and math for practical purposes, such as designing structures, machines, and systems, is a(n) ______________.

TEKS 5.3D

3. The standards a designer uses to measure the success of a design are ______________.

TEKS 5.3D

4. The process of applying the engineering design process to living things is ______________.

TEKS 5.3D

5. The original or test model a designer builds for a new product is a(n) ______________.

TEKS 5.3D

6. An engineer who designs artificial legs is engaged in the field of ______________.

## Science Concepts

Fill in the letter of the choice that best answers the question.

TEKS 5.2B

7. Suppose you are a bioengineer designing an artificial hand that can perform everyday tasks, such as picking up a spoon. What would you do first?

   (A) Build a prototype and have someone use it.

   (B) Make the hand lighter and more flexible.

   (C) Build a computer model to observe how the human hand works.

   (D) Take a survey to see how many people are interested.

TEKS 5.2B

8. What is the first step in the design process?

   (A) Brainstorm ideas for a product.

   (B) Ask questions to establish a need.

   (C) Identify criteria for the product.

   (D) Build a prototype and test it.

TEKS 5.2D, 5.3D

9. Engineers study materials for possible use in an artificial knee joint. They need a strong material with a mass/volume ratio in the range of 2.3–2.6. The graph shows data they collected on three materials.

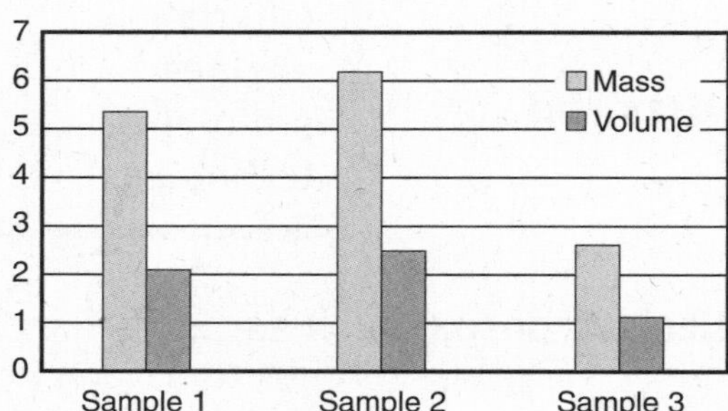


What can the engineers conclude using the data from the graph?

Ⓐ All of the samples meet the material design criterion that the engineers identified.

Ⓑ Sample 3 has the least volume and should not be considered for the knee.

Ⓒ Sample 2 has the greatest mass per volume ratio and is the densest material.

Ⓓ All samples are outside the acceptable range and show a mass of 5–6.

TEKS 5.2D

10. Use logical reasoning. Suppose you are designing a prosthetic shoulder joint. Which is the most important design criterion that you should include?

Ⓐ It should be realistic in color and appearance.

Ⓑ It should be capable of full movement within a shoulder socket.

Ⓒ It should keep the user from injuring himself again.

Ⓓ It should be stronger and more flexible than a natural shoulder joint.

TEKS 5.2D

11. A sports company wants to produce a profitable product that will benefit the wearer. The data below show the results of a survey about students' favorite sports activities.

**Sports Participation in High School**

| Sport | Fraction of Students |
|---|---|
| basketball | $\frac{4}{5}$ |
| bicycling | $\frac{3}{5}$ |
| soccer | $\frac{1}{2}$ |
| swimming | $\frac{3}{10}$ |

Which can you infer would be the most needed product among those students surveyed?

Ⓐ a helmet to protect against accidental head injuries

Ⓑ water-repelling racing swim trunks

Ⓒ shorts with padded backs

Ⓓ high-impact, ankle-supporting shoes

TEKS 5.2B

12. Which of the following is a testable hypothesis related to a new fabric prototype?

Ⓐ The fabric can be used for many products.

Ⓑ The fabric will be popular for use in clothing.

Ⓒ The fabric is stronger than other fabrics.

Ⓓ The fabric is easy to make and inexpensive.

Name ______________________________



TEKS 5.2D, 5.3D

**13.** Engineers want to develop a more efficient dishwasher by decreasing cycle time and the amount of water used per cycle. They design and test four different prototypes. The bar graph shows their results.

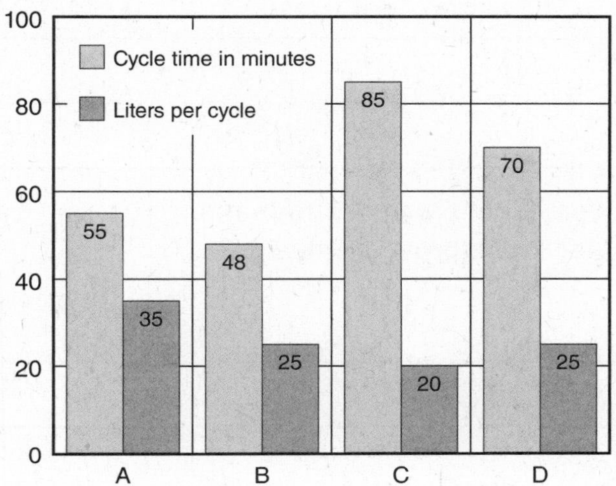


Based on this data, which model best meets the engineers' design criteria?

Ⓐ Model A
Ⓑ Model B
Ⓒ Model C
Ⓓ Model D

TEKS 5.2D, 5.3D

**14.** With further testing, engineers discover that the dishwasher model that best met the criteria didn't clean the dishes thoroughly. Which is the best next step for the engineers?

Ⓐ Start all over with a new dishwasher design.

Ⓑ Build another prototype and test it again.

Ⓒ Choose one of the other models to manufacture.

Ⓓ Figure out what is wrong with the model and redesign it.

TEKS 5.3B

**15.** A company claims that their MP3 players produce better sound than that of a competitor.

Which of the following best describes this claim?

Ⓐ If the company is reputable, it is probably true.

Ⓑ It can't be proven because "better" is an opinion.

Ⓒ It can be evaluated by experimental testing.

Ⓓ You could decide if it's true by testing the players.

TEKS 5.3B

**16.** A satellite TV company claims that they have more satisfied users than their competitor. How would you evaluate the accuracy of this claim?

Ⓐ Ask all of your friends and neighbors if they are satisfied with their company.

Ⓑ Read the claims of both companies and compare them.

Ⓒ Try both companies and decide which you like better.

Ⓓ Analyze a survey of satisfied satellite TV users.

# Apply Inquiry and Review the Big Idea

TEKS 5.2C, 5.2F

**17.** Javier wants to design a better pack to carry his books and sporting equipment back and forth to school.

**a.** What criteria will Javier use when choosing material for his bag? How will he test the criteria? What tools will he use?

**b.** Describe Javier's procedure in testing his prototype. What types of information will he collect? How will he decide whether he needs to improve his design? How will he select the final design?

Use the table to answer questions 18 and 19. It shows the result of an investigation to determine the range of the signal of four models of garage door remote openers and the time it takes for the doors to lift.

| Remote Range and Door Lift Time | | |
|---|---|---|
| **Model** | **Range (m)** | **Time (sec)** |
| A | 18 | 10 |
| B | 10 | 8 |
| C | 15 | 12 |
| D | 6 | 15 |

TEKS 5.2D

**18.** Analyze and interpret data. Which opener best meets the criteria for longest range and shortest lift time? Explain your answer.

TEKS 5.2D

**19.** How many times farther than the shortest-range remote was the longest-range remote able to activate the garage door?

UNIT 3

# Matter

## Big Idea

Matter has measurable physical properties which determine how matter is classified, changed, and used.

TEKS 5.2A, 5.2B, 5.2G, .5.5A, 5.5B, 5.5C, 5.5D

## I Wonder Why

This metal detector doesn't find objects made of glass, plastic, or wood. How does it detect only metal objects? *Turn the page to find out.*

**Here's why** A metal detector sends out signals. The signals bounce off hidden objects. The detector can tell the difference between the way metals and other materials reflect the signals. It lets the user know only when the object is made of metal.

In this unit, you will explore the Big Idea, the Essential Questions, and the Investigations on the Inquiry Flipchart.

Levels of Inquiry Key ■ DIRECTED ■ GUIDED ■ INDEPENDENT

**Big Idea** Matter has measurable physical properties which determine how matter is classified, changed, and used.

## Essential Questions



Now I Get the Big Idea!

**Science Notebook**

Before you begin each lesson, be sure to write your thoughts about the Essential Question.

**TEKS** **5.2A** describe, plan, and implement simple experimental investigations... **5.2G** construct appropriate...charts using technology, including computers... **5.5A** classify matter based on physical properties... **5.5B** identify the boiling and freezing/melting points of water on the Celsius scale

Lesson 1

Essential Question

# What Are Observable Physical Properties of Matter?

## Engage Your Brain!

As you read the lesson, look for the answer to the following question and record it here.

Bottled water and the snow from this snow machine are both water. How are these forms of water different?

______________________________

______________________________

______________________________

______________________________

## Active Reading

### Lesson Vocabulary

List the terms. As you learn about each one, make notes in the Interactive Glossary.

______________ ______________

______________ ______________

______________ ______________

______________ ______________

### Compare and Contrast

Many ideas in this lesson involve comparisons and contrasts—how things are alike and different. Active readers stay focused on comparisons and contrasts when they ask themselves, How are these things alike? How are they different?

# What's the Matter?

This book is made of matter, and so are you. You might think that matter can be seen and felt. But did you know that air is matter also? What is matter?

**Active Reading** As you read these two pages, draw two lines under each main idea.

The large pencil has more matter than the smaller pencils. It has more mass and more volume.

Breathe in and out. Can you feel air hitting your hand? You can't see air, and you can't grab it. Yet air is **matter** because it has mass and it has volume. Matter cannot be created or destroyed. It might change form, but it is still matter.

*Mass* is the amount of matter in something. Each of the tiny particles that make up matter has mass, even though the particles are so small you cannot see them. **Volume** is the amount of space something takes up. When air is blown into a balloon, you can see that it has volume.

## Name That Matter

Look at the matter in this picture.

1. What matter is soft and sticky?

_______________

2. What matter is hard and sharp?

_______________

Odor

Texture

## Matter Has Properties

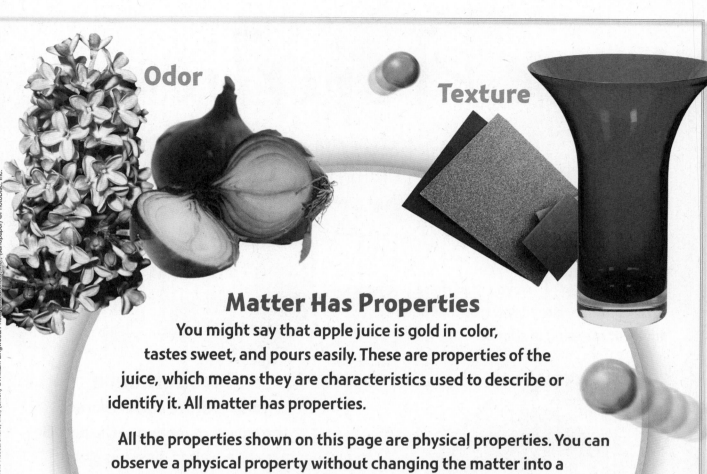

You might say that apple juice is gold in color, tastes sweet, and pours easily. These are properties of the juice, which means they are characteristics used to describe or identify it. All matter has properties.

All the properties shown on this page are physical properties. You can observe a physical property without changing the matter into a new substance. For example, texture is how something feels. In observing that sandpaper has a rough texture, you don't change the sandpaper.

Color

### Classify That Matter

Draw or use a computer to construct a chart to classify objects on these pages into two groups based on an observable physical property.

# More Properties

Color, texture, and odor are just a few physical properties. What are some other properties of matter?

**Active Reading** As you read these two pages, circle common everyday words that have a different meaning in science.

## Temperature

**Temperature** is a measure of the energy of motion of the particles in matter. Melted glass has a very high temperature. Temperature can be measured by using a thermometer.

## Volume

The food in the small bowl has less volume than the food in the large bowl because it takes up less space. Many tools can be used to measure volume.

## Mass

A bowling ball and a basketball have about the same volume. The bowling ball has a greater mass because it contains more matter. Mass can be measured by using a balance.

## Relative Density

The **relative density** of substances determines whether one will sink or float in another. The gas in these balloons is less dense than the air around them. That is why the balloons "float" in air.

# Do the Math!

### Use Comparison Symbols

Symbols are often used in math to compare quantities. The ">" symbol means *greater than,* and the "<" symbol means *less than.* Look at the picture. Then complete the chart by using the correct symbol.

| The relative density of | Comparison symbol | Layer or Object |
|---|---|---|
| the red liquid is | | the nut and bolt |
| the light blue liquid is | | the table tennis ball |
| the yellow liquid is | | all other liquids |

## Liquids

A **liquid** is a substance that has a definite volume but does not have a definite shape. The particles in a liquid move slower than the particles in a gas, and they slide by one another.

# States of Matter

Another physical property of matter is its state. Solid, liquid, and gas are the most common states of matter on Earth.

**Active Reading** As you read these two pages, draw boxes around the names of the three things that are being compared.

## Gases

A **gas** is a substance that does not have a definite shape or volume. The particles in a gas move very quickly and are far apart from one another.

Matter is made of tiny particles. The particles in solids, liquids, and gases have different amounts of energy. The amount of energy affects how fast the particles move and how close together they are.

The shape and volume of something depends on its state. Because each particle in a gas is affected little by the other particles, gas particles are free to move throughout their container. Gases take both the shape and the volume of their container.

Particles in a liquid cannot move as freely. A sample of a liquid keeps the same volume no matter what container it is in. However because the particles slide by one another, a liquid takes the shape of its container.

The particles in a solid do not move from place to place, so solids keep the same shape and volume.

## Solids

A **solid** is a substance with a definite shape and volume. The particles in a solid are very close to one another. They don't move from place to place. They vibrate where they are.

▶ Make a chart to classify the objects in the tank based on their states. Which are liquids, solids, or gases?

# Properties of Solids, Liquids, and Gases

Each different material has its own unique properties. However, properties can change depending on the state of the material.

**Active Reading** As you read these two pages, find and underline facts about each state of matter.

Each state of matter has different physical properties. Liquids and gases both flow, moving from place to place. Gases can expand, taking up more space, or compress, taking up less space. Solids have definite textures.

Liquid water flows much more quickly than honey.

### Flow

All liquids flow from one place to another. Different liquids may flow at different rates.

## Shape

Although the sugar, lemons, pitcher, and spoons are all solids, each one feels different. All solids have a shape, but the shape of some solids can be changed easily.

## Volume

A lot of gas has been compressed in this tank. It is under high pressure. Compressed gas from the tank expands, filling many balloons.

## Solubility

The water doesn't change the glass pitcher or the wooden spoon, but it does change the sugar. **Solubility** is the ability of a substance to dissolve when mixed in another.

▶ Number statements on these pages *1*, *2*, or *3* to indicate which of the numbered statements below they help support.

1. Liquids and gases are alike in some ways.
2. Not all solids dissolve in water.
3. Pressure can affect the volume of a gas.

# A Matter of Temperature

On a hot day, an ice cube melts. This is caused by a change in temperature. When matter changes state, the type of matter does not change.

**Active Reading** As you read these two pages, draw one line under a cause. Draw two lines under the effect.

When matter takes in or releases energy, its temperature changes. When enough energy is taken in or released, matter can change state.

When a gas releases energy, its temperature goes down until it *condenses,* or changes to a liquid. When a liquid releases energy, its temperature goes down until it *freezes,* or changes to a solid.

When a solid takes in energy, its temperature rises until it *melts*, or changes to a liquid. When a liquid takes in energy, its temperature rises until it *evaporates*, or changes to a gas. Evaporation and boiling are similar—both turn liquids into gases. Evaporation is slower and happens only at a liquid's surface. Boiling is faster and happens throughout the liquid.

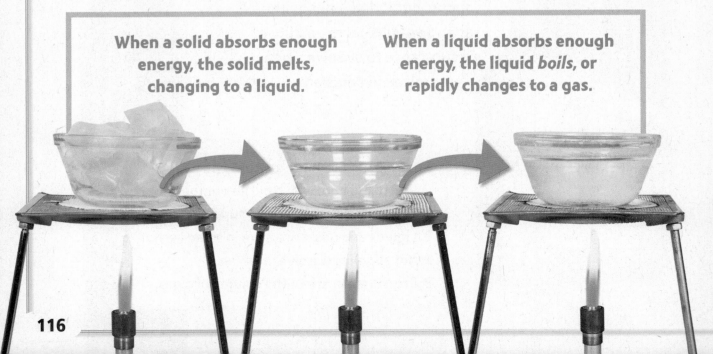

When a solid absorbs enough energy, the solid melts, changing to a liquid.

When a liquid absorbs enough energy, the liquid *boils*, or rapidly changes to a gas.

When a gas releases enough energy, the gas condenses, changing to a liquid. Particles of water vapor condense and form raindrops and dew.

When a liquid releases enough energy, the liquid freezes, changing to a solid. Dripping water that freezes can form icicles.

The temperature at which a certain type of matter freezes or melts is the same. The temperature at which a type of matter condenses or boils is also the same. For water, the melting and freezing points are 0 °C. The condensation and boiling points are 100 °C. Evaporation can happen at temperatures below the boiling point.

Lava is hot, melted rock that erupts from a volcano. Lava releases energy as it cools and becomes solid rock.

▶ Complete this graphic organizer.

As a solid takes in energy, its temperature _________. Eventually, it will ________, changing to a ________.

↓

If the liquid takes in enough ________, it will _________, changing to a ________.

# Useful Properties

You've learned that relative density can be used to classify objects. What other physical properties of matter can we use to sort objects into groups? Read on to find out!

**Active Reading** As you read these two pages, circle objects that *conduct*. Underline objects that *insulate*.

Have you heard the saying about how hard it is to find a needle in a haystack? Finding it would be much easier if we used physical properties. Magnetism and thermal and electrical conductivity are properties of matter that we use often.

## Magnetic vs. Nonmagnetic

Have you ever used a magnet to hang paper on your refrigerator? Magnets produce a force, a pull or push, called *magnetism*. They can pull together or push apart magnetic substances. A *magnetic* substance, such as iron and a few other metals, is attracted by a magnet. A magnet has no effect on nonmagnetic substances, such as paper, wood, or glass.

The magnet attracts the iron in the refrigerator. The nonmagnetic paper is pressed in between.

## Thermal Conductors

The metals in these pans are conductors. Metals *conduct*, or allow thermal energy to pass through them. Other substances, such as plastic pot handles, wood spoons, and cotton oven mitts, are poor conductors of thermal energy. They *insulate*, or keep energy from moving through them.

## Comparing Magnets

Describe the steps you would follow to investigate which refrigerator magnet is strongest.

_______________________________________________

_______________________________________________

_______________________________________________

_______________________________________________

_______________________________________________

_______________________________________________

_______________________________________________

## Electrical Conductors

Metals are also good conductors of electrical energy. In the diagram, the metals in the plug and wire conduct electricity into the toaster, where thermal energy is produced. The plastic in the plug, socket, and around the wire are electrical insulators. They keep the electrical energy away from your hand.

When you're done, use the answer key to check and revise your work.

**Read the summary statements below. Each one is incorrect. Change the part of the summary in blue to make it correct.**

1. A property is a characteristic of matter that is used to determine the state of the matter. ____________________________

2. A small plastic ball floats between two liquids. Its relative density is greater than both liquids. ____________________________

3. The particles in a solid are close together, but they can slide past one another. ____________________________

4. A solid changes to a liquid during a process known as freezing. ____________________________

5. Solids and liquids can be compressed when put under pressure. ____________________________

6. A substance's ability to spread or mix in another is called relative density. ____________________________

## Summarize

**Read the properties below. Write *S* for solid, *G* for gas, and *L* for liquid. Some properties may have more than one answer.**

7. Has a definite texture and shape ____

8. Can melt ____

9. Can freeze ____

10. Can boil ____

11. Takes the volume of its container ____

12. Can condense ____

13. Can flow ____

14. Takes the shape of its container ____

15. Has a definite volume ____

Answer Key: 1. describe or identify matter 2. one liquid but less than the other 3. liquid 4. melting 5. Gases 6. solubility 7. S 8. S 9. L 10. L 11. G 12. G 13. L, G 14. L, G 15. S, L

# Brain Check

Lesson 1

Name ______________________

## Word Play

**1** **Use the clues below to fill in the words in the puzzle.**

1. To squeeze a gas into a smaller space
2. A physical property that describes how something feels
3. The state of matter that keeps its shape and volume when it is placed in a different container
4. The measure of the energy of motion of particles of matter
5. Anything that has mass and volume
6. What happens to a liquid when it releases enough energy
7. A substance floats or sinks in another because of its relative ________.
8. The state of matter that has particles that slide by one another
9. The amount of space something takes up
10. The state of matter that expands to fill its container

1.
2.
3.
4.
5.
6.
7.
8.
9.
10.

**Read down the squares with red borders. The word you find will complete the riddle below.**

Perry the porcupine's portrait perfectly portrayed his pestering personality and prickly __ __ __ __ __ __ __ __ __ __.

# Apply Concepts

**2** Tell what property each of the following tools is used to measure.

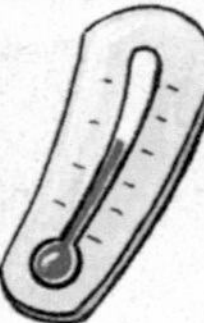

____________ ____________ ____________

**3** Complete these descriptions of the different states of matter. Then classify each of the following examples of matter according to their state: honey, pencil, helium in a balloon, water in a bottle, air bubbles in a fish tank, and rocks.

| ____________ | ____________ | Solids |
|---|---|---|
| *Particles are very far apart and move very fast.* | *Particles are closer together and move past one another.* | ____________ ____________ |
| *Examples:* ____________ | *Examples:* ____________ | *Examples:* ____________ |

**4** Fill in the name of the processes (such as freezing) that are represented.

(a) ____________ (b) ____________

SOLID —(a)→ LIQUID —(b)→ GAS

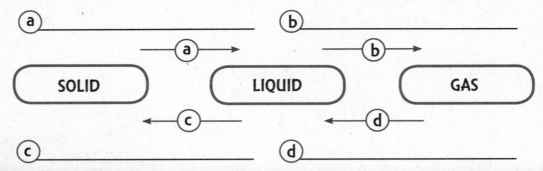

SOLID ←(c)— LIQUID ←(d)— GAS

(c) ____________ (d) ____________

Play a game of 20 Questions with members of your family. Have them choose a simple item that you can see in the room. Try to guess what the item is by asking yes/no questions about the item's properties.

TEKS 5.3D connect grade-level appropriate science concepts with the history of science, science careers, and contributions of scientists 5.5A classify matter based on physical properties

S.T.E.M.

Engineering & Technology

Carbon fiber is used to make this bike wheel strong and lightweight.

# Strong, Light, or Both?

What physical properties do you want in a bicycle wheel? It has to be strong, but also lightweight so it takes less energy to pedal the bike. You could easily bend one of these wheel spokes, but many, arranged together, make the wheel strong enough to support your weight and more!

Carbon fiber threads are woven into fabric.

Carbon fiber is smaller and stronger than a human hair!

Spider silk is the strongest, lightest natural material. It is stronger than steel! Carbon fiber is a strong, human-made thread that can be woven into fabric. A single carbon fiber is much finer than a human hair. Carbon fiber is one of the strongest and lightest materials made by people.

Circle a natural material. Put an X on a manufactured material. What are two physical properties these materials have in common?

______________________________

______________________________

# S.T.E.M.
continued

Every design has its upside and its downside. When a design for an object is chosen to meet one purpose, other features may not be as good. A quality that a designer must give up in order to get a desired quality is called a design trade-off. A designer needs to think of both the upside and the downside of a particular design.

Look at these shoes. List two examples of the upside and two of the downside for each shoe. Think of another type of shoe. Draw it in the empty space, and explain the trade-offs.

Upside

Downside

Upside

Downside

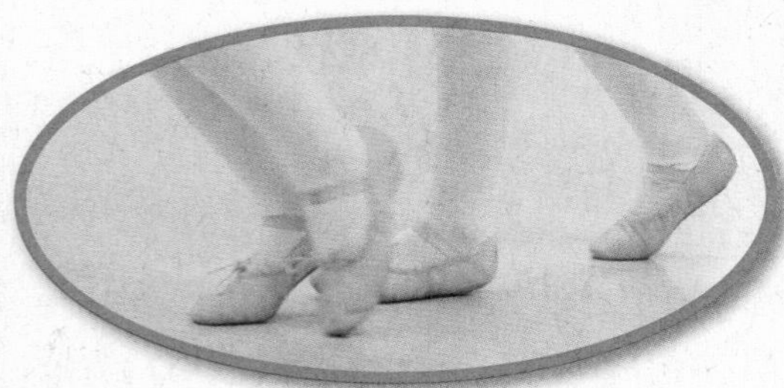

Upside

Downside

Upside

Downside

## Build On It!

Rise to the engineering design challenge—complete **Design It: Distillation Device** in the Inquiry Flipchart.

**TEKS** **5.2C** collect information by detailed observations... **5.2D** analyze and interpret information to construct...explanations... **5.5A** classify matter based on physical properties... **5.5C** demonstrate that some mixtures maintain physical properties of their ingredients **5.5D** identify changes that can occur in the physical properties of the ingredients of solutions

Essential Question

# What Are Mixtures and Solutions?

## Engage Your Brain!

As you read the lesson, look for the answer to the following question and record it here.

How are a smoothie and a salad alike? How are they different?

______________________________

______________________________

______________________________

______________________________

## Active Reading

### Lesson Vocabulary

List each term. As you learn about each one, make notes in the Interactive Glossary.

______________________________

______________________________

### Problem and Solution

Ideas in this lesson may be connected by a problem-solution relationship. Active readers mark a problem with a *P* to help them stay focused on the way information is organized. When multiple solutions are described, they mark each solution with an *S*.



Inquiry Flipchart p. 19 — An Inky Mixture / Does It Dissolve?

# Matter Mix-Up

A box of colored pencils. A basket of footballs, tennis balls, and hockey pucks. A toy box full of toys. All these things are mixtures. But what is a mixture?

**Active Reading** As you read the next page, draw two lines under the conclusion. Draw one line under each fact that leads to the conclusion.

This fruit salad is a mixture of different pieces of fruit.

Look at the mixtures on these pages. They have a few things in common. First, two or more substances or objects were combined. The fruit salad has several types of fruit. The laundry pile has several types of clothing. Second, each type of matter in a mixture keeps its own identity. The peach in the fruit salad is the same type of matter as it was before it was mixed into the fruit salad. The jeans in the laundry pile are still jeans.

By now, you've probably figured out that a **mixture** is a combination of two or more substances that keep their identities. The parts of a mixture don't undergo a chemical change. Making a mixture is a physical change.

A carbonated beverage is a mixture of water, gases, and other ingredients.

▶ These clothes are all jumbled together. How can you demonstrate that this pile of laundry is a mixture?

___________________________________

___________________________________

___________________________________

# Find a Solution!

In some mixtures, it's easy to see the individual pieces that are mixed together. In other mixtures, small parts are very evenly mixed. What are these special mixtures?

**Active Reading** As you read these two pages, underline lesson vocabulary words each time they are used.

Each bite of fruit salad contains different combinations of fruit. You can separately taste peaches and different kinds of berries. But what do you notice when you drink a glass of lemonade? Every sip tastes the same. This is because lemonade is a solution. A **solution** is a mixture that has the same composition throughout.

When food coloring is added to water, the two liquids evenly mix, forming a solution.

A solution forms when one ingredient *dissolves* in another. When something dissolves, it breaks up into particles so tiny they can't be seen even with a microscope. These particles then evenly mix with the other part of the solution. Not everything dissolves. If you put a rock and salt in water, the rock won't dissolve, but the salt will.

Solutions are commonly liquids, such as the mixture of the different liquids that make up gasoline. But not all solutions are liquids. Air is a solution of different gases. Tiny particles of nitrogen, oxygen, and other gases are evenly mixed in air. Brass is an example of a solid solution formed from solid copper and solid zinc.

A mixture of sand and water forms where waves wash over the sand. Such a mixture is not a solution.

Ocean water itself is a solution. It contains several different dissolved substances.

▶ What changes occur in the physical properties of ingredients in solutions?

_______________

_______________

# Separating Mixtures

Suppose you really don't like olives. How are you going to get them off that deluxe pizza your friend ordered? Sometimes you need to separate the components of a mixture.

**Active Reading** As you read this page, put brackets [ ] around the sentence that describes the problem and write *P* next to the sentence. Underline the sentence that describes the solution and write *S* next to it.

Mixtures are not always easy to separate. But since mixing is a physical change, each component in a mixture keeps most of its physical properties. Physical properties such as color, size, melting point, boiling point, density, and solubility can be used to separate mixtures. Separating a mixture can be very simple. Or it can involve several, complex steps when one method is not enough.

### Density

**Every substance has its own density. A less-dense substance will float on a denser substance. Objects will float in water if they are less dense than water. They will sink if they are denser than water.**

▶ What property was used to separate the items on this tray?

____________________

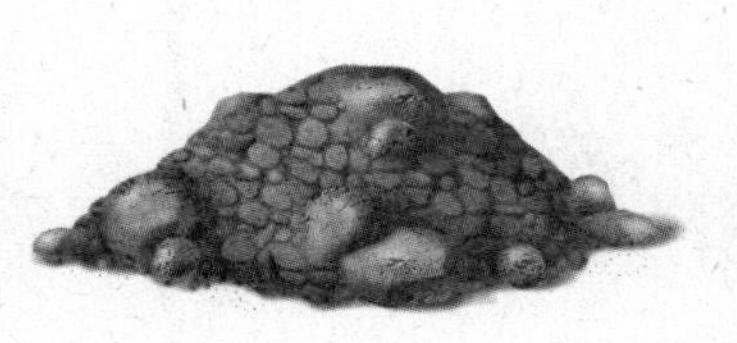

# When One Isn't Enough

## sieve/mesh screen

A sieve or mesh screen has holes that matter can pass through. Matter that is smaller than the holes passes through the mesh screen while matter that is larger than the holes stays above the mesh screen.

## magnetic force

A magnet attracts matter that contains iron, separating it from the other parts of the mixture.

## filtration

A filter works like a mesh screen with very tiny openings, or pores. Only the smallest bits of matter—like water particles and dissolved particles of salt—can pass through the pores.

## evaporation/boiling

Boiling is when a liquid rapidly changes to a gas at the boiling point of the liquid. Evaporation also changes a liquid to a gas, but it occurs at temperatures below the boiling point. During these processes, only the liquid particles leave the solution. Dissolved particles stay behind.

A magnet takes away bits of iron.

Water is added. Then the filter removes the soil.

The water is boiled away. Only salt is left behind.

Why It Matters

# Proportions and Properties

When you make lemonade, it's important to get the amounts of lemon and sugar right. If it's too sweet or too sour, it doesn't taste right. How do proportions affect the properties of a mixture?

Mixtures of metals are called *alloys.* The properties of the alloy depend on how much of each metal is in the mixture. Chemists first decide on the properties they need their alloy to have. Then they decide how much of which metals will give them those properties.

Steel is an alloy. It is made from iron and other substances. Different substances give steel different properties. For example, adding chromium will make steel shiny. Metals such as nickel and titanium can keep it from rusting. Carbon is often added to steel to make it stronger. Other substances help steel used in tools stay sharp or keep from wearing down.

To make an alloy, metals and other elements are melted together and then allowed to harden.

► For each steel object on this page, list at least two properties that the steel must have.
Kettle
Sculpture
Steel Building Frame

# Do the Math!

## Organize and Evaluate Data

**Use technology to construct a table, chart, or simple graph to organize, examine, and evaluate the data in the following statements: Stainless steel is composed of 74 parts iron, 18 parts chromium, and 8 parts nickel. Tool steel has 20 more parts iron than stainless steel does. It also has 1 part of both nickel and carbon and 4 parts of other substances.**

When you're done, use the answer key to check and revise your work.

**Write *S* if the photo and caption describe a mixture that is a solution. Write *M* if they describe a mixture that is NOT a solution.**

_____ (1) When you combine ingredients to make a sandwich, each ingredient keeps its identity. You could easily separate them.

_____ (2) Soft drinks are made by dissolving a gas and other ingredients in water. The dissolved particles are much too small to be seen.

_____ (3) The solid bits of orange pulp do not dissolve in the liquid. Because the pulp particles are large, they will eventually settle out.

_____ (4) Particles of several different gases make up air. Air on one side of a room is just like the air on the other side.

## Summarize

**Fill in the missing words to tell how to separate mixtures.**

To sort the items in your junk drawer, you'd use observable (5) ________________ such as size, color, shape, and (6) ________________ attraction. But how would you separate table sugar, sand, and pebbles? Because the pebbles are (7) ________________ than the grains of sugar and sand, you could remove them using a sieve, or mesh (8) ___________. You could then add water and shake until the sugar (9) ______________. If you poured this mixture through a coffee (10) ________________ into a beaker, the (11) ________________ would be left on the filter, but the sugar solution would pass through. Adding heat would cause the water to (12) ________________, leaving solid sugar behind.

Answer Key: 1. M 2. S 3. M 4. S 5. properties 6. magnetic 7. larger 8. screen 9. dissolves 10. filter 11. sand 12. evaporate or boil

Name ___________________________

## Word Play

1 Complete the crossword puzzle. Use the words in the box if you need help.

**Across**

1. Another name for a mesh screen
4. Type of change that doesn't involve the formation of a new kind of matter
5. Tool that attracts objects that contain iron
6. What an object that is less dense than water will do when placed in water
7. Object used to separate very small particles from a mixture
8. The amount of matter in a given volume

**Down**

1. A physical property; for example, round, square, rectangular, or flat
2. Process by which a liquid changes slowly to a gas
3. Kind of mixture that has the same composition throughout
5. A combination of two or more substances that keep their individual identities

| sieve | shape | evaporation | solution* | physical |
|---|---|---|---|---|
| magnet | mixture* | float | filter | density |

* Key Lesson Vocabulary

# Apply Concepts

2 Classify. Circle the substances below that are solutions.

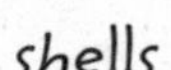

brass trumpet | trail mix | shells | sandwich | drink from a mix

3 Make a list of solid mixtures in your classroom.

4 Demonstrate that some mixtures maintain the physical properties of their ingredients. Draw and label a picture to show how you would separate each mixture.

Name ___________________________



5 Answer these questions in terms of what you know about mixtures.

a. How would changing the proportions of substances in an alloy change its properties?

_______________________________________________

_______________________________________________

_______________________________________________

b. Why is it possible to use physical properties to separate a mixture?

_______________________________________________

_______________________________________________

c. Recycling helps us conserve resources. Draw a line connecting each piece of garbage in a mixed bag with the bin it should be thrown in.

milk jug | soup can | envelope | cardboard box

soda can | water bottle | broken pencil

Garbage | Plastic | Aluminum and Tin | Paper

6 

Salt seems to disappear when it is poured into water. Use the terms *mixture, solution,* and *dissolve* to explain what happens.

_______________________________________________

_______________________________________________

_______________________________________________

7 Tell how you would use one or more of these tools to separate the mixtures.

Rice from dried soup mix

Salt from saltwater

Nails from gravel

8 Tell what would happen if you stirred each of these cups faster.

Water and Sugar

Share what you have learned about mixtures with your family. With a family member, identify examples of mixtures at mealtime, or in places in your home.

Inquiry Flipchart page 20

**TEKS** **5.2C** collect information by detailed observations and accurate measuring **5.2D** analyze and interpret information to construct reasonable explanations from... evidence **5.2F** communicate valid conclusions in both written and verbal forms **5.5A** classify matter based on physical properties, including... physical state... relative density, solubility in water... **5.5C** demonstrate that some mixtures maintain physical properties of their ingredients such as iron filings and sand **5.5D** identify changes that can occur in the physical properties of the ingredients of solutions such as dissolving salt in water or adding lemon juice to water

Name ______________________________

Essential Question

# How Do Substances Change When They Form a Solution?

## Set a Purpose

What will you learn from this investigation?

______________________________

______________________________

______________________________

## Think About the Procedure

What physical properties will you observe during the investigation?

______________________________

______________________________

______________________________

Making detailed observations and accurate measuring are important science skills. Why don't you have to subtract the mass of the beaker to find out whether the mass of the liquid-solid mixture has changed?

______________________________

______________________________

______________________________

## Record Your Data

Record your data for the first half of the investigation in the table below. Then use a computer to draw a table to record your data for the investigation's second half.

| Liquid-Solid Mixture | | |
|---|---|---|
| **Substance** | **Volume (mL)** | **Mass (g)** |
| water | | |
| powdered drink mix | | |
| water and powdered drink mix | | |

## Draw Conclusions

How did the appearance of the water, alcohol, and powdered drink mix change when they formed a solution?

Were there any observable changes in the mass or volume of the substances after they formed a solution? Explain.

## Analyze and Extend

1. How do you know when a solution forms? How could you prove that the powdered drink mix and the alcohol are still present in the solution?

2. Matter is made of tiny particles. Use indirect (inferred) evidence to explain any changes in the volume of the water-alcohol solution.

3. Would you classify powdered drink mix as soluble or insoluble in water? What about alcohol? Explain.

4. Think of other questions you would like to ask about what happens to properties when a substance dissolves.

TEKS 5.3D connect grade-level appropriate science concepts with the history of science, science careers, and contributions of scientists 5.5C demonstrate that some mixtures maintain physical properties of their ingredients…

# Meet the Property Pros

## Alfred Nobel

Alfred Nobel was born in Sweden in 1833. While studying to become a chemical engineer, Nobel met a chemist who had invented nitroglycerine. This was an explosive liquid that was too dangerous to use. Nobel mixed the liquid with a type of sand so that it could be shaped into rods. In 1866, Nobel got a patent on his new invention. It was called "dynamite." The properties of the nitroglycerine and sand worked together to form a mixture that could be safely used to blast rocks and build tunnels.

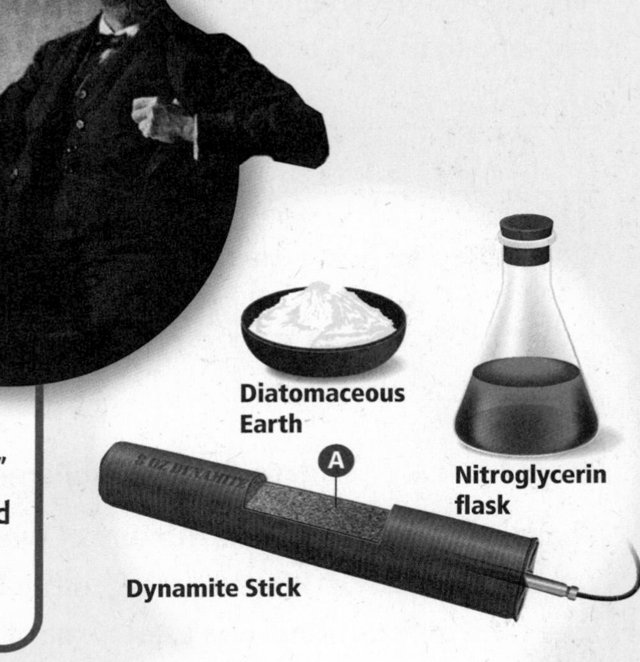


Dynamite made Alfred Nobel very rich. When he died, he left money to reward people for their contributions to art, peace, and science. The rewards are called the *Nobel Prizes*. Smalley's fullerenes won him one of these prizes in 1996.

## Richard E. Smalley

Richard Smalley was a materials scientist. A materials scientist studies the properties of matter to invent new substances with unique properties. Smalley and his teammates at Rice University found a way to make carbon particles form new structures called *fullerenes*. Fullerenes can have many shapes. Some fullerenes have repeating six-sided patterns, like soccer balls. Others are shaped like tiny tubes. Because fullerenes are hollow, they can hold other substances. Fullerenes are very strong and are good conductors of thermal and electrical energy. Now the question is, What can we do with them?

# Useful Properties

Nobel and Smalley analyzed and experimented with the properties of materials. Answer the questions below to review their contributions to science.

**How did Nobel's dynamite combine the properties of nitroglycerine and sand to make a useful product?**

_______________________________________________

_______________________________________________

**What are some properties of Smalley's fullerenes?**

_______________________________________________

_______________________________________________

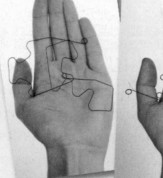

**What Now?** To date, Smalley's fullerenes have not been widely used.

**The picture shows nitinol, a mixture of two metals. At room temperature, you can bend or twist it. When warmed, nitinol returns to its original shape. It took a long time before nitinol was used to make things like eyeglass frames, dental braces, and golf clubs. What can you conclude about materials like fullerenes and nitinol?**

_______________________________________________

_______________________________________________

_______________________________________________

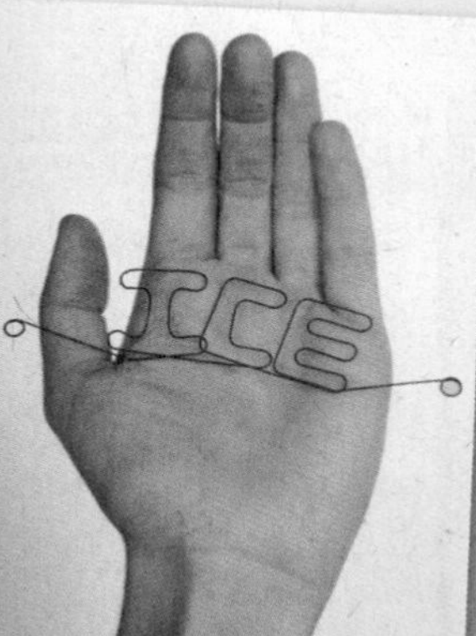


## Be a Materials Scientist!

Graphite and fullerenes are made of carbon. Graphite is a lubricant, a substance used to reduce friction between moving parts. Identify a property of fullerenes that would make them good lubricants and a machine part where it could be used. Communicate your ideas to your class.

# Unit 3 Review

Name ______________________

## Vocabulary Review

Use the terms in the box to complete the sentences.

| |
|---|
| freezing |
| gas |
| liquid |
| physical changes |
| solubility |
| solution |
| temperature |
| volume |

TEKS 5.5A

1. Matter that has a definite volume but no definite shape is a(n) ______________________.

TEKS 5.5A

2. A mixture that has the same composition throughout is called a(n) ______________________.

TEKS 5.5A

3. The amount of space that matter takes up is its ______________________.

TEKS 5.5A

4. The ability of a substance to dissolve in another is called ______________________.

TEKS 5.5A

5. Matter without a definite volume or shape is called a(n) ______________________.

TEKS 5.5B

6. A measure of the energy of motion of the particles in a substance is its ______________________.

TEKS 5.5A

7. Changes in which the form or shape of a substance changes but the substance keeps its identity are called ______________________.

TEKS 5.5A

8. A change of state from a liquid to a solid is ______________________.

## Science Concepts

Fill in the letter of the choice that best answers the question.

Use the following diagram to answer questions 9 and 10.

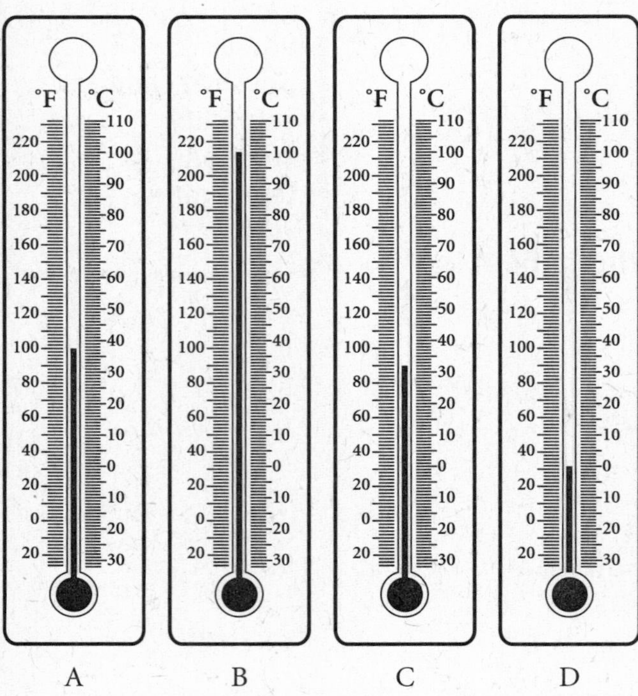


TEKS **5.5B, 5.4A**

**9.** Which thermometer shows the freezing point of water?

Ⓐ A
Ⓑ B
Ⓒ C
Ⓓ D

TEKS **5.5B, 5.4A**

**10.** Which thermometer shows the boiling point of water?

Ⓐ A
Ⓑ B
Ⓒ C
Ⓓ D

TEKS **5.5C**

**11.** Nadia has a mixture of oil and water. She wants to remove most of the oil from the mixture. How can she do this?

Ⓐ use a magnet to attract the oil
Ⓑ pour the mixture through a sieve
Ⓒ stir the mixture until the oil dissolves
Ⓓ let the oil float to the top and skim it off

TEKS **5.5A**

**12.** The rate at which a solid dissolves in water depends on many factors. Which of these factors has no effect on the rate at which a solid dissolves?

Ⓐ temperature of the liquid
Ⓑ the color of the solid
Ⓒ whether the liquid is stirred
Ⓓ the amount of the solid

TEKS **5.4A, 5.5A**

**13.** Peter places six balls of modeling clay on one side of a balance. He places a plastic cube on the other side. It takes 41 plastic cubes to balance the modeling clay. He then removes the clay, shapes it into a dinosaur, and puts it back on the balance. How many cubes will Peter most likely need to balance the dinosaur?

Ⓐ 35 cubes
Ⓑ 38 cubes
Ⓒ 41 cubes
Ⓓ 47 cubes

Name ______________________

TEKS 5.3A, 5.5A

14. The diagram shows three graduated cylinders, each containing two liquids.

Which statement is true?

Ⓐ The liquid with the greatest density is syrup.

Ⓑ The liquid with the greatest density is soap.

Ⓒ Oil and soap have the same density.

Ⓓ Water and syrup have the same density.

TEKS 5.3A, 5.5A

15. Lia dissolves sugar in water. She says that the sugar must have changed into another substance because it disappears. Which of the following could you use to support or contradict Lia's claim?

Ⓐ Add sugar to different amounts of water to see if the same thing happens.

Ⓑ Add different amounts of sugar to water to see if it all disappears.

Ⓒ Let the water evaporate to show that the sugar is still present.

Ⓓ Heat the sugar-water mixture to see if it produces bubbles.

TEKS 5.5A

16. The diagram shows what happened after Kwan added crystals of a solid to water.

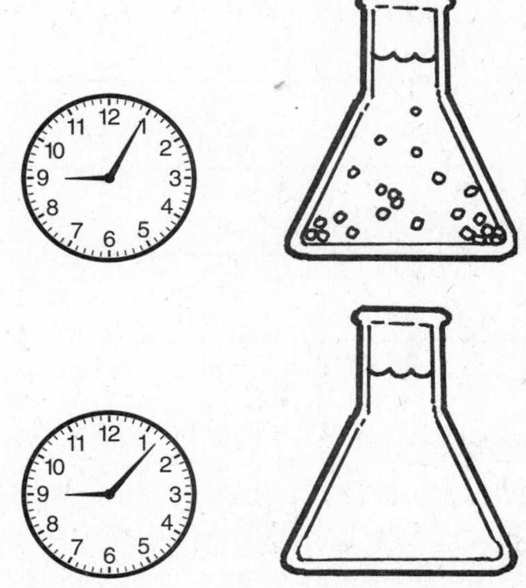

What can you infer about the solid?

Ⓐ The solid was sugar.

Ⓑ The solid was mixed evenly in water.

Ⓒ The solid was less dense than water.

Ⓓ The solid had a greater mass than the water.

TEKS 5.5A, 5.5C

17. Carlo mixes sand, salt, and iron filings. What tools could Carlo use to separate the mixture?

Ⓐ a balance and a hand lens

Ⓑ a thermometer and a hot plate

Ⓒ a magnet and a beaker of water

Ⓓ a sieve and tweezers

# Apply Inquiry and Review the Big Idea

Write the answers to these questions.

**TEKS 5.2A, 5.5A**

**18.** Janelle has three metal cubes that look the same and are the same size. Plan and describe an investigation that Janelle can use to determine if the cubes are made of the same substance. What tools will Janelle use? How will she decide if the substances are the same?

**TEKS 5.3A, 5.5A**

**19.** In Question 18, suppose Janelle finds that each cube sinks in water and has a volume of 8 $cm^3$. She knows that density is mass divided by volume. Using logical reasoning, tell how the mass of a cube compares to the mass of an equal volume of water.

**TEKS 5.3C**

**20.** Draw a time-lapse diagram to show what happens when a cube of sugar dissolves in water. Label the diagram to show why the sugar seems to disappear.

**TEKS 5.3A, 5.5B**

**21.** Hussein finds that a substance heats up at a rate of 1.8 °C per second and another at twice that rate. How long before the second substance reaches the boiling point of water if it starts at 0 ºC? Round and record your answer to the nearest whole number.

UNIT 4

# Forces and Motion

## Big Idea

Forces interact with objects to produce motion. Motion can be observed, measured, and described.

TEKS 5.2A, 5.2B, 5.2C, 5.2D, 5.2E, 5.2F, 5.2G, 5.3A, 5.3D, 5.6D



## I Wonder Why

Why does a pit crew need to replace a racecar's tires several times during the race? *Turn the page to find out.*

**Here's why** Friction gives the racecar traction and allows it to grip the track, but it also produces a lot of heat. The high speed and forceful turns of a race wear tires out quickly.

In this unit, you will explore the Big Idea, the Essential Questions, and the Investigations on the Inquiry Flipchart.

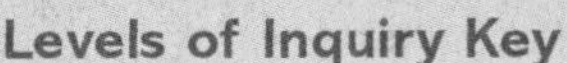

**Big Idea** Forces interact with objects to produce motion. Motion can be observed, measured, and described.

## Essential Questions



**Science Notebook**

Before you begin each lesson, be sure to write your thoughts about the Essential Question.

TEKS **5.2D** analyze and interpret information to construct reasonable explanations from... evidence **5.2F** communicate valid conclusions in both written and verbal forms **5.2G** construct appropriate simple graphs...using technology, including computers, to organize, examine, and evaluate information **5.6D** design an experiment that tests the effect of force on an object

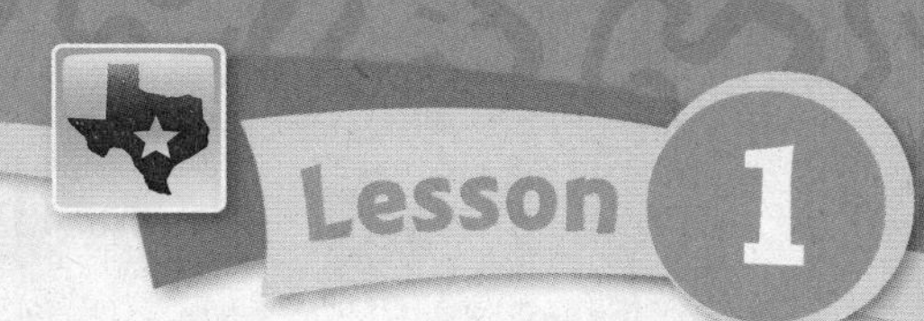


Essential Question

# What Are Forces?

## Engage Your Brain!

As you read the lesson, figure out the answer to the following question. Write the answer here.

What forces are acting on this cyclist? Are all the forces balanced?

______________________________

______________________________

______________________________

______________________________

______________________________

______________________________

## Active Reading

### Lesson Vocabulary

List the terms. As you learn about each one, make notes in the Interactive Glossary.

______________ ______________

______________ ______________

______________

### Cause and Effect

Some ideas in this lesson are connected by a cause-and-effect relationship. Why something happens is a cause. What happens as a result of something else is an effect. Active readers look for effects by asking themselves, What happened? They look for causes by asking, Why did it happen?



Inquiry Flipchart p. 21 — On a Roll / Make It Easier

# PUSHING and Pulling

You pull on a door to open it. You lift up a backpack. You push on the pedals of a bike to go faster. What is the effect of force on an object?

**Active Reading** As you read this page, underline the effects a force can have on an object.

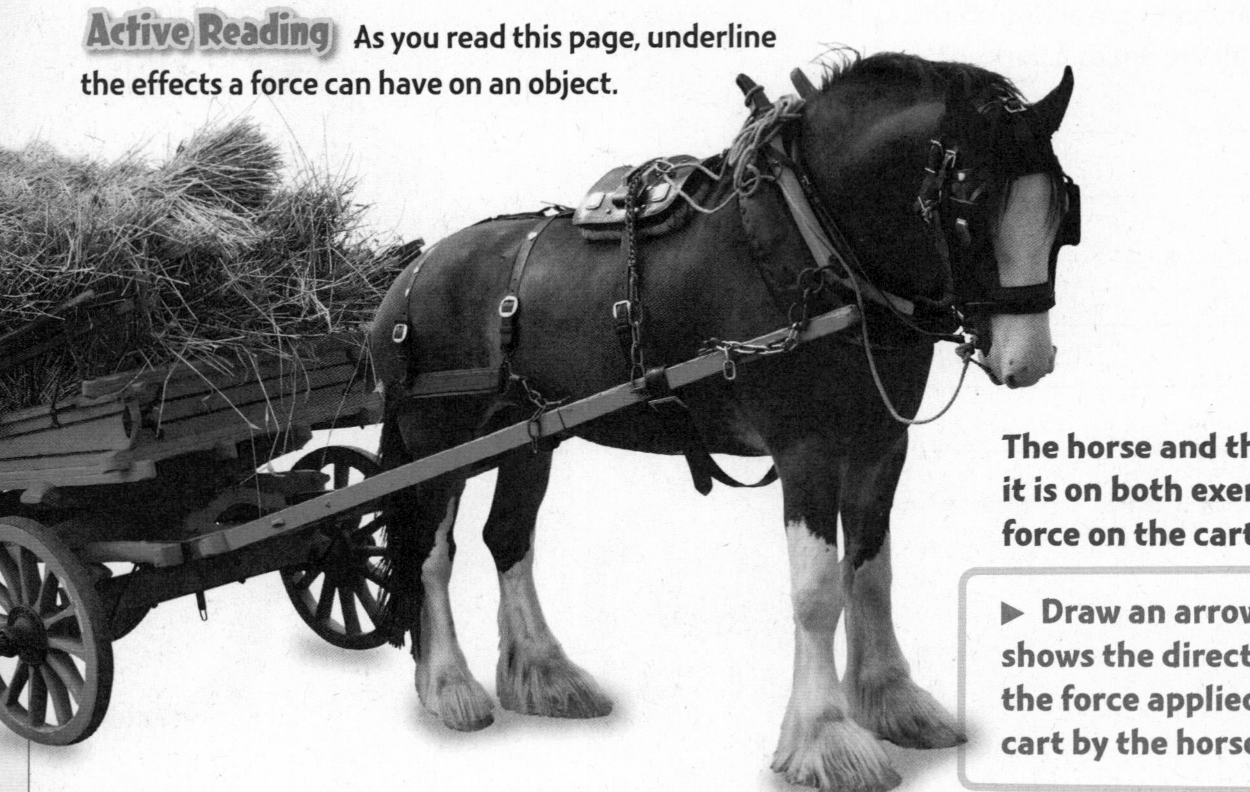

The horse and the road it is on both exert a force on the cart.

▶ Draw an arrow that shows the direction of the force applied to the cart by the horse.

Changes in motion all have one thing in common. They require a **force**, which is a push or a pull. Forces can cause an object at rest to move. They can cause a moving object to speed up, slow down, change direction, or stop. Forces can also change an object's shape.

Forces are measured with a spring scale in units called newtons (N). The larger the force, the greater the change it can cause to the motion of an object. Smaller forces cause smaller changes. Sometimes more than one force can act together in a way that does not cause a change in motion.

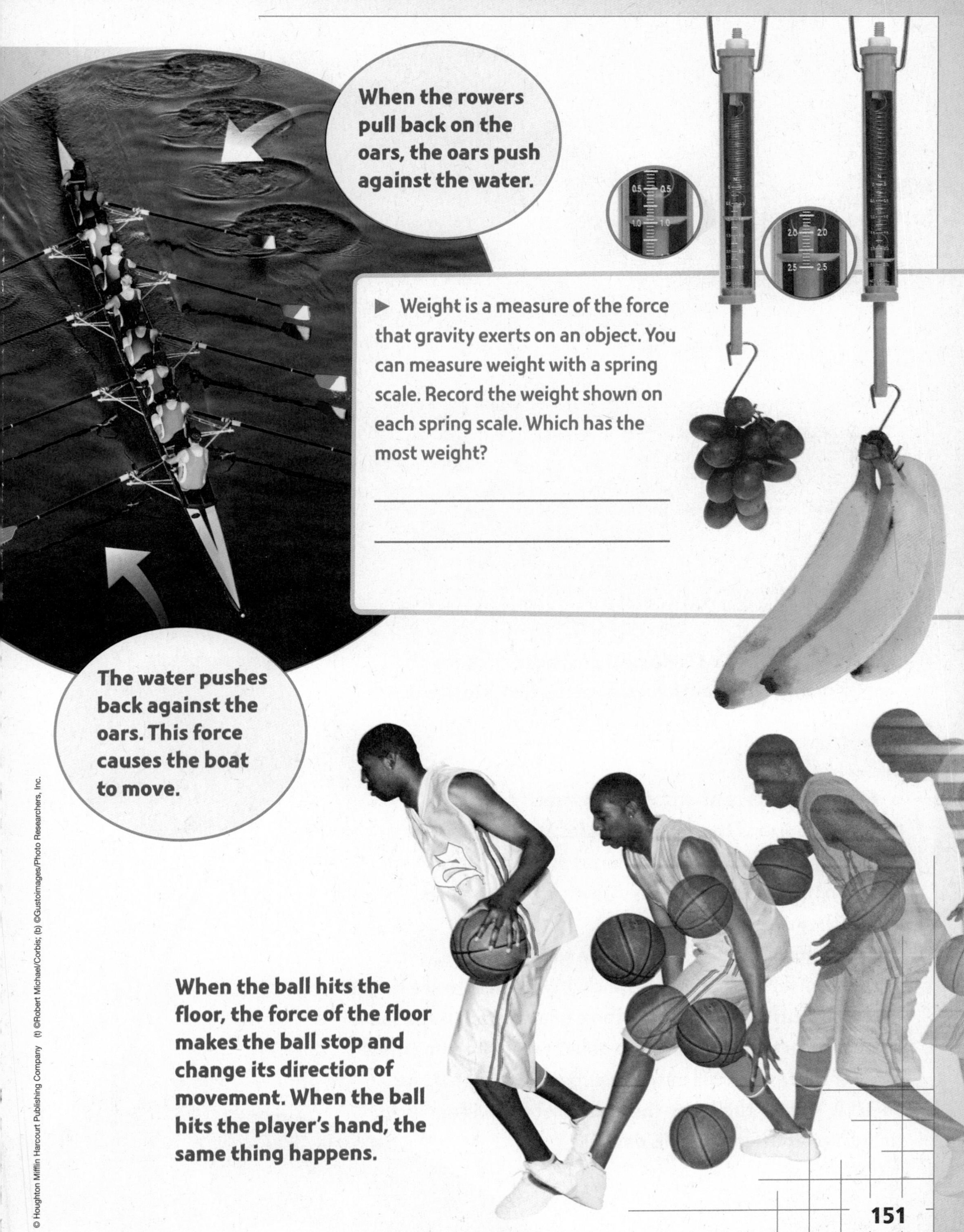

When the rowers pull back on the oars, the oars push against the water.
The water pushes back against the oars. This force causes the boat to move.
0.5
1.0
2.0
2.5


► Weight is a measure of the force that gravity exerts on an object. You can measure weight with a spring scale. Record the weight shown on each spring scale. Which has the most weight?

_______________________________________

_______________________________________

When the ball hits the floor, the force of the floor makes the ball stop and change its direction of movement. When the ball hits the player's hand, the same thing happens.

# TWO COMMON Forces

What do the skydivers and some of the flower petals have in common? They are both falling! What causes this?

**Active Reading** As you read these pages, circle the sentence that describes a force that causes things to slow down.

► Draw an arrow showing the direction of the gravitational force between Earth and the falling flower petals.

## Gravity

**Gravity** is a force of attraction between two objects. The size of this force increases as the mass of the objects increases. It decreases as the distance between the objects increases. Gravity acts on objects even if they are not touching.

Large objects such as Earth cause smaller objects, such as the skydivers, to accelerate quickly. We expect to see things fall toward Earth. However, the force of attraction is the same on both objects. If you place two objects with the same mass in outer space, they will move toward one another. If one object is "above" the other, the bottom object will appear to "fall up" as the other "falls down"!

Friction changes the energy of motion into thermal energy. When you use sandpaper to smooth wood, you can feel the temperature rise.

## → Friction

Is it easier to ride your bike on a smooth road or on a muddy trail? Why?

**Friction** is a force that opposes motion. Friction acts between two objects that are touching, such as the bike tires and the road. Friction can also exist between air and a moving object. This is called air resistance.

It is easy to slide across smooth ice because it doesn't have much friction. Pulling something across rough sandpaper is a lot harder because there is lots of friction.

An air hockey table blows air upward. This layer of air reduces the surface friction, so the pieces move quickly.

▶ In the pictures on this page, circle the places where there is friction between two objects. In the small boxes, write *Inc* if the object is designed to increase friction and *Dec* if the object is designed to decrease friction.

**The tires on this bike are designed to keep the rider from slipping. You have to pedal harder on a rough surface to overcome the force of friction.**

# BALANCED or Unbalanced?

The tug-of-war teams are both applying forces. So why isn't anyone moving?

**Active Reading** Draw a circle around a sentence that explains why objects don't always move when a force is applied.

When you sit on a chair, the force of gravity pulls you down. The chair pushes you up. You stay in one place because the forces on you are balanced. **Balanced forces** are forces on an object that are equal in size and opposite in direction. They cancel each other out.

The tug-of-war teams in the picture don't move because the forces are balanced. Friction keeps them from sliding. They won't move until one side exerts a larger force. Then, the forces are no longer balanced. **Unbalanced forces** are forces that cause a change in motion. A force must also overcome the force of friction before an object will move.

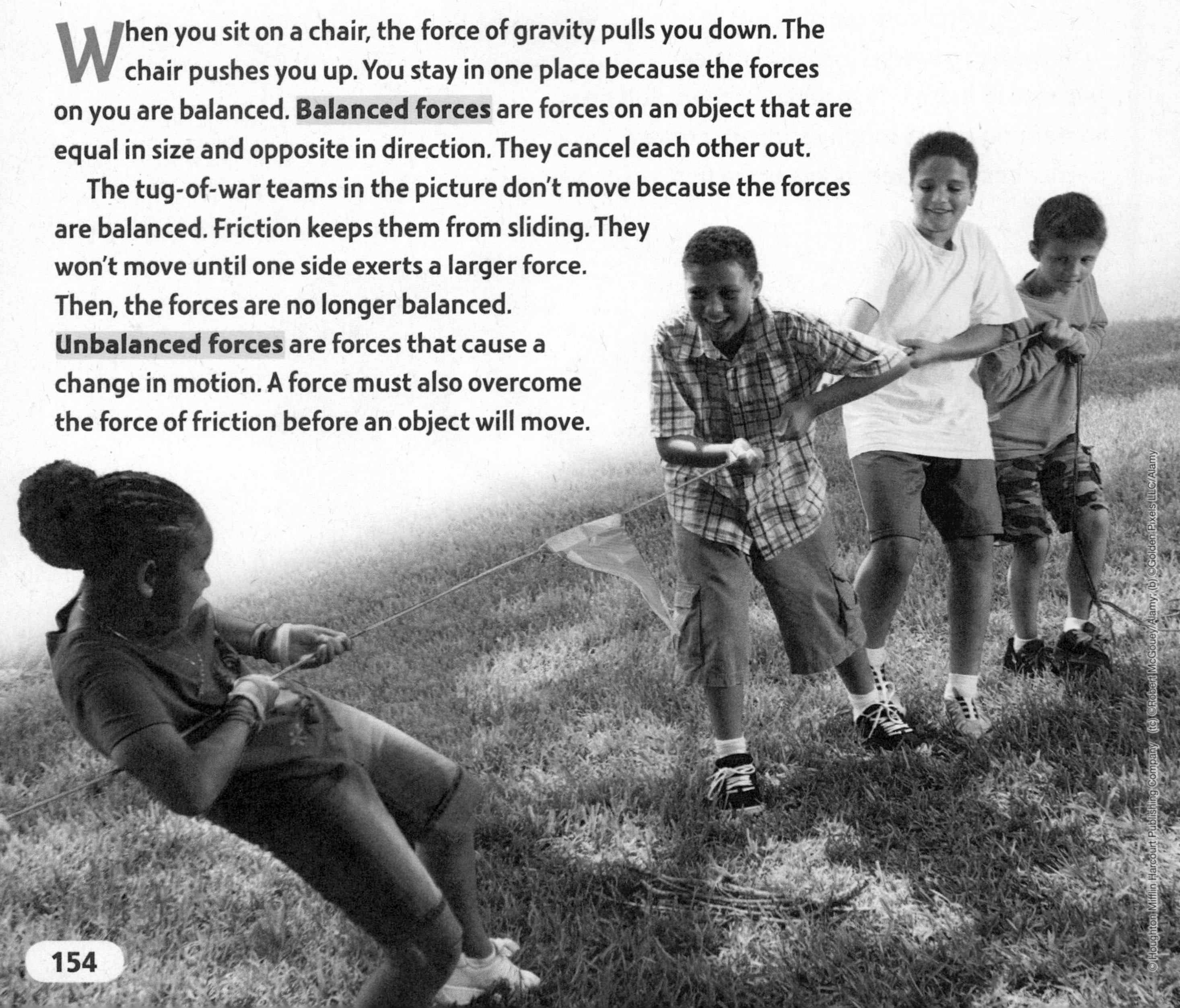

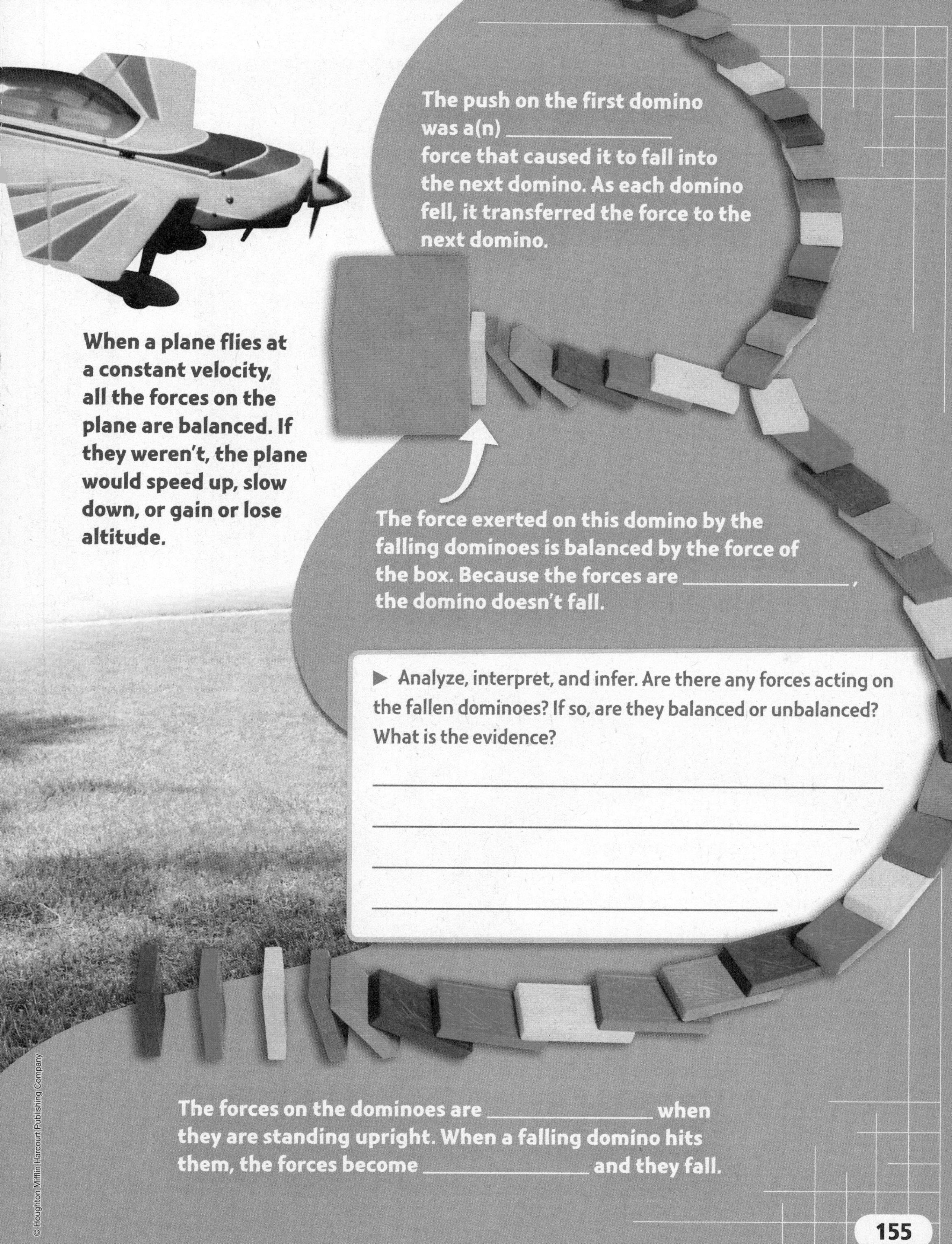

When a plane flies at a constant velocity, all the forces on the plane are balanced. If they weren't, the plane would speed up, slow down, or gain or lose altitude.

The push on the first domino was a(n) ________________ force that caused it to fall into the next domino. As each domino fell, it transferred the force to the next domino.

The force exerted on this domino by the falling dominoes is balanced by the force of the box. Because the forces are ________________, the domino doesn't fall.

▶ Analyze, interpret, and infer. Are there any forces acting on the fallen dominoes? If so, are they balanced or unbalanced? What is the evidence?

______________________________________________

______________________________________________

______________________________________________

______________________________________________

The forces on the dominoes are ________________ when they are standing upright. When a falling domino hits them, the forces become ________________ and they fall.

# PULL (or Push) Harder!

Would you expect a bunt in baseball to go out of the park? Why or why not?

**Active Reading** As you read, circle the sentences that explain the relationship between the size of a force and motion.

▶ Use forces to explain why the boy can't ring the bell.

_______________

_______________

_______________

When the man swings the hammer, he exerts a force on a plate. The plate transfers the force to a piece of metal that rises up the column and rings the bell.

The boy swings the same kind of hammer at the same kind of machine. Why doesn't the metal hit the bell?

TEST YOUR STRENGTH

TEST YOUR STRENGTH

If you want to make the cue ball knock another ball into a pocket, you hit the cue ball with a lot of force. This large force makes the cue ball change its velocity, or accelerate, quickly. It has lots of energy to transfer to the other ball. The energy causes the other ball to accelerate.

The greater the force applied to the cue ball, the more force it can transfer to the other ball. A large force will cause a large change in the motion of the other ball. A small force will cause little change. Changes in velocity can also include changes in direction.

## Do the Math!

### Display Data in a Graph

Use technology and the data below to construct a graph that shows the relationship between the force applied to an object and its acceleration.

| Force (N) | Acceleration ($m/sec^2$) |
|---|---|
| 1 | 0.5 |
| 2 | 1.0 |
| 5 | 2.5 |
| 8 | 4.0 |
| 10 | 5.0 |

1. Examine and evaluate the graph. Tell someone how an increase in the applied force affects the object's acceleration.

# I'M NOT Moving!

It's easy to lift your empty backpack off the ground. Could you use the same force to lift it when it's full of books?

**Active Reading** **As you read these pages, circle cause-and-effect signal words, such as *because*, *so*, or *therefore*.**

**The springs in the pictures all exert the same force on the balls, causing them to roll across the page. The ball with the least mass accelerates the fastest. Therefore, it travels the farthest. The same force has a greater effect on an object with a small mass than an object with a larger mass.**

▶ Rank the balls by writing *greatest*, *middle*, or *least* in the six blanks.

**Foam Ball**

**mass:** ________

**acceleration:** ________

**Baseball**

**mass:** ________

**acceleration:** ________



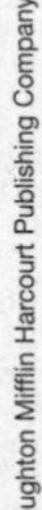

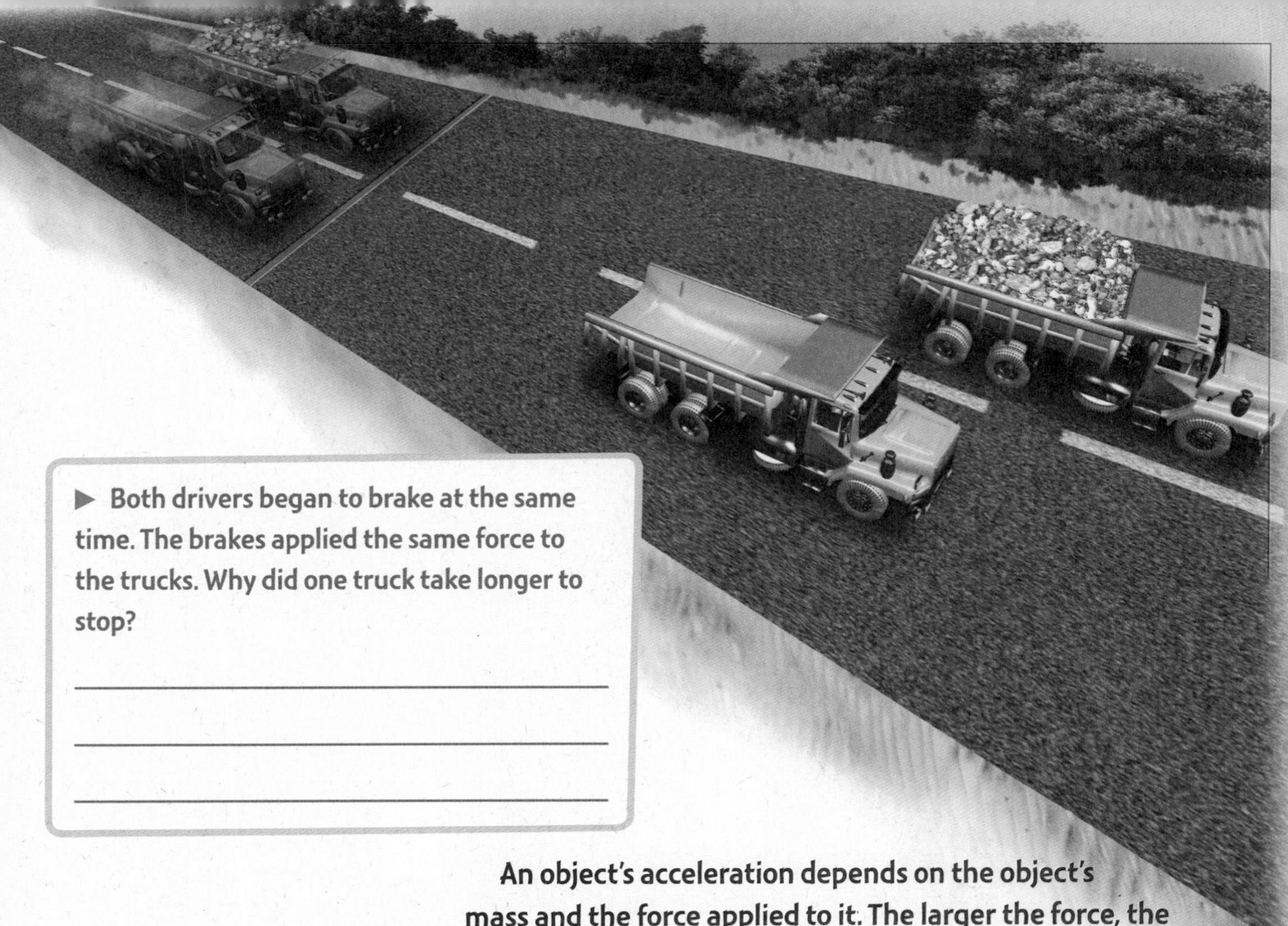

▶ Both drivers began to brake at the same time. The brakes applied the same force to the trucks. Why did one truck take longer to stop?

_______________________________________________

_______________________________________________

_______________________________________________

An object's acceleration depends on the object's mass and the force applied to it. The larger the force, the greater is the acceleration. Suppose you push a wagon gently. The wagon speeds up slowly. If you use more strength to push, then the wagon's speed changes quickly.

The less an object's mass is, the less force is needed to change its motion. It's easier to push an empty shopping cart than a full one. Light cars are used in drag races because a car with less mass speeds up faster than a car with more mass.

If you want to slide a heavy box across the floor faster, you have two options. You could take some items out of the box, which decreases its mass. Or you could have a friend help you, which increases the force you apply.

**Steel Ball**

**mass:** ________

**acceleration:** ________

Why It Matters

How did I get to Mars?

# LET'S GO to Mars!

How did an understanding of forces help to send a rover to Mars and safely land it there?

**1** The first force you need is an unbalanced force to oppose Earth's gravity. A huge booster rocket produces nearly 900,000 N of force that accelerates the rocket upward.

**2** After the booster rocket falls away, smaller rockets in the second stage fire. The rockets change the direction of the vehicle's motion and put it in orbit around Earth.

**3** The third-stage rocket firing produces enough force to reach "escape velocity." Earth's gravity can no longer pull it back down. We're on our way!

▶ What forces act on the rocket while it's at rest on Earth's surface? Are they balanced or unbalanced?

_______________

_______________

_______________

_______________

_______________

## Balanced

▶ At what points during the Rover's trip to Mars are the forces on it balanced?

______________________________

______________________________

______________________________

## Unbalanced

▶ What unbalanced forces are acting on the Rover as it lands on Mars?

______________________________

______________________________

______________________________

## Gravity

▶ Infer. Use forces to explain why the Rover required a parachute and "air bags."

______________________________

______________________________

______________________________

During much of the time it takes the spacecraft to travel to Mars, it travels at a constant velocity. The forces acting on the spacecraft are balanced, so its motion does not change.

Tiny rockets occasionally fire to keep the spacecraft on course. During these times, the forces are unbalanced.

As the spacecraft approaches Mars, gravitational attraction begins to accelerate it toward the surface. Like a person jumping from a plane, the Rover detaches from the spacecraft. Parachutes open to slow its fall. Then a big ball inflates around the Rover. When the Rover hits the surface of Mars, it bounces around until it comes safely to rest.

Mars Rover air bag testing

When you're done, use the answer key to check and revise your work.

**Change the part of the summary in blue to make it correct.**

|  |  |
| --- | --- |
| 1. Forces are pushes and pulls that increase the speed of objects. | ______________ |
| 2. Gravity is the force of attraction between a planet and another object. | ______________ |
| 3. An object moving through the air slows down because it is affected by the force of gravity. | ______________ |
| 4. When balanced forces act on an object, the object falls. | ______________ |
| 5. In order for an object to change its speed or direction, someone has to push it. | ______________ |

Answer Key: 1. can change the motion or shape of objects 2. any two objects 3. the force of friction 4. doesn't change its motion 5. an unbalanced force must act on it

# Brain Check

Lesson 1

Name ____________________

## Word Play

**1** A foreign-language teacher placed words from other languages into the following sentences. For each sentence, write the English word that means the same as the foreign word. Then use the circled letters to complete the riddle.

1. Italian — A push is an example of a forza. Another example is a pull.

   _ ◯ _ ◯ _
   (11, 3)

2. French — The force of attraction between Earth and objects on its surface is pesanteur.

   _ ◯ _ _ _ _ _
   (8)

3. Russian — The force between two moving objects that are touching is Трение.

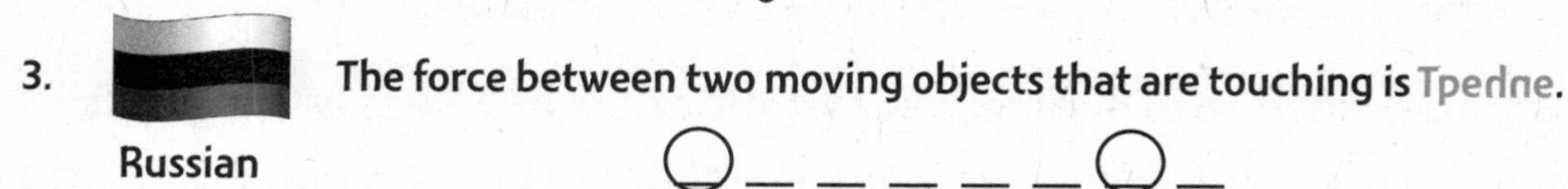

   ◯ _ _ _ _ _ _ ◯ _
   (4, 7)

4. German — Two forces that are equal in size but opposite in direction are ausgeglichene Kräfte.

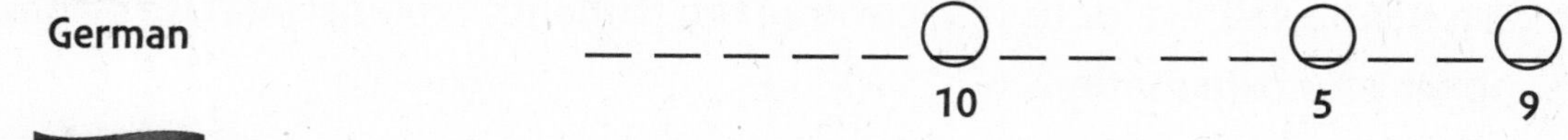

   _ _ _ _ _ ◯ _ _   _ _ ◯ _ _ ◯
   (10, 5, 9)

5. Portuguese — Two forces that are not equal in size are Forças desequilibradas.

   ◯ _ _ _ _ _ _ _ _ _   _ _ _ _ ◯ _
   (2, 6)

6. Chinese — A 彈簧秤 is a tool that can be used to measure the size of a force.

   ◯ _ _ _ _ _ _ ◯ _ _ _ ◯
   (1, 12, 13)

Riddle: What conclusion did the student draw?

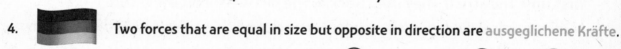

The _o_r_e of the _o_c_ is the h___e, of __ur__.
(1 2 3 — 4 5 6 — 7 8 9 — 10 11 — 12 13)

Try saying that five times fast!

# Apply Concepts

2 Draw pictures of two activities that you might do. In the first, draw a pushing force. In the second, draw a pulling force.

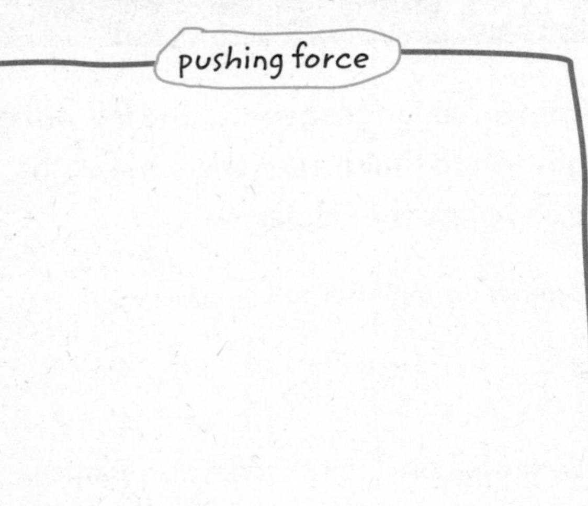


3 Two students designed an experiment to test the effect of a force on an object. They used a catapult to try and hit a target. The catapult has only one setting. The first time they tried, they used Rock B. The picture shows the result. Based on their empirical evidence, the students concluded that Rock A would help them hit the target. Analyze, evaluate, and critique the students explanation. Use evidence to support your explanation.

Name ______________________



4 Use the words *balanced* and *unbalanced* as you name and describe the forces acting in each of these pictures.

a. 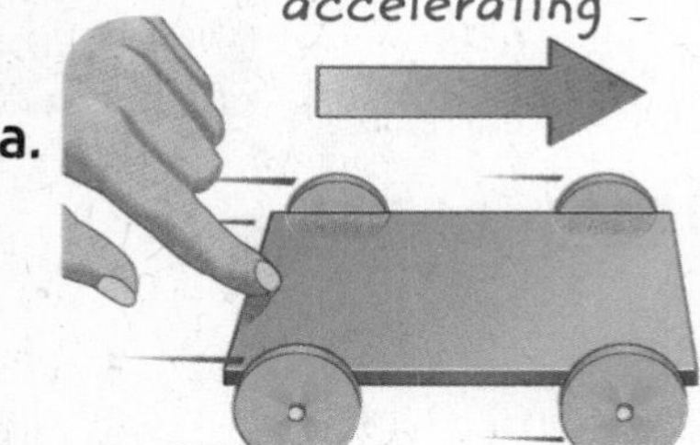


b. 

c. 

______________________ ______________________ ______________________

5 Draw what will happen to a ball that you throw straight up into the air. Explain why this happens.

______________________

6 Explain why it is easy to slip on a floor that is wet.

______________________

7 Analyze, interpret, and infer: Look at the drawings at right. Mary measured the distance each ball traveled. Draw lines to match the ball with the distance it traveled. Then explain why each ball traveled a different distance.

_______________________________________________

_______________________________________________

_______________________________________________

25 cm

15 cm

20 cm

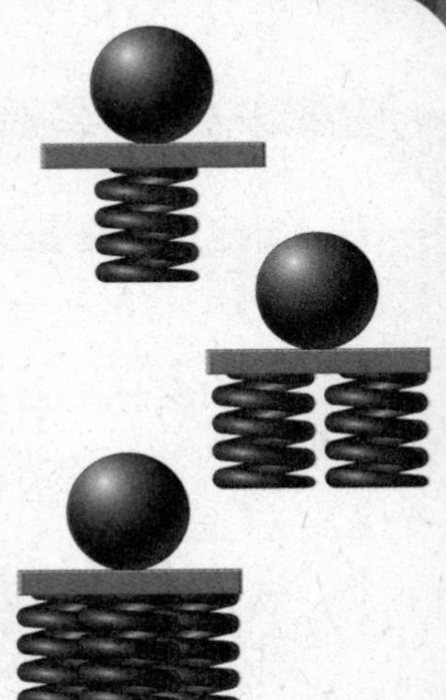

8 Give an example of each of the following.

a. A force is applied but nothing happens.

_______________________________

b. A force causes an object to change shape.

_______________________________

c. A force causes an object to change position.

_______________________________

d. A force causes an object to stop moving.

_______________________________

9 Circle the object(s) whose velocities are not changing. Draw an up arrow next to the object(s) whose speeds are increasing. Draw a down arrow next to the object(s) whose speeds are decreasing.

A car travels 35 miles per hour around a bend in the road.

A car comes to a stop when a traffic light turns red.

A race car accelerates when a race begins.

A car is driving 45 miles per hour down a straight road.

Take It Home!

Discuss with your family what you've learned about forces. Together, identify five forces that you use to change the motion of objects in your everyday life. Consider forces that weren't discussed in the lesson.

S.T.E.M.

Engineering & Technology

# Football Safety Gear

Football is a rough sport. Players often collide with great force. Designers have developed protective gear to protect players from injury.

The first helmets were custom made out of leather by horse harness makers. Later, ear holes and padding were added. These helmets had little padding and no face guards.

Hard plastic shells, fitted foam linings, and metal facemasks now make helmets more protective. Some helmets even contain sensors that transmit signals to warn if a player's head has been hit hard enough to cause a serious injury.

## Critical Thinking

How do modern materials make it possible to build a better helmet than one made of just leather?

______________________________________________

______________________________________________

# S.T.E.M.

continued

When engineers develop new materials, it can spark new and improved designs of all sorts of familiar objects.

Choose two pieces of safety gear from your favorite sport or activity. Draw each piece of gear. Do research to find out what material makes up each piece. Label the materials. Explain how one material's properties made it a good design choice.

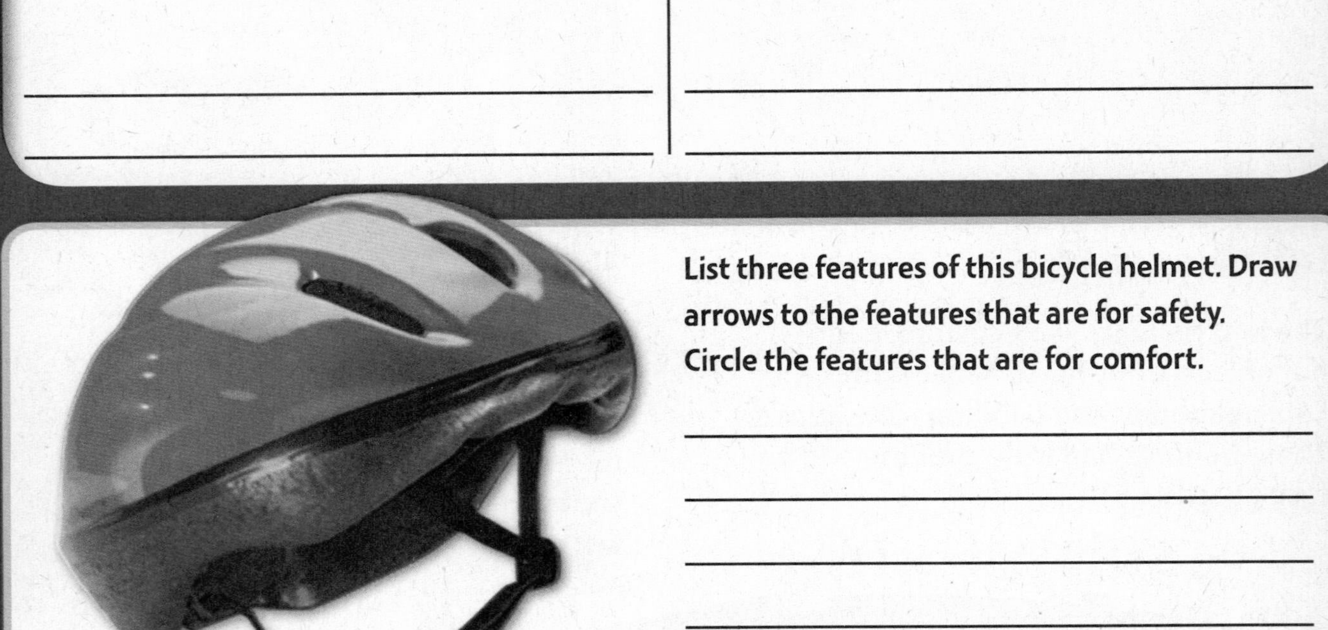

List three features of this bicycle helmet. Draw arrows to the features that are for safety. Circle the features that are for comfort.

## Build On It!

Rise to the engineering design challenge—complete **Design It: Balloon Racer** in the Inquiry Flipchart.

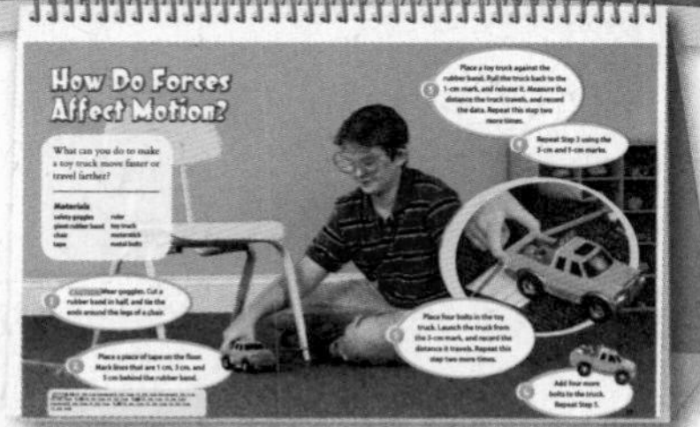

Inquiry Flipchart page 23

**TEKS** **5.2A** ...implement simple experimental investigations... **5.2B** ask well-defined questions, formulate testable hypotheses... **5.2C** collect information by...accurate measuring **5.2D** analyze and interpret information to construct reasonable explanations... **5.2E** demonstrate that repeated investigations may increase the reliability of results... **5.2G** construct...graphs...to organize, examine, and evaluate information **5.6D** design an experiment that tests the effect of force on an object

Name ________________________________

Essential Question

# How Do Forces Affect Motion?

## Set a Purpose

What will you learn from this experiment?

________________________________

________________________________

________________________________

## State Your Hypothesis

Write your hypothesis.

________________________________

________________________________

________________________________

## Think About the Procedure

Why do you use a rubber band to start the toy truck rather than your hand?

________________________________

________________________________

________________________________

Why do you think it is important to repeat each test three times?

________________________________

Why do you add bolts to the truck?

________________________________

________________________________

________________________________

________________________________

## Record Your Data

In the table below, record the information you collected by accurately measuring.

<table>
<tr><th colspan="10">How Forces Affect Motion</th></tr>
<tr><td>Part I:</td><td colspan="9">Distance rubber band was stretched</td></tr>
<tr><td></td><td colspan="3">1 cm</td><td colspan="3">3 cm</td><td colspan="3">5 cm</td></tr>
<tr><td>Distance traveled (cm)</td><td></td><td></td><td></td><td></td><td></td><td></td><td></td><td></td><td></td></tr>
<tr><td>Part II:</td><td colspan="9">Rubber band stretched to 3 cm</td></tr>
<tr><td></td><td colspan="3">Empty truck</td><td colspan="3">Truck with 4 bolts</td><td colspan="3">Truck with 8 bolts</td></tr>
<tr><td>Distance traveled (cm) Trial 1</td><td colspan="3"></td><td colspan="3"></td><td colspan="3"></td></tr>
<tr><td>Distance traveled (cm) Trial 2</td><td colspan="3"></td><td colspan="3"></td><td colspan="3"></td></tr>
<tr><td>Distance traveled (cm) Trial 3</td><td colspan="3"></td><td colspan="3"></td><td colspan="3"></td></tr>
</table>

## Draw Conclusions

Each time you changed a variable and launched the truck, you ran three trials. Calculate the average distance traveled by the truck in each experimental setting.

| Experimental settings | Average distance traveled (cm) |
|---|---|
| Rubber band at 1 cm | |
| Rubber band at 3 cm | |
| Rubber band at 5 cm | |
| | |
| Truck with 0 bolts | |
| Truck with 4 bolts | |
| Truck with 8 bolts | |

Draw two bar graphs to organize, examine, and evaluate your data.

## Analyze and Extend

1. Analyze and interpret collected information to construct a reasonable explanation. How is an object's mass related to its change in motion when acted on by a force?

2. How does the size of the force applied to an object affect its motion?

3. **REVIEW** Why is it important to repeat an experiment several times or to have several people perform the same experiment?

4. **REVIEW** Ask a well-defined question about motion and forces. Describe, plan, and (if allowed) implement a simple experiment that tests one variable.

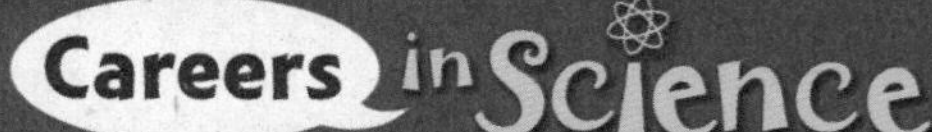

# 10 Things to Know About Safety Engineers

1. A safety engineer helps design and test devices to make them safer.

2. Safety engineers make changes to designs to avoid possible dangers.

3. I'm a crash test dummy. Some safety engineers use me as a model.

4. Safety engineers can make machines, such as cars, safer to use.

5. Safety engineers make cars safer with inventions such as seat belts and air bags.

6. Some safety engineers focus on stopping specific dangers, such as fires.

7. Safety engineers help society have fewer injuries and illnesses.

8. Some keep germs from spreading into our food and making us sick.

9. They may focus on protecting workers from getting hurt on the job.

10. To do their jobs, safety engineers need to study physics, chemistry, math, and human behavior.

# Now You Be the Engineer!

1. What do you think is the best thing about being a safety engineer?
2. How do safety engineers help society?

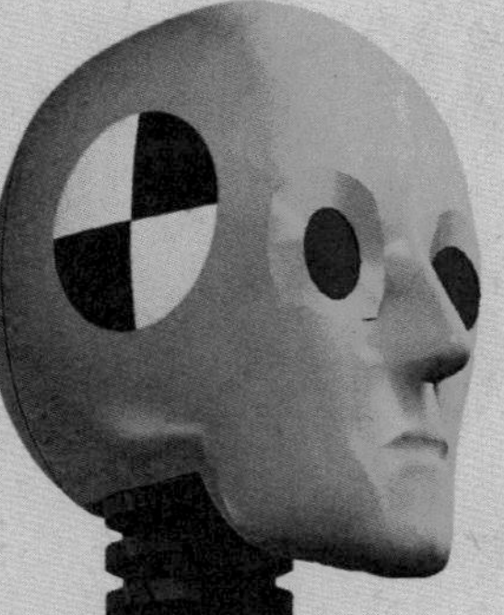

3. What safety features in cars have safety engineers helped to develop?
4. What question would you like to ask a safety engineer?

1 ________________________________
________________________________
________________________________
________________________________

2 ________________________________
________________________________
________________________________
________________________________
________________________________
________________________________

3 ________________________________
________________________________

4 ________________________________
________________________________
________________________________
________________________________

# Unit 4 Review

Name ______________________

## Vocabulary Review

Use the terms in the box to complete the sentences.

| balanced forces |
|---|
| force |
| friction |
| gravity |
| motion |
| unbalanced forces |

**TEKS 5.6D**

1. Forces that cause a change in motion are ________________.

**TEKS 5.6D**

2. A force of attraction between two objects, even if they are not touching, is ________________.

**TEKS 5.6D**

3. A change of position of an object is called ________________.

**TEKS 5.6D**

4. A push or a pull, which causes movement or change in an object's shape, is a(n) ________________.

**TEKS 5.6D**

5. Forces on an object that are equal in size and opposite in direction are ________________.

**TEKS 5.6D**

6. A force that opposes motion and acts between two objects that are touching is ________________.

## Science Concepts

Fill in the letter of the choice that best answers the question.

**TEKS 5.2D**

7. This table shows the masses of several different objects.

| Object | Metal washer | Plastic disk | Rock | Wooden block |
|---|---|---|---|---|
| Mass (g) | 1.5 | 34 | 16 | 22 |

Based on the observable evidence, which object will require the most force to toss it 2 meters?

Ⓐ rock
Ⓑ plastic disk
Ⓒ metal washer
Ⓓ wooden block

**TEKS 5.2B, 5.6D**

8. Which of the following is the best testable hypothesis about the effect of a force on an object's motion?

Ⓐ Pulling a heavy box is better than pushing it.

Ⓑ Objects that look heavy can exert more force than other objects.

Ⓒ The force needed to move an object increases as the object's mass increases.

Ⓓ You can use a metric ruler to measure the force applied to an object.

Use the diagram to answer questions 9 and 10. The diagram shows an experiment Lily performed to measure forces.

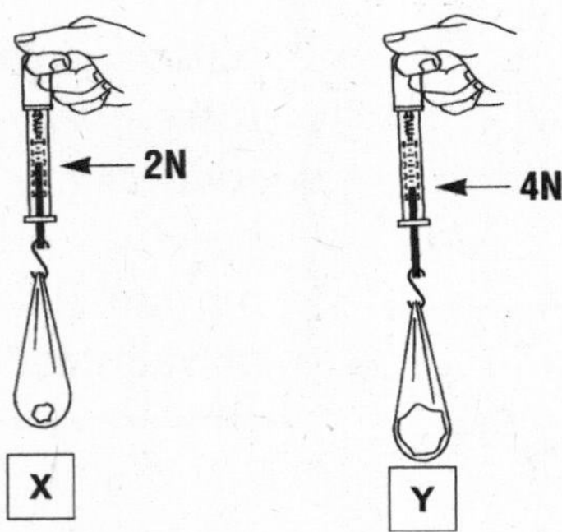


TEKS 5.4A, 5.6D

9. Analyze the readings on the spring scales. Which statement best describes the cause of the readings on the scales?

   (A) The amount of matter in object Y is twice that in object X.

   (B) The volume of object Y is twice the volume of object X.

   (C) The density of object Y is twice that of object X.

   (D) The pull of gravity on object Y is half that of object X.

TEKS 5.2A, 5.6D

10. How would you describe the variable being measured by this experiment?

   (A) the applied force

   (B) the force of friction

   (C) the gravitational force

   (D) the upward, or normal, force

TEKS 5.2D

11. An object is traveling in a straight line in space. No forces are acting on the object. Based on this evidence, what will happen to the object's motion?

   (A) It will move faster and faster because there is no force to stop it.

   (B) It will stop gradually because there is no force to keep it moving.

   (C) It will stop immediately when the force that started its motion has stopped.

   (D) Its motion will not change, and it will continue in the same direction at the same speed.

TEKS 5.2D

12. Four forces are acting on the block shown in the following illustration:

   - $F$ is the applied force.
   - $F_f$ is friction.
   - $F_g$ is the gravitational force.
   - $F_n$ is the normal force—the upward push of the table on the block.

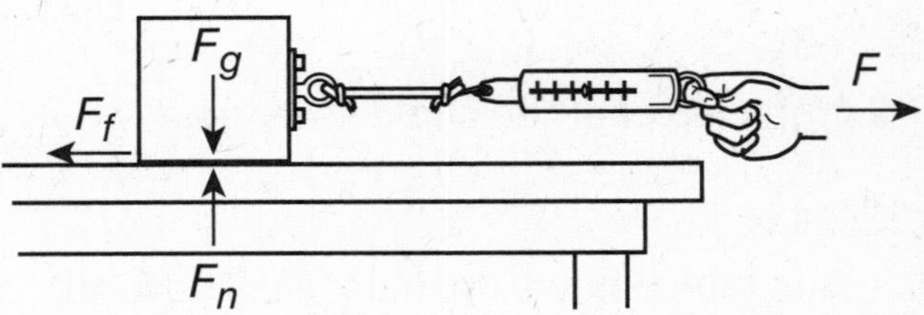


The block is not moving. Based on this evidence, which of the following statements is true?

   (A) $F$ and $F_f$ are equal.

   (B) $F$ and $F_g$ are equal.

   (C) $F$ is greater than $F_f$.

   (D) $F_g$ is greater than $F$.

Name ______________________________

Use the diagram to answer questions 13 and 14. Shawna designed an experiment like the one shown below.

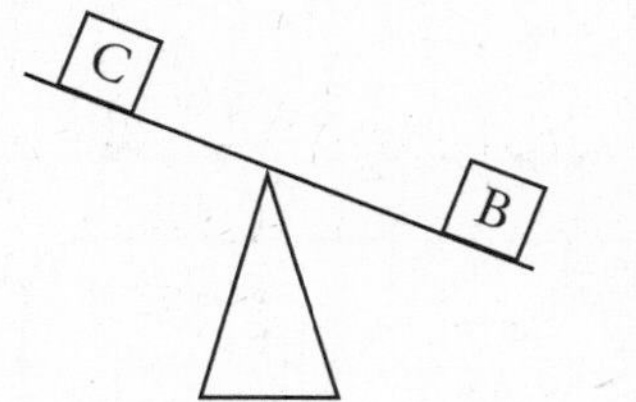

TEKS 5.2B, 5.6D

13. Which question is Shawna trying to answer with her experiment?

Ⓐ She wanted to measure the mass of the blocks.

Ⓑ She wanted to measure the weight of the blocks.

Ⓒ She wanted to know how the masses of the blocks compare.

Ⓓ She wanted to know how the volumes of the blocks compare.

TEKS 5.3A, 5.6D

14. Using logical reasoning and evidence from the experiment, which statement correctly describes the blocks?

Ⓐ The block with the largest mass is B.

Ⓑ The block with the largest mass is A.

Ⓒ The block with the smallest mass is C.

Ⓓ The block with the smallest mass is B.

TEKS 5.2D, 5.6D

15. Rosa designed an experiment to measure the effect of forces on an object. The table shows the data she collected.

| Block color | Mass (g) | Pushing force (N) | Friction (N) |
|---|---|---|---|
| Red | 50 | 24 | 6 |
| Green | 100 | 24 | 6 |
| Blue | 40 | 24 | 6 |
| Yellow | 75 | 24 | 6 |

Based on the data, which block will have the greatest change in motion?

Ⓐ red block

Ⓑ blue block

Ⓒ green block

Ⓓ yellow block

TEKS 5.6D

16. Raul plans an experiment to test the effect of forces on an object. He applied the forces shown in the diagram.

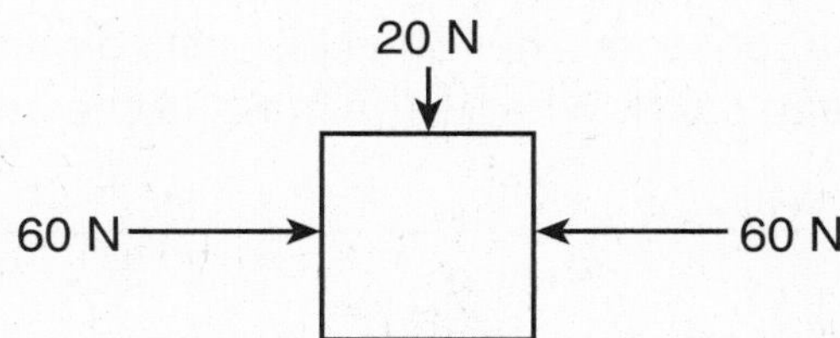


As a result of his experiment, what will Raul observe?

Ⓐ The box will remain in its current position.

Ⓑ The box will move downward in a straight line.

Ⓒ The box will move to the right in a straight line.

Ⓓ The box will move back and forth from left to right.

# Apply Inquiry and Review the Big Idea

Write the answers to these questions.

TEKS 5.2D, 5.6D

17. Naomi exerts a force of 20 N on a ball with a mass of 0.5 kg. Cyrus exerts a force of 30 N on the same ball. What is the difference in the acceleration of the ball in $m/s^2$. (Hint: Acceleration = force ÷ mass)

_______________

TEKS 5.3C

18. Draw a diagram of an object at rest with four forces acting on it: gravity; normal, or upward, force; applied force; and friction. Use arrows to show the direction and size of each force.

TEKS 5.2D, 5.4A

19. The spring scale shown has an object on the pan.

a. What does the reading on the scale measure?

_______________

_______________

b. Suppose another object is placed on the pan, making the scale read 5.0 N. What is the mass of the additional object?

_______________

_______________

TEKS 5.6D, 5.2B

20. Luis wants to know how the force needed to drag a box across a carpet differs from the force needed to drag the box across an icy pond. Use the space below to describe an experiment Luis could do to find out the answer to his question.

_______________

_______________

_______________

_______________

UNIT 5

# Forms of Energy

## Big Idea

Energy occurs in many forms and can be observed in cycles, patterns, and systems.

TEKS 5.2A, 5.2B, 5.2C, 5.2D, 5.2G, 5.3A, 5.3C, 5.3D, 5.4A, 5.5A, 5.6A, 5.6B, 5.6C, 5.7C

## I Wonder Why

The image shows a "solar farm." Why is it called a farm? What do you think is being "harvested"? *Turn the page to find out.*

**Here's why** A solar farm collects energy from the sun and converts it to electricity, which is carried by transmission lines to wherever it is needed. The electricity is then used in homes, businesses, and industries.

In this unit, you will explore the Big Idea, the Essential Questions, and the investigations on the Inquiry Flipchart.

Levels of Inquiry Key ■ DIRECTED ■ GUIDED ■ INDEPENDENT

**Big Idea** Energy occurs in many forms and can be observed in cycles, patterns, and systems.

## Essential Questions



**Science Notebook**

Before you begin each lesson, be sure to write your thoughts about the Essential Question.

TEKS 5.6A explore the uses of energy, including mechanical, light, thermal, electrical, and sound energy

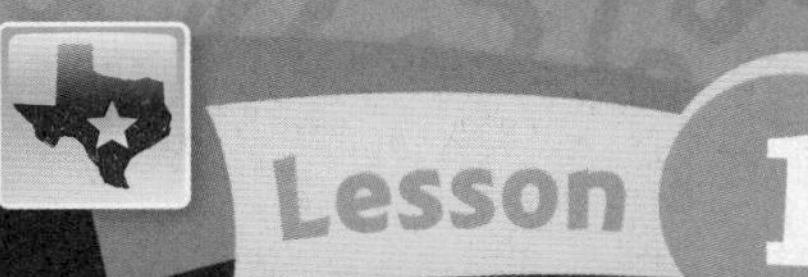


Essential Question

# What Is Energy?

## Engage Your Brain!

As you read the lesson, figure out the answer to the following question. Write the answer here.

What kinds of energy are represented in this picture?

______________________________

______________________________

______________________________

______________________________

## Active Reading

### Lesson Vocabulary

List the terms. As you learn about each one, make notes in the Interactive Glossary.

______________ ______________

______________ ______________

______________ ______________

### Compare and Contrast

Many ideas in this lesson are about ways that things are alike or different. Active readers stay focused on comparisons and contrasts by asking how things are alike and how they are different.



Inquiry Flipchart p. 24 — Seeing Sound Energy / Light Travels

# Energy All Around

What does a melting scoop of ice cream have in common with a kicked soccer ball? The ice cream and the ball both change in some way. What causes these changes?

**Active Reading** As you read this page, underline important details about energy.

▶ A soccer ball won't move unless something gives it energy. Energy changes the ball's motion. Circle the thing in the picture that gave the ball energy.

Think about all the ways that you use energy. **Energy** is the ability to cause changes in matter. Energy is involved when matter moves or changes its shape. A change in temperature also involves energy.

Energy can transform, or change, from one form into another. The boy in the picture is using energy to run. The energy came from food that he ate.

When the boy kicks the ball, his foot transfers energy to the ball. The moving ball transfers energy again. Energy moves to particles in the air and on the ground. These tiny particles begin to move faster.

The ball stops moving after it has transferred all its energy. Energy is never used up. It just changes from one form to another.

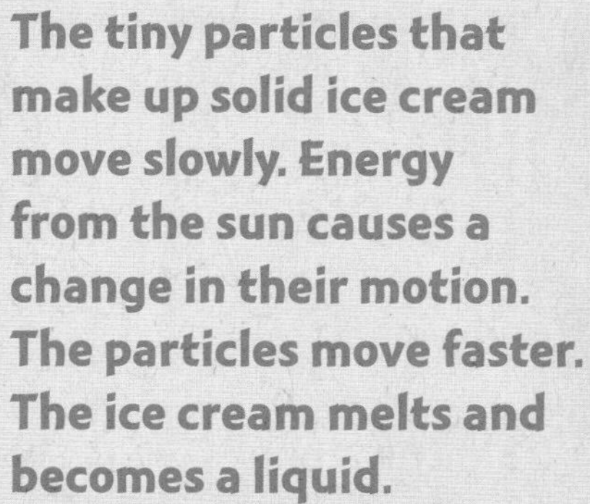

The tiny particles that make up solid ice cream move slowly. Energy from the sun causes a change in their motion. The particles move faster. The ice cream melts and becomes a liquid.

► What caused this ice cream to melt?

_______________

_______________

_______________

► For each statement, write *T* for true or *F* for false.

◯ 1. Energy can cause a change in matter.

◯ 2. Energy can change from one form to another.

◯ 3. Energy can be used up and destroyed.

◯ 4. Energy can be transferred from one object to another.

# The Ups and Downs of Energy

Does an object that is not moving have any energy? Let's find out!

**Active Reading** As you read this page, circle the sentences that tell how potential energy and kinetic energy are different.

Does a book sitting on a shelf have energy? Yes! Someone gave it energy by lifting the book to the shelf. The energy is now stored in the book. The energy an object has because of its position or condition is called **potential energy** (PE).

If the book falls off the shelf, it begins moving. Its potential energy changes to the energy of motion. The energy an object has because of its motion is called **kinetic energy** (KE).

When the roller coaster car is at the top of a hill, most of its energy is potential energy due to its position. Gravity will change this PE to KE as the car starts downhill.

________

When you compress a spring or stretch a rubber band, your energy is stored in the object as potential energy. The potential energy changes to kinetic energy when you release the spring or rubber band.

Position isn't the only way that energy can be stored. A match head has potential energy stored in chemical bonds between its particles. Striking the match releases the stored energy as heat and light. A charged battery also contains potential energy. A battery dies when all of its potential energy has been transformed to electrical energy.

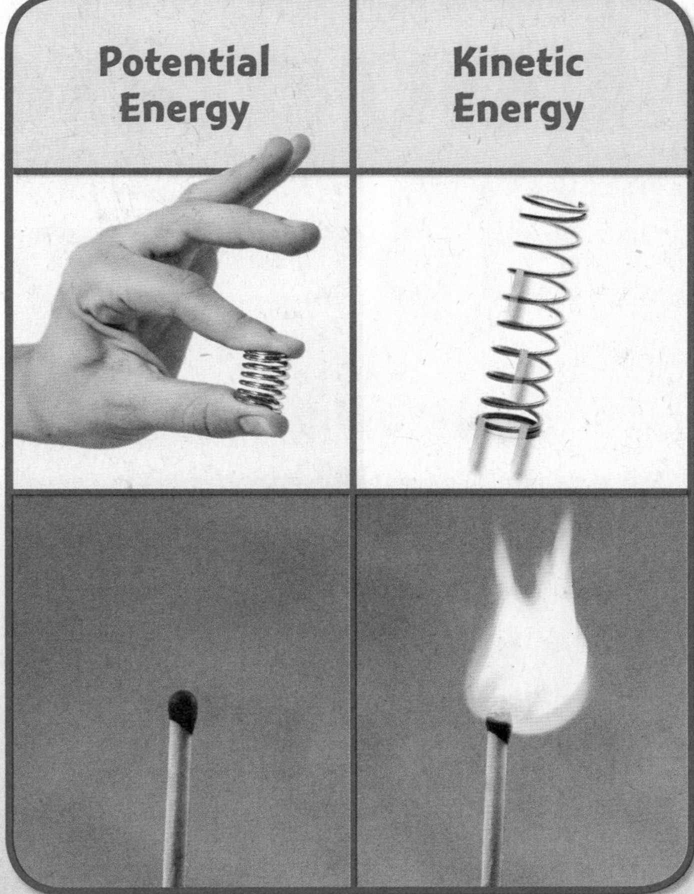


As the car moves downhill, its PE changes to kinetic, or moving, energy. At the bottom of the hill, the car's energy is kinetic. This KE becomes PE as the roller coaster car travels up the next hill.

▶ Fill in the three bubbles on the roller coaster track. Write *KE* if a coaster car at that position would have mostly kinetic energy. Write *PE* if it would have mostly potential energy.

▶ When does a roller coaster car have the most kinetic energy?

______________________________

______________________________

______________________________

______________________________

# Loud, Soft, Hot, Cold

The kinetic energy of a moving roller coaster car is easy to see. How can you sense energy in tiny particles of matter that are too small to see?

**Active Reading** **As you read these two pages, underline the sentences that tell you how sound energy and thermal energy are alike.**

When a trumpet makes noise, it vibrates, or moves back and forth. The trumpet transfers energy to tiny particles of air. Each particle of air moves back and forth, bumping into other particles. The sound travels outward.

► Draw an arrow to show the direction that sound waves are traveling.

If someone knocks on your door, the particles in the door vibrate. They bump into particles in the air on your side of the door. The sound travels through the door and through the air to you as a sound wave.

*Sound energy* is —

- a form of energy that is carried as waves in vibrating matter.
- a type of kinetic energy, because particles of matter are moving.
- the cause of all the sounds you hear.

Another type of energy that involves moving particles is thermal energy. *Thermal energy* is the total kinetic energy of the particles that make up a substance.

Thermometers measure thermal energy. You sense thermal energy as temperature. The more thermal energy an object has, the greater its temperature. Thermal energy helps you to stay warm, to cook your food, and to heat water for washing or bathing.

▶ In a hot-air balloon, the burning of propane produces thermal energy. This energy raises the temperature of the air particles inside the balloon to _______ °C.

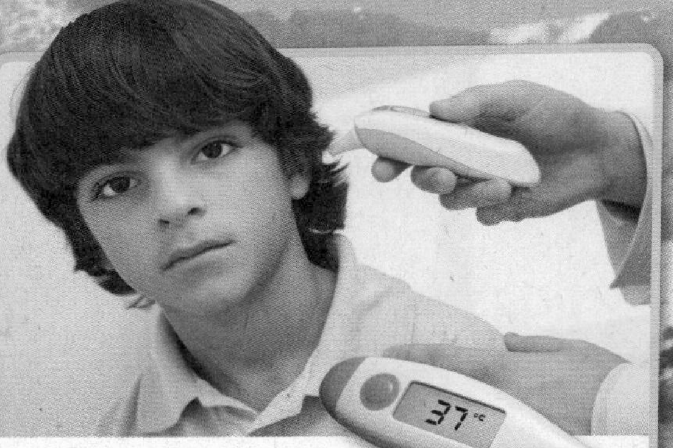


▶ This thermometer shows normal body temperature, which is _______ °C (98.6 °F).

▶ The air at the top of this icy mountain has very little thermal energy. Its temperature is _______ °C.

## Do the Math!

### Use Number Lines

Draw a number line. On the line, place the three temperatures (in °C) shown in the pictures on this page. Then add a point for normal room temperature, 22 °C.

# See a Sea of Energy

Your ears use sound energy to hear. What kind of energy allows your eyes to see?

**Active Reading** As you read, draw boxes around the descriptions of light energy and electrical energy.

The sun is the source of the light energy entering the cave.

Suppose you are using a flashlight in a dark room. You drop the flashlight and it breaks. What can you see? Nothing! Your eyes need light energy to work.

*Light energy* is a form of energy that can travel through space. Light can also pass through some types of matter, such as air or glass. Light energy travels as waves.

You can see light energy. Some objects give off light. You see all other objects when light reflects, or bounces off, from them and enters your eyes.

▶ List three sources of light.

________________________

________________________

________________________

You see the cave walls when light bounces off them and reaches your eyes.

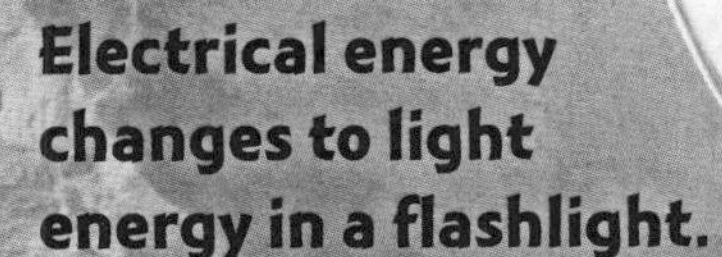

Electrical energy changes to light energy in a flashlight.

Objects that give off light energy often give off heat. But the two types of energy are different. You can tell them apart by the way you sense the energy. Your skin senses heat, but it cannot sense light energy. Your eyes sense light energy.

Flashlights and television sets produce light. To do this, they use another type of energy, called electrical energy. **Electrical energy** is energy caused by the movement of electric charges. When you use electricity, you are using electrical energy.

Electrical energy can change to other types of energy you can use. Electrical energy changes to thermal energy in a toaster or a stove. Cell phones and stereo speakers use electrical energy to produce sound. In lamps and spotlights, electrical energy changes to light energy.

**Computers and other devices that are plugged in use electrical energy.**

▶ List three objects that use electrical energy.

_______________

_______________

_______________

# Energy in Machines and Food

You have learned about machines that use electrical energy. Some machines don't need to be plugged in. What forms of energy do they use?

**Active Reading** Draw one line under things that have mechanical energy. Draw two lines under things that have chemical energy.

Many objects, such as a ball thrown in the air, have both kinetic and potential energy. **Mechanical energy** (ME) is the total energy of motion and position of an object. As a ball drops, its potential energy decreases as its kinetic energy increases. Its mechanical energy, though, stays constant. The relationship among these forms of energy is shown by the following equation.

Mechanical Energy = Kinetic Energy + Potential Energy

A machine uses mechanical energy to do work. For example, a fan plugged into the wall uses electrical energy. It changes that energy into the mechanical energy of the spinning fan blades. The spinning fan uses the mechanical energy to do work—moving the air in a room.

► Describe how energy in gasoline is transformed in a lawn mower.

______________________________

______________________________

______________________________

______________________________

______________________________

______________________________

Have you ever felt as if you were going to "run out of energy"? The energy your body uses comes from the food you eat. Food contains a kind of potential energy called chemical energy. **Chemical energy** is energy that is stored in matter and that can be released by a chemical reaction.

When your body needs energy, it breaks down food and releases potential chemical energy from it. If you use that energy to run or jump, it changes into kinetic energy. Your body also uses chemical energy stored in food to produce thermal energy. This keeps your body at a steady temperature.

Cars use chemical energy in liquid fuel such as gasoline. A flashlight uses the chemical energy stored in a battery to produce light. Some stoves change chemical energy to thermal energy by burning a gas called propane.

▶ Winding the key on the toy increases the toy's ______________ energy.

▶ Our bodies use the ________________ energy in food to move and stay warm.

▶ These gears make the hands of this watch move because they have ______________ energy.

Why It Matters

# Spotlight on Energy

A stage production requires different kinds of energy. How many are being used on this stage?

**Active Reading** As you read these pages, draw a box around each type of energy.

Some stage shows use fire, sparklers, and explosions. These elements turn stored chemical energy into light, heat, and sound energy.

Musicians use mechanical energy to play instruments. The instruments make sound energy that the audience hears as music.

These performers are high above the stage. They have a lot of potential energy due to their position.

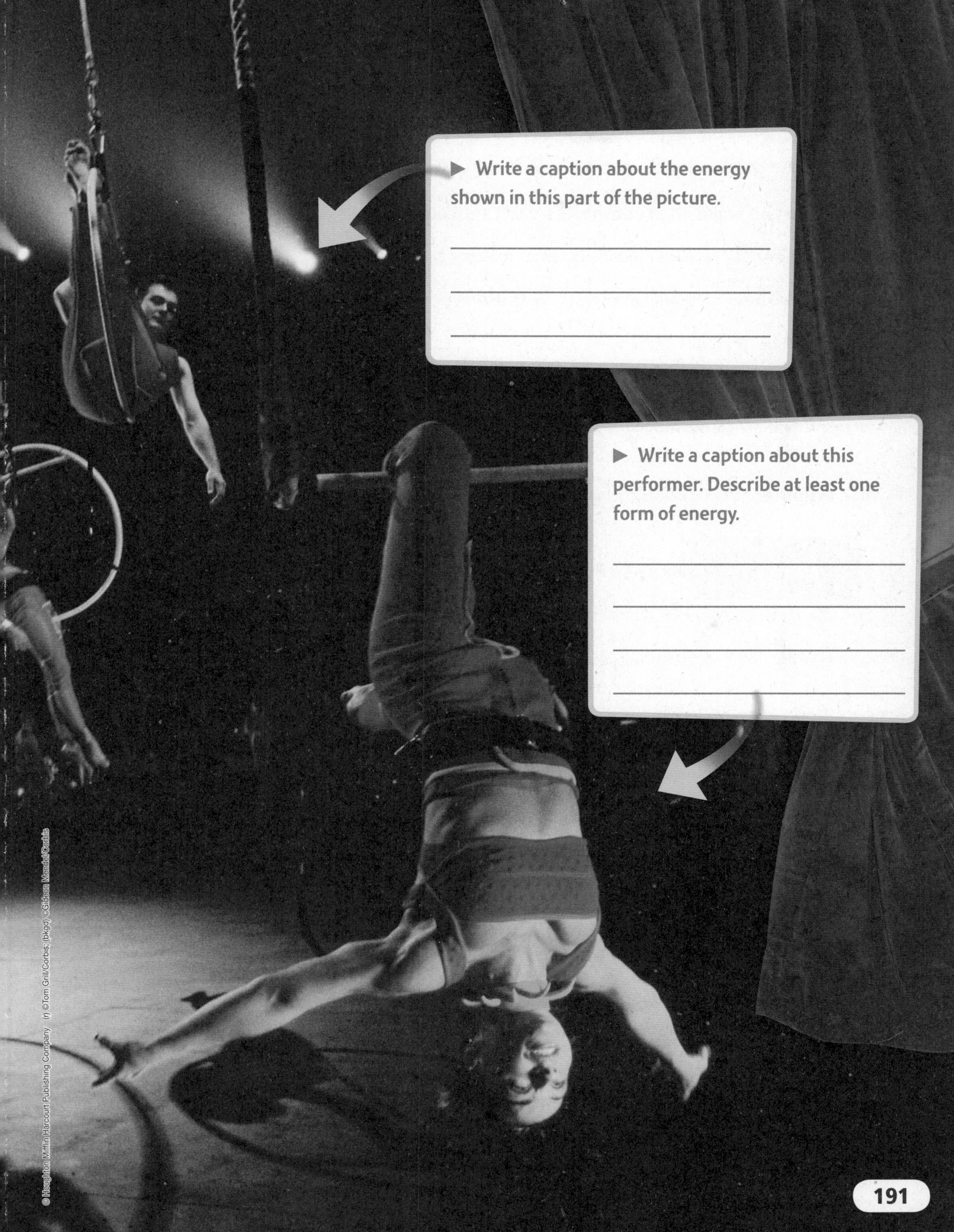

▶ Write a caption about the energy shown in this part of the picture.

_______________________________________

_______________________________________

_______________________________________

▶ Write a caption about this performer. Describe at least one form of energy.

_______________________________________

_______________________________________

_______________________________________

_______________________________________

When you're done, use the answer key to check and revise your work.

**Part I: Circle the word that completes each sentence.**

A. Energy is the ability to cause motion or create ( matter / change ).

B. There are two main categories of energy—potential and ( thermal / kinetic ).

C. Energy can't be created or ( destroyed / captured ).

D. Energy can change from one form to another, which is called energy ( transformation / conservation ).

**Part II: Complete the graphic organizer below.**

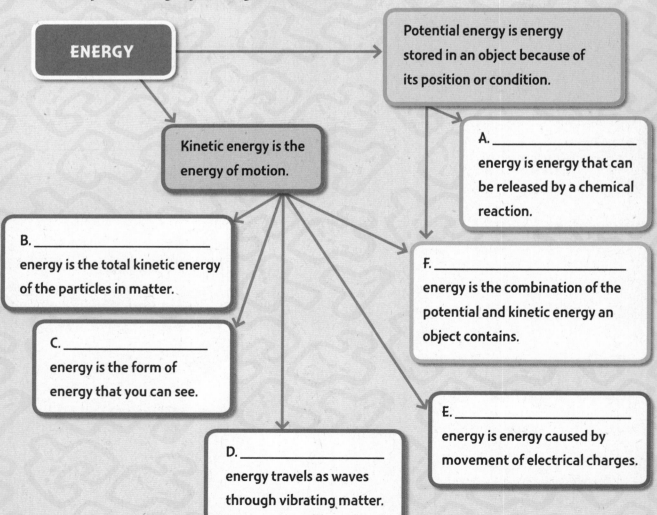

ENERGY

Potential energy is energy stored in an object because of its position or condition.

Kinetic energy is the energy of motion.

A. ______________ energy is energy that can be released by a chemical reaction.

B. ______________ energy is the total kinetic energy of the particles in matter.

C. ______________ energy is the form of energy that you can see.

D. ______________ energy travels as waves through vibrating matter.

E. ______________ energy is energy caused by movement of electrical charges.

F. ______________ energy is the combination of the potential and kinetic energy an object contains.

Answer Key: Part I: A. change B. kinetic C. destroyed D. transformation Part II: A. Chemical B. Thermal C. Light D. Sound E. Electrical F. Mechanical

Lesson 1

Name ____________________

## Word Play

1 Use the clues and the word bank to fill in the puzzle.

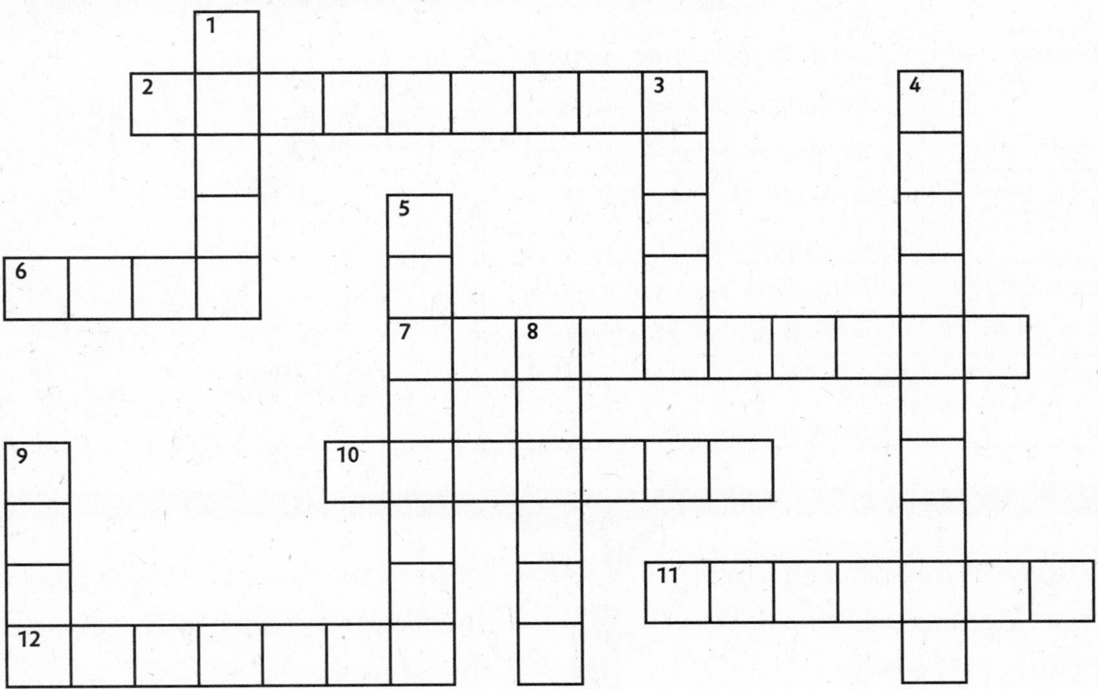


### Across

2. Stored energy due to position or condition
6. A substance that contains useful chemical energy
7. Energy caused by the movement of electric charges
10. Energy of motion
11. To move back and forth
12. Energy of moving particles of matter

### Down

1. Form of energy you can hear
3. Form of energy you can see
4. Total potential and kinetic energy of an object
5. Energy that can be released by a chemical reaction
8. Ability to cause changes in matter
9. What your body feels thermal energy as

| mechanical* | chemical* | electrical* | sound | light | energy* |
|---|---|---|---|---|---|
| potential* | kinetic* | thermal | vibrate | food | heat |

* Key Lesson Vocabulary

# Apply Concepts

**2** Complete the matching game. The first one is done for you.

| | | |
|---|---|---|
| Light Energy (E) (3) | A. The total kinetic energy of the particles in matter |  |
| Thermal Energy ◯◯ | B. Energy caused by motion of electric charges | |
| Sound Energy ◯◯ | C. Energy that is stored in matter and can be released during a chemical reaction | |
| Electrical Energy ◯◯ | D. Energy carried as waves of vibrating matter | |
| Mechanical Energy ◯◯ | E. Energy that travels as a wave and that you are able to see | |
| Chemical Energy ◯◯ | F. Sum of an object's potential and kinetic energy | |



**3** Use the terms *potential energy* and *kinetic energy* to tell what is happening to the skier.

**4** Identify the types of energy present or produced in each lettered part of the picture.

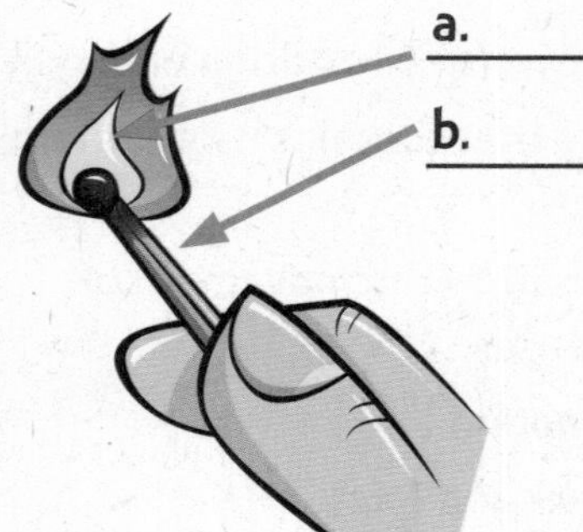

When you go home, ask your family to help you list all the kinds of energy you use around your house. Try to find at least one example of each type of energy you learned about in this lesson.

**TEKS** **5.3D** connect grade-level appropriate science concepts with the history of science, science careers, and contributions of scientists **5.6A** explore the uses of energy, including mechanical, light, thermal, electrical, and sound energy

# Ask a Windsmith

**Q.** What does a windsmith do?

**A.** A windsmith operates, maintains, and repairs the electrical and mechanical parts of wind turbines.

**Q.** What is a wind turbine?

**A.** A wind turbine is a modern windmill. It uses the energy of wind to do work and to generate electrical energy.

**Q.** How does a wind turbine work?

**A.** The wind's kinetic energy is transferred to the turbine's blades, causing them to spin. When the blades spin, a long shaft, or pole, also spins. The shaft is connected to a generator. In the generator, kinetic energy is transformed into electrical energy.

**Q.** Is it scary to climb a wind turbine?

**A.** If you are afraid of heights, it could be, but windsmiths are used to working high up. The first day a windsmith climbs a turbine is a day to celebrate.

## Now It's Your Turn!

What fields of science do you think can help choose the location of a wind turbine?

_______________

_______________

_______________

# SHOW WHAT YOU KNOW ABOUT Windsmiths

Answer these four questions about windsmiths.

**1**

What part of a windsmith's work do you find most interesting?

______________________________

______________________________

______________________________

**2**

How is energy transferred and transformed by a wind turbine?

______________________________

______________________________

______________________________

**3**

How do windsmiths help society?

______________________________

______________________________

______________________________

**4**

What questions do you have about windsmiths?

______________________________

______________________________

______________________________

TEKS 5.2D analyze and interpret information to construct reasonable explanations from... evidence 5.2G construct appropriate...charts using technology...to organize, examine, and evaluate information 5.3A ...analyze, evaluate, and critique scientific explanations by using... logical reasoning... 5.6A explore the uses of energy, including...thermal...energy

Lesson 2

Essential Question

# What Is Thermal Energy?

## Engage Your Brain!

As you read the lesson, look for the answer to the following question and record it here.

The person in the picture uses energy from the fire to keep warm and cook food. How does the fire's energy reach the person and the food?

___

___

___

## Active Reading

### Lesson Vocabulary

List each term. As you learn about each one, make notes in the Interactive Glossary.

___

___

___

### Compare and Contrast

Many ideas in this lesson are connected because they explain how things compare and contrast—how they are alike and different. Active readers stay focused on how things compare and contrast when they ask themselves, How are conduction, convection and radiation alike? How are they different?



Inquiry Flipchart p. 25 — Where Is the Energy?/Heating from Afar

# Lively Particles!

Why do some substances feel cold while others feel hot? What causes this difference? Moving particles!

**Active Reading** As you read these two pages, underline the definitions of vocabulary terms.

Although you can't see them, the tiny particles that make up all matter are constantly moving. They buzz around like a swarm of bees, bouncing in every direction as they collide. These particles have *kinetic energy*, or energy of motion. **Thermal energy** is the total amount of kinetic energy of the particles in a substance.

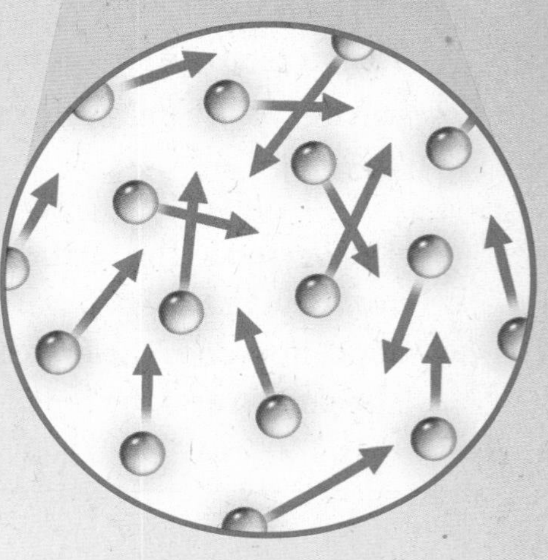

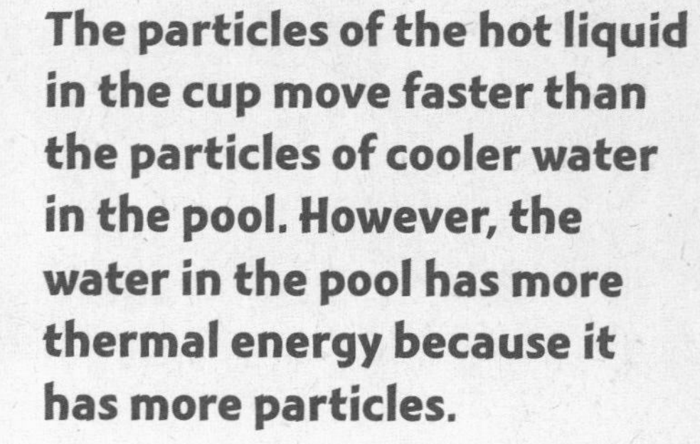

The particles of the hot liquid in the cup move faster than the particles of cooler water in the pool. However, the water in the pool has more thermal energy because it has more particles.

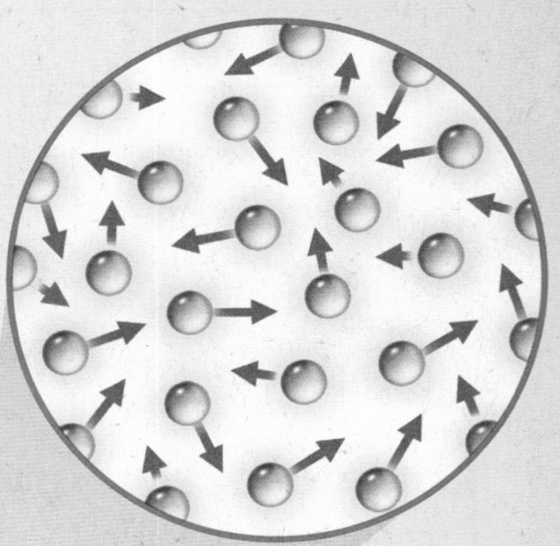

## Temperature

**Temperature** is a measure of the average kinetic energy of the particles in a substance. A thermometer helps you compare the average kinetic energy of different substances. The faster the particles move in a substance, the higher its temperature. In a traditional liquid-filled thermometer, the height of the liquid in the tube increases as temperature increases. The thermometer in this beaker uses a heat sensitive metal.

## Do the Math!

### Use a Calculator

An average is the sum of the numbers in a set divided by the number of items in that set. Use a calculator to help you collect, record, and analyze the information in the table.

| Student | Sit-ups /minute |
|---|---|
| A | 30 |
| B | 25 |
| C | 40 |
| D | 33 |

What is the sum of the numbers in the set?

_______________

What is the number of items in the set?

_______________

What is the average number of sit-ups done by the four students in one minute?

_______________

The iceberg and ice cube have the same temperature. The iceberg contains more thermal energy because it has many more vibrating particles.

# Move It Around

In order to use thermal energy, we must move it from place to place. How does it move?

**Active Reading** As you read these two pages, underline information that compares and contrasts ways that energy is transferred.

Energy is transferred between substances with different temperatures. We call this transfer of energy **heat**. Heat always moves from a substance with a higher temperature to one with a lower temperature.

## Conduction

*Conduction* is the transfer of energy between particles that are in contact. When the girl holds the ice cube against her skin, fast-moving particles in her skin collide with slower moving particles in the ice cube. Heat flows from her skin to the ice cube by conduction. This lowers the temperature of her skin, so she feels cooler. What happens to the ice?

When cooking food over a campfire, heat transfers from the burning logs to the pot by conduction.

## Analyze Energy Transfer

Label each type of energy transfer in the diagram. Draw arrows to show the direction of energy transfer.

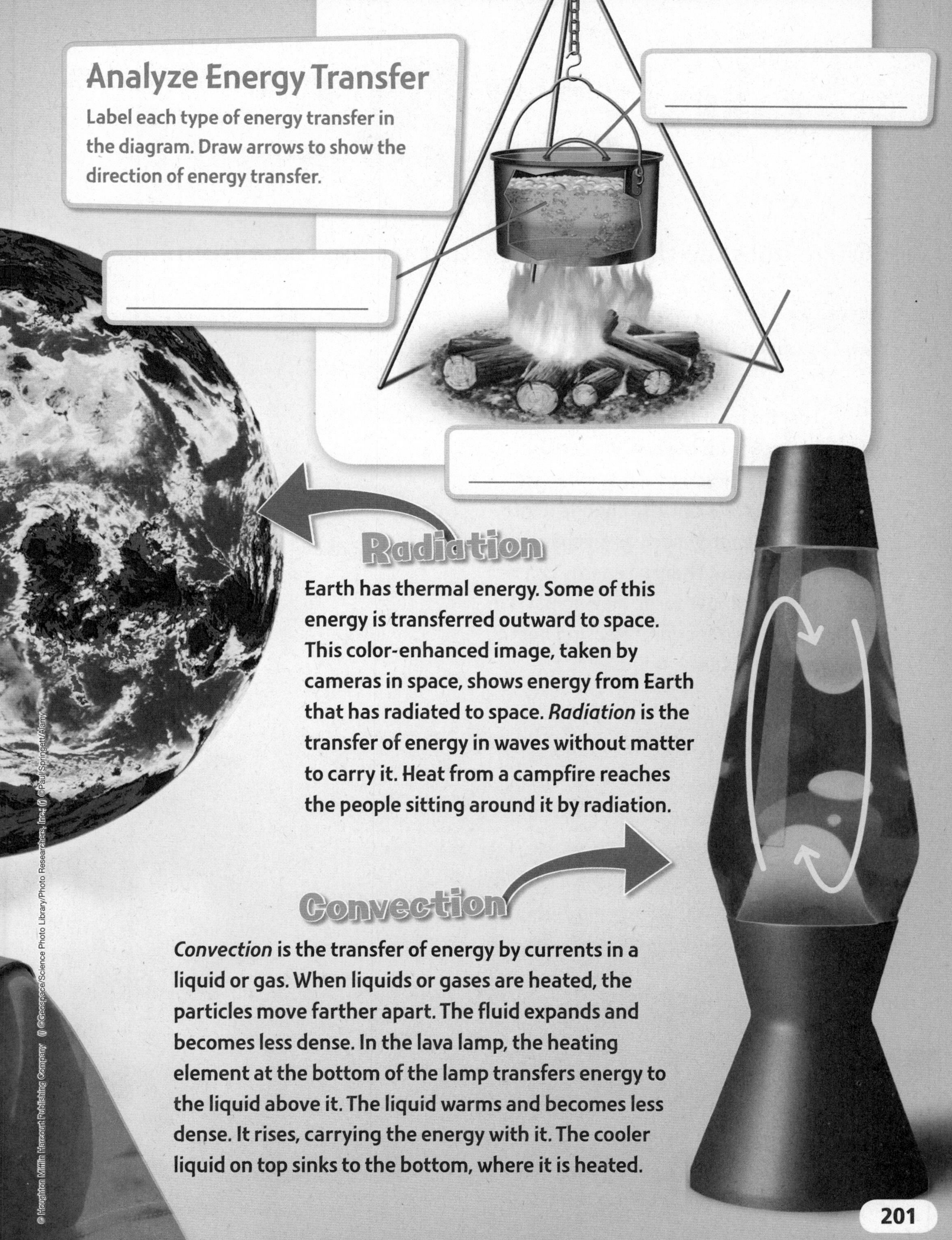

### Radiation

Earth has thermal energy. Some of this energy is transferred outward to space. This color-enhanced image, taken by cameras in space, shows energy from Earth that has radiated to space. *Radiation* is the transfer of energy in waves without matter to carry it. Heat from a campfire reaches the people sitting around it by radiation.

### Convection

*Convection* is the transfer of energy by currents in a liquid or gas. When liquids or gases are heated, the particles move farther apart. The fluid expands and becomes less dense. In the lava lamp, the heating element at the bottom of the lamp transfers energy to the liquid above it. The liquid warms and becomes less dense. It rises, carrying the energy with it. The cooler liquid on top sinks to the bottom, where it is heated.

# Going to the Source!

## Where does the thermal energy that we use come from?

**Active Reading** As you read these two pages, draw a box around sources of thermal energy.

Most thermal energy used on Earth comes from the sun. We can use thermal energy directly, such as when we warm ourselves. We can also change it into other forms of energy, such as mechanical or electrical energy. Thermal energy can be "lost" when it changes form. Moving parts in machines produce friction, releasing heat to the environment that is not used.

### Solar Radiation

The sun's energy reaches Earth by radiation. Solar radiation is the most important energy source on Earth. Only a tiny fraction of the sun's energy reaches Earth. Yet it enables life to exist on our planet. Solar radiation and Earth's atmosphere help keep Earth within the narrow range of temperatures needed for life to survive and thrive.

# Combustion of Fuels

A *fuel* is a substance that can burn. *Combustion* occurs when a fuel rapidly combines with oxygen. This process produces light and thermal energy. Combustion of fuels is the second most important source of energy on Earth. The most common fuels are fossil fuels, such as petroleum, coal, and natural gas. Fuels made from living organisms, such as trees or corn plants, are called *biofuels*.

## Construct a Chart Using Technology

Use the chart to organize, examine, and evaluate information about two of the sources of thermal energy described on these pages.

# Geothermal Energy

*Geothermal energy* is thermal energy naturally produced under Earth's surface. Below Earth's cool surface, there are regions so hot that rocks melt. In some places, we can directly observe geothermal energy. Volcanoes, geysers, and hot springs are visible examples of geothermal energy.

# Uses of Energy

So much energy! But what can we do with it? Let's find out.

**Active Reading** As you read these two pages, put brackets [ ] around the detail sentences. Draw arrows from the details to the main idea being explained.

How many ways can you think of to use thermal energy? You might think of keeping warm, cooking your food, or ironing your clothes. That's just a start!

Examine the information in the simple circle graph. What percentage of energy use could come from solar panels? Explain.

_______________

_______________

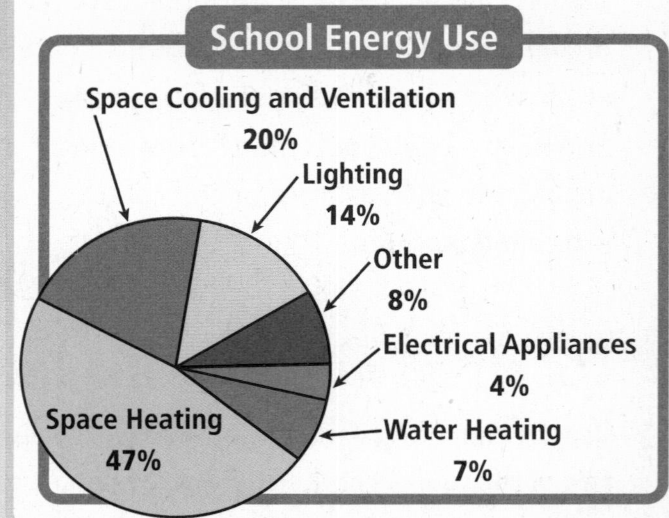


## Energy from the Sun

One way to use the sun's energy is to heat water for homes and businesses. Water runs through pipes in a solar panel, where it is heated by solar radiation. The hot water is then stored until it is needed. You have to pay for the panel, but the energy to heat the water is free!

During colder weather, solar radiation passing through windows warms a room. The energy makes the room warmer than the temperature outside. A plant nursery's greenhouse works in the same way.

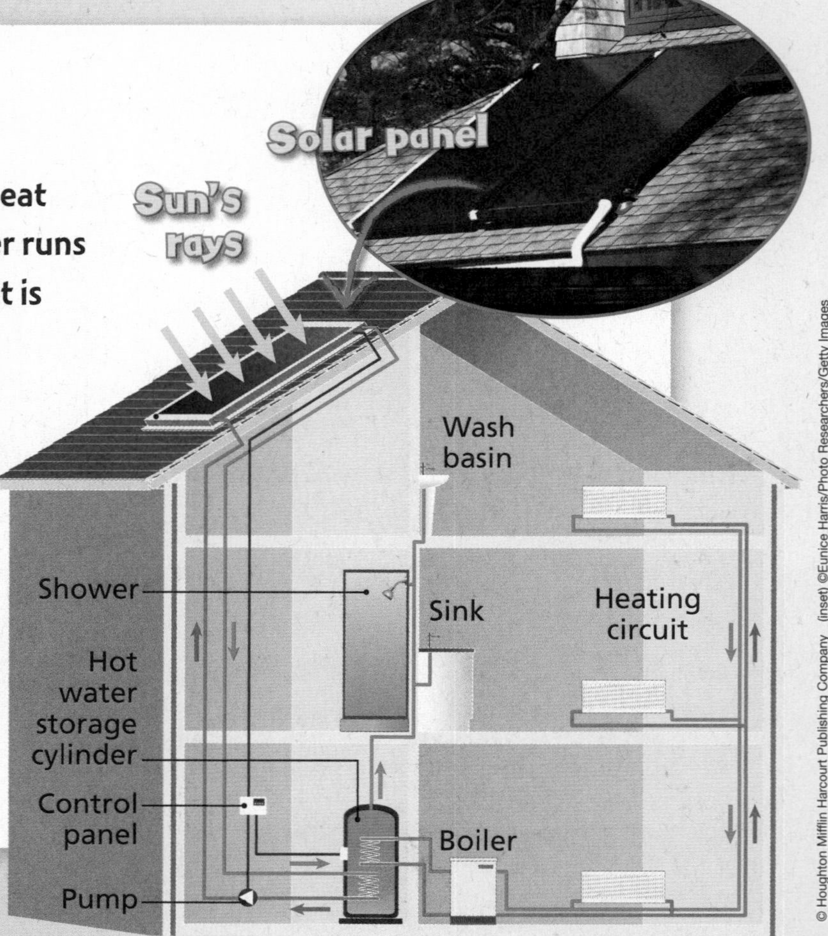

# Geothermal Energy

The diagram shows how geothermal energy is transformed into electrical energy. First, super-hot groundwater is pumped to the surface, where it changes into steam. The steam turns a fan-like device called a *turbine*. Then the steam loses energy and changes back to water, which is pumped back to the ground to be reheated. The turbine turns a *generator*—a machine that uses magnets to change mechanical energy into electricity. The electricity travels through wires to homes, businesses, factories, and other consumers.

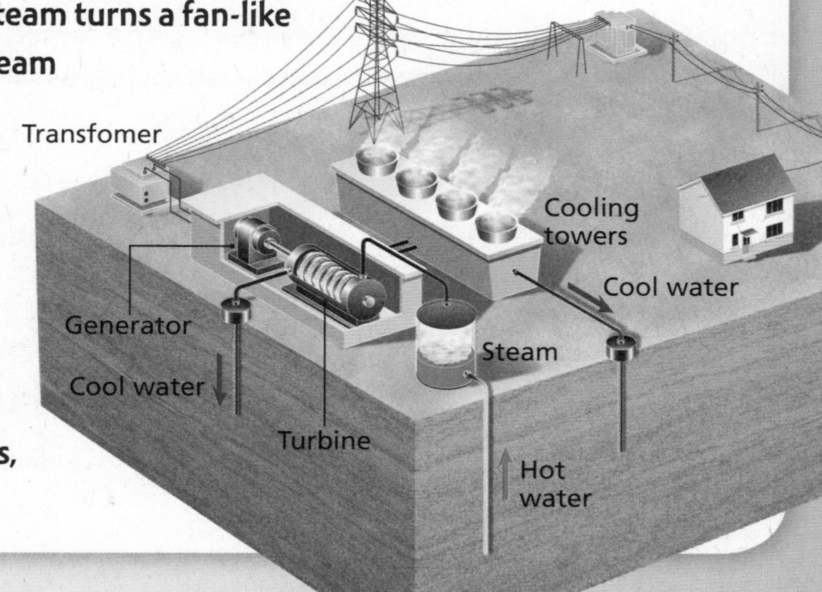


# Thermal Energy from Combustion

Thermal energy is used to process products such as foods, plastics, and metals. In many cities, fossil fuels are burned to produce the electricity used in factories. Thermal energy from combustion also is important in transportation. Engines in vehicles change the thermal energy of fossil fuels into motion. Some of this energy is wasted, though. It heats fluids that are then air-cooled to prevent the engine from overheating. Energy produced by the combustion of fossil fuels is used in many ways.

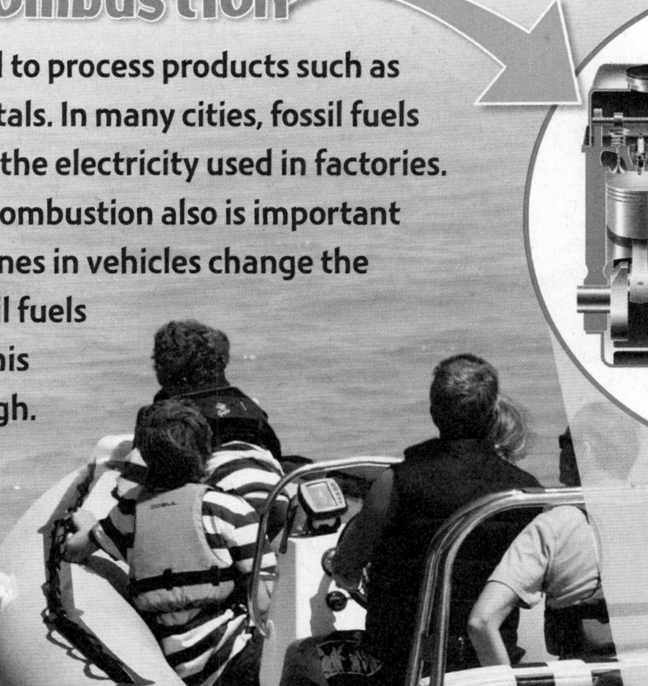

When you're done, use the answer key to check and revise your work.

**Complete the outline below to summarize the lesson.**

## 1

I. Thermal Energy

A. Thermal energy is (1) ______________________________

B. (2) ____________ is a measure of the average kinetic energy of the particles in a substance.

II. Transfer of Energy

A. (3) ____________ is the transfer of energy between substances at different temperatures.

B. Energy travels from place to place by:

1. (4) ____________
2. Convection
3. (5) ____________

III. Sources of Thermal Energy

A. Solar Radiation

B. (6) ____________ of Fuels

C. Geothermal Energy

IV. Uses of Thermal Energy

A. Roof panels can use (7) ____________ to heat water.

B. Geothermal energy can be changed to (8) ____________.

C. Engines in vehicles use combustion to produce energy of motion

## Summarize

**Fill in the missing words to tell what happens when heat moves from one substance to another.**

9. Heat always travels from a substance with a ____________ temperature to a substance with a lower temperature.
10. When particles are touching, heat moves by ____________.
11. Heat moves by convection in a ____________ or gas.
12. Energy that can travel through empty space is called ____________.

Answer Key: 1. the total kinetic energy in the particles of a substance; 2. temperature; 3. heat; 4. conduction; 5. radiation; 6. Combustion; 7. solar radiation; 8. electricity; 9. higher; 10. conduction; 11. liquid; 12. radiation

# Brain Check

Lesson 2

Name ____________________

## Word Play

**1** Use the clues to unscramble the science terms and solve the riddle below.

| Clue | Scrambled term | Answer boxes |
|---|---|---|
| 1. Total kinetic energy of the particles of a substance | RALTHEM GYENER | ☐☐☐☐☐☐☐ ☐☐☐☐☐☐ (15, 5) |
| 2. Transfer of energy between substances with different temperatures | TAEH | ☐☐☐☐ (7, 11) |
| 3. Measure of the average kinetic energy of the particles in a substance | PERMETRETUA | ☐☐☐☐☐☐☐☐☐☐☐ (9) |
| 4. Transfer of energy between solids | COUNONDITC | ☐☐☐☐☐☐☐☐☐☐ (14, 4) |
| 5. Makes up most of Earth's energy | OALRS DIATRIONA | ☐☐☐☐☐ ☐☐☐☐☐☐☐☐☐ (2, 12, 16) |
| 6. Transfer of thermal energy through a liquid or gas | NOCTECVONI | ☐☐☐☐☐☐☐☐☐☐ (8) |
| 7. Transfer of thermal energy in waves without matter | TAANOIDIR | ☐☐☐☐☐☐☐☐☐ (3) |
| 8. Energy produced and stored under Earth's crust | LOTHEGRAEM REGNEY | ☐☐☐☐☐☐☐☐☐☐ ☐☐☐☐☐☐ (6, 10, 13, 17, 18) |
| 9. Rapid combining of a fuel with oxygen | NOUMISTOCB | ☐☐☐☐☐☐☐☐☐☐ (1) |

Place the numbered letters in order to find out what you are doing when you cook food over a campfire.

☐☐☐☐☐ ☐☐☐☐☐☐☐ ☐☐☐☐☐☐

1 2 3 4 5 6 7 8 9 10 11 12 13 14 15 16 17 18

# Apply Concepts

2 A student says that four cups of boiling water have the same thermal energy as two cups of boiling water. Critique the student's explanation. Is she correct?

_______________

_______________

_______________

_______________

3 Explain how energy is transferred from the cup.
Draw arrows showing the movement of energy.

_______________

_______________

_______________

4 5. Name one way in which thermal energy from each of the following sources is used. If thermal energy is changed into another form of energy, describe the changes.

a. solar radiation _______________

_______________

b. combustion of fuels _______________

_______________

c. geothermal energy _______________

_______________

Work with an adult to identify examples of conduction, convection, and radiation around your home. Explain how energy moves from one location to another.

Lesson 3
INQUIRY

Inquiry Flipchart page 26

**TEKS** **5.1A** demonstrate safe practices and the use of safety equipment...during...outdoor investigations **5.2A**...implement... investigations testing one variable **5.2C** collect information by detailed observations and accurate measuring **5.3A** ...analyze...scientific explanations by using...experimental testing... **5.4A** collect...analyze information using tools, including... Celsius thermometers... **5.6A** explore the uses of energy, including...thermal, electrical...energy

Name ______________________

Essential Question

# What Changes Can Energy Cause?

## Set a Purpose

How will this investigation help you observe changes in matter?

______________________

______________________

______________________

## State Your Hypothesis

Write your hypothesis.

______________________

______________________

______________________

## Think About the Procedure

How hot do you predict the solar cookers will become?

______________________

______________________

What is the purpose of the aluminum foil?

______________________

______________________

What variable will you change in this experiment?

______________________

______________________

What outdoor safety steps should you practice?

______________________

______________________

## Record Your Data

Use technology to draw a data table to record your temperature measurements in degrees Celsius.

## Draw Conclusions

Was your hypothesis supported? Why or why not?

## Analyze and Extend

1. Analyze and interpret results to make an inference. How would your results differ if you had made the cooker just from the poster board? Explain.

2. How might a solar cooker be useful in places where there is no electricity?

3. How could you improve your solar cooker to make it heat faster?

4. Using the setup shown below, Dwayne concludes that the solar cooker on the left is the best because it heats up the fastest. Based on the result of your own experiment, analyze, evaluate, and critique Dwayne's conclusion.

5. What other questions would you like to ask about using solar energy? What investigations could you do to answer the questions?

**TEKS** **5.3C** draw or develop a model that represents how something works or looks that cannot be seen... **5.5A** classify matter based on physical properties, including...the ability to conduct or insulate...electric energy **5.6A** explore the uses of energy, including mechanical, light, thermal, electrical, and sound energy

Lesson 4

Essential Question

# What Is Electricity?

## Engage Your Brain!

Find the answer to the following question in this lesson and record it here.

What causes the girl's hair to stand out from her head?

______________________________

______________________________

______________________________

______________________________

## Active Reading

### Lesson Vocabulary

List the terms. As you learn about each one, make notes in the Interactive Glossary.

______________________________

______________________________

### Main Ideas

The main idea of a paragraph is the most important idea. The main idea may be stated in the first sentence, or it may be stated elsewhere. Active readers look for the main idea by asking themselves, What is this section mostly about?



Inquiry Flipchart p. 27 — Static Cereal! / Invent a Use

# All Charged Up

You can charge a battery. A football player can charge downfield. How is an electric charge different?

**Active Reading** As you read these two pages, underline the main idea on each page.

What do you, this book, and your desk all have in common? You are all made of atoms. *Atoms* are the building blocks of all matter. Atoms are so small that you cannot even see them without a special microscope. Atoms are made up of even smaller particles called protons, neutrons, and electrons.

The main difference between protons, electrons, and neutrons is their electric charge. *Electric charge* is a property of a particle that affects how it behaves around other particles.

- Protons have a positive charge (+1).
- Electrons have a negative charge (–1).
- Neutrons are neutral. They have no charge.

When an atom has equal numbers of protons and electrons, the positive charges and negative charges cancel each other. The atom itself has no charge.

Protons and neutrons are found in a region of the atom called the nucleus. Electrons are found in a region of mostly empty space called the electron cloud.

**Legend**

= neutron  = proton  = electron

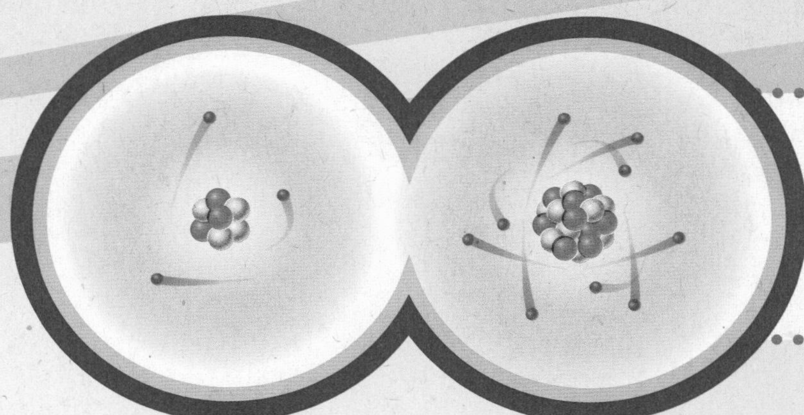

Each of these atoms has the same number of protons and electrons. Both atoms are neutral.

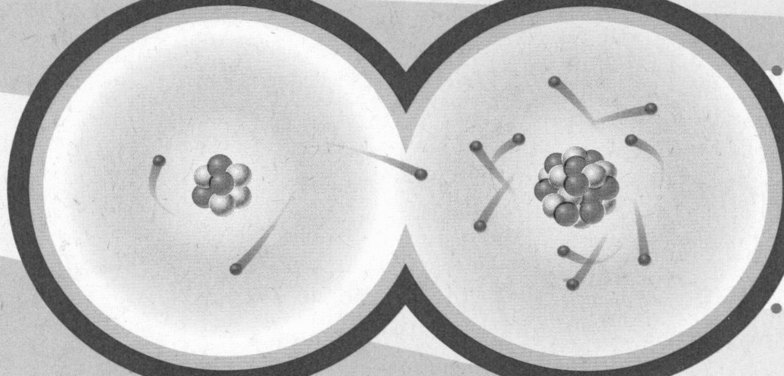

An electron from the atom on the left moves to the atom on the right.

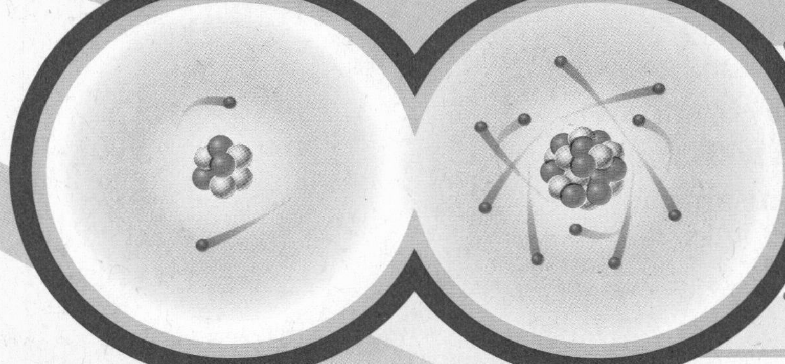

The atom on the left now has a charge of +1. The atom on the right has a charge of –1.

Atoms sometimes gain or lose electrons. This gain or loss causes an atom to have an unequal number of positive and negative charges. For example, if an atom with nine protons and nine electrons gains an electron, the atom will have a charge of –1.

If a neutral atom loses an electron, the number of protons will no longer balance the number of electrons. The atom will have a charge of +1.

▶ Draw an atom with three protons, four neutrons, and two electrons.

What is the charge of this atom?

# Opposites Attract

Have you ever had a "bad hair day"? Your hair sticks out in every direction and won't lie flat. What causes that?

**Active Reading** As you read this page, circle the definitions of *repel* and *attract*. On the next page, draw a box around the sentence with the main idea.

+ ⟷ +
+ →← −
− ⟷ −

**Particles with the same charge repel, or push away from, one another. Particles with opposite charges attract one another, or pull together.**

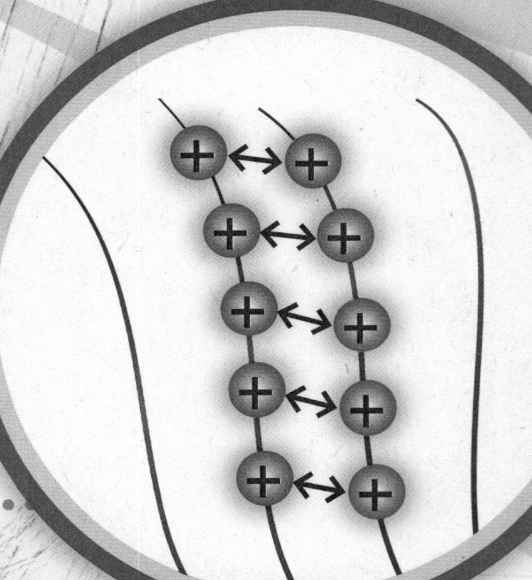

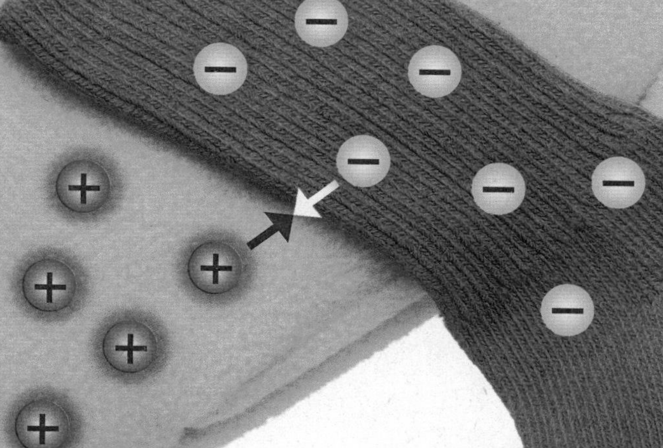

## Do the Math!

### Positive and Negative Numbers

Fill in the missing squares in the table.

| Original charge on an object | Electrons gained or lost | Final charge on the object |
|---|---|---|
| +300 | Gains 270 | |
| −300 | Loses 525 | |
| −270 | | −500 |

In the dryer, atoms in clothing gain and lose electrons. Each piece of clothing becomes charged. The positively charged surfaces attract the negatively charged surfaces. As a result, the clothes stick together.

Electric charges can build up on objects. This buildup is **static electricity**. *Static* means "not moving." Objects with opposite electric charges attract each other. Objects with the same charge repel each other.

When you brush your hair, electrons move from each strand of hair to the brush. Soon, all the strands are positively charged. All the strands having the same charge causes them to repel one another and stick out.

A charged object can attract a neutral object. If you rub a balloon on your hair, the balloon picks up extra electrons that give it a negative charge. When you bring the balloon near a wall, electrons in a small part of the wall are repelled and move away, leaving a positive charge at the wall surface. As a result, the balloon sticks to the wall.

Why It Matters

# Lightning Strikes

Thunderstorms can be scary. Lightning can be dangerous. What is lightning? How can you stay safe during a thunderstorm?

**Active Reading** As you read these two pages, underline the main idea on each page.

Static electricity is a buildup of charges on an object. Charges stay on an object until it comes close to an object that has a different charge.

As you walk across a carpet, electrons move from the carpet to you. Because electrons repel each other, they spread out all over your body. When you touch something, the electrons jump from your finger to the object. This jumping is called an electrostatic discharge. You feel it as a tiny shock.

Zap! Electrons jump from a person with a negative charge.

▶ Complete this cause-and-effect graphic organizer.

| Cause: An object with a negative charge is placed near an object with a positive charge. | → | Effect: ______________ |
|---|---|---|

Not all electrostatic discharges cause small shocks. Some result in huge shocks. During a thunderstorm, tiny raindrops or ice particles bump into each other. These collisions cause an electric charge to build in the clouds. Positive charges form at the top of a cloud and on the ground. Negative charges form near the bottom of a cloud.

When the difference in charge between a cloud and the ground is great enough, there is a huge electrostatic discharge that we call lightning. A lightning spark can jump between two clouds, between a cloud and the air, or between a cloud and the ground. The temperature inside a lightning bolt can reach 27,760 °C (50,000 °F), which is hotter than the surface of the sun!

## Lightning Safety

- Stay inside during thunderstorms.
- Turn off electrical appliances and stay away from windows.
- If you can't get inside a safe structure, wait in a car with a metal top for the storm to pass.
- Know the weather forecast. If you will be outside, have a plan in case a thunderstorm develops.

**When lightning strikes, it can catch objects on fire. A tree struck by lightning may split.**

▶ Draw a cloud in the sky. Then, draw positive and negative charges to show what causes lightning to form.

# Current Events

Electrostatic discharges may be exciting to watch, but flowing charges are more useful.

**Active Reading** As you read these two pages, draw a box around the sentence that contains the main idea.

When electric charges have a path to follow, as they do in the wire below, they move in a steady flow. This flow of charges is called an **electric current.**

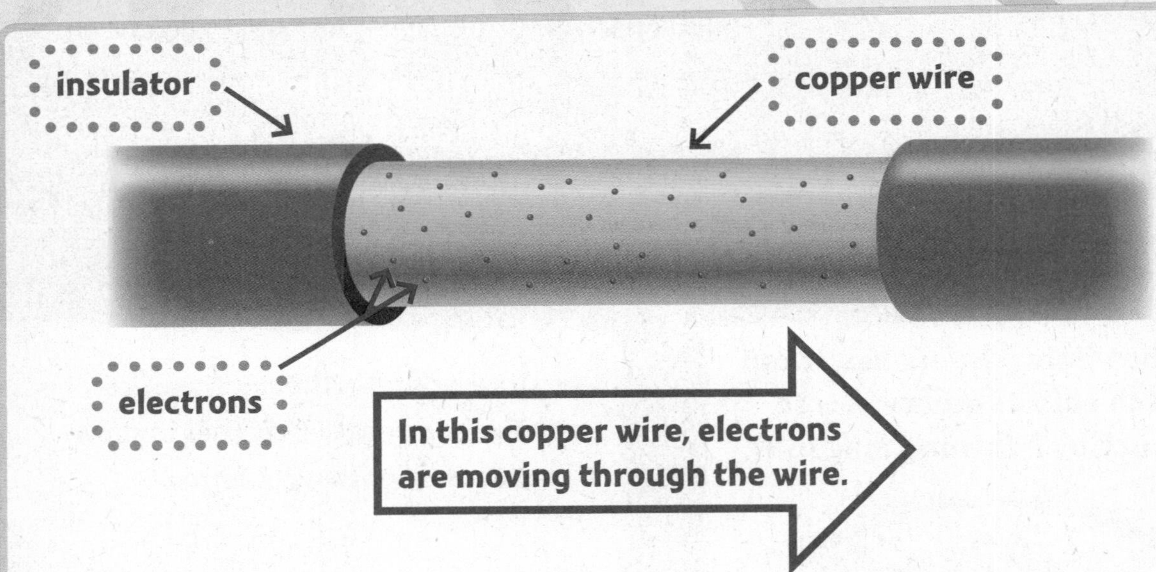

insulator
copper wire
electrons
In this copper wire, electrons are moving through the wire.

An insulator is a material that resists the flow of electrons. Electric currents can flow easily through conductors, such as a copper wire.

▶ What do the blue dots on this wire represent? What is the flow of these blue dots called?

_______________

_______________

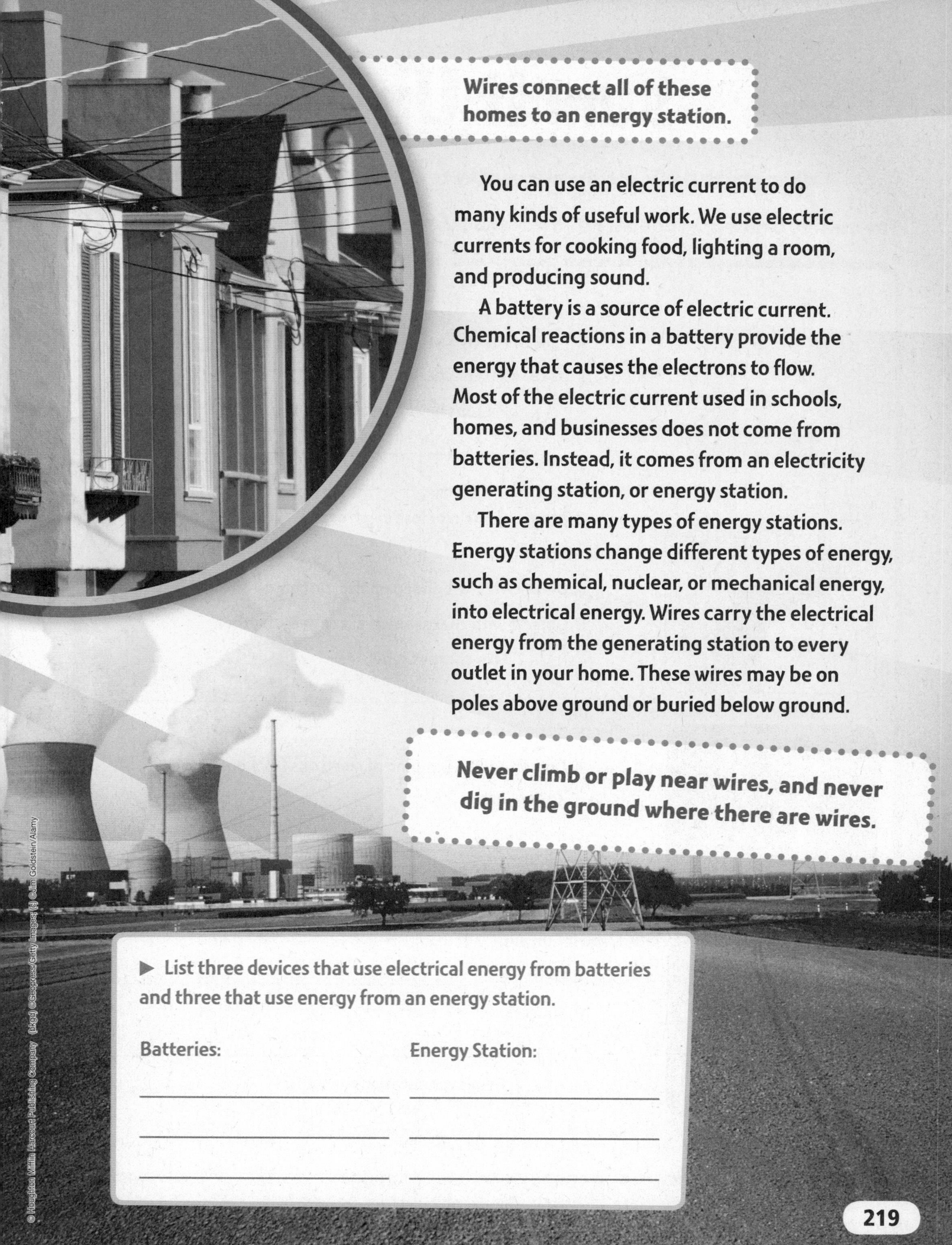

Wires connect all of these homes to an energy station.

You can use an electric current to do many kinds of useful work. We use electric currents for cooking food, lighting a room, and producing sound.

A battery is a source of electric current. Chemical reactions in a battery provide the energy that causes the electrons to flow. Most of the electric current used in schools, homes, and businesses does not come from batteries. Instead, it comes from an electricity generating station, or energy station.

There are many types of energy stations. Energy stations change different types of energy, such as chemical, nuclear, or mechanical energy, into electrical energy. Wires carry the electrical energy from the generating station to every outlet in your home. These wires may be on poles above ground or buried below ground.

**Never climb or play near wires, and never dig in the ground where there are wires.**

▶ List three devices that use electrical energy from batteries and three that use energy from an energy station.

| Batteries: | Energy Station: |
| --- | --- |
| ______________ | ______________ |
| ______________ | ______________ |
| ______________ | ______________ |

When you're done, use the answer key to check and revise your work.

**The outline below is a summary of the lesson. Complete the outline.**

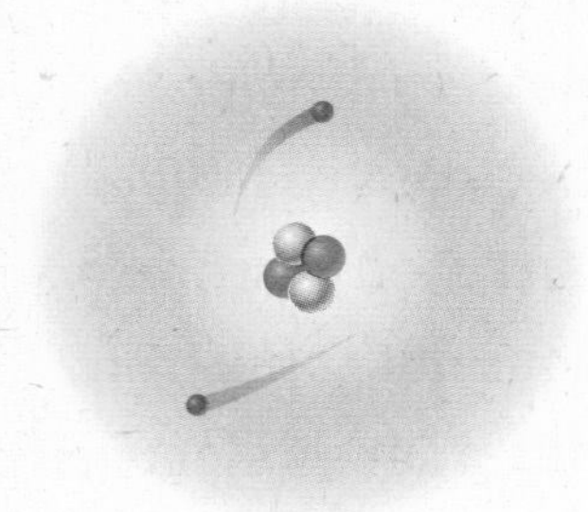

I. Electric Charges

A. Each of the three types of particles that make up atoms has a different charge.

1. Protons have a positive charge.

2. ______________________________

3. ______________________________

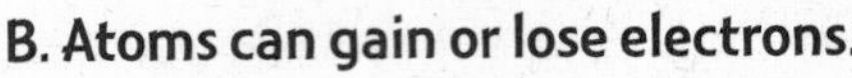

B. Atoms can gain or lose electrons.

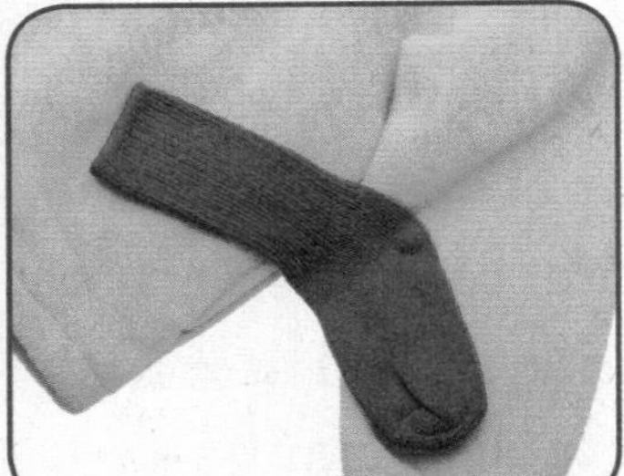

II. Static Electricity

A. Definition: the buildup of electric charge on an object.

B. Objects with charges interact with each other.

1. Like charges repel.

2. ______________________________

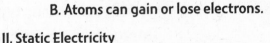

III. Electrostatic Discharge

A. Definition: the jumping of electrons from one object to another.

B. Examples

1. Getting shocked after walking across a rug

2. ______________________________

IV. Electric Current

A. Definition: ______________________________

B. Sources

1. ______________________________

2. Generating stations



Answer Key: I. A. 2. Electrons have a negative charge. I. A. 3. Neutrons have no charge. II. B. 2. Opposite charges attract. III. B. 2. Lightning IV. A. the flow of electrons IV. B. 1. Batteries

Name ___________________________

## Word Play

**1** **Fill in the blank in each sentence. Then, find the words in the blanks in the word search below.**

a. Two positive charges ________________ each other.

b. A positive charge and a negative charge ________________ each other.

c. The buildup of electric charge on an object is ________________ electricity.

d. The flow of electric charges along a path is electric ________________.

e. A proton has a ________________ charge.

f. A neutron is ________________ because it has no charge.

g. An electron has a ________________ charge.

h. Electricity is produced at a generating ________________.

| | | | | | | | | |
|---|---|---|---|---|---|---|---|---|
| C | N | E | G | A | T | I | V | E |
| U | F | R | E | P | E | L | R | V |
| R | I | G | H | T | E | N | I | I |
| R | N | A | T | T | R | A | C | T |
| E | G | C | I | T | A | T | S | I |
| N | E | U | T | R | A | L | L | S |
| T | I | G | H | T | N | I | N | O |
| S | T | A | T | I | O | N | G | P |

**Find the letters you didn't circle in the word search. Write them in order from left to right in the blanks below.**

Riddle: What do you call a very scary electrostatic discharge?

_ _ _ _ _ _ _ _ _ _ _ _ _ _ _ _ _ _ _

# Apply Concepts

**2** List the three particles that make up an atom. Describe the charge of each particle.

| Parts of an Atom | |
|---|---|
| Particle | Charge |
| | |
| | |
| | |

Where are these particles found in an atom?

______________________________________________

______________________________________________

**3** Explain why the balloons are sticking to this cat.

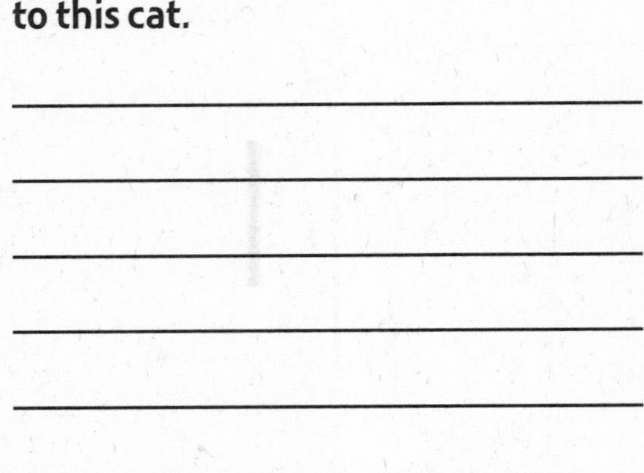

**4** List three ways you can use an electric current. Describe the energy change that takes place.

______________________________________________

______________________________________________

______________________________________________

______________________________________________

______________________________________________

5 Fill in the blanks to complete the sequence graphic organizer.

A wool sock and a cotton shirt ________________ against each other in a dryer.

↓

Electrons move from the wool to the ______________ .

↓

The two pieces of clothing have ________________ charges and they ________________ each other.

6 Explain why the event in the picture takes place.

_______________________________________________

_______________________________________________

_______________________________________________

_______________________________________________

_______________________________________________

_______________________________________________

_______________________________________________

_______________________________________________

_______________________________________________

**7** Draw a line from each picture to its description. Circle the pictures that show sources of current used by people every day.

| electric current | static electricity | electrostatic discharge | battery |
|---|---|---|---|

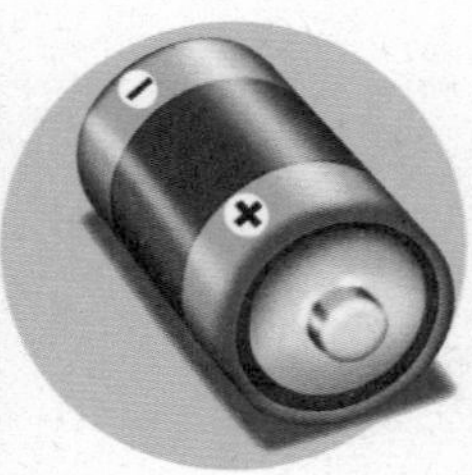
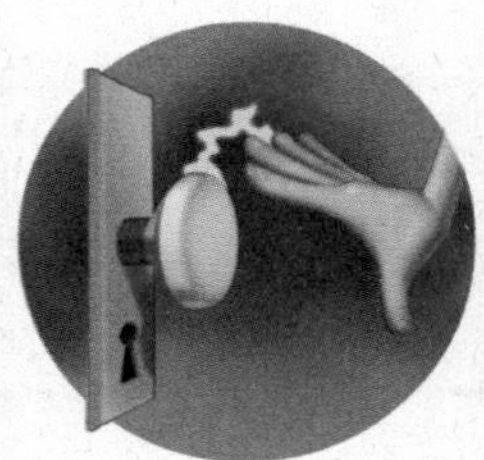

**8** Suppose you are playing soccer at a park, and you hear thunder that sounds far away. Describe some things you should and should not do to stay safe.

______________________________________________

______________________________________________

______________________________________________

______________________________________________

______________________________________________

______________________________________________

**Take It Home!**

Do your clothes stick together when they come out of the dryer? If so, how could you prevent this from happening? Use Internet resources to learn how dryer sheets work to reduce static electricity in your clothes.

TEKS 5.2D analyze and interpret information to construct reasonable explanations from… evidence 5.3C draw…a model that represents how something works… 5.5A classify matter based on physical properties, including…the ability to conduct or insulate…electric energy 5.6B demonstrate that the flow of electricity in circuits…can produce light, heat, and sound

Lesson 5

Essential Question

# How Do Electric Circuits, Conductors, and Insulators Work?

## Engage Your Brain!

Find the answer to the following question and record it here.

From this electrical energy control center, workers can shut off electrical energy to parts of their city while leaving others on. How can they do that?

_______________

_______________

_______________

_______________

## Active Reading

### Lesson Vocabulary

List each term. As you learn about each one, make notes in the Interactive Glossary.

_______________ _______________

_______________ _______________

_______________

### Cause and Effect

Some ideas in this lesson are connected by a cause-and-effect relationship. Why something happens is a cause. What happens as a result of something else is an effect. Active readers look for effects by asking themselves, What happened? They look for causes by asking, Why did it happen?



Inquiry Flipchart p. 28—Test the Load!/High, Low, and Just Right

# Some Go with the Flow

Would you be surprised to see the prongs on an electrical plug made of plastic? You should be! There's a very good reason why plugs and electrical cords are made of certain materials.

**Active Reading** As you read these two pages, underline the definitions of key words.

When it comes to working with electricity, knowing the properties of materials is important. Some materials allow electricity to pass through them freely. Others block its flow.

## Conductors and Insulators

You would do well to stay away from electrical poles. They're safe enough when they're in good working order. But if one of the wires they carry were to get free, you'd be in trouble! These wires are made of metals, such as copper, which conduct electrical energy. **Conductors** allow electricity to easily travel through them. Some materials prevent the flow of electricity. These materials are called **insulators.** Materials such as plastics, rubber, concrete, glass, and wood insulate electrical energy. Their low cost and flexibility make plastics and rubber great for covering electrical plugs and cords.

# Identify Conductors and Insulators

In each box, write *conductor* or *insulator.*

Copper Wire

____________________

Electrical Gloves

____________________

Lightning Rod

____________________

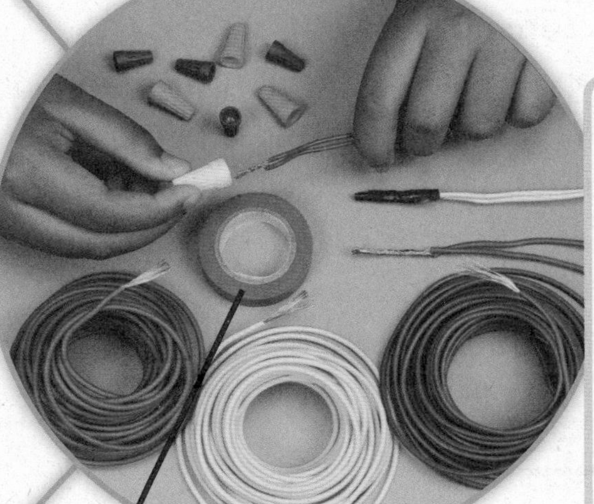

Electrical Tape

____________________

▶ The brightly-colored "caps" are twist-on connectors. They are used to hold two or more wires together. These connectors are made of a conductor and an insulator. Where do you think the insulator is? The conductor? Explain.

________________________________________

________________________________________

________________________________________

________________________________________

# A Path to Charge

Suppose you flip on a light switch and nothing happens. What's wrong?

**Active Reading** As you read these two pages, draw one line under a cause and two lines under an effect

Electricity requires a closed path to flow. An electric **circuit** is a complete pathway made of conductors through which electric current can flow. A battery or other electrical energy source makes electric charges in wires begin to move. When the charges reach a device like a light bulb or a fan, they provide energy to make the device work. The path must go from the energy source to the device and back again to keep the charges moving. This is a complete circuit.

## Parts of a Circuit

Opening a switch in a circuit causes a gap, so charges can't flow. Closing, or turning the switch "on," closes the gap. Devices in a circuit such as lamps, buzzers, or appliances are called *resistances* or *loads*. You can draw a circuit diagram using the symbols in the key. Notice how each device in the circuit matches a symbol in the circuit.

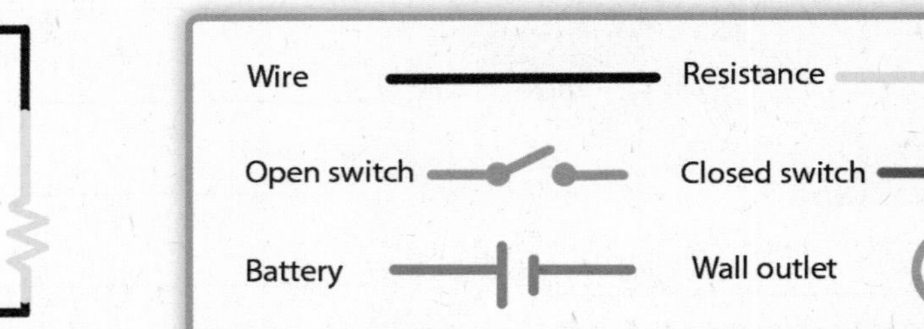

# Electricity Changes in Circuits

Electric circuits convert electricity to other forms of energy. For example, circuits in this train change electricity into mechanical energy (motion), light energy, and sound energy. Thermal energy is also produced from electricity to heat the interior of the train cars on cold days.

The hair dryer changes electrical energy into heat and motion as it heats and blows hot air.

## Draw a Circuit

Use the key on the previous page to draw a circuit diagram for a complete circuit containing a battery, a switch, and a resistance. Then explain what energy changes take place when the resistance is a light bulb.

_______________

_______________

_______________

_______________

_______________

_______________

_______________

# Which Path to Take?

One path or many? How do electric charges flow through circuits?

**Active Reading** As you read these two pages, draw boxes around the names of the two things that are being compared.

There are many electric circuits in your home. The lights and sockets in one room might be on one circuit. An electric oven uses a lot of electricity, so it might be on its own circuit. There are two main types of circuits.

## Series Circuit

Can you identify the parts of this circuit? Look at the key at the bottom of this page for help. In a **series circuit**, electric current has only one path to follow to and from the energy source. In this circuit, current passes through both light bulbs, so they both light up. What happens if one light bulb burns out? The other light goes out, too, because the circuit is broken.

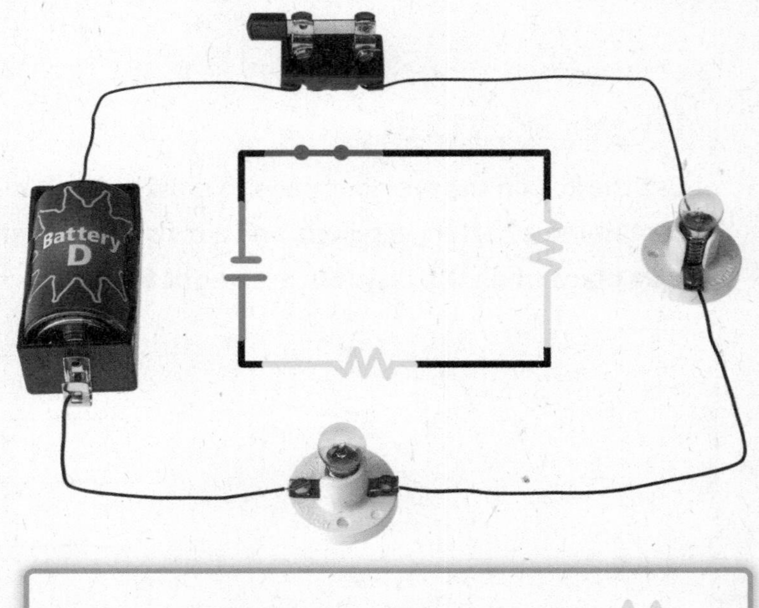

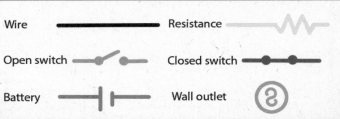

Wire — Resistance

Open switch — Closed switch

Battery — Wall outlet

## Circuits at Home

At home, you need to turn lights on and off individually. The same is true for other electrical devices. A series circuit only works if all of the devices in the circuit are on. So, which type of circuit do you think is mostly used in homes?

## Where's That Load?

Redraw the emergency flashlight circuit. Include the missing load that represents the siren.

**Emergency Flashlight Radio and Siren**

## Parallel Circuit

How can you keep the other devices in a circuit working if one stops working? A **parallel circuit** contains two or more paths for electric charges to follow. This emergency flashlight has a light, a radio, and a small siren. Each device is connected to the battery through its own parallel circuit. Three separate switches are used to turn the devices on and off, so that they can work independently of one another.

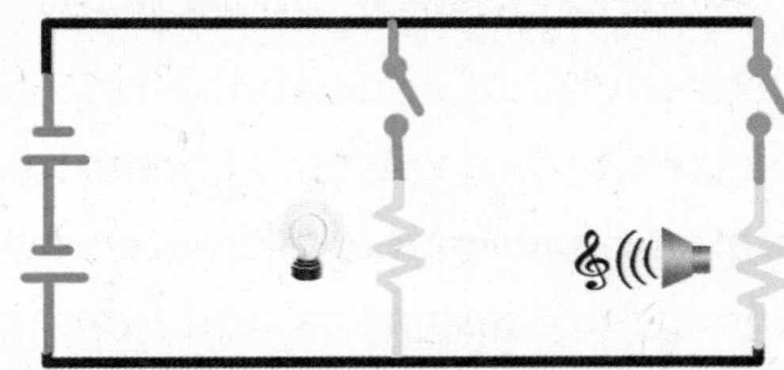

Why It Matters

# Home Circuits

Look around a room in your house. How many electrical outlets, light fixtures, and switches are there? Are they all in the same circuit? How can you find out?

**Active Reading** As you read these two pages, draw a line under the main idea.

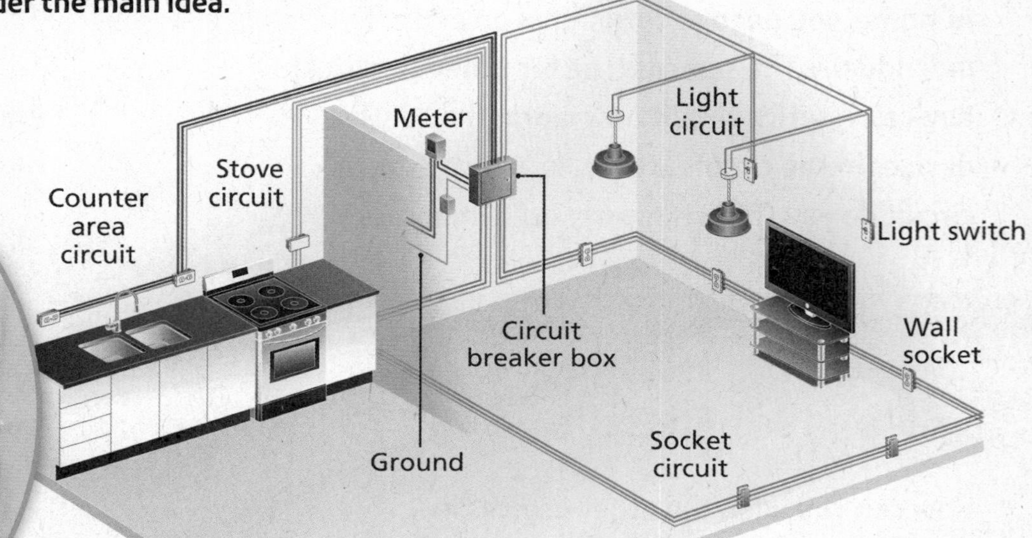


▶ Examine the circuits in the diagram. Circle two resistances wired in the same circuit. Box a resistance that is on its own circuit.

Your home electrical system is a small part of a larger system that includes your city, state, and national region. The electricity that you use at home might come from generating stations hundreds of kilometers away. At home, a network of conductors, insulators, and switches are arranged into circuits. It carries electricity into every room. Many meters of wiring make up your home electrical system. However, this is a small fraction of the amount of wiring it takes to bring electricity into your home.

## Changing Electrical Energy

Many of the forms of energy you see around your house begin as electricity. Television sets and karaoke machines can convert electricity into light, sound, and thermal energy. Fans, blenders, and can openers change electrical energy into energy of motion. These machines also waste electrical energy as heat and sound. Look at the picture. Can you tell where electrical energy is being changed?

## Do the Math!

### Interpret a Simple Graph

The symbol % means *percent*, or "out of a hundred." For example, *8%* means "8 out of a hundred." Examine the information in the graph. Then answer the questions below.

1. Which activity consumed the most energy in the home?

_______________

2. Which two activities combine to consume 29 out of 100 units of energy?

_______________

_______________

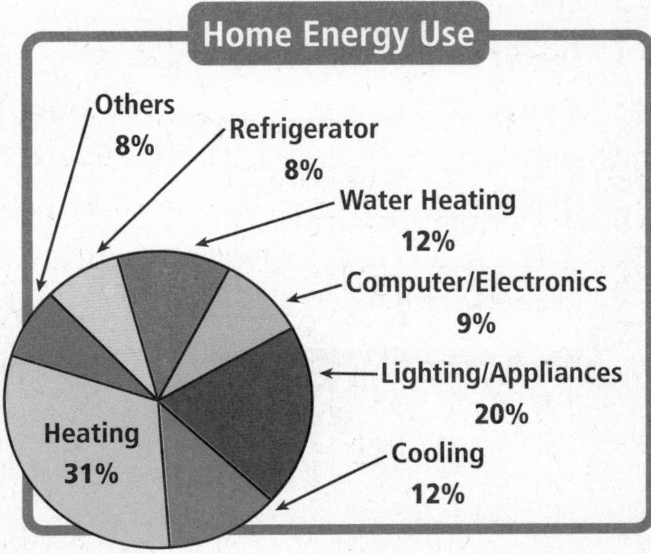

When you're done, use the answer key to check and revise your work.

**Label the parts of the circuit.**

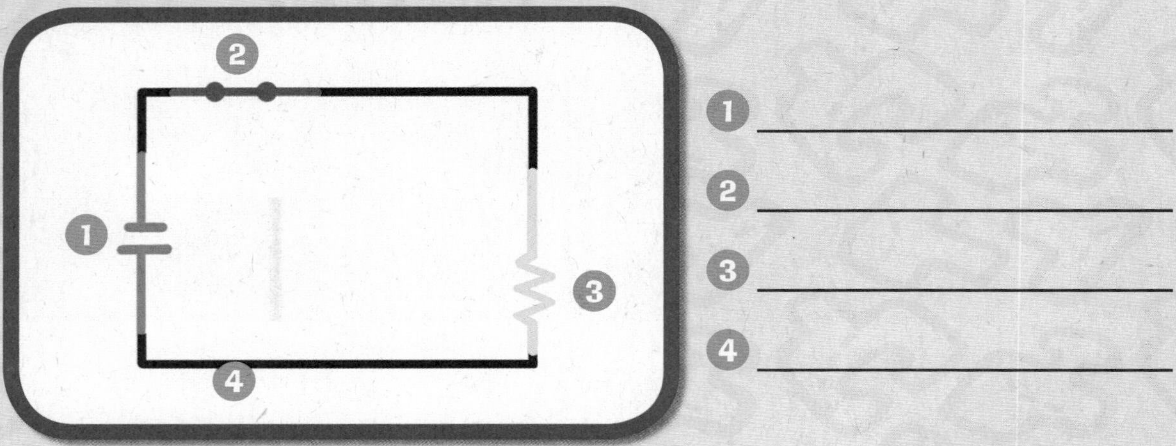


1 ______________________

2 ______________________

3 ______________________

4 ______________________

5 Assume that the load in the circuit above is a light bulb. Explain what would happen if you open the switch. What is the cause?

______________________________________________

______________________________________________

## Summarize

**Fill in the missing words to describe conductors, insulators, and electric circuits.**

Electric current easily passes through (6) ________________, such as silver and copper. All metals are good (7) ________________ of electricity. Non-metal materials such as wood, glass, plastic, and (8) ________________ block the flow of (9) ________________. These materials are called (10) ________________. The wires connecting the battery, switch, and resistance in a (11) ________________ have a (12) ________________ at their center to conduct electricity and a covering made of a (13) ____________________ to make the wires safe to handle.

Answer Key: 1. battery 2. switch 3. resistance or load 4. wire 5. the light bulb would go out because the electric charges no longer have a complete path to flow through 6. metals 7. conductors 8. rubber 9. electricity 10. insulators 11. circuit 12. metal/conductor 13. non-metal/insulator

Name ______________________

## Word Play

**1** Use the clues to complete the puzzle.

**Across**

3. Complete path for electric charge
5. Circuit with one path for electric charges
6. Circuit with two or more paths for electric charges
7. Material that allows electrical charges to flow easily
8. Device that changes electricity to other forms of energy

**Down**

1. Used to open and close a circuit
2. Source of power for a circuit
4. Material that blocks the flow of electric charges

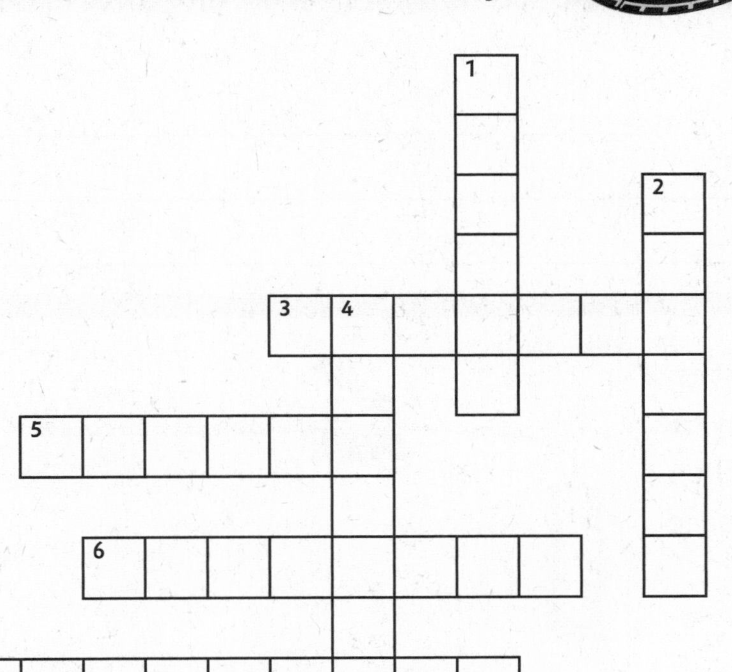

# Apply Concepts

2 Select and circle the appropriate equipment that would be safe to use when working with electric current. Explain why some are safer than others.

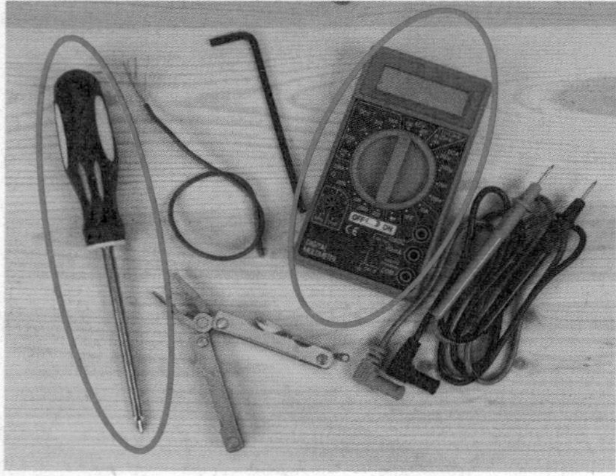

3 A wall switch is connected to a wall outlet. A lamp with a switch is plugged into the outlet. You turn the wall switch on, but the lamp stays off. Give three reasons why this might happen.

4 Analyze the circuit. On the lines below, explain why the circuit isn't complete. Then draw in whatever you need to complete the circuit.

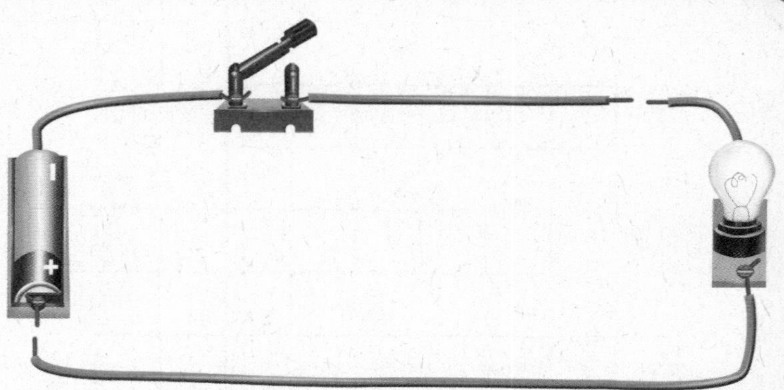

Name ____________________



5 Convert this circuit to a parallel circuit that has a light bulb and a buzzer. Show in your circuit a picture of the resistances in each part of the circuit.

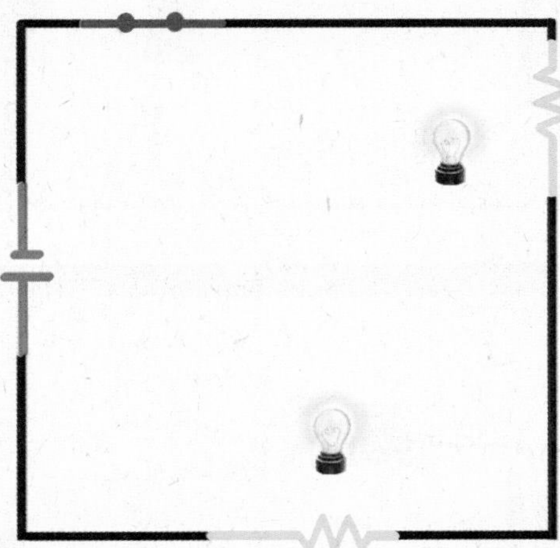

6 In each circuit, electrical energy is being transformed into other forms of energy. Identify the forms of energy produced in each circuit.

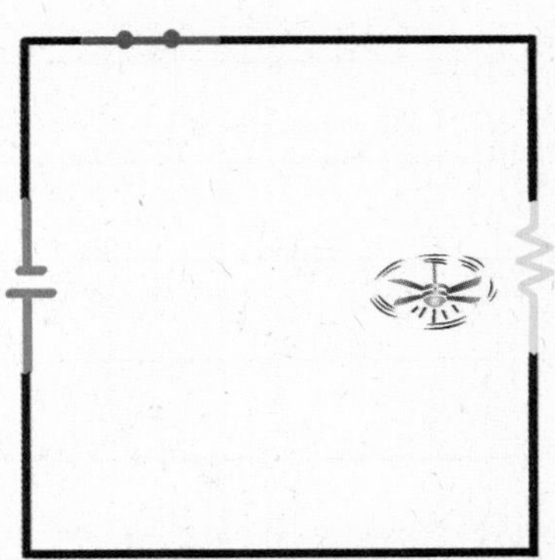

# Apply Concepts

**7** Analyze the circuit. Name two possible reasons why one light bulb is not lit.

**8** Circuits convert electrical energy into other forms of energy. Analyze and evaluate the brightness of the light bulbs in the diagrams. Use logical reasoning and empirical evidence to explain the differences in brightness.

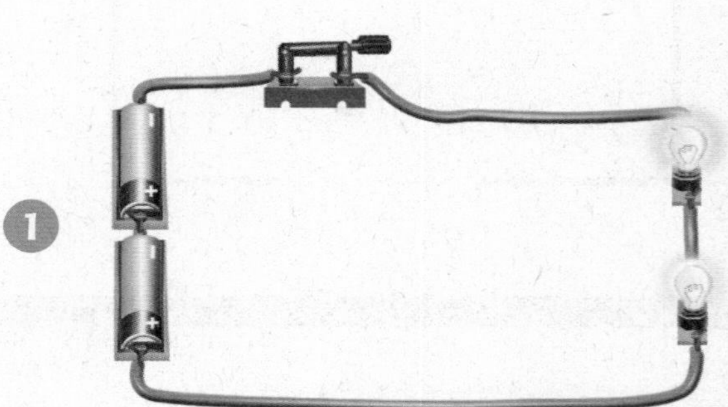

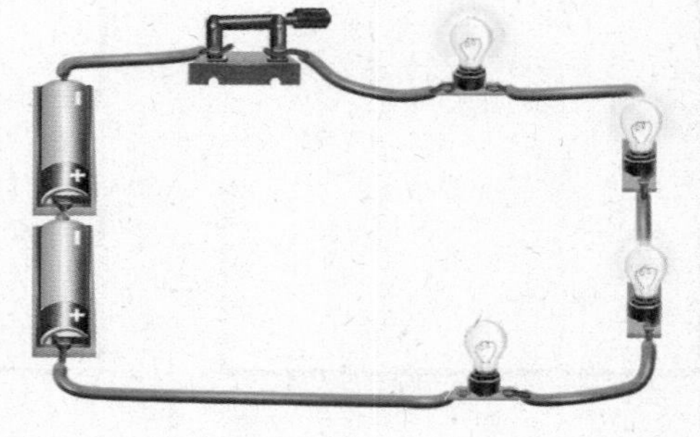

With an adult, find your home's circuit breakers. A circuit breaker is like a switch. Have the adult open one of the breakers. Look around to find which lights are in that circuit. Explain why the lights won't work.

Inquiry Flipchart page 29

**TEKS** **5.2D** analyze and interpret information to construct reasonable explanations…from evidence **5.3A** analyze, evaluate…scientific explanations by using empirical evidence…and experimental testing **5.3C** draw a model that represents how something works or looks… **5.6B** demonstrate that the flow of electricity in circuits requires a complete path through which an electric current can pass and can produce light, heat, and sound

Name ______________________________

Essential Question

# How Does an Electric Circuit Work?

## Set a Purpose

**What will you learn from this investigation?**

______________________________

______________________________

______________________________

## Think About the Procedure

**Look at the circuit diagram you drew in Step 2. Where in the circuit is the switch?**

______________________________

______________________________

______________________________

**Switches turn on and off loads in circuits. Does it matter where you put the switch in your circuit? Explain.**

______________________________

______________________________

______________________________

______________________________

______________________________

## Record Your Data

**Use the space to draw a circuit diagram. Revise your drawing based on your classmates' feedback and your final working circuit.**

## Draw Conclusions

A complete path is needed for electricity to flow in a circuit. What empirical evidence did you gather to conclude that the circuit you built was a complete circuit?

Examine your final circuit. Can you improve it? Describe a design for an alternative circuit that could produce the same results.

## Analyze and Extend

1. Electricity can be transformed into other forms of energy. Use the evidence you gathered during experimental testing to explain how electricity changed in your circuit.

2. Look at your circuit. Observe how it works. Use this information to explain how you could change your circuit so that the buzzer could be turned off and on separately from the light bulbs. Draw a circuit diagram to show how you would do it.

3. Infer. Do you think there is a limit to the number of devices you can put in a circuit? Explain.

4. Think of other questions you would like to ask about how electrical energy flows in circuits.

**TEKS** **5.2D** analyze and interpret information to construct reasonable explanations from... evidence **5.3C** draw a...model that represents how something works or looks... **5.6A** explore the uses of energy...including...electrical...energy **5.6B** demonstrate that the flow of electricity... requires a complete path through...and can produce light, heat, and sound

S.T.E.M.

Engineering & Technology

# How It Works:

## Electric Clothes Dryer

You turn the dials on the front of the dryer to open and close circuits. The circuits regulate temperature and how long the dryer will run.

You press the start switch to start the dryer. The switch closes a circuit that turns on an electric motor, an electric heating coil, and a fan. The motor turns the drum.

A thermostat connected to the heating circuit turns the heating elements off and on to keep the temperature you have chosen.

When you open the door, the door switch opens the circuit and stops the drum from spinning.

The motor in the dryer changes electrical energy into energy of motion, thermal energy, and sound energy.

## Troubleshooting

The dryer won't start. Put an *X* on two parts that could be broken. Why did you choose those parts?

_______________________________________________

_______________________________________________

continued

## Show How It Works:

Draw a circuit diagram to show how the door switch might work. Label all the parts of your diagram to show what parts of the dryer they correspond to. Use your circuit to explain why opening the door stops the drum from turning.

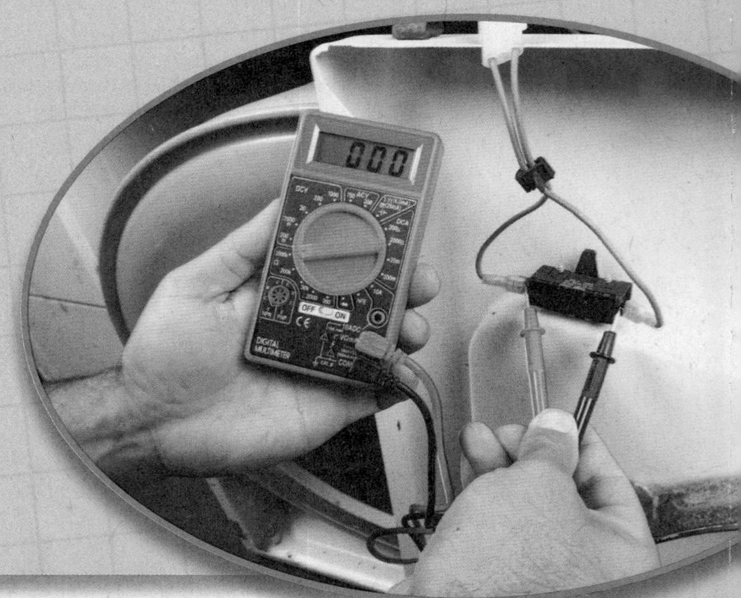

## Saving Energy!

Think of a device you could invent to make the dryer stop when the clothes are dry rather than after a fixed length of time. What would be the triggers or inputs for this device? Which of the dryer's systems would be connected to the new device? Draw a circuit diagram and explain how the device would work.

_______________________________________________

_______________________________________________

_______________________________________________

_______________________________________________

Draw Here

## Build On It!

Rise to the engineering design challenge—**Build in Some Science: Circuit Tester** on the Inquiry Flipchart.

# Unit 5 Review

Name ______________________

## Vocabulary Review

Use the terms in the box to complete the sentences.

| |
|---|
| chemical energy |
| electrical energy |
| electric current |
| mechanical energy |
| sound energy |
| thermal energy |

TEKS 5.6A

1. The flow of electrons through a wire is a(n) ______________________.

TEKS 5.6A

2. When the string of a guitar vibrates, it produces ______________________.

TEKS 5.6A

3. When the sun increases the total kinetic energy of the particles in your skin, your ______________________ increases.

TEKS 5.6A

4. The type of energy released when a match burns is ______________________.

TEKS 5.6A

5. Energy that allows a lightbulb to glow is ______________________.

TEKS 5.6A

6. The total amount of potential and kinetic energy in a moving car is its ______________________.

## Science Concepts

Fill in the letter of the choice that best answers the question.

TEKS 5.6A

7. Which of these appliances is **designed** to convert electrical energy into sound energy?

   Ⓐ printer

   Ⓑ refrigerator

   Ⓒ electric heater

   Ⓓ music amplifier

TEKS 5.2D, 5.6A

8. The water in a swimming pool tends to be warmer in the daytime and cooler at night. What natural source of energy causes this difference?

   Ⓐ chemical energy

   Ⓑ solar energy

   Ⓒ mechanical energy

   Ⓓ sound energy

Use the diagram to answer questions 9, 10, and 11. It shows thermometers in four cups of water.

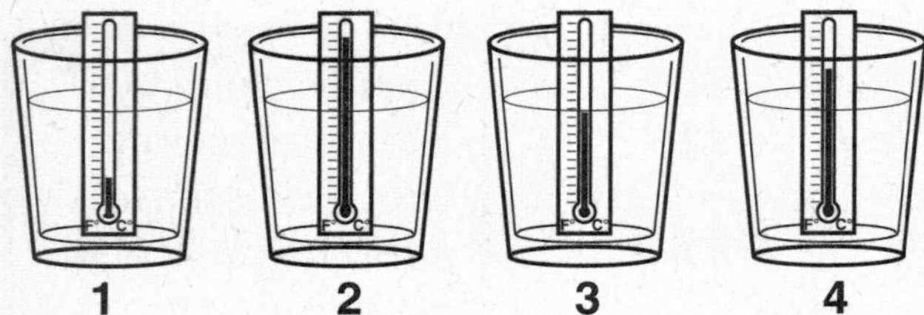


TEKS 5.2D, 5.3C

9. Which is the best explanation for the differences in the temperatures?
   - Ⓐ The water in each cup came from a different source.
   - Ⓑ The average kinetic energy of the particles in each cup is different.
   - Ⓒ There are different numbers of particles in each cup.
   - Ⓓ There are different types of particles in each cup.

TEKS 5.2D, 5.4A

10. Which of the following shows the correct order of the amount of thermal energy in the cups from greatest to least?
    - Ⓐ 1, 2, 3, 4
    - Ⓑ 1, 4, 3, 2
    - Ⓒ 3, 2, 4, 1
    - Ⓓ 2, 4, 3, 1

TEKS 5.2D

11. If the containers in the diagram were touching, which of these describes the flow of heat between them?
    - Ⓐ from container 2 to container 1
    - Ⓑ from container 1 to container 2
    - Ⓒ from container 3 to container 2
    - Ⓓ from container 3 to container 4

TEKS 5.5A

12. Which statement best describes the difference between an electrical insulator and conductor?
    - Ⓐ A conductor is a metal, and an insulator is a nonmetal.
    - Ⓑ A conductor contains more electrons than an insulator.
    - Ⓒ An insulator has a static charge, and a conductor does not.
    - Ⓓ An insulator does not contain electrons, and a conductor does.

TEKS 5.6A, 5.6B

13. The diagram shows a circuit containing a battery and two doorbells.

Which statement about the circuit is TRUE?

- Ⓐ The bells will ring because it is a series circuit.
- Ⓑ The bells will ring because they are attached to the battery.
- Ⓒ The bells won't ring because the circuit isn't complete.
- Ⓓ The bells won't ring because the battery isn't big enough.

Name ___________________________

TEKS 5.2B, 5.5A

14. Ariel wants to build an electric circuit with a device that can be turned on and off. Which list contains all of the materials she will need for her circuit?

Ⓐ battery, wire, lightbulb, switch

Ⓑ string, buzzer, battery, switch

Ⓒ buzzer, wire, switch, lightbulb

Ⓓ wire, ruler, switch, battery

TEKS 5.2D, 5.6B

15. The diagrams show four different electric circuits.

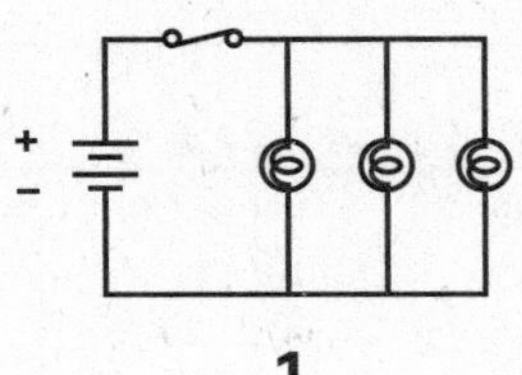


1

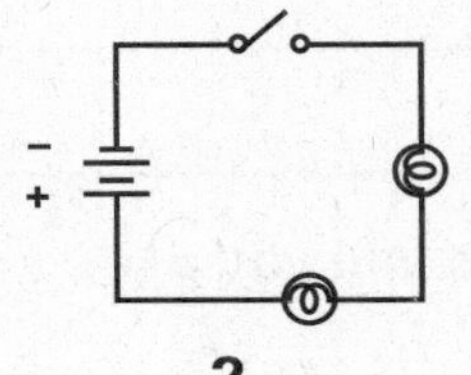


2

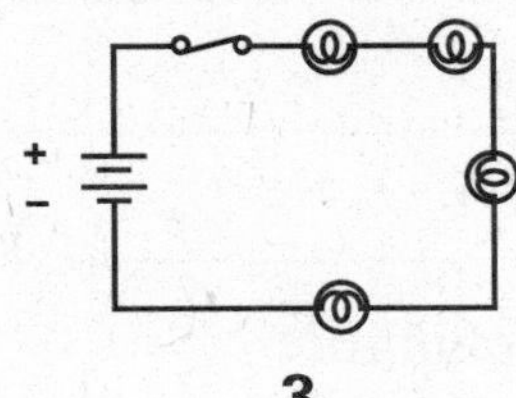


3

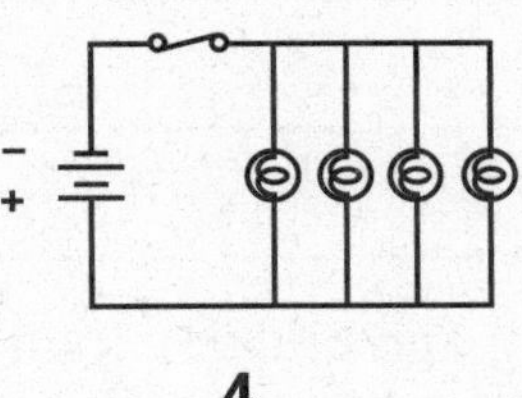


4

In which of the circuits will other bulbs remain lit when one burns out?

Ⓐ only circuit 1

Ⓑ only circuits 1, 3, and 4

Ⓒ only circuits 2 and 3

Ⓓ only circuits 1 and 4

TEKS 5.2D, 5.6A

16. You rub two balloons on your hair on a dry day. Your hair is attracted to both balloons. Then, you bring the balloons near each other. What would you observe?

Ⓐ They repel each other.

Ⓑ They attract each other.

Ⓒ They neither attract nor repel each other.

Ⓓ Opposite charges make one balloon become larger and one become smaller.

TEKS 5.2D, 5.6A

17. The diagram shows what happens in a pot of water heated on a stove. Which of the following types of heat transfer is shown by the arrows?

Ⓐ conduction

Ⓑ convection

Ⓒ radiation

Ⓓ evaporation

# Apply Inquiry and Review the Big Idea

Write the answers to these questions.

TEKS 5.3C, 5.6A

**18.** Draw and label a diagram that shows how energy changes form in a television.

TEKS 5.2B, 5.3A, 5.6B

**19.** Raul claims that thicker wire will carry more electrons to a lightbulb in an electric circuit, so the bulb will look brighter than when a thin wire is used. Plan and describe an investigation that will provide data to help you analyze and evaluate Raul's explanation.

**a.** Formulate a testable hypothesis.

**b.** How will you test your hypothesis? What equipment will you use?

**c.** How would you use your data to analyze, evaluate, and critique Raul's explanation?

TEKS 5.2D, 5.6A

**20.** Energy is measured in units called *joules* (J). Suppose a roller coaster car starts with 78,000 J of potential energy. In a few seconds, it converts two-thirds of this energy into kinetic energy. As it takes a curve, the car doubles its kinetic energy. How much mechanical energy does the car now have?

UNIT 6

# Light and Sound

## Big Idea

Light and sound are useful forms of energy that travel in waves.

TEKS 5.2A, 5.2B, 5.2C, 5.2D, 5.2F, 5.3A, 5.3D, 5.4A, 5.6A, 5.6C

## I Wonder Why

Why does the shape of the bandshell help concertgoers hear the orchestra's music? *Turn the page to find out.*

**Here's why** Sound energy can reflect, or bounce off, surfaces. The curved, hard surface of the bandshell helps to reflect sound toward the audience. A well-designed bandshell enables concertgoers far from the stage to hear the music just as well as those who are close to it.

In this unit, you will explore the Big Idea, the Essential Questions, and the investigations on the Inquiry Flipchart.

Levels of Inquiry Key ■ DIRECTED ■ GUIDED ■ INDEPENDENT

**Big Idea** Light and sound are useful forms of energy that travel in waves.

## Essential Questions



**Science Notebook**

Before you begin each lesson, be sure to write your thoughts about the Essential Question.

TEKS 5.6A explore the uses of energy, including mechanical, light, thermal, electrical, and sound energy

Lesson 1

Essential Question

# What Is Sound?

## Engage Your Brain!

Find the answer to the following question in this lesson and record it here.

How does a drummer make music?

________________________________

________________________________

________________________________

________________________________

## Active Reading

### Lesson Vocabulary

List the terms. As you learn about each one, make notes in the Interactive Glossary.

______________ ______________

______________ ______________

### Compare and Contrast

In this lesson, you'll read about how characteristics of sound are alike and different from one another. Active readers stay focused on comparisons and contrasts when they ask themselves, How are these things alike? How are they different?



Inquiry Flipchart p. 31—Good Vibrations/Thick or Thin

You may have seen water waves that look like this. Water waves move in an up-and-down motion as shown here. No matter how a wave is shaped, it carries energy.

# Waves of SOUND

Some waves are long and flat. Other waves are tight and tall. But all waves move from place to place in a regular way.

**Active Reading** As you read these pages, underline the effect of plucking a guitar string.

Water waves carry energy as they move, one after another, across a lake. A **wave** is a disturbance that transmits energy. There are other kinds of waves that you can't see. Sound energy is a series of vibrations traveling in waves. *Vibrations* are the back-and-forth movements of an object. When you pluck a guitar string, the string vibrates, causing sound waves. The vibrating body of the guitar makes the sound louder.

## Musical Vibrations

Use arrows to indicate the parts of the guitar that vibrate.

Thinking of a spring toy can help you understand compression waves.

1 The coils in one area become bunched up, or compressed. They then stretch out, or separate.

2 and 3 These compressions and separations occur along the length of the spring as the wave moves away from its starting point.

Musical instruments aren't the only things that make sound. Striking the head of a nail with a hammer causes sound vibrations, too. Many animals make sounds by moving a column of air up through the throat and mouth.

All sound vibrations travel in compression waves. As a compression wave moves, particles of air or other matter are pushed together, or compressed. Then the particles spread apart. Sound energy moves away from its source as this bunching and spreading of particles is repeated over and over. Your ears detect sound waves when the waves make parts of your ears vibrate. Your brain interprets these vibrations as sound.

► Tell how a compression wave and a water wave are alike and different.

______________________________

______________________________

______________________________

______________________________

______________________________

______________________________

______________________________

A bird's song has a high pitch and a high frequency. Its sound waves have many vibrations per second.

This dog's bark has fewer vibrations per second. It has a low pitch and a low frequency.

# It Sounds LIKE . . .

Our world is full of sounds—many of them pleasant, others harsh or annoying.

**Active Reading** As you read these two pages, underline the definitions of *pitch, frequency,* and *volume.*

People measure characteristics of sound in order to understand, describe, and control how sounds affect our ears. Pitch and volume are two useful ways to measure sound. The highness or lowness of a sound is its **pitch**. A flute produces high-pitched sounds. A tuba produces low-pitched sounds. **Frequency** is the number of vibrations that occur during a unit of time. A sound with a high pitch has a high frequency. Low-pitched sounds have lower frequencies.

The loudness of a sound is its **volume**. Volume is measured in units called *decibels* [DES•uh•buhlz], abbreviated *dB*. The softest sounds that humans can hear are near 0 dB. The humming of a refrigerator is 40 dB. Heavy city traffic is about 85 dB. Any noise at this level can cause hearing loss if a person listens for a long period of time. It's wise to wear earplugs if your ears will be exposed to 15 minutes or more of noise at 100 decibels. No more than one minute of noise at 110 decibels is safe without ear protection.

120 dB If you are close to a lightning strike, the resulting thunder can be loud enough to cause pain.

100 dB Sounds that are 85 dB or louder can damage your ears.

80 dB

20 dB

## Turn That Down!

Analyze the chart. Then order the sounds from 1, the quietest, to 6, the loudest. Put a star next to any sound that could damage your ears.

**Decibel Scale of Common Sounds**

| Source of Sound | Decibel Level |
|---|---|
| _________ normal conversation | 60 dB |
| _________ firecracker | 150 dB |
| _________ whispered voices | 20 dB |
| _________ ambulance siren | 120 dB |
| _________ power lawn mower | 90 dB |
| _________ personal stereo system at highest volume | 105 dB |

# The TRAVELS of Sound

Sound can travel through walls, windows, and floors, as well as air and water. Does sound travel at the same speed through solids, gases, and liquids?

**Active Reading** As you read these two pages, **underline** places where solids, liquids, and gases are compared or contrasted.

**The sound of this boy's voice moves through a gas (air) and a liquid (water) before reaching the other boy's ears underwater.**

Sound travels in waves. But sound can only travel if there are particles that the waves can cause to vibrate. Most of the sounds you hear move though the air. Air and other gases have particles that vibrate as sound energy hits them. Liquids and solids are also made of particles, so sound waves can move through these materials, too. However, if there are no particles to move, then sound cannot travel. What would happen if an astronaut dropped a heavy rock on the moon? Would it produce a sound? Since the moon doesn't have an atmosphere, sound waves wouldn't be carried to the astronaut's ears. She might feel vibrations at her feet, but she wouldn't hear a sound.

# Do the Math!

## Multiply Whole Numbers

Use a calculator and the information in the table to calculate how long it will take a sound to travel 4,575 m through each type of matter.

| Type of Matter | Approximate Speed of Sound (m/s) |
|---|---|
| Pure water | 1,525 |
| Dry air | 300 |
| Cast iron | 4,575 |

Pure water: ______________________

Dry air: ______________________

Cast iron: ______________________

Sound waves travel through different kinds of matter at different rates. The speed at which sound waves pass through solids, liquids, and gases has to do with how their particles are arranged. Particles in a solid are packed closely together. The particles in gases are far apart. Liquids are in between. For this reason, sound travels through gases more slowly than it travels through liquids and solids.

**When you knock on a door, the sound moves through a solid (wood) and through a gas (air) on the other side of the door.**

# SOUND Off!

Imagine a world without sound! What kinds of things wouldn't you be able to do? Wait—I can't hear you!

**Active Reading** As you read these two pages, draw one line under an example of sound traveling through a gas, two lines through a liquid, and three lines through a solid.

Talking on the phone or listening to music would be things you wouldn't be able to do. You wouldn't even be able to hear the grumbling of your own stomach! Let's take a look at how many different ways people use sound energy.

## Exploration

When sound energy strikes matter, some of it bounces back toward the source. Materials reflect sound in different ways. Geologists use sound waves to locate underwater resources such as oil. Tools called *sonar* help researchers map the ocean floor or locate sunken ships.

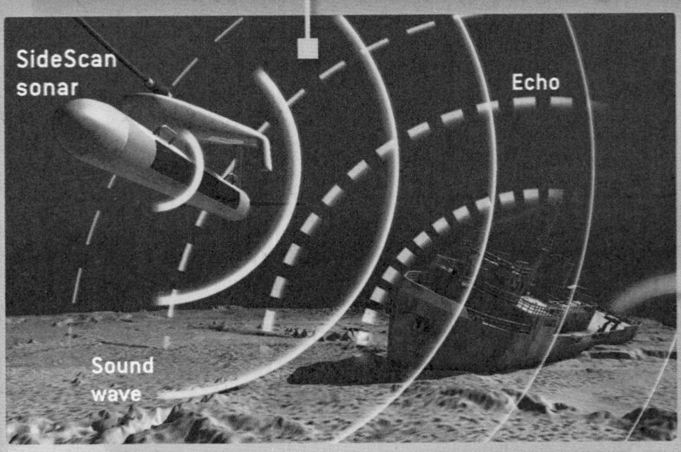


## Everyday Uses

Sound energy plays a major part in communication and entertainment. You know that sound energy must travel through matter. In many devices, such as cell phones, sound waves from your voice travel through air to a microphone. The sound waves are changed to other forms of energy. When the energy reaches the receiving phone, a speaker changes it back to sound waves that you can hear.

## Medicine

Doctors use a simple tool called a stethoscope to listen to your heart. They also use high-frequency sound waves called *ultrasound* to produce images of structures inside the body. This picture shows a heart. Ultrasound can also be used to treat some medical problems. For example, the vibrations from ultrasound can break up hard deposits in the kidneys. As a result, a doctor doesn't have to operate to remove them.

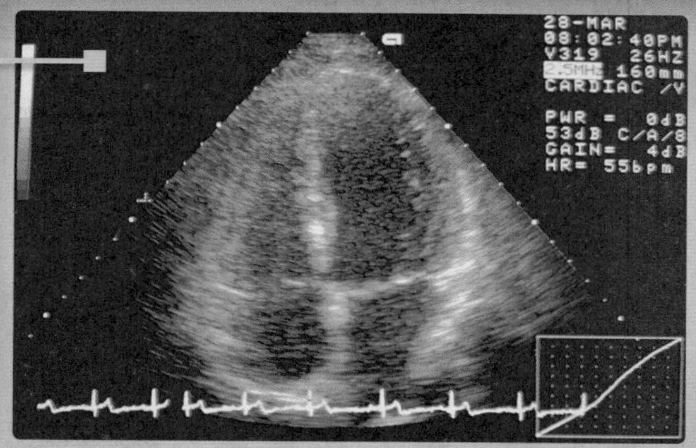


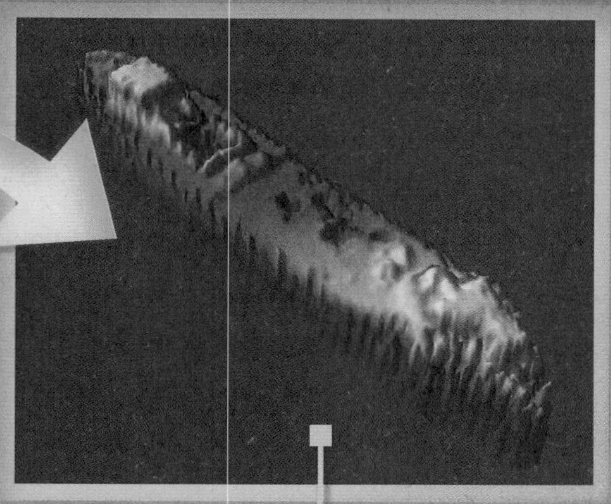

As the waves from a sonar bounce back from a submerged ship, they arrive at different times back to listening devices. A computer changes the collected signals to form a picture of the ship (above).

## Fun Sound Facts

Submarines use sonar to locate the position of other ships. Sound moves about five times faster in water than it does through air. Sound travels about 300 m/s in air.

Suppose a sonar signal sent by a submarine takes 2 s to travel from the ship and back again. How far is the submarine from the bottom? Show your work.

______________________________

______________________________

______________________________

______________________________

# Sound All Around

Understanding the properties of sound energy allows people to use and control sound.

Sometimes people want sounds to be softer or to not be heard at all. At other times, people want sounds to be louder or clearer. Engineers design rooms and buildings to reduce outside noise and to make indoor sounds more pleasant.

Sound insulation contains tiny air cells. Sound is absorbed as the cells trap sound waves. This keeps the sound inside the room. Similar technology is used in apartment buildings to help limit the amount of noise you hear from your neighbors!

Engineers use knowledge of sound's properties as they record music, voices, and other sounds in studios. Sound engineers also combine the singer's voice with the background music.

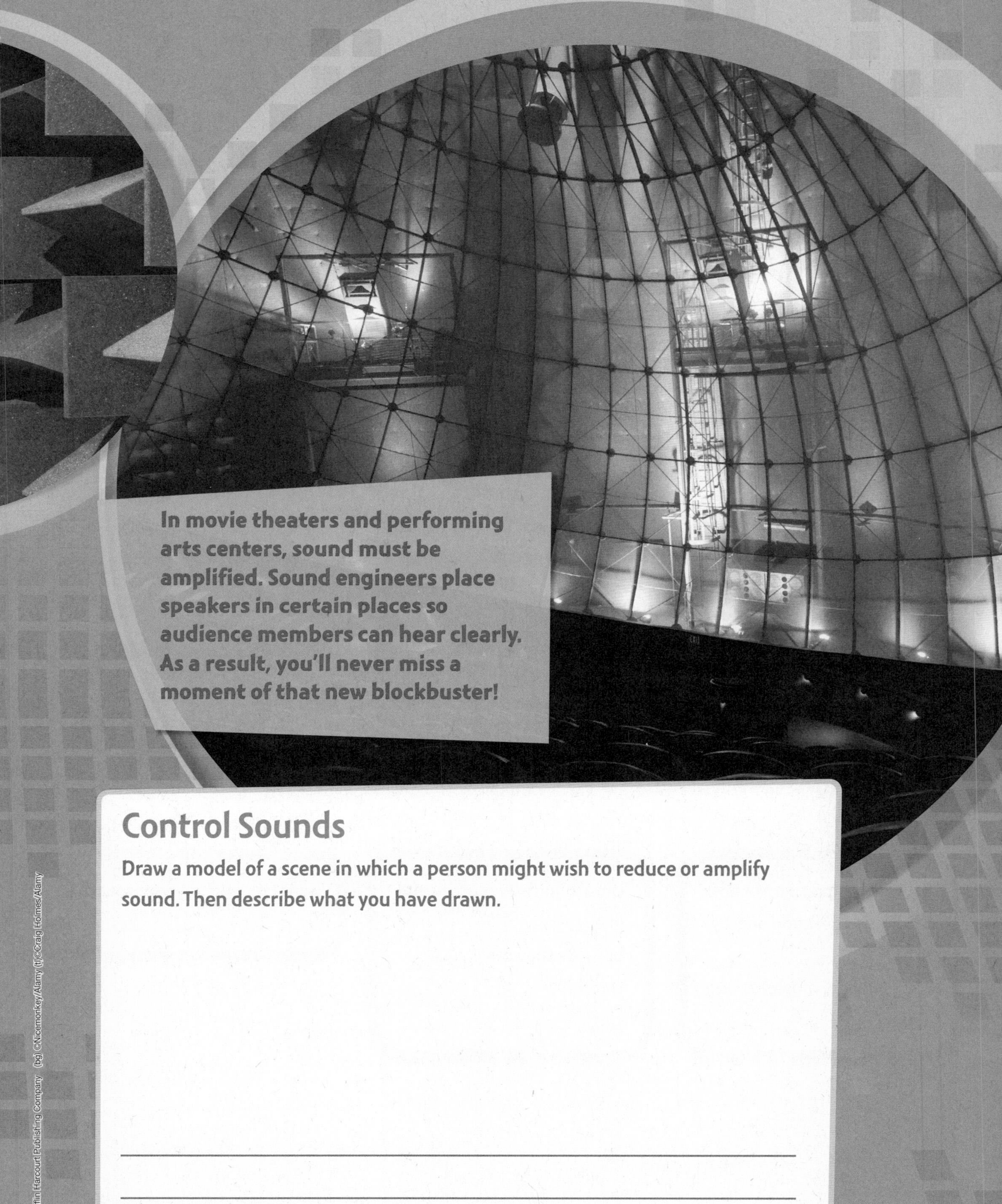

In movie theaters and performing arts centers, sound must be amplified. Sound engineers place speakers in certain places so audience members can hear clearly. As a result, you'll never miss a moment of that new blockbuster!

## Control Sounds

Draw a model of a scene in which a person might wish to reduce or amplify sound. Then describe what you have drawn.

______________________________________________

______________________________________________

When you're done, use the answer key to check and revise your work.

**Fill in the blanks to complete the statements that describe the characteristics and uses of sound energy.**

**Characteristics of Sound**

The loudness of a sound is its 1. ____________________. It is measured in 2. ____________________.

The highness or lowness of a sound is called 3. ____________________.

The number of vibrations in a unit of time is 4. ____________________. A sound with a high frequency has a 5. ____________________

**Uses of Sound Energy**

Barking, singing, and sirens, are all uses of sound energy to 6. ____________________. Sound energy moves through air by 7. ____________________.

Ultrasound waves are useful in 8. ____________________, because they can travel through 9. ____________________, ____________________.

Sonar technology uses sound waves for 10. ____________________

Answer Key: 1. volume 2. decibels 3. pitch 4. frequency 5. high pitch 6. communicate 7. compression 8. medicine 9. living tissue without causing harm 10. exploration

# Brain Check

Lesson 1

Name ____________________________

## Word Play

**1** Match each picture to a term, and each term to its definition.

| Picture | Term | Definition |
|---|---|---|
|  | decibel | the loudness of a sound |
|  | frequency | disturbances of particles in matter as a sound wave travels forward |
|  | pitch | the number of vibrations that occur in a given unit of time |
|  | vibrations | a disturbance that carries energy |
|  | volume | the highness or lowness of a sound |
| 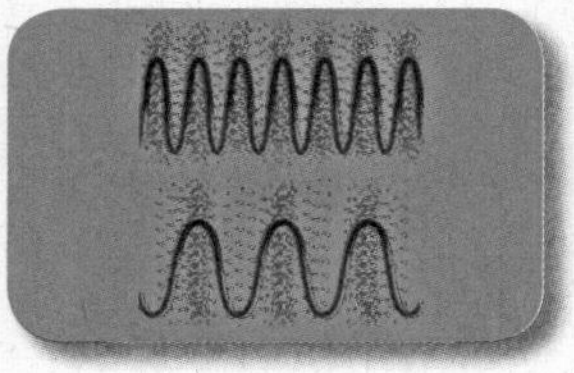 | wave | the unit of measure for the volume of sound |

# Apply Concepts

**2** Define *wave*. Then explain how vibrations, waves, and energy are related to sound.

______________________________________________

______________________________________________

**3** Label the pictures *1*, *2*, and *3* to indicate the speed at which sound waves travel through each kind of matter. Let *1* be fastest and *3* be slowest.

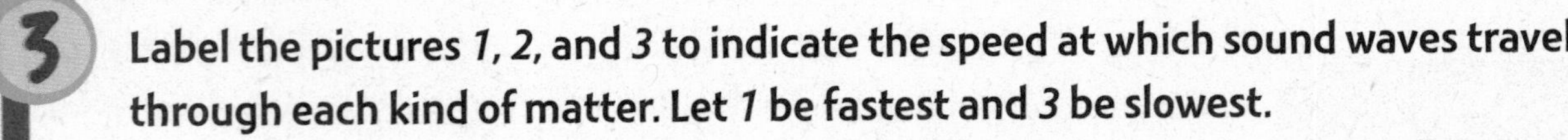

________  ________  ________ 

**4** Explain how a sound's pitch and frequency are related.

______________________________________________

______________________________________________

______________________________________________

**5** Examine the picture. Which properties of sound are used?

______________________________________________

______________________________________________

______________________________________________

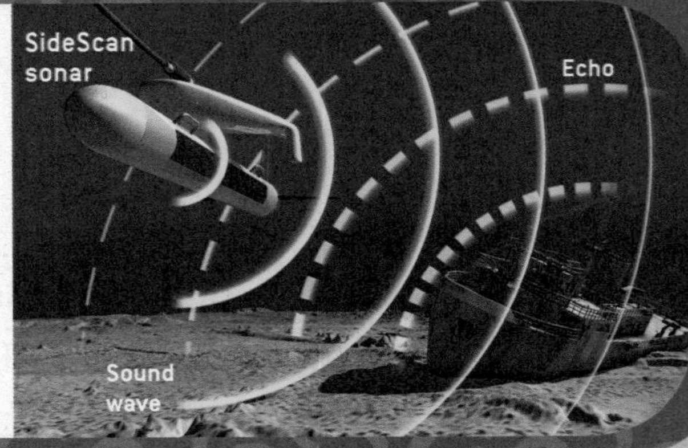

Spend time walking slowly from room to room. List and classify the sounds you hear with a family member. For example, you might classify them as *loud* and *soft*, or *electronic*, *mechanical*, *human*, or *natural*.

# Ask a Sound Designer

**Q. What does a sound designer do?**

**A.** The sound designer plans and provides the sounds you hear in a play or movie. They are in charge of making noises and sound effects. They make every sound from the slam of a car door to the roar of a lion.

**Q. How do designers come up with the sounds?**

**A.** They start by studying the script. They gather information about the settings of the play or movie, and what sounds a person might hear in those places. They also think about the mood. An audience might not even notice some sounds that provide mood and feelings. Music can give information about a character or a story. It can also help the viewer know when something in a play or movie is about to happen.

**Q. What do sound designers need to know about sound?**

**A.** They need to know a lot about the quality of sounds and how they are made. Sound designers have to understand pitch, volume, and how sound travels and lasts.

# Did You Hear That?

Can you figure out the sound each object makes? Read the description of each sound. Write the number of the sound next to the picture that matches it.

1. This object makes a warning sound with a very high volume and a high pitch so people are sure to hear it.
2. This makes a low-pitched sound when you strike it.
3. This makes sounds when you strum it.
4. This can make high- or low-pitched sounds when you blow into it.
5. This object makes a sound with a low pitch and a high volume.
6. This organism can make a high-volume sound with a high pitch.

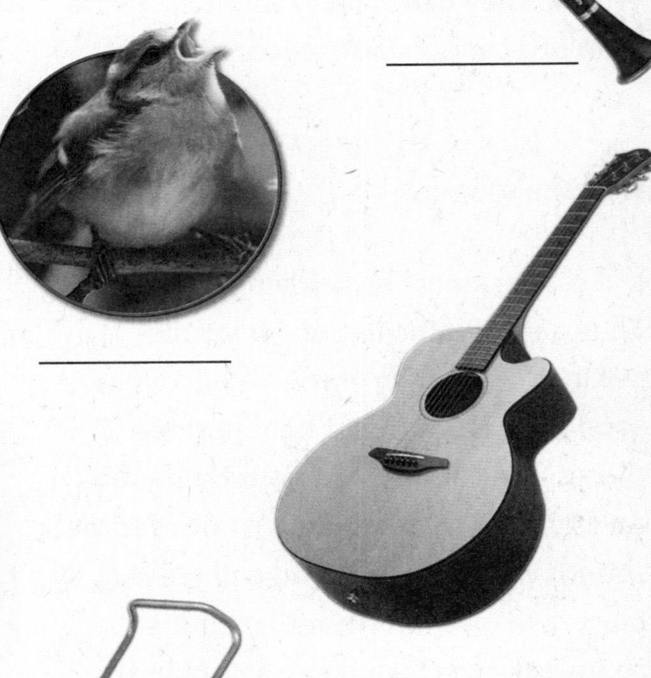

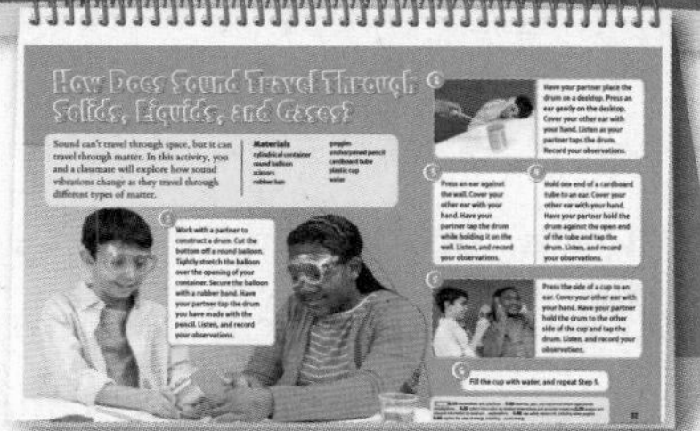

Inquiry Flipchart page 32

**TEKS** **5.2A** describe, plan, and implement simple experimental investigations testing one variable **5.2B** Ask well-defined questions... **5.2C** collect information by detailed observations **5.3A**...analyze, evaluate, and critique scientific explanations by using empirical evidence...and experimental testing... **5.6A** explore the uses of energy, including...energy

Name ______________________________

Essential Question

# How Does Sound Travel Through Solids, Liquids, and Gases?

## Set a Purpose

At the end of this experiment, what will you understand better about sound energy?

______________________________

______________________________

## Think About the Procedure

What stays the same in all of the trials?

______________________________

______________________________

What variable will you change in each trial?

______________________________

______________________________

______________________________

Why will you start by listening to the sound without pressing your ear against any surface?

______________________________

______________________________

## Record Your Data

Record your observations in the table below.

| How do sound waves travel to your ear? | Describe each sound. |
|---|---|
| Step 1 From the drum through air (gas) | |
| Step 2 | |
| Step 3 | |
| Step 4 | |
| Step 5 | |
| Step 6 | |

## Draw Conclusions

Why did you place a hand over your free ear in Steps 2–5?

Did the sound change from Step 1 to Step 2? Explain.

Were your descriptions of the sounds in Step 1 and Step 4 different? Why?

Why do you think the sounds produced in Steps 5 and 6 were different?

## Analyze and Extend

1. Based on your empirical evidence, construct a scientific explanation about how gases, liquids, and solids can change the way we hear a sound.

2. Analyze, evaluate, and critique the explanations offered by other groups. Why might the results you got differ from theirs?

3. Most of the sounds you hear travel through air. If you could, how would you change the procedure to better hear sounds transmitted through solids and liquids?

4. What other questions would you like to ask about how sound travels in different types of matter?

**TEKS 5.2D** analyze and interpret information to construct reasonable explanations... **5.2F** communicate valid conclusions in both written and verbal forms **5.6A** explore the uses of energy, including...light...energy **5.6C** demonstrate that light travels in a straight line...

Essential Question

# What Is Light?

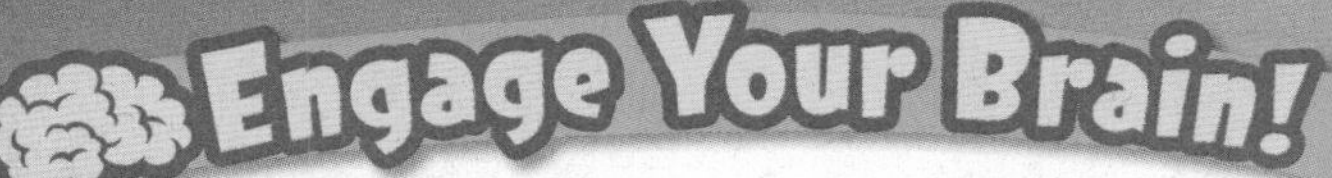


Find the answer to the following question in this lesson and record it here.

What kind of light is used to produce these hologram images?

______________________________

______________________________

______________________________

______________________________

## Lesson Vocabulary

List the terms. As you learn about each one, make notes in the Interactive Glossary.

______________________________

______________________________

______________________________

______________________________

## Main Idea and Details

In this lesson, you'll read about light and its uses. A few sentences contain main ideas about light, while others give details that add information to these ideas. Details can include facts, examples, or features of a topic. Active readers remain focused on the topic as they ask, What information does this detail add to the main idea?

# LIGHT Energy

Have you ever made shadow figures with your hands? If you have, you have experienced one of the characteristics of light.

**Active Reading** Draw a box around the main idea of the paragraph. Draw circles around three details that add information about this idea.

**Light** is a form of energy that moves in waves and can travel through space. Light waves are *transverse waves.* As these waves move forward, energy is carried perpendicular to their forward motion, forming an S shape. Light spreads out in all directions, traveling in straight lines from its source. Light can move through a vacuum because it does not need matter to transmit its energy. This is why light can reach Earth from space. Light travels faster than anything else in the universe. It takes only about 8 minutes for light to travel the more than 149 million km (93 million mi) from the sun to Earth. All life on Earth depends on energy from sunlight.

A wave moving on a rope is an example of a transverse wave. Each part of the rope moves up and down as the wave travels to the right.

Shadows form when a solid object blocks light.

Light naturally spreads outward in all directions as it travels.

Light travels in a straight line until it hits the lampshade.

► Draw arrows to show how light travels away from the bare bulb in the photo on the right. Tell someone how the shade affects the path of light in the photo on the left.

## Do the Math!

### Divide Whole Numbers

Light travels at a rate of about 300,000 km/s. Calculate how long it would take light to travel from Earth to Mars, a distance of 56 million km.

_______________________________________

_______________________________________

Radio waves can have wavelengths as long as several football fields.
"Night vision" instruments use infrared waves to make objects visible in dark settings.
Low Frequency
RADIO
INFRARED
Long Wavelength
MICROWAVE
Wireless phones transmit and receive microwaves, which have some of the longest wavelengths and lowest frequencies in the electromagnetic spectrum.

# Now You SEE IT Now You Don't

You may think of light as the energy that allows your brain, with the help of your eyes, to perceive the world around you. But there's a lot more to light than that! Most of the wavelengths of light are invisible to our eyes.

**Active Reading** As you read these pages, **underline** the sentences that tell how light waves differ.

Humans can see visible light, which has intermediate wavelengths and frequencies near the middle of the electromagnetic spectrum.

Sunscreen helps protect human skin from the sun's ultraviolet rays.

VISIBLE LIGHT

ULTRAVIOLET

High Frequency

X-RAYS

Short Wavelength

X-rays have very short wavelengths.

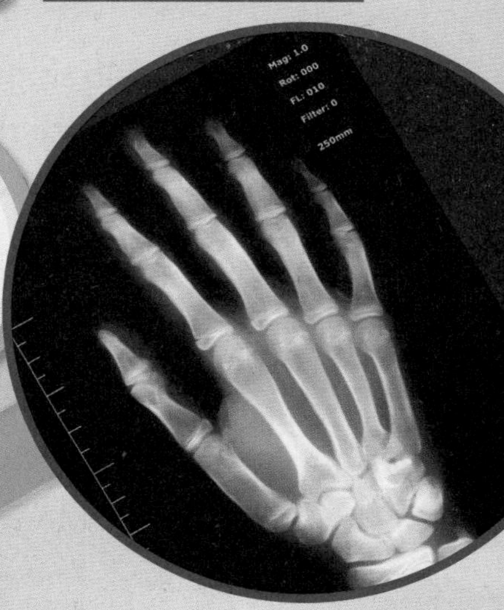


► How would you describe the position of visible light in the electromagnetic spectrum?

______________________________

______________________________

______________________________

Light waves are all around us, but many of them are invisible. The **electromagnetic spectrum** is a range of light waves organized by frequency and wavelength. At one end of this spectrum, waves have long wavelengths, or a wide distance between one high point to the next, and low frequencies. These include radio waves, microwaves, and infrared waves. At the other end, waves have short wavelengths and high frequencies. These include ultraviolet rays from the sun and X-rays.

The light that our eyes detect is called visible light. Visible light forms one very narrow section in about the middle of the electromagnetic spectrum. Visible light looks white to our eyes, but it is actually made up of many colors. Red light has the longest wavelength in the visible spectrum, and violet has the shortest.

Why It Matters

# LASER Light

Lasers have many uses in schools, hospitals, stores, and homes. What exactly is a laser? Why are lasers important to people in so many different fields?

Light from a bulb shines in straight lines in all directions. Laser light is different. A *laser* is a beam of light focused in only one direction. Also, a laser beam contains only one wavelength of light. These features make a beam of laser light very precise and powerful.

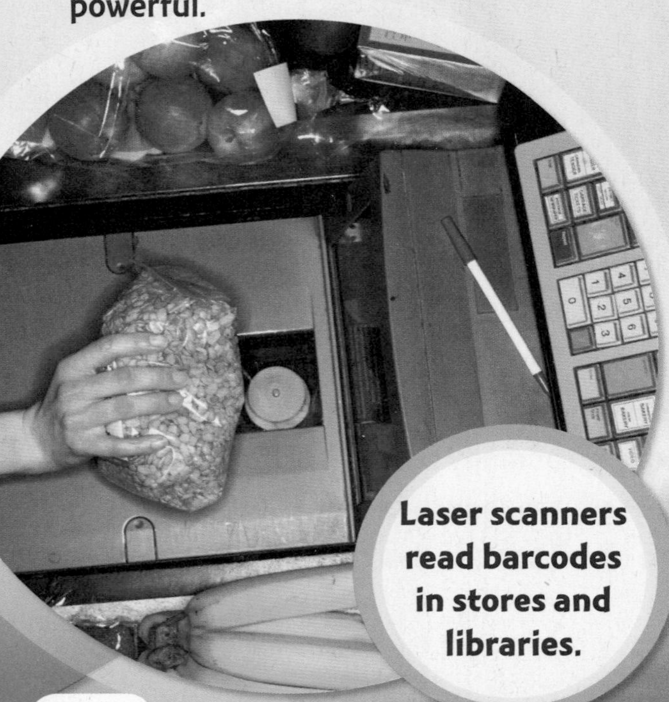

Laser scanners read barcodes in stores and libraries.

▶ Write a caption for this photo.

______________________________

______________________________

Identify a property that light from bulbs and lasers have in common.

______________________________

______________________________

▶ Write a caption for this photo. Describe how lasers are being used.

_______________________________________________

_______________________________________________

_______________________________________________

_______________________________________________

_______________________________________________

Artists use lasers to make three-dimensional images called holograms. Some doctors use lasers as cutting tools in surgery. Lasers are used to cut steel in factories and metal shops. Laser pointers help teachers in classrooms. Police detectives use lasers to analyze fingerprints at crime scenes. In all of these cases, lasers must be used safely. You should never look into the source of a laser's light, as it can damage your eyes.

**Lasers read digital information on compact discs and DVDs.**

When you're done, use the answer key to check and revise your work.

**Use what you've learned about light to complete the following.**

## Summarize

1.____________________ is a form of energy that travels in waves. As 2. ____________________ move forward, energy moves perpendicular to the forward motion. Infrared waves, ultraviolet waves, microwaves, radio waves, X-rays, and visible light are organized by wavelength and frequency in the 3.____________________. The power of 4.____________________ comes from the fact that they contain a single wavelength of light focused in just one direction.

Describe three new things that you learned about light.

________________________________________

________________________________________

________________________________________

________________________________________

________________________________________

Answer Key: 1. Light 2. transverse waves (or light waves) 3. electromagnetic spectrum 4. lasers

# Brain Check

Lesson 3

Name ______________________________

## Word Play

**1** Use the words in the box to complete the puzzle.

### Across

1. A form of electromagnetic energy, some of which is visible
4. A dark area where light is blocked by an object
7. The direction energy is carried as a light wave moves forward
8. The range of electromagnetic waves from radio waves to X-rays

### Down

1. A beam of light of a single wavelength focused in a single direction
2. A type of wave that forms an S shape
3. A type of wave that comes from the sun and may harm human skin
5. The type of light that helps humans see the world
6. A type of wave that is used in "night vision" equipment

| | | | | |
|---|---|---|---|---|
| electromagnetic* | infrared | laser | light* | perpendicular |
| shadow | transverse | ultraviolet | visible | |

* Key Lesson Vocabulary

2 Explain how light travels. Include as many details as you can.

3 Describe the part of the electromagnetic spectrum that people *can* see. Then name three devices that use electromagnetic waves that people *can't* see.

4 Circle the light that would be best for pointing out details on a map hanging high on a wall. Then explain your choice.

5 Analyze and interpret information. Explain why light produced by the sun reaches Earth, but sound produced by the sun does not.

**Take It Home!**

With a family member, go on an electromagnetic wave scavenger hunt. List items that use light waves to function. Organize the objects in your list by the terms *infrared*, *ultraviolet*, and *visible light*.

TEKS 5.2C collect information by detailed observations... 5.2D analyze and interpret information to construct reasonable explanations from...evidence 5.6C demonstrate that light travels in a straight line until it strikes an object or travels through one medium to another...light can be reflected...and refracted such as the appearance of an object when observed through water

Lesson 4

Essential Question

# What Are Some Properties of Light?

## Engage Your Brain!

Find the answer to the following question in this lesson and record it here.

Why do lighthouses use lenses?

______________________________

______________________________

______________________________

______________________________

## Active Reading

### Lesson Vocabulary

List the terms. As you learn about each one, make notes in the Interactive Glossary.

______________ ______________

______________ ______________

______________ ______________

### Compare and Contrast

Many ideas in this lesson are connected because they explain comparisons and contrasts—how things are alike and different. Active readers stay focused on comparisons and contrasts when they ask themselves, How are these things alike? How are these things different?



Inquiry Flipchart p. 34 — Coins in a Fountain/Bending Light

# Just Passing Through

Light acts differently when it strikes windows, thin curtains, or brick walls. How does each material affect the light that strikes it?

**Active Reading** As you read these two pages, underline sentences that provide details about how light acts when it strikes different materials.

Light travels outward, in all directions, in straight lines from its source until it strikes something. Light behaves in different ways depending on the kind of matter it meets. Most objects absorb some of the light that hits them. The amount of light absorbed depends on the material the object is made of.

**Opaque** materials do not let light pass through them. Instead, the material absorbs light—light enters the material but doesn't leave it. When a material absorbs light, the energy from the light is transferred to the material. Many solid objects are opaque because they are made of materials such as metal, wood, and stone that do not allow light to pass through. Objects that are opaque cause shadows to occur because the objects absorb or reflect all of the light that hits them.

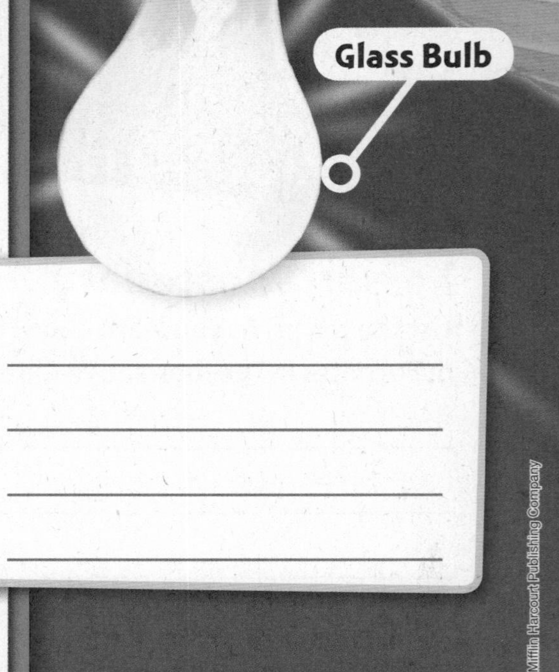

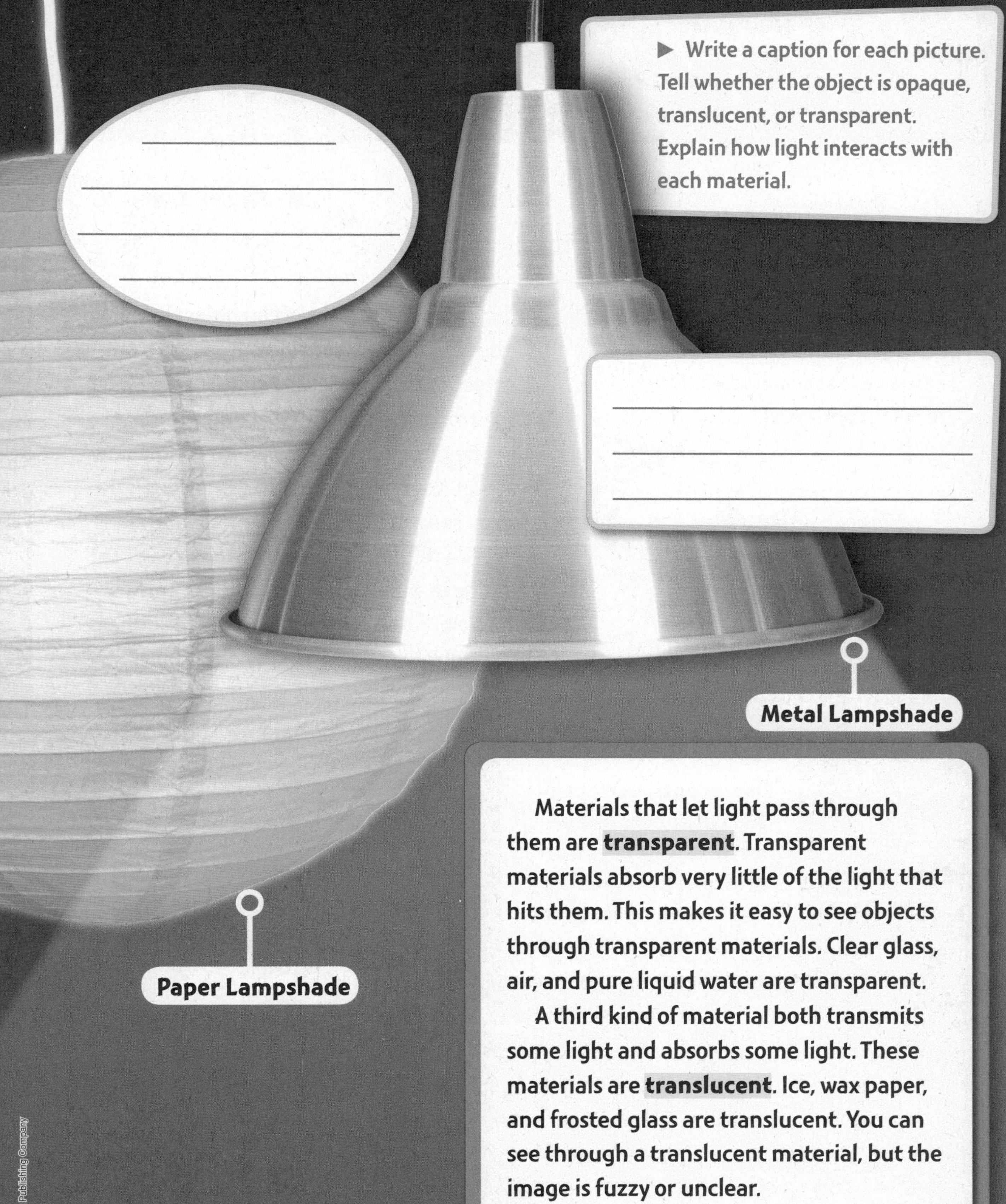

▶ Write a caption for each picture. Tell whether the object is opaque, translucent, or transparent. Explain how light interacts with each material.
Metal Lampshade
Paper Lampshade


Materials that let light pass through them are **transparent**. Transparent materials absorb very little of the light that hits them. This makes it easy to see objects through transparent materials. Clear glass, air, and pure liquid water are transparent.

A third kind of material both transmits some light and absorbs some light. These materials are **translucent**. Ice, wax paper, and frosted glass are translucent. You can see through a translucent material, but the image is fuzzy or unclear.

# Mirror, Mirror

Did you look at yourself in a mirror as you got ready for school? The properties of light enabled you to see your image.

**Active Reading** As you read these two pages, draw boxes around the words or phrases that signal when things are being contrasted.

The bouncing of light off an object is known as **reflection**. When light traveling from an object strikes a smooth, shiny surface, such as a mirror, all of the light striking the surface from one direction is reflected in a single new direction. Your eyes detect the reflected light, and you see a clear, reversed image of the object—a reflection. In contrast, you can't see an image in something with a rough surface, such as cloth or wood, because the roughness causes light to reflect in many directions.

**The smooth surface of the water acts like a mirror. Light rays are reflected back in a way that enables you to see a clear, reversed image.**

**The backpack appears yellow because its material reflects yellow light and absorbs all other colors of light.**

▶ Compare the surfaces of the metal container and the paper bag. The smooth surface reflects light in a single direction back to your eyes. The rough surface reflects light in all directions. Identify the material that would produce the better reflection.

_______________________________________________

_______________________________________________

How an object reflects light also determines what colors you see. As light strikes the surface of an object, the object absorbs certain colors of light and reflects others. A ripe strawberry absorbs nearly all colors of light, but it reflects red light. So, your eyes see the strawberry as red. Grass reflects green light while absorbing all other colors.

Black objects absorb all colors of light. They also absorb more of the energy in light. White objects, though, reflect all colors of light and absorb less energy. Because white clothes don't absorb as much energy, wearing white rather than dark clothes on a bright, hot day will keep your body cooler.

▶ When we look at these fruits and vegetables, we see a variety of colors.

Choose one fruit or vegetable. Explain why it's the color it is.

_______________________________________________

_______________________________________________

_______________________________________________

_______________________________________________

_______________________________________________

_______________________________________________

# Light Bends

What happened to the straw in the glass? Did someone break it? No! What you are observing is another property of light—refraction.

**Active Reading** As you read these pages, underline words that identify the cause of refraction. Circle words that identify an effect of refraction.

The bending of light as it passes at an angle from one type of matter into another is called **refraction**. Refraction occurs because the speed of light varies depending on the material through which the light travels. As the light changes speed, it bends. Look at the straw at the top of this page. Light from the top of the straw passes through the air and the glass to your eyes. But light from the bottom part starts out in the water and passes into the glass and then into the air. Each time the light enters a new material, it bends slightly because it changes speed. By the time this light reaches your eyes, it is coming from a different angle than the light from the top of the straw. As a result, the straw appears to be bent or broken.

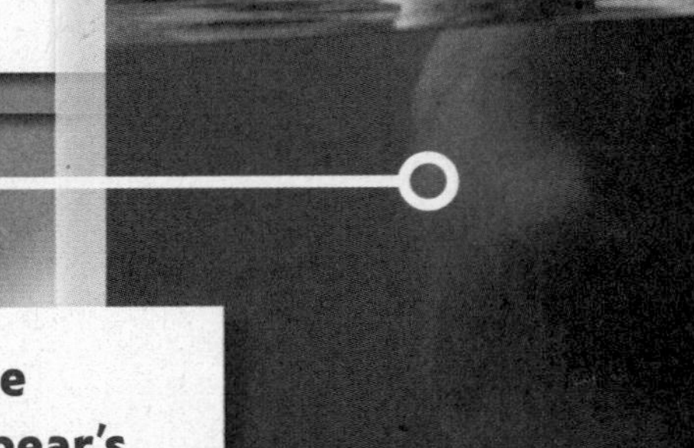

**Refraction produced the illusion that this polar bear's head is separate from its body.**

A **prism** is a transparent material that separates white light into its component colors by refraction. When white light enters a prism, the different colors of light bend at different angles. The light moves through the prism and exits it as a rainbow.

Light bends in other ways. *Diffraction* is the bending of light around barriers or through openings. If you look at the edges of a shadow cast in bright sunlight, you may notice that the edges of the shadow are blurry. This blurriness is caused by light bending around the edge of the object. The colors of the sunset are a result of diffraction as sunlight bends around particles in the air.

## Do the Math!

### Angles of Refraction

The diagram shows how light bends as it enters and then exits a transparent material. Use a protractor to measure the angles formed as the light is refracted.

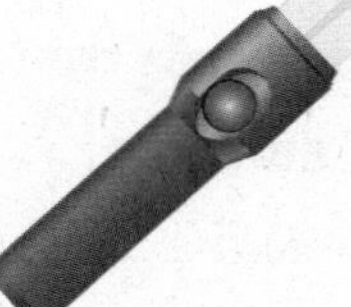

_______________________________________________

_______________________________________________

_______________________________________________

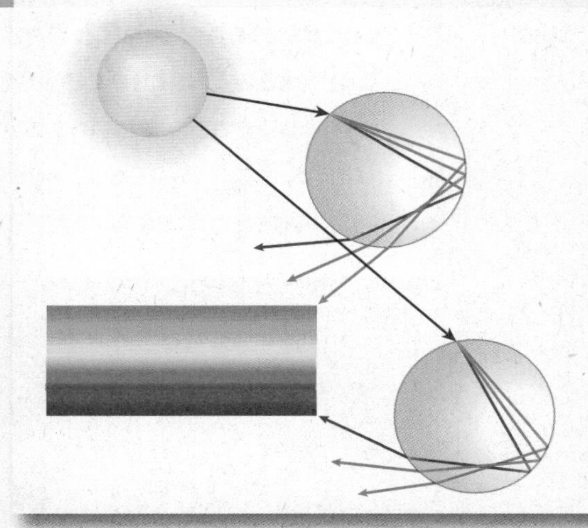

**Rainbows are a product of refraction and reflection. Sunlight separates into colors as it passes from the air into a water droplet. The colored light is reflected off the back of the drop, and it is refracted again as it passes into the air. Light from many droplets forms the arcs of color in a rainbow. Red light comes from droplets higher in the air, and violet light comes from lower droplets.**

# Lenses

Cameras, telescopes, and eyeglasses all contain lenses. Even your eyes have a lens inside each of them! What do lenses do?

**Active Reading** As you read the next page, put brackets [ ] around the details that describe convex and concave lenses. Draw a line under the main idea that the details help explain.

Lenses are curved transparent objects that refract light. You can find lenses in DVD players, photocopiers, and binoculars. Even the microscope you use in many science activities has a lens. Most lenses are circular and are made of clear glass or plastic. Many devices use a series of lenses to make images clearer. Lenses vary greatly in size. Microscopes use several tiny lenses to magnify small objects. The Yerkes Observatory in Wisconsin has a reflecting telescope with a lens that is over a meter in diameter!

**Telescopes use lenses to magnify objects. Incoming light moves through a convex lens, which bends light toward the center of the tube and brings it into focus. The concave eyepiece lens magnifies the image.**

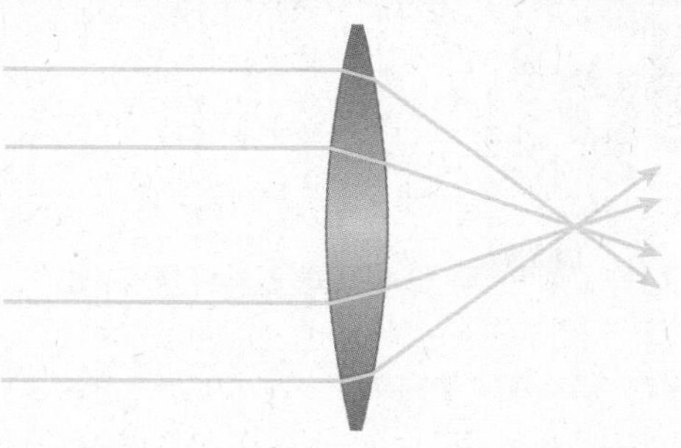

Convex lenses have an outward curve on at least one side. The other side may be curved or flat. These lenses refract light toward a focus, or focal point.

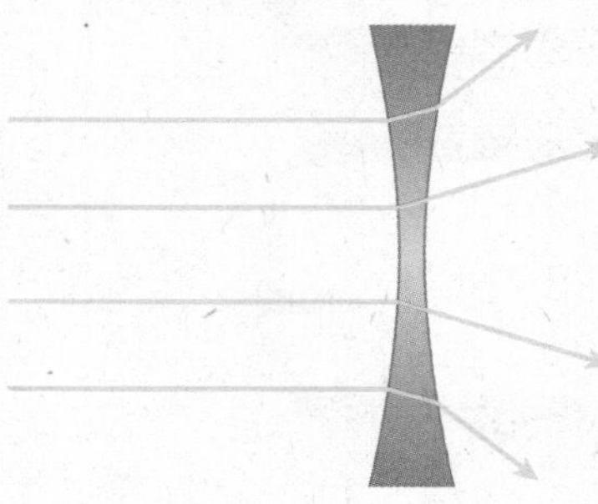

Most concave lenses have an inward curve on both sides. These lenses spread light waves apart.

A *convex lens* is a lens that is thicker at the center and thinner at the edges. Convex lenses are sometimes called positive lenses because they bring light waves together. In other words, a convex lens focuses light. This bending allows an image to form at a point called the focal point.

A *concave lens* is a lens that is thicker at the edges and thinner at the center. Sometimes called negative lenses, concave lenses spread light waves apart from a focal point.

Eyeglasses may have concave or convex lenses, depending on the type of vision correction needed.

## Concave, Convex, or Both?

Fill in the Venn diagram to compare and contrast concave and convex lenses.

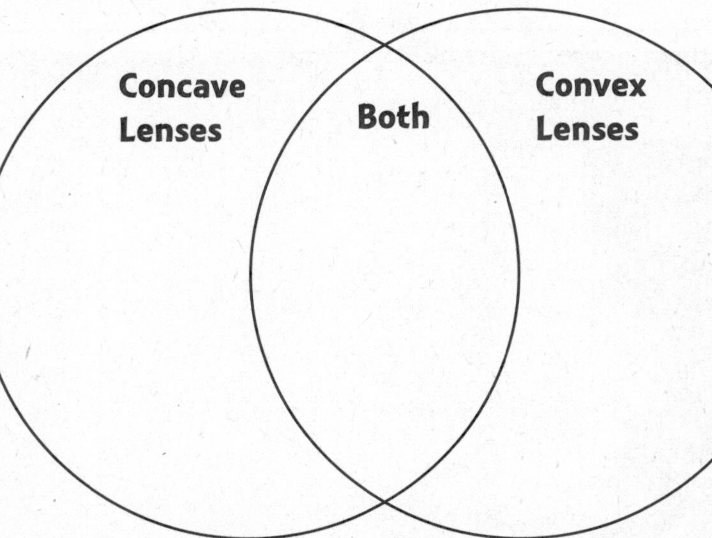

When you're done, use the answer key to check and revise your work.

**Use the terms below to fill in the graphic organizers about some properties of light.**

| | | |
|---|---|---|
| reflection | translucent | diffraction |
| opaque | refraction | transparent |

**Descriptions of Ways Different Materials Absorb Light**

1. ________________

2. ________________

3. ________________

**The Bouncing or Bending of Light**

4. ________________

5. ________________

6. ________________

Answer Key: 1, 2, and 3: transparent, translucent, and opaque in any order 4, 5, and 6: reflection, refraction, and diffraction in any order

# Brain Check

Lesson 4

Name ______________________________

## Word Play

**1** Use the clues to help you write the correct word in each row. Some boxes have already been filled in for you.

| | | | | | | | | | | | |
|---|---|---|---|---|---|---|---|---|---|---|---|
| a. | | | | F | R | | | | I | | |
| b. | | | | F | R | | | | I | | |
| c. | | | | F | | | | | I | | |
| d. | | | | | | | | R | I | | |
| e. | | | A | | | | | R | | | |
| f. | | | A | | | | | | | | |
| g. | | | A | | | | | | | | |

### Clues

a. This makes the edges of a shadow look blurred.

b. It's another way of saying "the bending of light."

c. This is the word for the bouncing of light off an object.

d. This object will separate light into the colors of the spectrum.

e. This word describes objects that let light pass through them.

f. This word describes objects that let only some light pass through them.

g. This word describes objects that let little or no light pass through them.

| | | | |
|---|---|---|---|
| transparent* | reflection* | prism* | diffraction |
| translucent* | opaque* | refraction* | |

* Key Lesson Vocabulary

### Bonus

**The prefix *con-* means "with." What words with this prefix can you find in the lesson?**

______________________________________________

# Apply Concepts

2 Which is better: checking your appearance in a regular mirror or checking it in a sheet of crumpled aluminum foil? Explain why one reflective surface is better than the other.

_______________________________________________

_______________________________________________

_______________________________________________

3 Construct an explanation. Why is the fisherman having a hard time catching the fish?

_______________________

_______________________

_______________________

_______________________

4 Circle the image that shows an opaque material.

With a family member, walk through the rooms of your home and identify opaque, transparent, and translucent objects. See how many surfaces you can find in which you can see a reflection.

**TEKS 5.3D** connect grade-level appropriate science concepts with the history of science, science careers, and contributions of scientists **5.6A** explore the uses of energy, including...sound energy

## S.T.E.M.

### Engineering & Technology

# Play It Again

The hand-cranked Victrola was one of the first machines to play back recorded sound. The grooves on a flat disk send a sound vibration through a needle.

A record player makes sound the same way a Victrola did, but it is powered by electricity.

Instead of coming from physical grooves, the sound on a reel-to-reel player comes from signals recorded on magnetic tape.

Cassette tapes are magnetic like reel-to-reels, but they are small and portable. So are cassette players.

An MP3 is a type of computer file. It contains the digital code for recorded sounds. Many devices, from computers to phones to pocket-sized music players, can play back MP3 files.

Compact discs have grooves like records. But a CD player reads the grooves with a laser beam instead of a needle.

**Circle the sound devices that use discs. How are the players alike? How are they different?**

_______________________________________________

_______________________________________________

continued

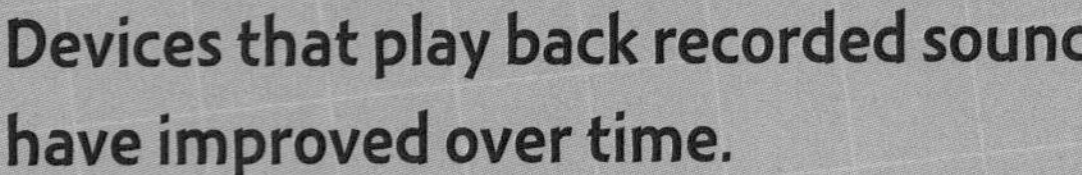
Devices that play back recorded sound have improved over time.

| | |
|---|---|
| | How is an electric record player an improvement over a hand-cranked Victrola?<br>________________________________________ |
| | How is a cassette tape an improvement over a reel-to-reel tape?<br>________________________________________ |
| | You have to rewind a cassette tape to get back to the beginning after it plays. How is a CD easier to play?<br>________________________________________ |
| | What makes MP3 files the most convenient way to play back recorded sound?<br>________________________________________ |
| | Draw a sound playback device that would be even better. What features might it have?<br>________________________________________ |

## Build On It!

Rise to the engineering design challenge—complete **Design It: Looking Around a Corner** on the Inquiry Flipchart.

Inquiry Flipchart page 36

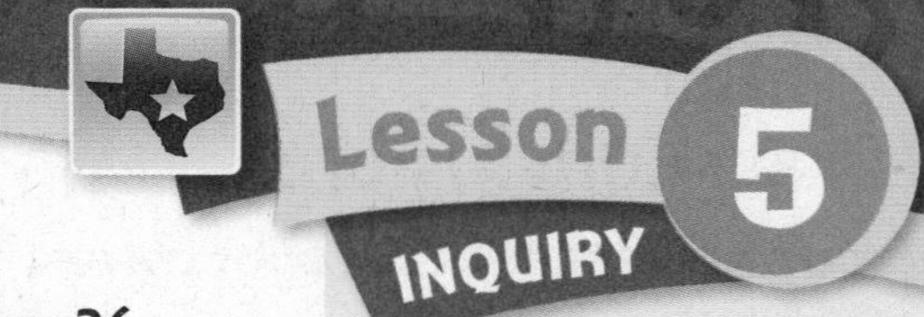


**TEKS 5.2C** collect information by detailed observations and accurate measuring **5.3A** ...analyze, evaluate, and critique scientific explanations by using empirical evidence, logical reasoning, and experimental and observational testing **5.4A** collect, record, and analyze information using tools, including...prisms, mirrors...and notebooks... **5.6C** demonstrate that light travels in a straight line until it strikes an object or travels through one medium to another and demonstrate that light can be reflected such as the use of mirrors or other shiny surfaces and refracted such as the appearance of an object when observed through water

Name ______________________________

Essential Question

# What Happens When Light Is Reflected and Refracted?

## Set a Purpose

**What do you expect to understand about light after you complete this investigation?**

______________________________

______________________________

______________________________

## Think About the Procedure

**What is the purpose of the mirror in the investigation?**

______________________________

______________________________

______________________________

**What is the purpose of the prism in the investigation?**

______________________________

______________________________

______________________________

## Record Your Data

**Draw a diagram of the setup showing the path of the light beam. Record the angles you measured on the diagram.**

## Draw Conclusions

You have learned that light travels in straight lines. How does the investigation support that statement? Use empirical evidence to support your answer.

How do the angles you measured in Step 6 compare?

## Analyze and Extend

1. Suppose the angle at which the light strikes the mirror is 50°. Infer the angle at which the light will reflect.

2. The speed of light changes as it enters and leaves a substance. Use empirical evidence from this investigation to explain how this was observed.

3. Why would a mirror be less useful to people if it scattered light?

4. What other questions would you like to explore about how light travels when it strikes a mirror or passes through a transparent medium such as water or glass.

# Unit 6 Review

Name ______________________

## Vocabulary Review

Use the terms in the box to complete the sentences.

| |
|---|
| light<br>opaque<br>reflection<br>refraction<br>translucent<br>volume |

TEKS 5.6C

1. Materials that do not let light pass through them are ______________________.

TEKS 5.6C

2. A form of energy that moves in waves and can travel through space is ______________________.

TEKS 5.6A

3. The loudness or softness of a sound is its ______________________.

TEKS 5.6C

4. The bending of light as it passes at an angle from one type of matter to another is called ______________________.

TEKS 5.6A, 5.6C

5. Materials, such as wax paper, that absorb some light and allow some light to pass through them are ______________________.

TEKS 5.6C

6. When light strikes a smooth, shiny surface, it bounces back in a process called ______________________.

## Science Concepts

Fill in the letter of the choice that best answers the question.

TEKS 5.6A

7. Which term best describes the form sound takes as it travels away from a drum?
   - (A) gas
   - (B) music
   - (C) waves
   - (D) particles

TEKS 5.6A

8. Which of the following uses light energy and can be found in binoculars, cameras, and eyeglasses?
   - (A) a lens
   - (B) a laser
   - (C) a prism
   - (D) a CD

TEKS 5.4A, 5.6C

9. Julio wants to know what happens when light strikes a prism. The diagram shows his investigation.

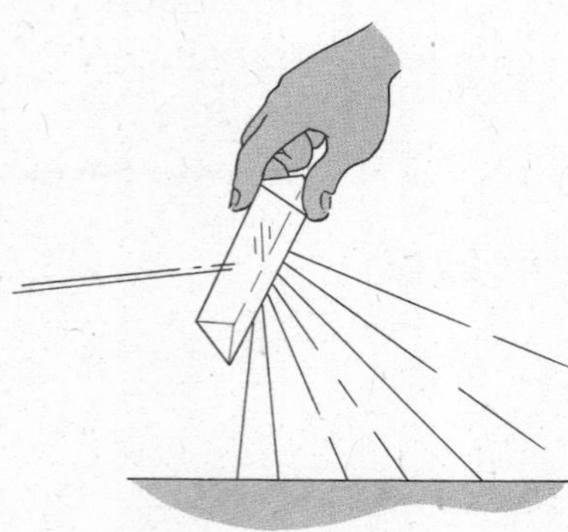

Which statement best describes what Julio observes?

Ⓐ a prism focusing light

Ⓑ a prism diffracting light

Ⓒ a prism reflecting light in straight lines

Ⓓ a prism refracting light into its component wavelengths

TEKS 5.3A, 5.6C

10. Kwan says that Julio's investigation proves that light doesn't travel in straight lines. Which statement best analyzes and interprets the diagram to evaluate Kwan's claim and produce an alternative explanation?

Ⓐ The prism causes the light to curve around it.

Ⓑ The prism reflects the light back to its source.

Ⓒ The light scatters in straight lines as it strikes the prism.

Ⓓ The light changes direction but always travels in straight lines.

TEKS 5.2D, 5.6A

11. People often use sounds to identify objects they can't see. What properties of sound help you identify a referee's whistle?

Ⓐ low frequency, high volume

Ⓑ high frequency, high volume

Ⓒ low frequency, low volume

Ⓓ high frequency, low volume

TEKS 5.2C, 5.6C

12. Which diagram shows what will happen to the light when Alain shines a flashlight at a mirror?

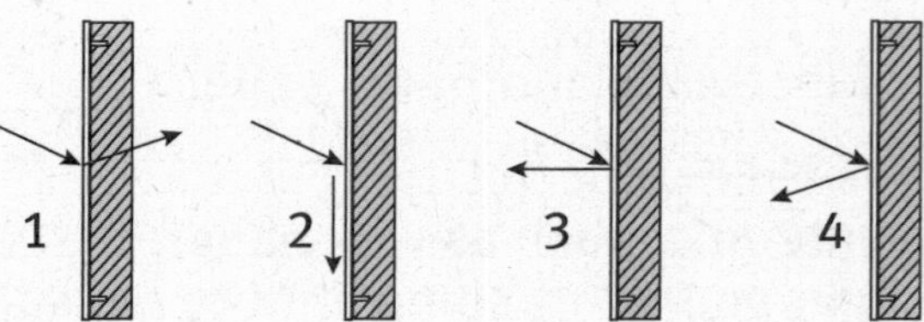


Ⓐ Diagram 1

Ⓑ Diagram 2

Ⓒ Diagram 3

Ⓓ Diagram 4

TEKS 5.6A, 5.6C

13. What happens to white light when it strikes a red shirt?

Ⓐ Red light is reflected and all other colors are absorbed.

Ⓑ Red light is absorbed and all other colors are reflected.

Ⓒ White light breaks into different wavelengths as it is reflected.

Ⓓ White light breaks into different wavelengths as it is absorbed.

Name ______________________________

TEKS 5.2D, 5.6A

**14.** Based on this diagram of the electromagnetic spectrum, which of the following statements is correct?

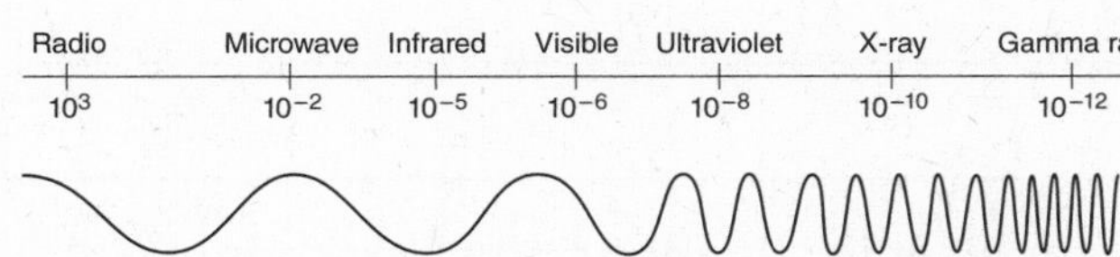


Ⓐ Radio waves have the highest frequency of all electromagnetic waves.

Ⓑ X-rays have a lower frequency than microwaves.

Ⓒ The frequency of visible light is greater than the frequency of radio waves.

Ⓓ As wavelength increases, frequency increases.

TEKS 5.2D, 5.6A

**15.** Giorgio connects the bottom of two cans with a string. Giorgio and a friend each take one of the cans and stand apart until the string is taut. Placing the can to his ear, Giorgio can hear what his friend whispers into his can. How is the string being used in this activity?

Ⓐ The string produces sound waves.

Ⓑ Sound waves move along the string.

Ⓒ Thermal energy is absorbed by the string.

Ⓓ Light waves travel along the string between the cans.

TEKS 5.6A

**16.** While swimming underwater in a pool, Hamid hears the honking of a truck's horn. What happened as the sound waves traveled from the horn to Hamid's ears?

Ⓐ The waves stopped as they reached the water.

Ⓑ The waves did not change speed as they passed from the air to the water.

Ⓒ The waves slowed down as they passed from the air to the water.

Ⓓ The waves sped up as they passed from the air to the water.

TEKS 5.2B, 5.6A

**17.** Beth wants to know more about rainbows. Which of the following is a question Beth might answer with an investigation?

Ⓐ Do all animals see rainbows?

Ⓑ What is the order of colors in a rainbow?

Ⓒ Why can't you reach the end of a rainbow?

Ⓓ How many rainbows appear in a year?

TEKS 5.2B, 5.4A

**18.** Which tools might you use to collect and record observations in an investigation on sound?

Ⓐ a microphone, a notebook, and a computer

Ⓑ test tubes, water, and a magnet

Ⓒ mirrors, prisms, and a notebook

Ⓓ a drum, a calculator, and a flashlight

## Apply Inquiry and Review the Big Idea

Write the answers to these questions.

TEKS 5.2B, 5.2F, 5.6C

19. Curt wants to know more about how the shape of a mirror affects the angle at which the mirror reflects light.

    a. What is a testable hypothesis that Curt might use for his investigation?

    b. What tools and equipment should Curt select for his investigation? What procedure will he use? What data will he collect? How will he decide if his hypothesis is correct?

TEKS 5.3A, 5.6A

20. In a movie, Hua saw a man put his ear on a railroad track and announce that a train was coming. No one else could see or hear the train. Based on what you have learned, how would you evaluate the man's claim?

TEKS 5.6A

21. The speed of sound in air at 20 °C is 343 m/s. Its speed in water at 20 °C is 1,483 m/s. How much longer would it take for sound in air to travel 10 km than in water? Round your answer to the nearest second.

UNIT 7

# Changes to Earth's Surface

**Big Idea**

Earth's surface is constantly changing. Fossils help us understand Earth's history.

TEKS 5.2A, 5.2B, 5.2C, 5.2D, 5.2F, 5.2G, 5.3A, 5.3C, 5.7A, 5.7B, 5.7D



## I Wonder Why

As a stream flows over dinosaur tracks, they change shape or disappear. Why do you think this happens? *Turn the page to find out.*

**Here's Why** The dinosaur tracks were made in soft mud that later hardened into rocks. Tiny bits of these rocks are broken down and carried away by the processes of weathering and erosion. Over time, these processes change the shapes of some tracks, completely erase others, and expose new tracks.

In this unit, you will explore the Big Idea, the Essential Questions, and the investigations on the Inquiry Flipchart.

Levels of Inquiry Key ■ DIRECTED ■ GUIDED ■ INDEPENDENT

**Big Idea** Earth's surface is constantly changing. Fossils help us understand Earth's history

## Essential Questions



Now I Get the Big Idea!

**Science Notebook**

Before you begin each lesson, be sure to write your thoughts about the Essential Question.

**TEKS** **5.7A** explore the processes that led to the formation of sedimentary rocks and fossil fuels **5.7B** recognize how landforms such as deltas, canyons, and sand dunes are the result of changes to Earth's surface by wind, water, and ice

Essential Question

# What Are Processes That Shape Earth's Surface?

## Engage Your Brain!

Find the answer to the following question in this lesson and record it here.

What natural processes can shape rock in such a curious way?

______________________

______________________

______________________

______________________

## Active Reading

### Lesson Vocabulary

List each term. As you learn about each one, makes notes in the Interactive Glossary.

______________________

______________________

______________________

______________________

### Visual Aids

A photo adds information to the text that appears on the page with it. Active readers pause their reading to review the photo and decide how the information in it adds to what is provided in the running text.



Inquiry Flipchart p. 37 — Gone with the Wind/*X* Marks the Landform

# Breaking It Down

Glance out your window. That landscape likely looked very different 10,000 years ago. What features are found on Earth's surface and what makes them change over time?

**Active Reading** As you read these two pages, circle clue words or phrases that signal a detail, such as an example or an added fact.

Tall mountains, deep canyons, and flat plains are all kinds of landforms. *Landforms* are features on Earth's surface. They are made and changed by natural processes, one of the most important of which is weathering. **Weathering** is the physical or chemical process that breaks down rock on or near Earth's surface. Weathering is often a slow process. In fact, it can take millions of years to weather an exposed rock layer.

Most rocks form in uniform, horizontal layers. The deep grooves and cracks in these rocks are indirect evidence of physical weathering.

These towering rock pillars and the huge sinkhole below were formed by chemical weathering. Weak acids in rainwater cause the rocks around the pillars and below the ground to weather.

There are two main kinds of weathering: physical weathering and chemical weathering. *Physical weathering* occurs when a mechanical process breaks down rocks. For example, you can physically weather a rock by hitting it with a hammer. *Chemical weathering* occurs when chemical reactions cause rocks to weaken and wear away. For instance, if you drop certain acids on some rocks, the rocks will dissolve and break down.

## Analyze and Interpret

Circle indirect (inferred) evidence of weathering on this rock. Construct a reasonable explanation for the rock's appearance using your inferred evidence.

_______________

_______________

_______________

_______________

_______________

# Agents of Weathering

Most rocks are as hard as . . . well, rocks! What can cause solid rocks to break apart?

**Active Reading** As you read these two pages, draw a line from each photo or diagram to the sentence in the text that describes it.

Mosses and other plants get nutrients from rocks by releasing substances that can chemically weather the rocks.

Agents of weathering include living things, water, wind, ice, and heat. Plant roots, for example, can give off chemicals that dissolve rocks over time. Roots also can grow in the cracks of rocks and break the rocks apart.

Water, too, contains substances that dissolve the bonds in the particles that make up rocks. Flowing water causes rocks to smack together and break apart. Wind causes weathering when it carries sand that blasts against rock. Ice weathers rocks when it repeatedly freezes and melts in the cracks of rocks. Heat can do the same thing when rocks are repeatedly warmed and cooled.

## Ice Wedging

Water enters the cracks in a rock. It freezes and expands, pushing against the cracks. The cracks widen. → The water thaws and moves deeper into the cracks of the rock. → As this cycle repeats again and again, the rock eventually breaks.

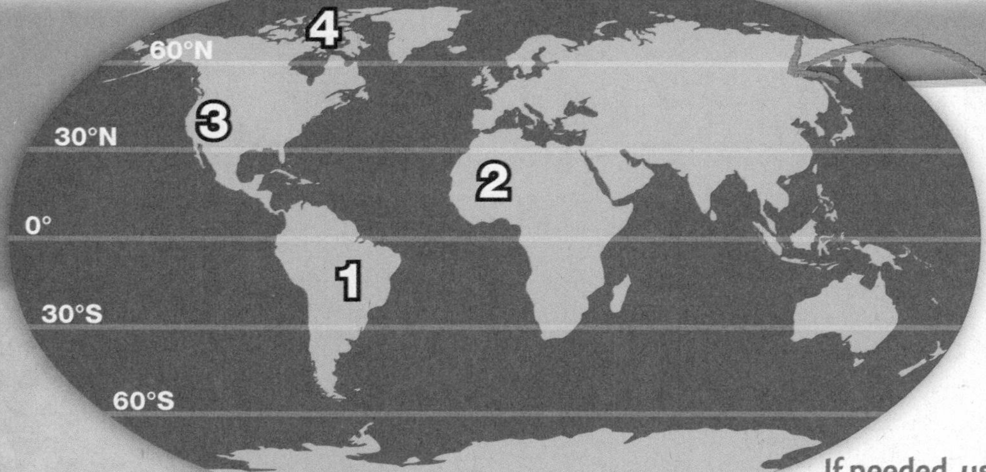


## Map It!

Examine information from these pages and this map to draw an inference about the rate of weathering in each of the numbered regions. If needed, use reference materials to identify the climate of each region.

_______________

_______________

_______________

Different factors affect how quickly weathering takes place. For example, climate has a big effect on rates of weathering. Places that are wet and hot have high rates of weathering because water and heat increase chemical reactions. In contrast, places that are cold or dry have lower rates of weathering. Weathering by ice wedging occurs in wet places that experience freezing temperatures. Other factors that influence weathering are:

- **Surface area** Weathering happens on the surfaces of landforms. Rocks with a lot of exposed surface have higher rates of weathering than rocks with less exposed surface.
- **Type of rock** Hard rocks, such as granite, are more resistant to weathering than softer rocks, such as limestone. As softer rocks wear away, hard rocks become the highest elevation points in an area.
- **Slope** Steep hills tend to have higher rates of weathering than gentle hills.
- **Time** The longer a landform has been exposed to agents of weathering, the higher its rate of weathering.

Flowing water causes physical weathering as rocks bounce and tumble along the bottom of a riverbed.

# Etch a Shape on Earth

You don't see big piles of broken rock everywhere you look. What happens to broken rock after it is weathered?

**Active Reading** As you read these two pages, find and underline three facts about erosion.

Some of the same agents that cause weathering also move materials from place to place. This process is called **erosion.** The agents of erosion include water, wind, ice, and gravity. Weathering and erosion are related processes. For example, a flowing river bangs rocks together, producing bits of weathered material called *sediment*. At the same time, the sediments are carried away to a new place, or eroded, by the energy of the moving water.

► Identify the landform and the agent of erosion in each photo.

Gravity is the force that pulls all things toward Earth's center. Gravity can cause rock materials on hillsides to move quickly downward. The result is a landslide, mudslide, or rockslide.

_______________

_______________

Glaciers can weather and erode large amounts of rock. Deep, smooth grooves in solid rock are often evidence of erosion by glacier.

______________________________

______________________________

Ocean waves also can cause weathering and erosion. As waves beat against a rocky shore, they turn rock into sediment, which is then carried away. Storm waves can cause severe beach erosion.

*Glaciers*, or huge sheets of slow-moving ice, are another agent of erosion. As a glacier moves forward, it can erode and flatten mountains, carving out a U-shaped valley.

Wind can blow sand and dry soil great distances. When the conditions are right, windblown sand can produce ridges, or hills of sand, called *sand dunes*. Plants can reduce soil erosion. Their roots draw ground moisture, which helps hold soil together.

A bit of breeze is all it takes to lift and move dry soil and sand. Shifting wind speed and direction constantly change the shape and location of sand dunes.

______________________________

______________________________

## Predict the Canyon's Future

A river is weathering and eroding this *canyon*, or deep valley with steep sides. Draw on the diagram to show what the canyon will look like thousands of years in the future.

# Drop It Now!

How long can an agent of erosion carry its load of sediments? When and why does it drop the sediments? Read on to find out.

**Active Reading** As you read these two pages, circle lesson vocabulary each time it is used.

Weathering and erosion work together to produce and shape landforms. But a third process, called *deposition,* works along with these two. **Deposition** occurs when an agent of erosion drops, or deposits, its load of sediment in a new place. Deposition can occur for different reasons. Wind and running water deposit the sediment they carry when their currents lose energy. Glaciers can melt and deposit their load of rocks and soil. The sediment may be dropped in front of, behind, or alongside the glacier in piles called *moraines.*

A moraine is a hill or ridge that forms when sediments are deposited by a glacier. The sediments may be a mixture of boulders, rocks, gravel, soil, and sand.

▶ Circle the moraine.

Sand grains in dunes can range in size from 0.2 mm to 1 mm. They are often well rounded and made of a single kind of material.

▶ Name the agent of deposition.

___

# Do the Math!

## Calculate Dune Movement

Collect and analyze information using a calculator. Wind erosion and deposition cause a sand dune to move at a rate of 1.7 m per month. How far does the dune move in one and a half years? Show your work.

___

___

The energy an agent of erosion has affects the distance sediment is eroded before being deposited. A fast-moving river, for example, can deposit sediment farther from its source than a slow-moving river. In general, large sediments, such as gravel or boulders, are deposited before smaller sediments, such as sand or silt.

The deposition of sediment creates different kinds of landforms on Earth's surface. For example, a river deposits its load of sediment at its mouth, or the place where it flows into the sea. The deposition of this sediment forms a *delta*, or fan-shaped feature, at the mouth of the river.

The Mississippi River slows down as it enters the Gulf of Mexico. The river loses energy and drops its load of sediment, forming a fan-shaped delta.

▶ Circle the agent of deposition.

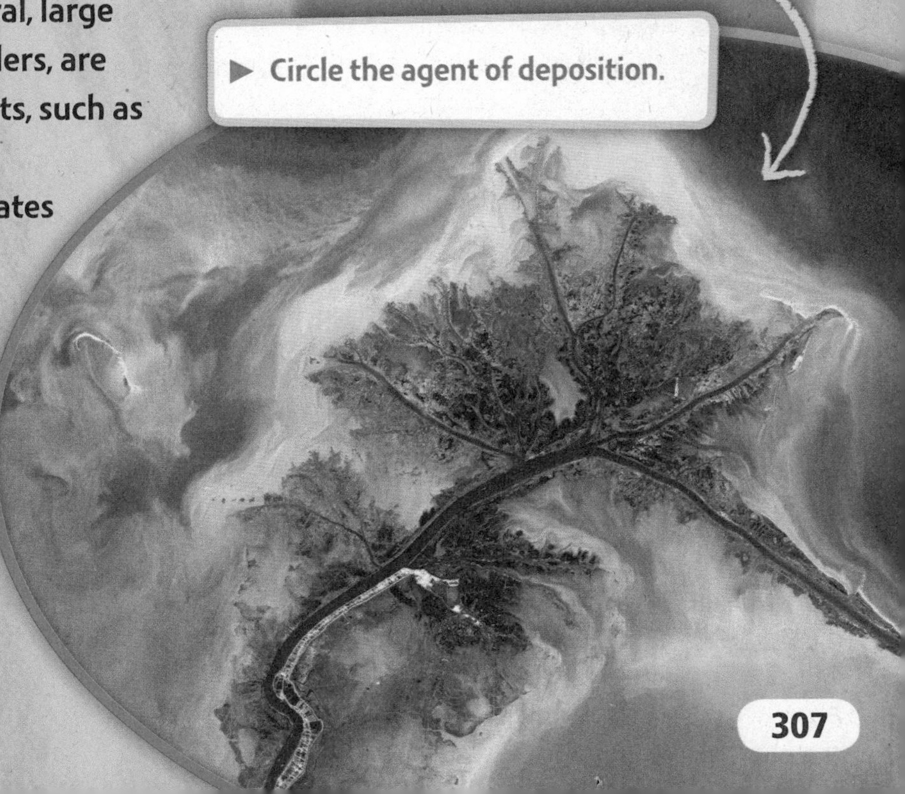

# Warning: Rock Construction

Weathering, erosion, and deposition break down, transport, and deposit rocks. But they also play a role in forming rocks.

**Active Reading** As you read these two pages, write numbers next to the appropriate sentences to show the order of events in the formation of sedimentary rock.

Weathering, erosion, and deposition lead to the formation of one of the three main kinds of rock: sedimentary rock. As you might guess from its name, **sedimentary rock** is made of sediment. These rocks can form when existing rock is weathered, eroded, and deposited in layers on land or underwater.

Pressure from overlying layers of sediment compacts, or squeezes together, the bottom layers. Substances called minerals act like glue, helping to cement the squeezed sediment into hard rock. Sedimentary rocks that form from compaction and cementation include shale and sandstone.

Layers of sediment were deposited one atop the other. Over time, the sediments in each layer were compacted and cemented together to form sedimentary rock.

Weathered and eroded rock form layers of sediment when deposited on land or underwater.

Pressure from overlying layers compresses the bottom layers into sedimentary rock.

Sometimes, the remains of dead plants and animals are part of the layered material that becomes sedimentary rock. The remains may form *fossils*, or traces of ancient organisms, in the rock. Sedimentary rocks that form from once-living things include coquina and coal.

Sedimentary rocks can also form when a body of water dries up and leaves behind deposits of dissolved minerals. These kinds of sedimentary rocks include rock salt and gypsum.

► A layer of sedimentary rock is exposed to wind, water, and extreme temperatures. What might eventually happen to the sedimentary rock?

______________________________

______________________________

______________________________

______________________________

Sedimentary rocks are made of different-sized sediment. Coquina is made mainly of pieces of shells that have been cemented together. Sandstone is made of bits of rock the size of salt crystals. Shale is made of tiny particles of clay.

shale

coquina

sandstone

Why It Matters

# Build It to Last

Erosion and flooding can cause the foundation of a house and roads to collapse.

Weathering, erosion, and deposition change landforms on Earth's surface. And they can make changes to human-made structures, too. What can be done about this?

Waterfront homes are lovely places to live. But flooding can sometimes erode the land. As shown above, a home that once stood perched aboveground now teeters on the edge of a raging flood!

As you can see, weathering and erosion influence where people can build homes, roads, and other structures. In areas that get a lot of floods or beach erosion, people often build their houses on stilts. The water rushes under the house, leaving the foundation of the house untouched.

On steep hillsides, people can plant vegetation to slow rates of weathering and erosion. They can also build terraces, or steps, into the hillside to slow the downward movement of sediments. The steps can be made of stones or logs. Concrete walls are expensive, but they, too, stop sediment from sliding downhill.

Building homes on stilts is one way to reduce problems associated with flooding and beach erosion.

▶ Suppose you want to build a house on the edge of a hill that overlooks a deep valley. What measures could you take to be sure your home will not have problems due to weathering and erosion?

_______________________________

_______________________________

_______________________________

Floods and landslides can wash away roads. Concrete retaining walls that reduce weathering and erosion can help solve this problem.

When you're done, use the answer key to check and revise your work.

**Fill in the missing words about weathering, erosion, and deposition.**

1. _______________ is the process that breaks down rock on or near Earth's surface.
2. _______________ weathering occurs when rocks are mechanically broken down.
3. _______________ weathering occurs when chemical reactions cause rocks to weaken and wear away. The agents of weathering include living things, wind, water, 4. _______________, and heat. Factors that influence rates of weathering include 5. _______________, surface area, type of rock, slope, and time. Erosion is the process that moves 6. _______________ from place to place. Agents of erosion include water, wind, ice, and 7. _______________. These agents drop their load of sediment in a process called 8. _______________. Landforms such as 9. _______________, 10. _______________, and moraines are made by deposition.

## Summarize

**Use the information in the summary to complete the graphic organizer.**

Sedimentary rocks are one of the three main kinds of rock found on Earth. They are formed by the processes of weathering, erosion, and deposition.

First: A rock is broken into smaller pieces by weathering.

↓

11. Then: _______________

↓

12. Next: _______________

↓

13. Last: _______________

Answer Key: 1. Weathering 2. Physical 3. Chemical 4. ice 5. climate 6. sediment 7. gravity 8. deposition 9. sand dunes or deltas 10. sand dunes or deltas 11. Erosion transports the sediment to a new location. The sediment is deposited on land or underwater. 12. Overlying layers of sediment are deposited and press down on the bottom layers. 13. Substances called minerals act like glue, helping to cement the squeezed sediment into hard rock.

Name ______________________

## Word Play

1 **Use the words from the lesson to complete each sentence.**

1. Plant roots that grow in the cracks of rocks can cause physical __ __ __ __ __ __ __ __ __ __.
2. Weathering, erosion, and deposition can lead to the formation of __ __ __ __ __ __ __ __ __ __ __ rock.
3. Wind __ __ __ __ __ __ __ on a farm can carry soil to a new place.
4. A moraine is associated with a slow-moving sheet of ice called a __ __ __ __ __ __ __.
5. When wind drops its load of sand, it can form a hill called a __ __ __ __ __ __ __ __ __ __.
6. A __ __ __ __ __ is a fan-shaped feature at the mouth of a river.
7. A deep, steep-sided valley formed by weathering and erosion is called a __ __ __ __ __ __.
8. Plants that get nutrients from rocks give off chemicals that can cause __ __ __ __ __ __ __ __ __ weathering.

**Figure out how to place the answers in the boxes below so that the letters in the red boxes answer the riddle.**

**Riddle: What do you make when you hit a rock with a hammer?**

| | | | | | | | | | | | |
|---|---|---|---|---|---|---|---|---|---|---|---|
| | | | | | | | d | d | | | |
| | | | h | | m | | | | | | |
| | | | | | | | t | | | | |
| | | | c | | e | | | | | | |
| | e | d | | | e | | t | | | | |
| | | | | | | | s | | | | |
| | | | | | | | n | | | | |
| | | | a | | | e | r | | | | |

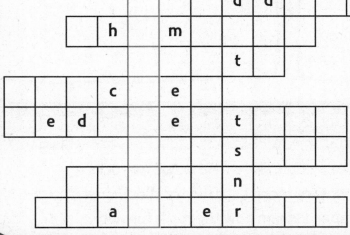

# Apply Concepts

2 Circle the rock layer that is most resistant to weathering. Explain your reasoning.

3 Draw and describe examples of landforms formed by deposition from wind, water, or ice.

4 In the boxes below, draw a two-step diagram showing how the deposition of sediment can form sedimentary rock.

Make a sedimentary rock collection. Use a field guide for rocks to identify and gather sedimentary rocks. Label your collection and share it with a family member. Explain how the rocks formed.

Inquiry Flipchart page 38

**TEKS** **5.2A** describe...simple experimental investigations testing one variable **5.2B**...select and use appropriate equipment and technology. **5.3A**...analyze, evaluate...scientific explanations by using empirical evidence, logical reasoning... **5.3C** draw or develop a model that represents how something works... **5.7B** recognize how landforms...are the result of changes to Earth's surface by...water...

Name ______________________________

Essential Question

# How Does Water Change Earth's Surface?

## Set a Purpose

**What will you learn from this activity?**

______________________________

______________________________

______________________________

## Think About the Procedure

**1. What do the materials in the activity represent?**

______________________________

______________________________

______________________________

**2. Why do you position the tray to produce a slope?**

______________________________

______________________________

______________________________

## Record Your Data

**Use the table below to record your observations. Draw or describe your model's appearance before and after you pour the water.**

| | Top view | Front view | Side view |
|---|---|---|---|
| Before water | | | |
| After water | | | |

## Draw Conclusions

What happened to the sugar under the clay?

Describe how your model demonstrates that water can change Earth's surface to produce landforms.

## Analyze and Extend

1. What would you expect to happen in places with steeper slopes where water moves downhill faster?

2. What would you expect to happen to rock in places where it rains often compared to places that receive very little rain?

3. Use empirical evidence and logical reasoning to analyze and evaluate the following scientific explanation: Some rocks weather more easily than others.

4. REVIEW What additional factors, or variables, could affect the rate of weathering?

5. REVIEW

A. Plan a simple experimental investigation to test the effect of one of the variables you listed.

B. Identify the equipment and technology you would select and how you would use them to complete the investigation.

TEKS 5.3C draw or develop a model that represents how something works or looks that cannot be seen... 5.7A explore the processes that led to the formation of sedimentary rocks and fossil fuels 5.7D identify fossils as evidence of past living organisms and the nature of the environments at the time using models

Essential Question

# What Are Fossils?

**Find the answer to the following question in this lesson and record it here.**

These animals no longer live on Earth. What can scientists learn about Earth's history by studying these animals?

______________________________

______________________________

______________________________

______________________________

## Active Reading

### Lesson Vocabulary

List the terms. As you learn about each one, make notes in the Interactive Glossary.

______________________________

______________________________

______________________________

______________________________

### Main Ideas

The main idea of a paragraph is the most important idea. The main idea may be stated in the first sentence, or it may be stated elsewhere. Active readers look for main ideas by asking themselves, What is this section mostly about?



Inquiry Flipchart p. 39 — What Made it/All that Came From OIL

Insects can get trapped in tree sap. Hardened sap is called amber. Insect parts and even whole insects are often preserved in amber.

Sometimes, whole organisms can be preserved as fossils. This baby mammoth was frozen in ice. Its soft tissues were preserved along with its bones and teeth.

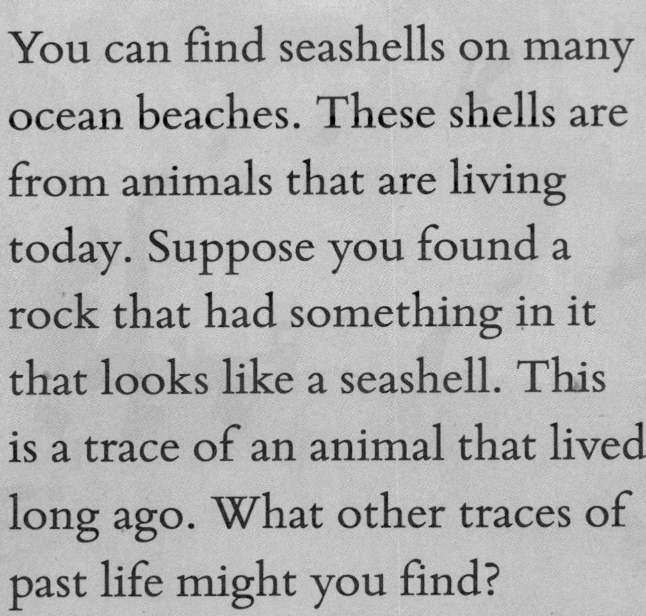

# Traces of the Past

You can find seashells on many ocean beaches. These shells are from animals that are living today. Suppose you found a rock that had something in it that looks like a seashell. This is a trace of an animal that lived long ago. What other traces of past life might you find?

**Active Reading** As you read, underline each type of fossil discussed.

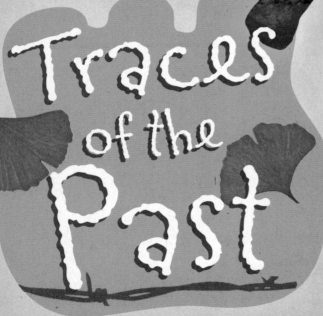

All living things contain the element carbon. Some plant tissues get preserved as *carbon films* in rock.

Footprints are examples of trace fossils. These features show that an animal was there, even though none of its parts were preserved.

The preserved remains or traces of a living thing is called a **fossil**. Fossils are evidence of past living organisms. They can be made of an organism's hard parts or its soft parts. Hard parts include bones, teeth, and shells. Soft parts are tissues such as skin and organs. Because bacteria quickly break down soft tissue, soft parts are rare as fossils. Soft-part fossils can be original tissue if it has been frozen or dried out as in a mummy. They can also be preserved as an impression in a rock.

Most fossils are found in sedimentary rock. One common way that fossils form is shown at right. Another way fossils form occurs as minerals, such as quartz, replace the shell or plant material that made up the organism. This is how *petrified* wood forms. Sometimes, the replacement is so perfect that even the bark and wood grain are visible.

These mold and cast fossils were made when a leaf was pressed into soft mud, leaving a hollow space called a **mold**. A **cast** can form if the mold is later filled with mud that hardens.

## What Might You Leave Behind?

Draw a set of footprints or other trace that you might leave. Explain what part of your body would make the trace and what your trace fossil would tell future scientists.

_______________________________________________

_______________________________________________

## Fossil Formation

1. An animal dies and settles on the bottom of a body of water.

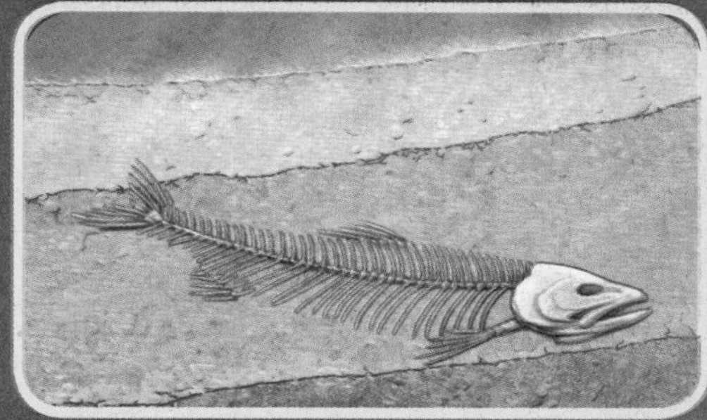

2. Sediment buries the animal. Over time, the soft parts of the animal decay.

3. Hard parts are preserved in sediment as a fossil.

The plants and animals shown on these pages are fossils. Scientists study many types of fossils to help them learn about ancient life on Earth.

## How Coal Forms

1. Plants die and settle to the bottom of a body of water. They are buried by sediment.

2. The temperature and pressure rise. Much of the water in the remains is squeezed out. The remains change into peat. Peat doesn't give off a lot of heat. It produces a lot of smoke when it burns.

3. Peat continues to be compressed and heated. Over time, all of the water is gone. Coal forms. It is hard and made of pure carbon. Coal produces a lot of heat and little smoke.

# Fossils That Burn

Not all organisms are fossilized in rock. What else may happen to organisms when they die? Let's explore the processes that led to the formation of fossil fuels.

**Active Reading** As you read these pages, draw two lines under the main idea of each paragraph.

Coal forms from dead plants. When plants die, they sometimes end up at the bottom of a lake or pond. Sediment buries the plants. Over many years, the heavy layers of sediment cause the temperature and pressure underground to rise. This causes the plant material to change into coal. The higher the temperature and pressure, the better the type of coal that forms. Because the coal we use today comes from ancient plants, it is a fossil fuel. A **fossil fuel** is an energy-rich resource formed from the buried remains of once-living organisms. Coal formation is continuing in peat bogs found around the world.

# How Oil and Natural Gas Form

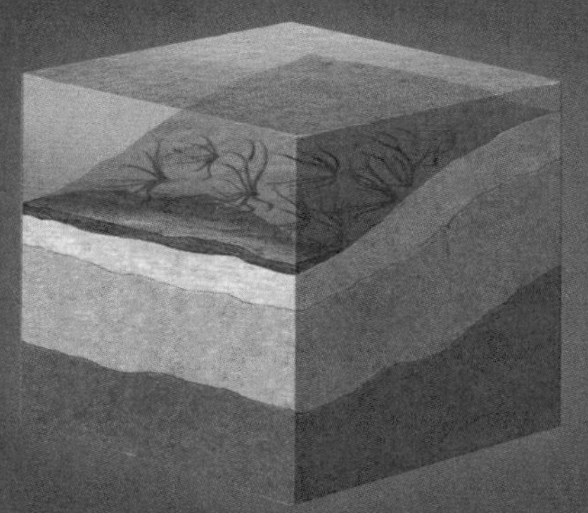

1. Many tiny sea organisms die and settle to the bottom of the ocean where they are buried by sediment.

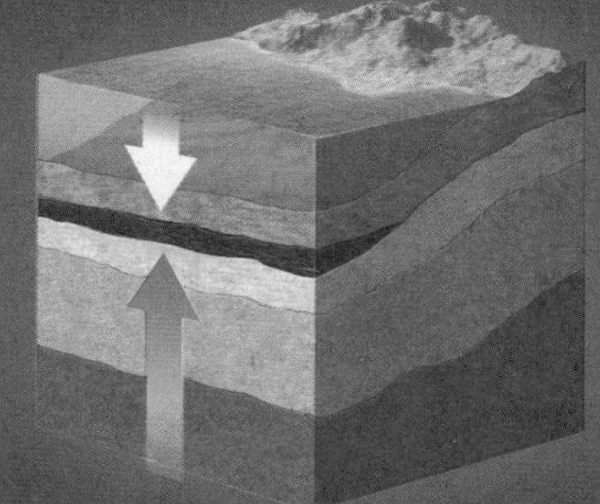

2. Over time, the weight of both the sediment and the water above it cause the temperature and pressure to rise.

3. Eventually, all that's left of the organisms is hydrogen and carbon. Oil and natural gas form from these elements.

Tiny diatoms are organisms that help form oil and natural gas. Imagine how many millions of them were needed to produce the fossil fuels we use today!

Oil and natural gas take millions of years to form. So the organisms that made the fuels we are using today are very old. Just like coal, oil and natural gas are fossil fuels. Today, large amounts of oil and natural gas are trapped beneath layers of rock deep below Earth's surface. Pumps remove the oil and natural gas from the ground.

## Do the Math!

### Use a Data Table

| Products Made from a Barrel of Crude Oil (Liters) | |
|---|---|
| Diesel Fuel | 35 L |
| Jet Fuel | 15 L |
| Other Products | 40 L |
| Gasoline | 70 L |

Oil that is pumped from the ground is called crude. Crude oil is refined to make many different products, such as gasoline for cars and fuel for jets.

About how many total liters are refined from a barrel of crude oil?

______________________________

How much crude oil remains after gasoline is refined from the oil?

______________________________

Why It Matters

# What Fossils Tell Us

Jawless fish

Armored fish

Fossils can tell us a lot about what life on Earth was like in the past.

Scientists who study fossils are called *paleontologists*. They study fossils to learn what life on Earth was like long ago. Fossils show that some types of plants and animals have changed a lot. Other plants and animals have hardly changed at all.

The woolly mammoth is related to modern elephants. It lived during the Ice Age when the climate was very cold. Today's elephants live mostly in warm climates.

Modern fish

Fish have changed a lot over time. The first fish had no jaws. Over time, fish developed jaws and became larger. Some fish developed heavy armor plates that covered their bodies. Fish today have jaws but no armor.

The ginkgo tree has been around for at least 420 million years. The leaves of today's ginkgos look very similar to those that grew long ago. Organisms that look as if they have not changed much over time are sometimes called living fossils.

## Changes Over Time

How might an animal or plant change over time? Draw a plant or animal that lives on Earth today. Then draw how its descendents might look 1 million years from now. Tell how your organism has changed.

______________________________

______________________________

When you're done, use the answer key to check and revise your work.

**Complete the outline below to summarize the lesson.**

## Summarize

I. Traces of the Past

A. Fossils are evidence of past living organisms.

B. One Way Fossils Form

1. Organisms die and settle on the bottom of a lake or ocean.
2. ______________________________.
3. ______________________________.

C. Kinds of Fossils

1. preserved in amber or ice
2. ______________________________
3. carbon film or trace fossil

II. Fossils That Burn

A. Fossil fuels are fuels that come from the decay and change of ancient organisms.

**B. How Coal Forms**

1. Plants' remains settle to the bottom of a lake or pond and are buried.
2. ______________________ drive off water and change the remains into peat.
3. More compression and heat results in ______________________.

C. How Oil and Natural Gas Form

1. Tiny ocean organisms die and settle to the bottom and are buried.
2. The weight of overlying sediment and water causes ______________________.
3. ______________________ form from the hydrogen and carbon that remain.

III. What Fossils Tell Us

A. Scientists called paleontologists study fossils.

B. How life has changed on Earth

Answer Key: I.B.2. Sediment buries the animal. I.B.3. Soft parts decay; hard parts are preserved. I.C.2. mold and cast fossils II.B.2. Temperature and pressure II.B.3. very hard coal made of pure carbon. II.C.2. pressure to rise. II.C.3. Oil and natural gas

Lesson 3

Name ______________________

## Word Play

**1** Read the summary statements below. Each statement is incorrect. Change the part of the statement in blue to make it correct. Use the word bank if you need help.

| carbon film | fossil* | fossil fuels* | mold* |
|---|---|---|---|
| mud | paleontologist | petrified wood | trace fossil |

* Key Lesson Vocabulary

1. A carbon film can be footprints preserved in rock. ______________________
2. A cast forms when a shell leaves its shape in the mud. ______________________
3. A mummy is a scientist who studies fossils. ______________________
4. Coal, oil, and gas are trace fossils. ______________________
5. The preserved remains or traces of a once-living organism is a mold. ______________________
6. A fossil leaf that is made only of carbon preserved between two rock layers is called a fossil fuel. ______________________
7. A cast forms when minerals fills a mold and hardens. ______________________
8. A paleontologist forms when minerals replace the plant material in a piece of wood. ______________________

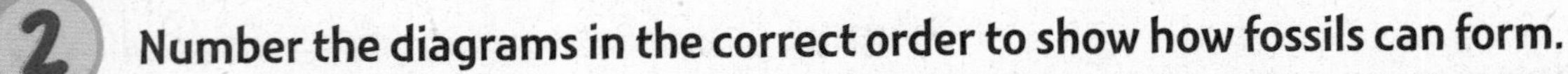

# Apply Concepts

2 Number the diagrams in the correct order to show how fossils can form.

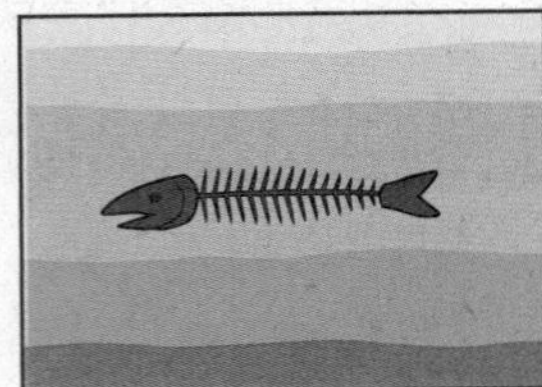
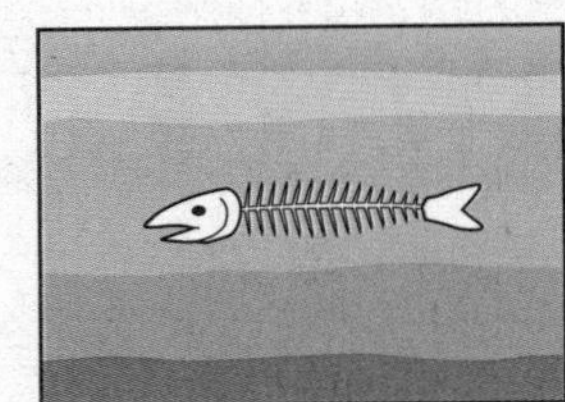

_____ _____ _____

3 Which would have a better chance of becoming a fossil: a fish that dies and settles to the ocean floor or a mouse that dies on the ground in a forest? Explain your answer.

_______________

_______________

4 What can you conclude about a time in Earth's past when only marine fossils formed?

_______________

_______________

5 Choose one type of fossil. Draw a three-panel comic strip to show how the fossil forms. Write a description and labels for each picture to show how the fossil forms.

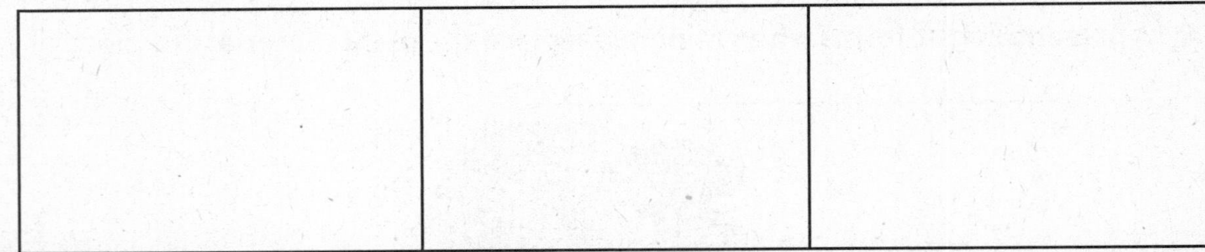

Make one kind of fossil using a grape. Set up an area where you can leave the grape sitting undisturbed for several days. Examine the grape each day and note any changes. When would you consider the grape a fossil?

S.T.E.M.

Engineering & Technology

# Tools That Rock

Geologists study Earth materials and often work outdoors. They use some tools you are probably familiar with, but they might use them in unexpected ways.

Hand-held GPS device

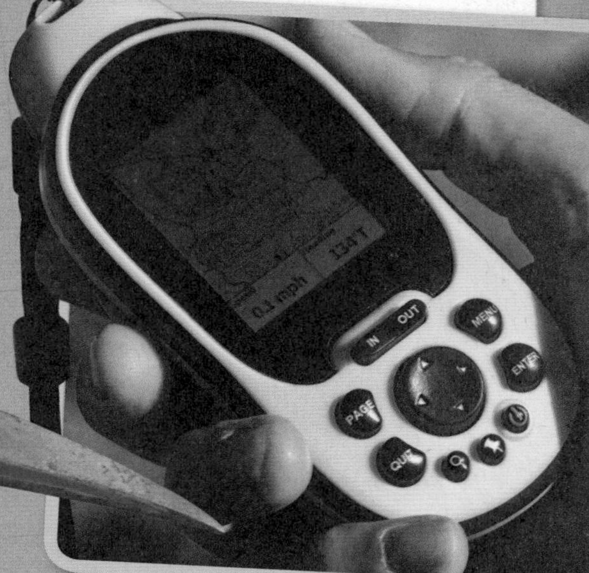

Geologists use physical tools such as this rock hammer to collect rock samples. They also use electronic technology, such as GPS for mapping and computers for recording and processing data.

## Critical Thinking

Name three tools a geologist uses that are not shown here. Describe what each tool is used for.

______________________________

______________________________

______________________________

continued

After collecting rocks, a geologist uses different tools to identify the samples.

How can a geologist use each of these tools below to identify a rock sample? Do research to find out, and write your explanations below.

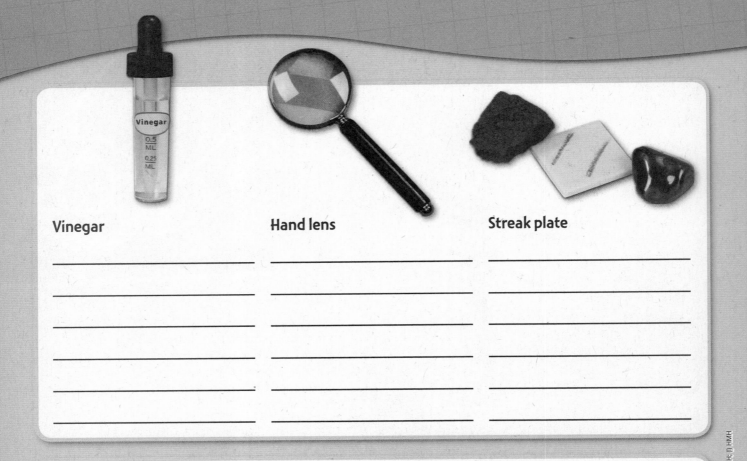

Vinegar

Hand lens

Streak plate

One new technology geologists use is GPS. First find out what GPS stands for. Then research how geologists use GPS, and write about why they find it useful.

## Build On It!

Rise to the engineering design challenge—complete **Improvise It: Separating By Size** in the Inquiry Flipchart.

TEKS **5.3C** draw or develop a model that represents how something works or looks that cannot be seen such as how a soda dispensing machine works **5.7D** identify fossils as evidence of past living organisms and the nature of the environments at the time using models

Lesson 4

Essential Question

# What Was Ancient Earth Like?

## Engage Your Brain!

Find the answer to the following question in this lesson and write it here.

This scene shows an environment on Earth millions of years ago. How are scientists able to make inferences about what Earth looked like long ago?

_______________

_______________

_______________

_______________

_______________

## Active Reading

### Lesson Vocabulary

List each term. As you learn about each one, make notes in the Interactive Glossary.

_______________

_______________

_______________

_______________

### Main Ideas and Details

In this lesson, you will read about Earth's ancient environments. Detail sentences throughout the lesson will provide information about this topic. The information may be examples, features, characteristics, or facts. Active readers stay focused on the topic when they ask, What fact or information does this sentence add to the topic?

# How Rocks and Fossils Tell a Story

Sedimentary rock forms in layers. Many sedimentary rocks contain fossils. How can you tell the age of these layers and of the fossils within them?

**Active Reading** Underline the sentences on this page that provide details about relative age.

You can learn about an area's history by studying its rocks and fossils. For example, you can tell how old the rock is compared to other rocks. You can also tell how living things and environments changed in that area over time. If you study rocks in different places, you can tell about large changes to Earth's surface and to life on Earth.

Imagine making a stack of newspapers in the order they were printed. When you look at the stack, you'll find the oldest paper on the bottom and the newest on the top. This models how rock layers form. The oldest rock layers are at the bottom and the youngest rock layers are at the top. The *relative age* of a layer of rock is the age of that layer when you compare it to other layers—older, younger, or the same.

The rock layers of the Grand Canyon formed at different times in Earth's history and under different conditions.

# Rock Layers of the Grand Canyon

Fossils form when sediment buries dead organisms. As a result, fossils are often found in sedimentary rocks. Scientists use fossils they find in rocks to help figure out the relative age of rock layers.

The *fossil record* is made up of all the fossils in Earth's rock layers. Fossils show how life on Earth has changed over time. So the *fossil record* contains information about Earth's history and the history of life on Earth.

Over time, movement of Earth's crust can cause layers of rock to become tilted. These movements can also lift rocks that were formed in the ocean to new positions high above sea level. The rock layers of the Grand Canyon were tilted and lifted millions of years ago.

The fossils in this layer of rock show that they were formed in an ocean.

This layer of rock is older than the layers above it, but younger than the layers below. It shows a fossil imprint, or mold, of a plant.

Fossils like these are found in another layer of rock also formed in the ocean.

This layer of rock is one of the lower layers of the canyon, and is older than all of the rocks above. It contains fossils of trilobites, small animals like horseshoe crabs, that lived in ancient seas.

## Relative Age

Suppose you find a fossil that looks like the second one, from the top, shown on this page. What can you say about its relative age?

_______________________________

_______________________________

_______________________________

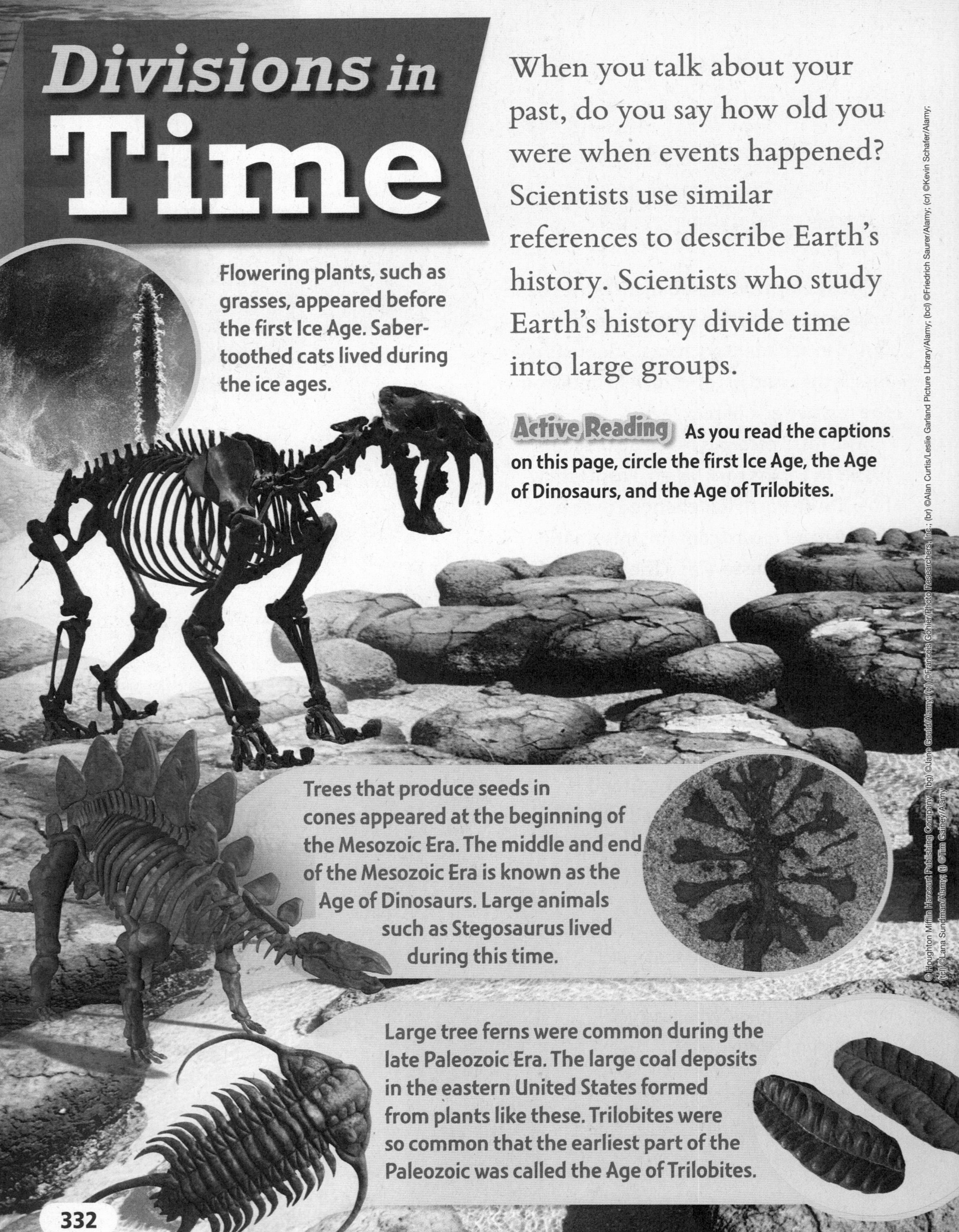

# Divisions in Time

When you talk about your past, do you say how old you were when events happened? Scientists use similar references to describe Earth's history. Scientists who study Earth's history divide time into large groups.

**Active Reading** **As you read the captions on this page, circle the first Ice Age, the Age of Dinosaurs, and the Age of Trilobites.**

**Flowering plants, such as grasses, appeared before the first Ice Age. Saber-toothed cats lived during the ice ages.**

**Trees that produce seeds in cones appeared at the beginning of the Mesozoic Era. The middle and end of the Mesozoic Era is known as the Age of Dinosaurs. Large animals such as Stegosaurus lived during this time.**

**Large tree ferns were common during the late Paleozoic Era. The large coal deposits in the eastern United States formed from plants like these. Trilobites were so common that the earliest part of the Paleozoic was called the Age of Trilobites.**

All the rocks on Earth are a record of Earth's long history. Scientists developed the *geologic time scale* to divide Earth's history into manageable units. The fossils each unit contains define it.

Some fossils are more help than others. **Index fossils** help to identify a very short period of Earth's history. Index fossils must meet four requirements.

1. The organisms from which they formed lived during a short period of Earth's history.
2. The organisms must have had large populations so that many fossils formed.
3. The fossils must be widespread.
4. The fossils must be easily recognized.

Pterosaurs lived during the Mesozoic. These animals were not dinosaurs. They were flying reptiles. The largest pterosaur had a wingspan of at least 12 m (39 ft)!

## Do the Math!

### Read the Geologic Time Scale

**Geologic Time Scale**

| million years ago (mya) | Era | Period | |
|---|---|---|---|
| Cenozoic Era 65 mya–present | | | Age of Mammals |
| 146 | Mesozoic Era | Cretaceous | Age of Dinosaurs |
| 200 | | Jurassic | |
| 251 | | Triassic | |
| 299 | Paleozoic Era | Permian | Age of Fishes |
| 359 | | Carboniferous | |
| 416 | | Devonian | |
| 444 | | Silurian | |
| 488 | | Ordovician | |
| 542 | | Cambrian | |
| Precambrian time 4,600–542 mya | | | 1st life on Earth [stromatolites] |

Use the geologic time scale to answer the questions.

Which time interval was the longest?

______________________

Which time is the shortest?

______________________

How many years did each of the three eras last?

______________________

______________________

______________________

How long did Precambrian time last?

______________________

# BIG *Changes on Earth*

Fossils tell about how life on Earth has changed over time. They also can give clues to how Earth's continents have changed.

***Mesosaurus*** **fossils are found in South America, Africa, Antarctica, Australia, and India.**

**Active Reading** As you read these pages, underline details that provide evidence for continental drift.

Fossils can tell us about the relative ages of rocks. From fossils we can learn about changes in life through the divisions of geologic time. Fossils can also provide evidence about other larger changes to Earth's surface. Using fossils, you can identify areas of Earth that are now in different places than they once were.

Scientists have found the same type of fossil on both sides of the Atlantic Ocean. They are fossils of a small lizard-like reptile called *Mesosaurus* that lived in fresh water. At first, scientists thought that *Mesosaurus* swam from one side of the ocean to the other. But *Mesosaurus* was too small to have been able to swim across the salty Atlantic!

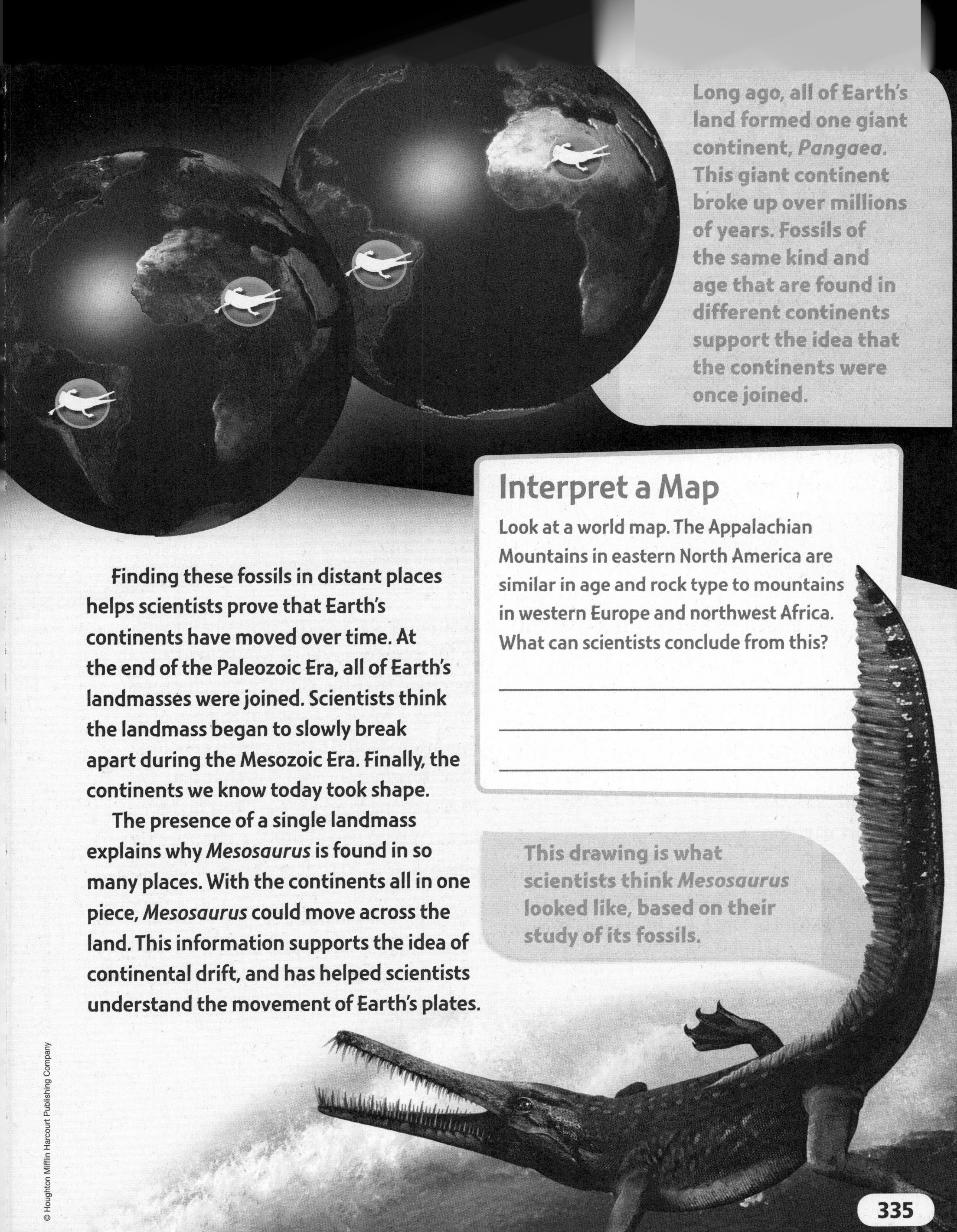

Long ago, all of Earth's land formed one giant continent, *Pangaea*. This giant continent broke up over millions of years. Fossils of the same kind and age that are found in different continents support the idea that the continents were once joined.

## Interpret a Map

Look at a world map. The Appalachian Mountains in eastern North America are similar in age and rock type to mountains in western Europe and northwest Africa. What can scientists conclude from this?

_______________________________________________

_______________________________________________

_______________________________________________

Finding these fossils in distant places helps scientists prove that Earth's continents have moved over time. At the end of the Paleozoic Era, all of Earth's landmasses were joined. Scientists think the landmass began to slowly break apart during the Mesozoic Era. Finally, the continents we know today took shape.

The presence of a single landmass explains why *Mesosaurus* is found in so many places. With the continents all in one piece, *Mesosaurus* could move across the land. This information supports the idea of continental drift, and has helped scientists understand the movement of Earth's plates.

This drawing is what scientists think *Mesosaurus* looked like, based on their study of its fossils.

# Changing *Environments*

Use this map to help you locate California and Indiana.

The La Brea Tar Pits 40,000 years ago

You can use fossils to tell how old a rock layer is and how a landmass might have moved. What else can you learn from fossils? Fossils provide clues about changing environments, too.

**Active Reading** As you read these pages, turn each heading into a question in your mind, and underline sentences that answer it.

Rancho La Brea today

Finding fossils of trees in the middle of some grasslands would lead you to conclude that the climate has changed. Finding a fossil sea snail at the top of a mountain would cause you to conclude that the environment has changed. The fossil record in an area is like a history book, telling you about the changes the environment in that area has undergone.

▶ Suppose you find a fossil seashell in rocks in your local park. Draw or develop a model to identify the nature of the environment at the time of the fossil.

## The La Brea Tar Pits

The La Brea Tar Pits are located in Los Angeles, California, where tar still seeps from the ground. About 40,000 years ago, the area looked like the picture shown on the facing page. Scientists have collected fossils of thousands of plants and animals from the pits. Scientists know that those plants lived in a climate only a little wetter and cooler than it is today. In other words, the climate has not changed much in this area over the last 40,000 years.

## Falls of the Ohio

Today the Falls of the Ohio is a state park in Indiana, tucked into a bend of the Ohio River where the land is flat and often dry. The summers are hot, and the winters are cold and snowy. But the rocks at the Falls of the Ohio State Park tell a different story. The rocks are filled with fossils of coral, clams, and other organisms that lived in shallow, warm, tropical seas. You can see on the map that Indiana is far from the ocean today. These fossils show that the climate in this area has changed a lot over the last 380 million years.

# The Great Die Offs

Scientists often compare fossils to organisms living today. They have discovered that many organisms have disappeared, or become extinct. There are times in Earth's history when a great many organisms became extinct all at once. How did this happen?

**Active Reading** As you read these pages, circle the possible causes of mass extinctions.

Sometimes only one species becomes extinct at a time. The passenger pigeon became extinct in 1914. Hunting and loss of habitat are likely causes. At several times during Earth's history, many species became extinct at the same time. These large events, caused by climate change, are called **mass extinctions.**

Worldwide volcanic eruptions can cause mass extinctions. These eruptions blow large amounts of ash and dust into the air. Sunlight is blocked, so plants can't grow. Other plants die when the ash settles on

Changing climate affects rainfall. Too much rain can cause flooding, which can destroy habitats. Too little rainfall means no plant growth and no water to drink. The result is death for many living things.

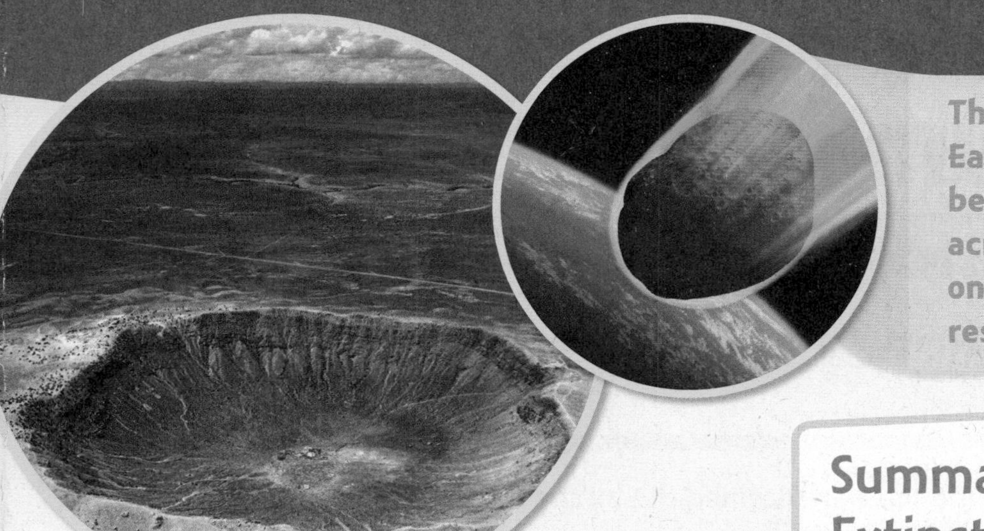

The last large meteor to hit Earth is thought to have been at least 16 km (10 mi) across. Craters such as this one in Arizona show the result of meteor impacts.

them and smothers them. If plants die, the animals that eat them also die.

Objects from outer space can cause mass extinctions. At the end of the Mesozoic, an asteroid crashed into what is now Mexico. The impact sent huge amounts of dust into the air. The dust blocked out sunlight. Changes in climate occurred that were similar to those caused by large volcanic eruptions. These changes may have caused the extinction of many animals, including the last of the dinosaurs.

## Summarizing Mass Extinctions

Fill in the chart to explain some causes of mass extinctions.

| Cause | Effect | Result |
|---|---|---|
| volcanic eruption | | |
| | flooding | |
| no rain | | |
| | dust and ash in the air | |

Volcanic ash can change climate.

**When you're done, use the answer key to check and revise your work.**

**The statements below are incorrect. Replace the words in blue to correct each statement.**

1. The units of the geologic time scale are defined the by the thickness of the rock layers. ____________________
2. The relative age of a fossil tells whether it is 1,000 years old or 1 million years old. ____________________
3. Rocks that contain fossils of brachiopods, crinoids, and jawless fish formed in a desert environment. ____________________
4. The Age of Dinosaurs is known for the large number of animals, such as the saber-toothed cat, that were able to live in a cold environment. ____________________
5. Index fossils must be found over a large area, be easily recognized, have lived during the Paleozoic, and have large populations. ____________________
6. Support for continental drift includes different fossils found on the same continents. ____________________
7. Fossils of the reptile *Mesosaurus* are used to explain the movement of continents because this reptile lived in the desert. ____________________
8. When volcanic eruptions send dust and ash into the air, increases in animal and plant populations can occur. ____________________



Answer Key: 1. fossils that are in the rocks 2. younger or older than another fossil 3. ocean environment 4. Ice Age 5. lived during a geologically short period of time 6. the same, different 7. in fresh water and could not swim across salt water 8. mass extinctions

# Brain Check

Lesson 4

Name ____________________

## Word Play

1 Use the clues to complete the puzzle.

### Clues

**Across**

2. can be used to help identify the relative age of a rock layer
4. unit of time that contains the Age of Dinosaurs
6. occurs when many species die out at the same time
7. a geologic chart that divides Earth's history into units
8. common fossil animal from the Paleozoic

**Down**

1. used to describe if a fossil is older or younger than another fossil
3. all of the fossils in Earth's rock layers
5. giant continent that existed in Earth's past

| | |
|---|---|
| fossil record | Mesozoic Era |
| geologic time scale | Pangaea |
| index fossil* | relative age |
| mass extinction* | trilobite |

* Key Lesson Vocabulary

# Apply Concepts

2 What does this fossil tell you about Antarctica's past environment?

3 The county is building a new road near your school. Bulldozers have dug up fossils of trees, leaves, and horses. Draw a picture of what the environment might have looked like when these plants and animals were living.

4 Place the following geologic time units in their correct order from oldest to most recent.

Cenozoic Era    Precambrian Time    Mesozoic Era    Paleozoic Era

Name ______________________________



5 What information in the picture supports the idea that Earth's continents have moved over time?

______________________________________________________________

______________________________________________________________

6 Read each description. Circle the fossil that is an index fossil.

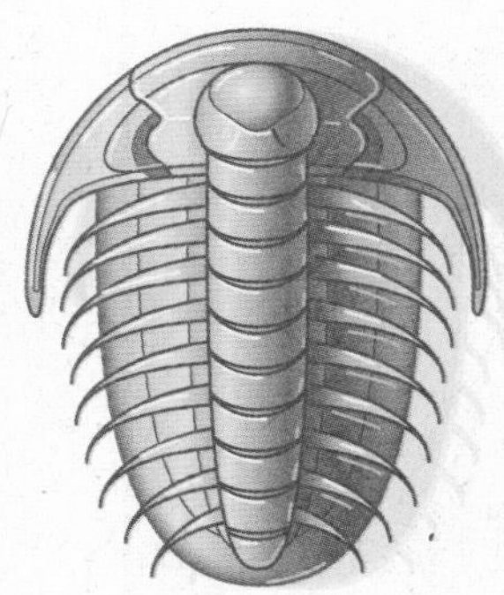

This animal lived for a short time during the late Paleozoic. Many of its fossils are found all over the United States.

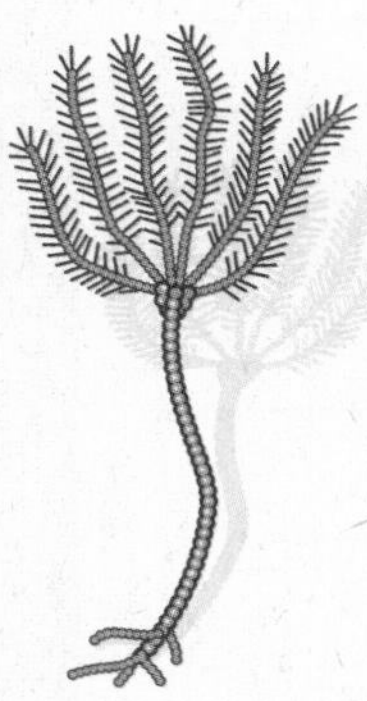

This animal lived during the early and middle Paleozoic. Its fossils have only been found in a few parts of Indiana.

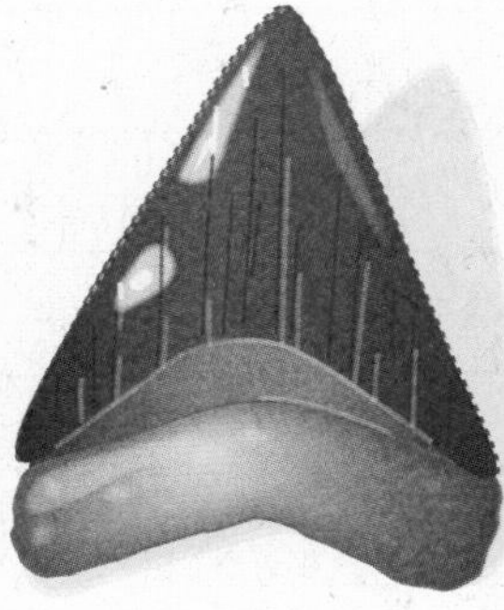

This tooth is from a shark that is living today. Many similar teeth have been found on the shores of Virginia.

7 Draw a three-panel comic strip that shows one way that a mass extinction might occur.

| Cause | Effect | End Result |
|---|---|---|
| | | |

8 Which rock layer is the oldest? Which is the youngest? Explain how you know.

___

___

___

___

___

___

___

___

Take a walk with an adult around your neighborhood. Think about how the area might change over the next 5, 10, 50, 100, or 1,000 years. What clues would tell future paleontologists about how your area looks today?

Inquiry Flipchart page 42

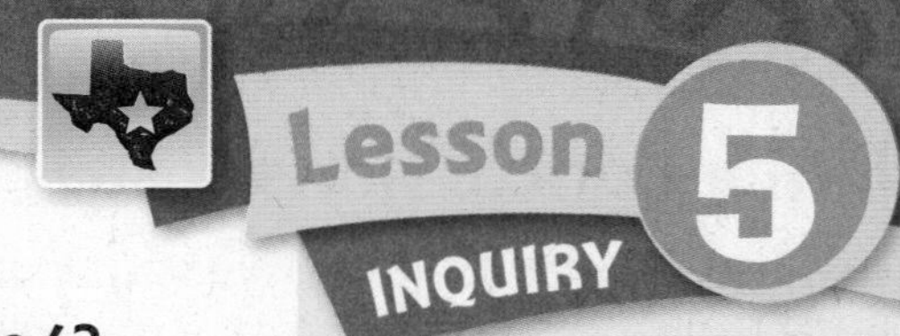


**TEKS** **5.2C** collect information by detailed observations and accurate measuring **5.2D** analyze and interpret information to construct reasonable explanations from direct (observable) and indirect (inferred) evidence **5.7D** identify fossils as evidence of past living organisms and the nature of the environments at the time using models

Name ______________________

Essential Question

# How Can Scientists Use Fossils?

## Set a Purpose

**What will you learn from this activity?**

______________________

______________________

______________________

______________________

## State Your Hypothesis

**Write your hypothesis or testable statement.**

______________________

______________________

______________________

______________________

## Think About the Procedure

**Why is it important to examine the fossil symbols carefully?**

______________________

______________________

______________________

**How would the results change if only one fossil symbol was drawn on each card?**

______________________

______________________

______________________

## Record Your Data

**Record your results in the space below.**

| Sequence of Rock Layers (Oldest to Youngest) | Fossil Symbols |
|---|---|
| Youngest | |
| ↑ | |
| | |
| | |
| | |
| | |
| | |
| Oldest | ▲ ☆ |

## Draw Conclusions

Use the results of your investigation and logical reasoning to order the fossils, from oldest to youngest, according to when they last appeared in the rock record.

| Oldest to Youngest | Fossil Symbols |
|---|---|
| Youngest | |
| ↑ | |
| | |
| | |
| | |
| | |
| | |
| | |
| | |
| | |
| Oldest | |

Share your answers above with another group. Explain how you determined the order of the ★, ■, and ●. Then, ask them to explain how they determined theirs.

_______________

_______________

_______________

_______________

_______________

## Analyze and Extend

1. Scientists use time-space relationships to compare rock layers around the world. What can you tell about the age of the fossil ✚ using this information?

   Fossil ○ is 25 to 50 million years old.
   Fossil ● is 75 to 110 million years old.

   _______________

   _______________

   _______________

2. What has most likely occurred if a fossil that appeared in an older rock layer does not appear in a younger rock layer?

   _______________

   _______________

   _______________

3. Suppose fossil # appeared in each rock layer. Would fossil # make a good index fossil? Explain.

   _______________

   _______________

   _______________

4. What other questions do you have about how scientists use fossils?

   _______________

   _______________

   _______________

# Meet Some Paleontology Pioneers

## Luis and Walter Alvarez

In 1980, a father-and-son geology team had an idea. They knew that dinosaurs may have become extinct around 65 million years ago when a huge asteroid hit Earth. To look for evidence of this, they looked at the layer of rock from that time period. The rock had a lot of the same chemical elements as asteroids. The Alvarezes inferred that an asteroid impact sent enough smoke and dust into the atmosphere to block out sunlight. Now many scientists agree with their idea.

## Karen Chin

Karen Chin knows that we learn about animals by studying what they eat. That is why she studies the fossils of dinosaur dung! She learns a lot about dinosaurs this way. She can tell how they interacted with the plants and animals in their ecosystems. Dr. Chin was the first person to identify and study *Tyrannosaurus rex* poop! From her research, she could show that *Tyrannosaurus rex* ate *Triceratops*. And it didn't just eat meat from its prey. It ate bones and all.

# Describe Dinosaurs

Look at each skeleton below. Answer the questions to compare and contrast the dinosaurs.

What do you think the plates on *Stegosaurus's* back were for?

_______________________________

_______________________________

_______________________________

Why do you think *Stegosaurus's* tail was so long?

_______________________________

_______________________________

_______________________________

What do you think *Tyrannosaurus rex* ate? Why do you think so?

_______________________________

_______________________________

_______________________________

Why do you think *Tyrannosaurus rex's* legs were longer than its arms?

_______________________________

_______________________________

_______________________________

How do scientists find data to answer these questions?

_______________________________

_______________________________

_______________________________

What do scientists learn from locations of dinosaur fossils?

_______________________________

_______________________________

_______________________________

# Unit 7 Review

Name ______________________________

## Vocabulary Review

Use the terms in the box to complete the sentences.

| |
|---|
| cast |
| deposition |
| erosion |
| fossil |
| index fossil |
| mold |
| sedimentary rock |
| weathering |

TEKS 5.7B

1. It can take millions of years for water, wind, and ice to break down rock through the process of ______________________.

TEKS 5.7D

2. The remains or traces of a plant or animal that lived long ago is a(n) ______________________.

TEKS 5.7A

3. Coal, a fossil fuel, forms when the remains of once-living organisms are part of the layered material that hardens into ______________________.

TEKS 5.7D

4. An impression of an organism, formed when sediment hardens around the organism, is called a(n) ______________________.

TEKS 5.7D

5. A model of an organism, formed when sediment fills a mold and hardens, is a(n) ______________________.

TEKS 5.7B

6. Wind slows down and drops its load of sediments in a process known as ______________________.

TEKS 5.7D

7. A fossil of a type of organism that lived in many places during a relatively short time span is called a(n) ______________________.

TEKS 5.7B

8. As a glacier moves forward, it carries earth materials to new places in a process called ______________________.

## Science Concepts

**Fill in the letter of the choice that best answers the question.**

**TEKS 5.2.D, 5.3A, 5.7D**

**9. Josh read about a land animal whose fossils were found in similar rock layers in Africa and South America. What can he conclude from this discovery?**

Ⓐ Animal fossils all look alike.

Ⓑ The landmasses were once joined.

Ⓒ The animals swam across the ocean.

Ⓓ The fossils formed in an ocean and washed ashore.

**TEKS 5.2D, 5.7D**

**10. Nikomo found a piece of amber. Which past-living organism shown below would the amber most likely contain?**

Ⓐ

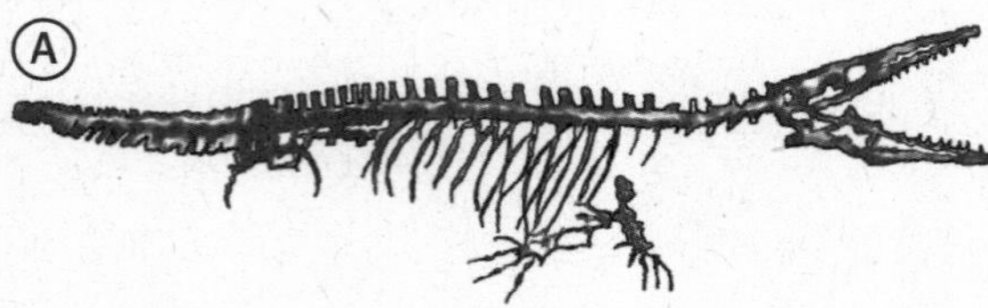

Ⓑ

Ⓒ

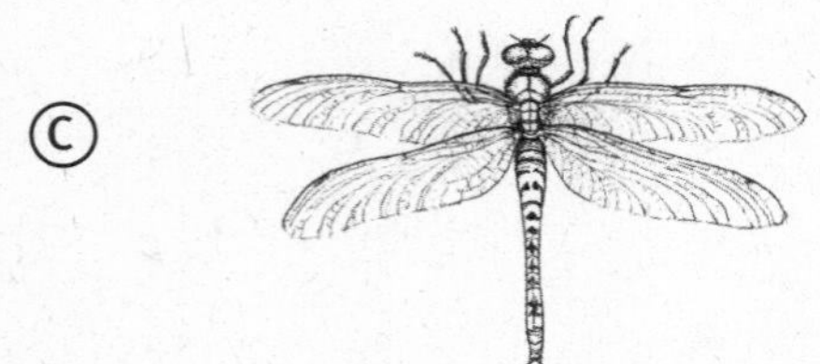

Ⓓ

**TEKS 5.7A**

**11. Over time the materials that form coal change. What was once a material that burns with a lot of smoke and little heat changes to a sedimentary rock that produces a lot of heat with little smoke. Which graph correctly shows what happens during the formation of coal as it improves in quality and hardens into sedimentary rock?**

Ⓐ Ⓒ

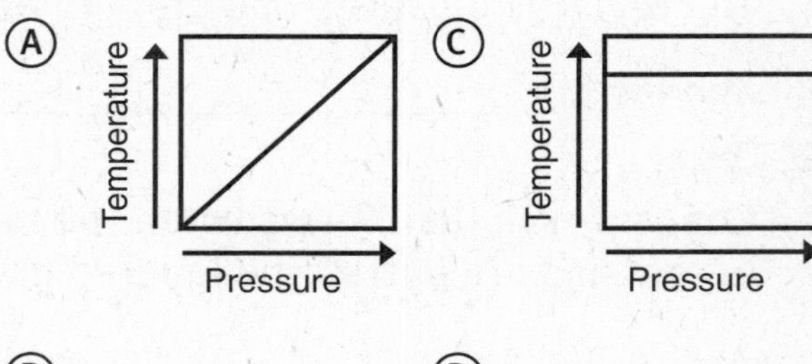


Ⓑ Ⓓ

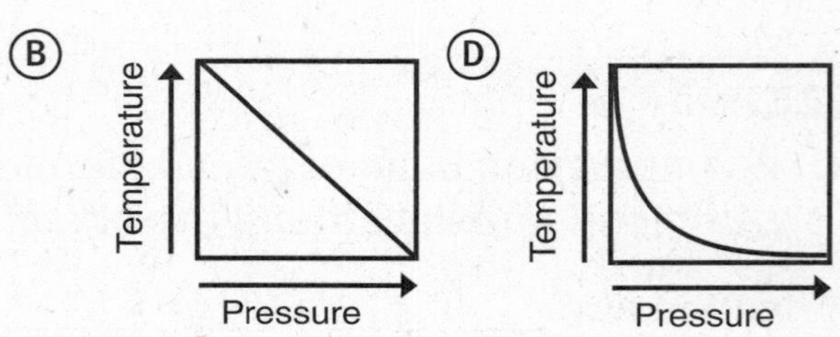


**TEKS 5.7B**

**12. Which statement best describes how landforms are the result of changes to Earth's surface?**

Ⓐ A delta is a hill that forms when water erodes and deposits soil.

Ⓑ A sand dune is a fan-shaped feature that forms when ice weathers rocks.

Ⓒ A moraine is a ridge that forms when a glacier deposits soil, rocks, and sand.

Ⓓ A canyon is a steep-sided valley that forms when wind deposits large-sized sediments.

Name ______________________

TEKS 5.2D, 5.7D

**13.** Suppose you found fossils of sharks and other fish in a nearby forest. What could you infer about the history of the area from these discoveries?

Ⓐ The area was once a valley.

Ⓑ The area was once a desert.

Ⓒ The area was once an ocean.

Ⓓ The area was once covered by ice.

TEKS 5.3C, 5.7B

**14.** Sasha wants to model a type of physical weathering, which takes place over long periods of time and can be difficult to directly observe. Which would make the best model?

Ⓐ Drop weak acids on a rock to wear it away.

Ⓑ Hit a rock with a hammer to break it apart.

Ⓒ Pour water over a pile of sand to carry the sand away.

Ⓓ Drop a pile of silt on the ground and measure its height.

TEKS 5.2D, 5.7D

**15.** Study the rock layers in the picture. The rocks formed when layers of sediment were weathered, eroded, and deposited. Which rock layer is most likely the oldest?

Ⓐ Layer A

Ⓑ Layer B

Ⓒ Layer C

Ⓓ Layer D

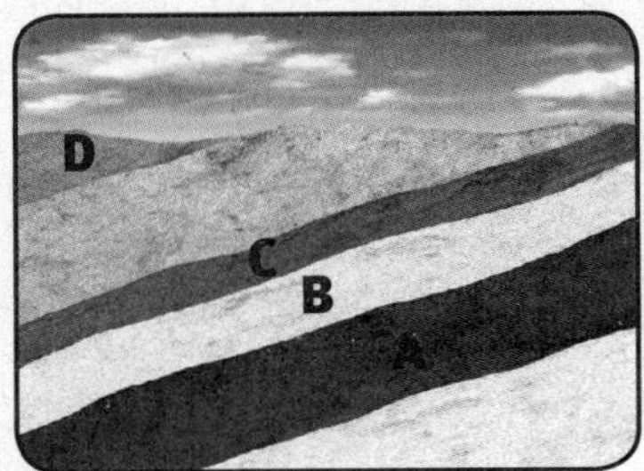


TEKS 5.2D, 5.7D

**16.** The map shows Paul's stops on a recent trip. He says that he found index fossils at each of his stops.

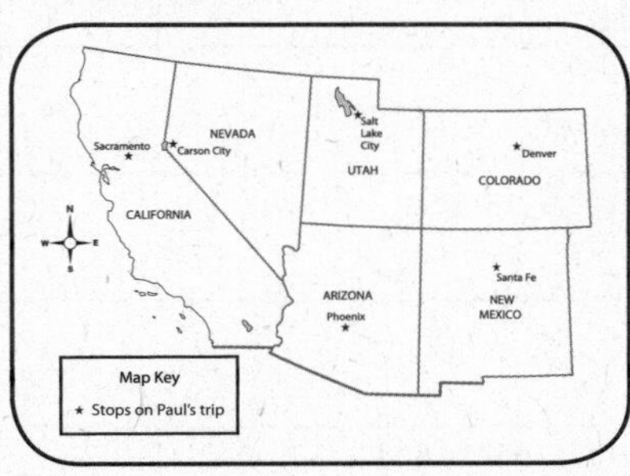


Which one requirement for an index fossil had Paul completely satisfied?

Ⓐ The fossil is from an organism that lived for a short geologic period.

Ⓑ The fossil is from an organism that had a large population.

Ⓒ The fossil is hard to recognize.

Ⓓ The fossil is widespread.

TEKS 5.7B

**17.** The picture shows a fast-moving stream.

What will most likely happen to this stream over time?

Ⓐ It will widen because of erosion.

Ⓑ It will become deeper because of deposition.

Ⓒ It will dry up because of physical weathering.

Ⓓ It will become narrower because of chemical weathering.

## Apply Inquiry and Review the Big Idea

Write the answers to these questions.

TEKS 5.2F, 5.7A

**18.** Leeza wanted to know the relative age of a fossil she found. How can she use the sedimentary rock layers shown here to help determine the fossil's relative age?

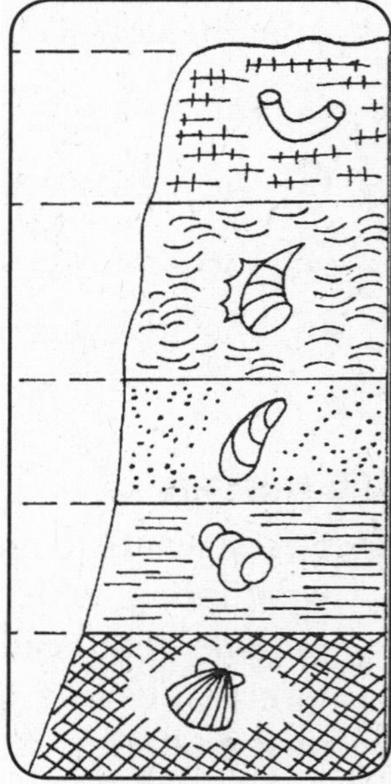

TEKS 5.3A, 5.7D

**19.** In a rock layer far inland, a scientist finds a fish fossil with large fins. She concludes that a sea must have once covered the area. Another scientist looks at the same fossil and notices that its body structures are similar to a type of fish found in nearby streams. He concludes that a freshwater lake once covered the area. Write a statement critiquing these scientific explanations and examining all sides of the scientific evidence.

TEKS 5.7B

**20.** A glacier is eroding the land over which it passes. It moves at a rate of 2 m per day. Currently, the glacier is 80 km from a small village. At current rates of movement, how many years before the glacier reaches the village?

UNIT 8

# Natural Resources

## Big Idea

Natural resources are essential to life and must be used with care.

TEKS 5.1B, 5.3C, 5.3D, 5.7C

## I Wonder Why

Rice can be grown almost anywhere, even on steep hills. Why do people build terraces on which to grow rice? *Turn the page to find out.*

**Here's why** Rice fields are kept very wet after they are planted. The water makes sure that only the strongest plants survive. Terraces allow farmers to flood the fields and use fewer chemicals to control weeds.

In this unit, you will explore the Big Idea, the Essential Questions, and the Investigations on the Inquiry Flipchart.

Levels of Inquiry Key ■ DIRECTED ■ GUIDED ■ INDEPENDENT

**Big Idea** Natural resources are essential to life and must be used with care.

## Essential Questions



**Science Notebook**

Before you begin each lesson, be sure to write your thoughts about the Essential Question.

TEKS 5.7C identify alternative energy resources such as wind, solar, hydroelectric, geothermal, and biofuels

Lesson 1

Essential Question

# How Do People Use Resources?

## Engage Your Brain!

As you read the lesson, look for the answer to the following question and record it here.

What types of resources do you see here? Which type is more easily replaced?

_______________

_______________

_______________

_______________

_______________

## Active Reading

### Lesson Vocabulary

List the terms. As you learn about each one, make notes in the Interactive Glossary.

_______________ _______________

_______________ _______________

_______________ _______________

_______________

### Compare and Contrast

In this lesson, you'll read about renewable and nonrenewable resources. As you read about resources, ask yourself how they are alike and different. Active readers stay focused on comparisons and contrasts when they ask themselves, How are these things alike? How are they different?



Inquiry Flipchart p. 43 — Catch That Dirt!/What's in Your Water?

# Natural Resources

Water, wind, sunshine, soil, coal—these may not seem to have much in common. However, they are *all* natural resources. Every living thing uses natural resources each day.

Wind, or moving air, is a renewable energy resource. Wind turns this turbine to produce electricity.

**Active Reading** As you read these two pages, draw boxes around the names of the two kinds of resources that are being compared.

Did you use water this morning when you brushed your teeth? Did you eat some fruit with your breakfast? If you did, then you used a natural resource! A **natural resource** is anything useful or necessary for living beings that occurs naturally on Earth. Human beings depend on natural resources all the time. You use many of them without even thinking about it.

Scientists classify resources into two groups. **Renewable resources** are resources that nature can replace when they are used. New trees grow to replace trees that get cut down. The water cycle constantly replaces water. Air, plants, animals, wind, and sunlight are other renewable resources.

Farmers use natural resources such as soil, air, water, and sunlight to produce food.

## Know Your Resources

Identify each resource as renewable or nonrenewable. Explain your answer.

______________ ______________ ______________ ______________

______________ ______________ ______________ ______________

**Nonrenewable resources** are resources that nature cannot replace after they are used. Someday they may disappear completely. Minerals and soil are nonrenewable resources. If used carefully, soil can last a long time, but if it is destroyed, it cannot be replaced.

Fossil fuels are also nonrenewable resources. A fossil fuel is an energy source formed deep inside Earth from the remains of organisms that lived long ago. Coal, natural gas, and oil are fossil fuels. Most of the energy we use comes from fossil fuels. Fossil fuels power cars and trucks, and they are also burned in many energy stations to produce electricity.

Natural resources are used to make products of all sorts. Every product you use started out as a natural resource.

Some oil is pumped from deep below the ocean floor.

# Resources on the Move

The United States and many other countries produce oil. Tanker ships and pipelines move oil to places where it is needed.

Where do natural resources come from? Some occur near where you live. Other resources occur in other parts of the world and are transported long distances to get to the places where they are used.

**Active Reading** As you read these pages, find and underline the definitions of *import* and *export*.

**Wyoming is tops for coal production. Coal is mainly used to generate electricity.**

**Iowa grows about 18 percent of the corn in the U.S. Corn is now used to make a fossil-fuel alternative.**

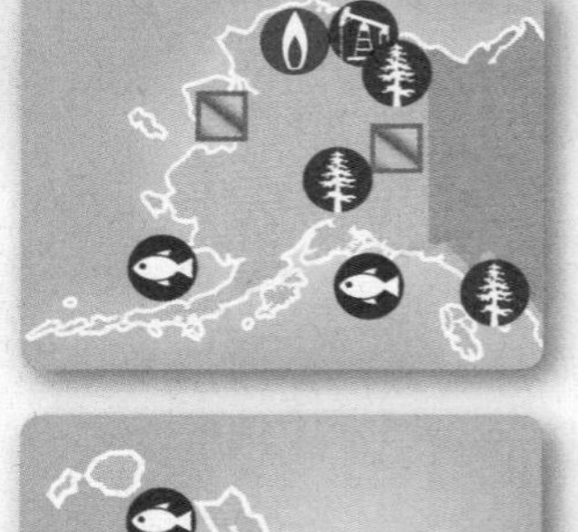

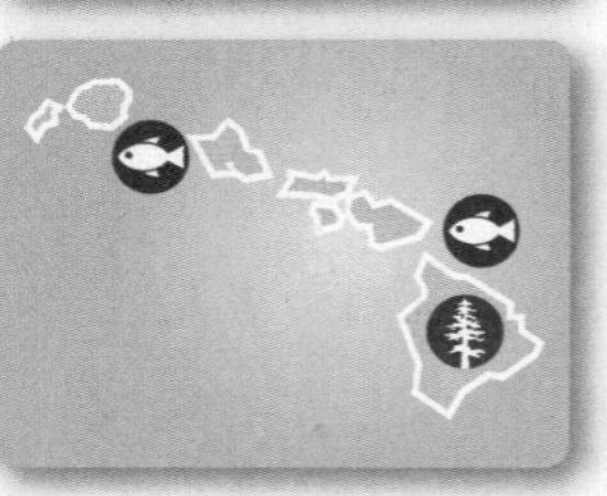

| | |
|---|---|
| Farming | Fishing |
| Ranching | Gold |
| Coal | Granite |
| Copper | Hydroelectric |
| Iron ore | Oil |
| Limestone | Silver |
| Logging | Uranium |
| Natural Gas | |

**Where's the beef? You can find a lot of it in Texas! 17 percent of beef cattle in the U.S. are raised there.**

**Next time you enjoy your favorite rice cereal, think of Arkansas. This is where nearly half of all rice is grown in the U.S.**

Have you ever visited a farmers' market? Local farmers bring their goods to the market soon after crops are harvested or products are made. Customers come to the market to buy fresh goods that are produced nearby. Goods sold at a farmers' market travel only short distances between where they are produced and where they are sold.

Most natural resources travel long distances between the places where they occur and the places where they are needed. For example, the United States uses more oil than it produces. The United States must import oil. An *import* is something brought into a country to be sold or traded. Other countries produce more oil than they use. These countries can sell the extra oil they produce. They export some of it to the United States. An *export* is something sent out of a country to be sold or traded.

Most imported oil arrives in the United States on huge tanker ships. These ships can carry large quantities of the natural resource. When the oil arrives in the United States, it is converted into fuel and other products. These products are carried around the country in pipelines and on trains and tanker trucks.

## Do the Math!

### Interpret a Circle Graph

This graph shows the amount of oil produced in different parts of the world. Each section shows production in one region. Label each section with the correct region and percentage.

- Middle East: 30%
- North America: 20%
- Eurasia (former Soviet Union): 15%
- Central and South America: 10%
- Asia and Oceania: 10%
- Africa: 10%
- Europe: 5%

Huge oil tankers move large amounts of oil across long distances.

# Alternative Energy

Fossil fuels may run out someday. What energy sources can we rely on in the future?

**Active Reading** As you read these two pages, draw a circle around each instance of the three-word phrase that is key to understanding the main idea.

Alternative energy sources are renewable. Often, they don't release substances that harm the environment. As our fossil fuel supply decreases, we will need to use more alternative energy sources. Each source has advantages and disadvantages. Some are costly. Some are only suited to certain places. As a result, a combination of different energy sources may work best for many places.

**Geothermal energy** is heat from inside Earth. In areas that have geysers or volcanoes, hot, molten rock is close to the surface. Geothermal plants can tap into this heat and produce electricity on a large scale.

**Hydroelectric energy** comes from the energy of flowing water. A dam is built across a river to make a reservoir. Water released from this reservoir flows through a hydroelectric energy station. The flowing water spins turbines that are connected to generators that produce electricity.

In a single minute, Earth gets enough solar energy to meet the world's yearly energy needs! Solar energy stations, such as this one, are built in places with lots of sunlight, such as deserts. Solar energy can be used to heat water or to produce electricity. However, the equipment used to collect solar energy is costly.

Wind can be used to generate electricity. Wind farms are built in open, flat places where the land elevation increases slightly over long distances and wind speeds are high. Wind energy is the fastest growing alternative energy source because it is the least expensive to harness.

**Biofuels** are fuels that are made from living things, such as corn or sugar cane. They can be used to power vehicles. They help reduce the harmful emissions from cars, trucks, planes, and other vehicles that use fossil fuels.

## What Works for You?

In the chart below, decide which alternative energy sources might work in your area. Explain your choices.

| Alternative Energy | | |
|---|---|---|
| Energy Source | Feasible in your area? (Yes or No) | Why or why not? |
| Geothermal | | |
| Hydroelectric | | |
| Solar | | |
| Wind | | |
| Biofuel | | |

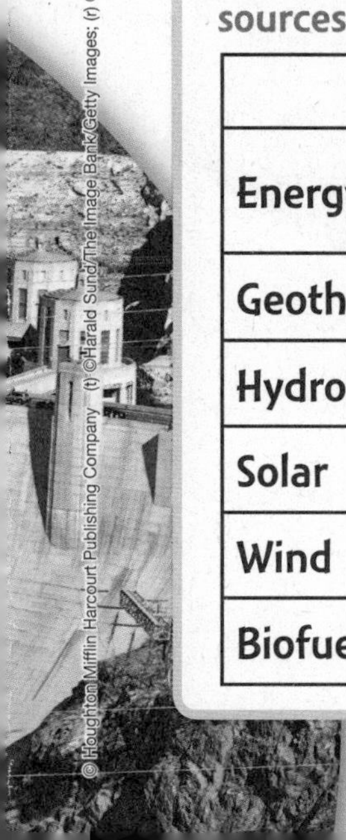

# What's That Smell?

Smoke from resources burned by factories contributes to air pollution.

Smog, trash, and dirty water are ways our use of natural resources can harm the environment.

**Active Reading** As you read these pages, draw a circle around the definition of *pollution*.

Cities and homes often draw water from underground. Waste from human activities can pollute underground water sources.

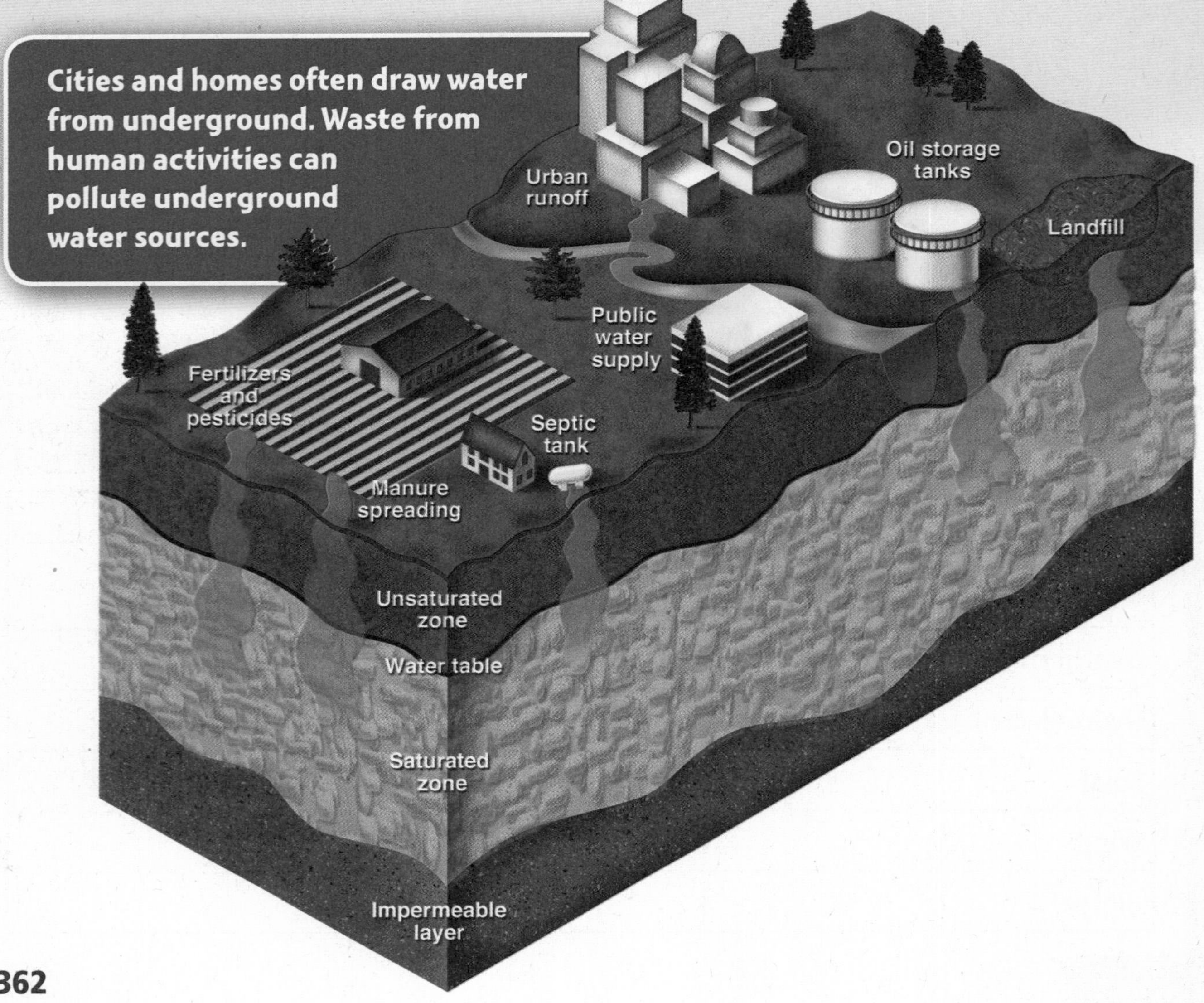

Natural resources help people do and make many things, but the use of natural resources can also cause pollution. **Pollution** is the contamination of air, water, or soil by materials that are harmful to living things. Air, water, and soil are some of the most important natural resources.

Most air pollution comes from the burning of fossil fuels. Cars and trucks are the greatest source of air pollution, but many factories and energy stations also pollute. Air pollution can harm the health of people, plants, and animals.

Water can become polluted when trash, eroded soil, or chemicals from manufacturing, farming, and landfills get into rivers, lakes, and oceans. These pollutants can also enter groundwater. Water pollution harms organisms, including people, that need water to live.

Soil can be polluted, too. Chemicals leaking from storage sites or runoff from roads and parking lots can soak into soils, making them unusable for growing crops.

## Pollution Affects Earth

Write two types of pollution in the *Effect* box. In the *Cause* box, explain the cause of each.

| Cause | | Effect |
|---|---|---|
| | → | |

## Why It Matters

# Using Resources at Home

You use natural resources all day every day—without even realizing it!

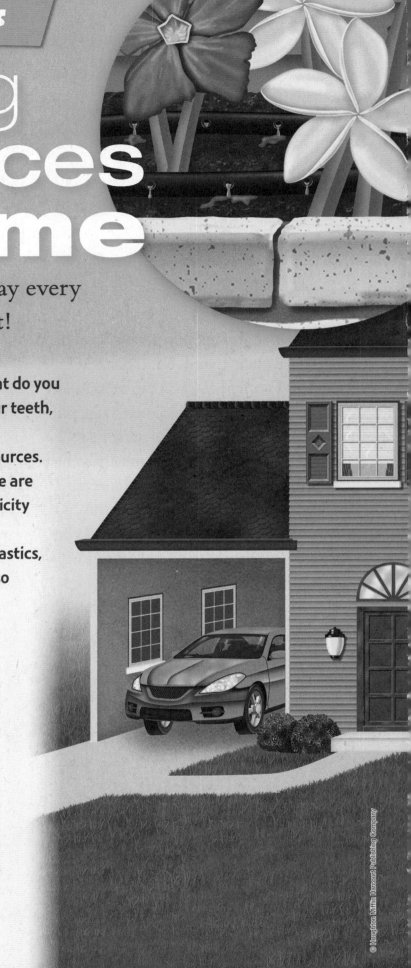

When you wake up in the morning, what do you do? You may eat breakfast, brush your teeth, and listen to the radio.

Each of these activities uses natural resources. The food that you eat and the water you use are renewable resources. Your radio uses electricity that may have been generated from the nonrenewable resource coal. The metals, plastics, and other materials the radio is made of also come from nonrenewable resources.

People do not use most natural resources in their original form. Although you can eat some fruits and vegetables just as they are picked, most foods are cooked. Every product you use was made from one or more natural resources. For example, the paper you use to print your homework probably comes from trees. What about the plastic fork you used to eat lunch? Plastic can be made from oil. How many ways can you find resources being used in this home?

Water-saving products such as a drip irrigation system can help your family use less water.

A computer runs on electricity. Electrical energy is often generated in energy stations by the burning of coal. The computer itself is made of minerals and plastic.

In the bathroom, you use water to keep clean. You also use electricity to run appliances.

## Name That Resource

Pick a room in your home. Describe how natural resources are used in that room.

**When you're done, use the answer key to check and revise your work.**

**Read the summary statements. Then draw a line to match each statement with the appropriate picture.**

1. Renewable resources are resources that nature can replace after they are used.

2. Some renewable resources can be used to generate electrical energy.

3. Natural resources can be imported and exported throughout the world.

4. Pollution occurs when waste and chemicals harm land, air, and water.

## Summarize

**Fill in the Venn diagram by writing the correct number of each item in the appropriate category.**

5. Natural resources
6. Solar energy
7. Water
8. Soil
9. Fossil fuels
10. Minerals
11. Plants

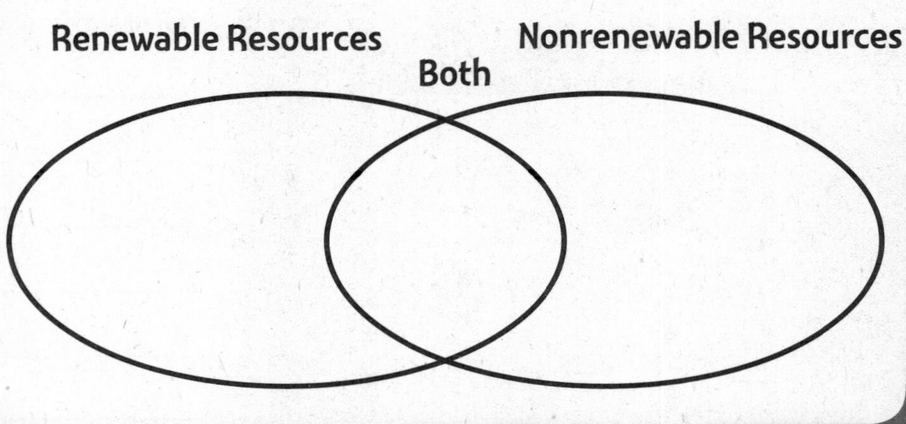




Answer Key: 1. (farm) 2. (wind turbines) 3. (cargo ship) 4. (factory)
Venn diagram: Renewable Resources—6, 7, 11; Both—5; Nonrenewable Resources—8, 9, 10

# Brain Check

Lesson 1

Name ______________________________

## Word Play

**1** Use the words in the box to complete each sentence. Then unscramble the circled letters to solve the riddle at the bottom.

| chemicals | food | landfills | nonrenewable* |
|---|---|---|---|
| replaced | pollution* | resource | wind |

*Key Lesson Vocabulary

1. Renewable resources include air, water, sunlight, and ◯ _ ◯ _ .

2. Minerals are a _ _ _ _ _ _ ◯ _ _ _ _ _ resource because minerals cannot be replaced after they are used.

3. _ _ _ _ _ _ _ _ ◯ used on farms can pollute lakes and rivers.

4. A natural _ _ ◯ _ _ _ _ _ is something useful to living things that occurs naturally on Earth.

5. Some turbines use _ ◯ _ _ to generate electrical energy.

6. Renewable resources can be _ _ _ ◯ _ _ _ _ by nature.

7. Smog is a form of air _ _ ◯ _ ◯ _ _ _ _ caused by the burning of fossil fuels.

8. Much of the trash that humans generate ends up in _ _ _ _ ◯ _ _ _ _ .

What do dinosaurs use to run their cars?

_ _ _ _ _ _ _ _ _ _ _ !

# Apply Concepts

**2** Circle the renewable resource.

**3** Identify and list the sources of five alternative energy resources.

**4** Explain why people are researching ways to use biofuels made from plants to power cars.

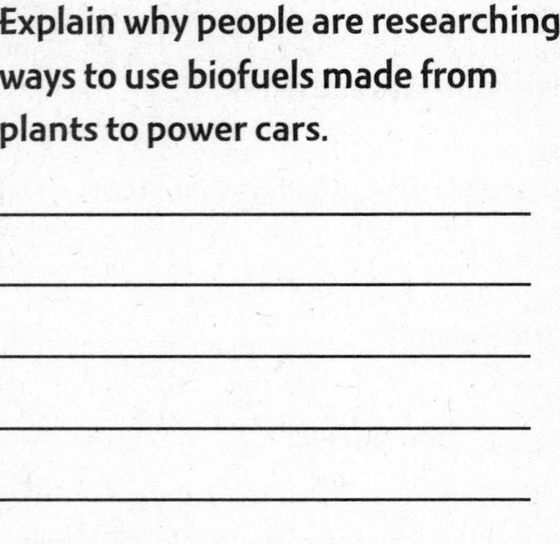

**5** Draw a picture that shows land, air, or water pollution. Label the source of the pollution.

Even though renewable resources will not run out, they can run short. Make a list of all the ways you use water in one day. Think of three ways that you could use less water. Share your results with your family.

TEKS **5.3C** draw or develop a model that represents how something works or looks that cannot be seen... **5.3D** connect grade-level appropriate science concepts with the history of science, science careers, and contributions of scientists

S.T.E.M.

Engineering & Technology

# How It Works:

## Getting to Oil

Oil forms deep below Earth's surface. To get oil, you have to drill a well. Then you need a pump to draw the oil up to the surface. Oil wells are drilled both on land and underwater into the ocean floor. Underwater drilling must be done carefully. Pipes to carry the oil must be in place before the well is drilled, or else the oil will escape into the water.

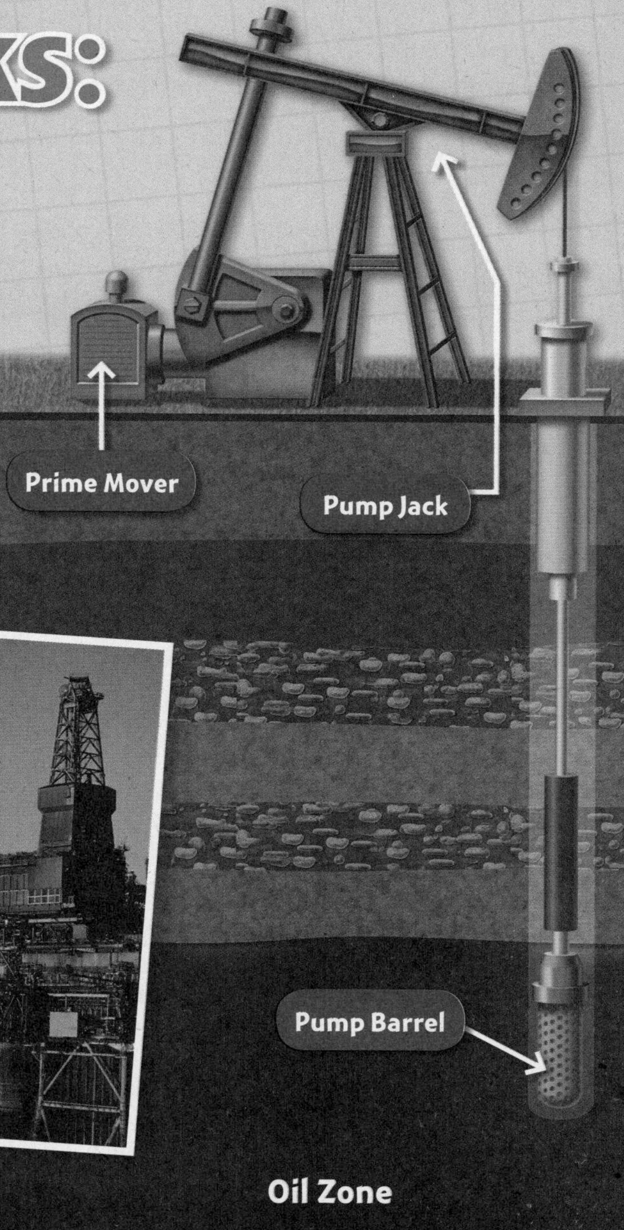

Prime Mover

Pump Jack

Offshore oil rigs operate from a platform in the ocean.

Pump Barrel

Oil Zone

## Critical Thinking

Is it more difficult to pump oil from a well on dry land or an underwater well? Why?

______________________________________________

______________________________________________

______________________________________________

# S.T.E.M.
continued

Drilling an oil well and pumping oil out of it are two different jobs. Both must be done carefully so that oil does not spill into the environment.

Find out more about the oil drilling process. Draw a model showing what happens below the surface that can't be easily seen, either on land or at sea. Label the parts.

What technology allows these workers to produce a drill long enough to reach the oil? Do more research to find out.

___

___

___

## Build On It!

Rise to the engineering design challenge—complete **Solve It: Separating Waste Materials** in the Inquiry Flipchart.

**TEKS 5.1B** make informed choices in the conservation, disposal, and recycling of materials
**5.7C** identify alternative energy resources such as wind, solar, hydroelectric, geothermal, and biofuels

Lesson 2

Essential Question

# How Do People Conserve Resources?

## Engage Your Brain!

As you read the lesson, look for the answer to the following question and record it here.

Which of the 3 Rs did the artist use when making this sculpture?

_______________

_______________

_______________

_______________

## Active Reading

### Lesson Vocabulary

List the term. As you learn about the term, make notes in the Interactive Glossary.

_______________

### Main Idea and Details

The main idea of a paragraph is the most important idea. The main idea may be stated in the first sentence of a paragraph, or it may be stated somewhere else. Active readers look for main ideas by asking themselves, What is this paragraph mostly about?



Inquiry Flipchart p. 45 — Hydroponics for the Future!/Recycling Rates

# It's Cool to Conserve

People in the United States throw away millions of tons of trash every year. Landfills are overflowing. What can *you* do to help keep our Earth clean?

**Active Reading** As you read this page, draw a box around problems that are caused by too much trash. Underline the solutions.

These chairs were made from reused snow skis.

Using your own bag over and over saves resources and reduces trash.

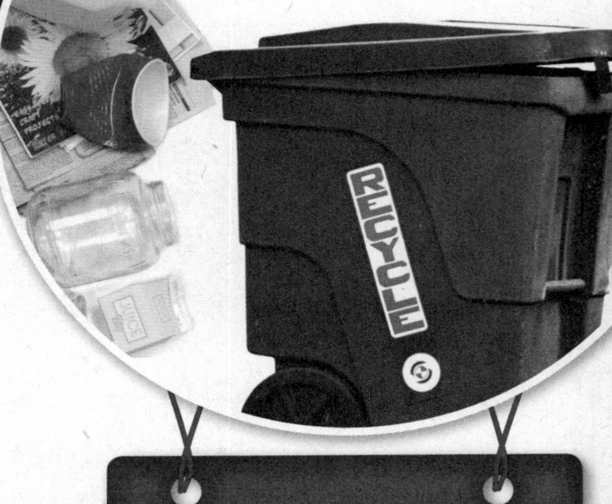


All of these items can be recycled. Next time you want to throw something away, check to see if you can recycle it instead.

You probably don't think about where trash goes after it is picked up from the curb. The truth is that trash is a big problem in our country. There is too much trash, and not enough places to put it. Garbage that is not disposed of properly pollutes natural resources—especially soil and water. So conservation is more important than ever. **Conservation** is using resources carefully and not wasting them. The 3 Rs—reducing, reusing, and recycling—help conserve our natural resources.

To *reduce* means to use less. When you reduce the amount of waste you make, less of it ends up buried in landfills or burned in incinerators. Try using the same cloth shopping bag instead of a new plastic or paper bag every time you go to the grocery store.

You can *reuse* an item by turning it into something else. That old tire? It would make a great tree swing! Your brother's old T-shirts? Tear them into squares and use them to wash the car. Reusing takes time and creativity.

A *recycled* product is one made from materials recovered from discarded items by reprocessing them. Your backpack may be made from recycled plastic bottles! Car bumpers and carpeting are a few other products that can be made from recycled materials. By making informed decisions about what to dispose of and what to recycle, you can conserve resources.

## Make Informed choices!

Look at the objects shown below and think about what each is made of. To demonstrate conservation, explain why these objects should not be disposed of. Describe how one object can be reused or recycled.

___

___

___

___

At a recycling center, discarded items are sorted for reprocessing.

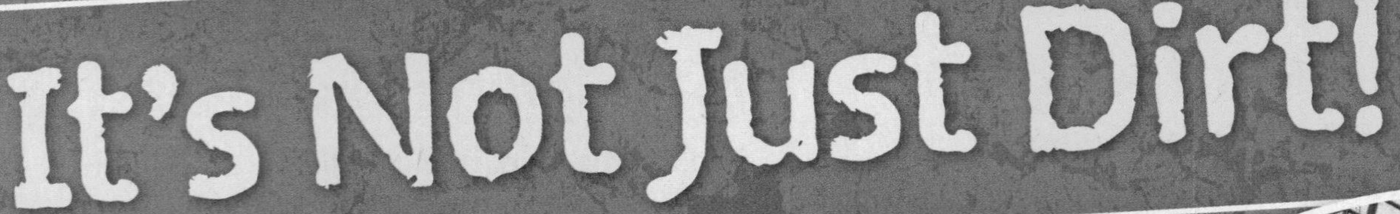

# It's Not Just Dirt!

Soil is one of the world's most valuable natural resources. What can we do to protect it?

**Active Reading** As you read these two pages, draw one line under each main idea and two lines under each supporting detail.

Dirt. You track it in on your feet. You may have played in it as a child. Why is it important to conserve dirt? Dirt, or soil, contains nutrients that plants need in order to grow. Most of our food comes from crops that grow in soil. Animals also depend on soil to provide the food they eat. Many organisms, such as earthworms, live in soil.

Natural events can cause soil to dry out, strip it of nutrients, and carry it away. Pollution, deforestation, road construction, and land development are some ways that humans harm soil.

Hydroponics

Intercropping

Contour plowing follows the natural curves of the land, preventing soil from washing away in heavy rains.

People have developed ways to help conserve soil. Some farmers rotate crops, or plant a different crop every other year. For example, one year a farmer may plant corn. Corn removes nitrogen from soils. The next year, the farmer plants soybeans. These plants return nitrogen to the soil.

Intercropping is the planting of more than one crop in the same field at the same time. The crops protect each other from insects and disease. They also protect the soil from erosion.

Did you know you can grow plants *without* soil? Using hydroponics, people can grow certain plants in water or another material, such as sand or gravel. Hydroponics actually conserves water and soil and uses less space than traditional farming.

Crop rotation with corn and soybeans

## Soil Smarts

Pick a type of soil conservation. Fill in the chart.

| Type of Soil Conservation | Draw It or Describe It | Tell How It Helps |
| --- | --- | --- |
| | | |

# Wonderful Water

Think of all the ways you use water. Scientists estimate that every person in the United States uses about 380 L (100 gal) of water every day. That's about 1,600 glasses of water!

**Active Reading** As you read these pages, underline the definition of *xeric landscaping.*

It's easy to take water for granted. After all, water's almost always there when you need it! Water is a renewable resource, but only some of it is available for use. It is important to keep an eye on how much water we use to make sure we always have enough.

Water conservation can start at home. Fixing a leaky faucet that drips at the rate of one drop per second can save more than 31 L (8 gal) of water every day! Do you have a garden that needs watering regularly? Your family can collect rainwater in a barrel or use a drip irrigation system. Drip irrigation slowly delivers water right to a plant's roots, so water is not lost due to evaporation or runoff.

Turning off the water when you brush your teeth can save about 11 L (3 gal) of water per day.

Rain barrel

One method of gardening that helps conserve water in areas with little rainfall is xeric landscaping. Xeric landscaping is using native plants that match the natural growing conditions of an area. The result is—you guessed it!—less water is needed to keep plants alive. People who live in desert regions and plant desert plants in their yards do not have to waste water on thirsty lawns.

Xeric landscaping can reduce watering by 50 to 75 percent.

## Do the Math!

### Solve Real-World Problems

Items such as low-flow shower heads, low-flush toilets, and front-loading washing machines can help reduce water use. Use the data to complete the chart and find out just how much water can be saved.

| | Traditional (water use in gal) | Water-Saving (water use in gal) | Water savings in one day | Water savings in one week |
|---|---|---|---|---|
| Shower head (assume 2 showers per day) | 70 gal per shower (10-minute shower) | 25 gal per shower (10-minute shower) | | |
| Toilet (assume 10 flushes per day) | 5 gal per flush | 2 gal per flush | | |
| Washing machine (assume 1 load per day) | 40 gal per full load | 20 gal per full load | | |

# Who Turned Out the Lights?

Every time you ride in a car or bus, turn on a light, work on your computer, or turn on the heat on a cold day, natural resources go to work for you!

**Active Reading** As you read these pages, draw a box around the name of each natural resource that provides energy. Then underline the energy it provides.

Electricity and heat are forms of energy that you use in your home. Energy doesn't just appear out of nowhere, though. Fossil fuels—coal, natural gas, and oil—help provide that energy. These resources are limited and burning them causes pollution, so using less both conserves them and helps clean the environment.

You have probably seen those new, bumpy light bulbs. They are called LEDs, or light-emitting diodes. LEDs use about a tenth of the electricity that regular bulbs use, and they last more than 40 times longer. Changing the bulbs in your home is an easy was to conserve energy. It can help your family save money, too!

## How Can We Help?

Each picture on these pages shows a way to conserve energy. On the lines by the picture, tell how the item reduces energy use.

These turbines change the energy of moving air into electricity.

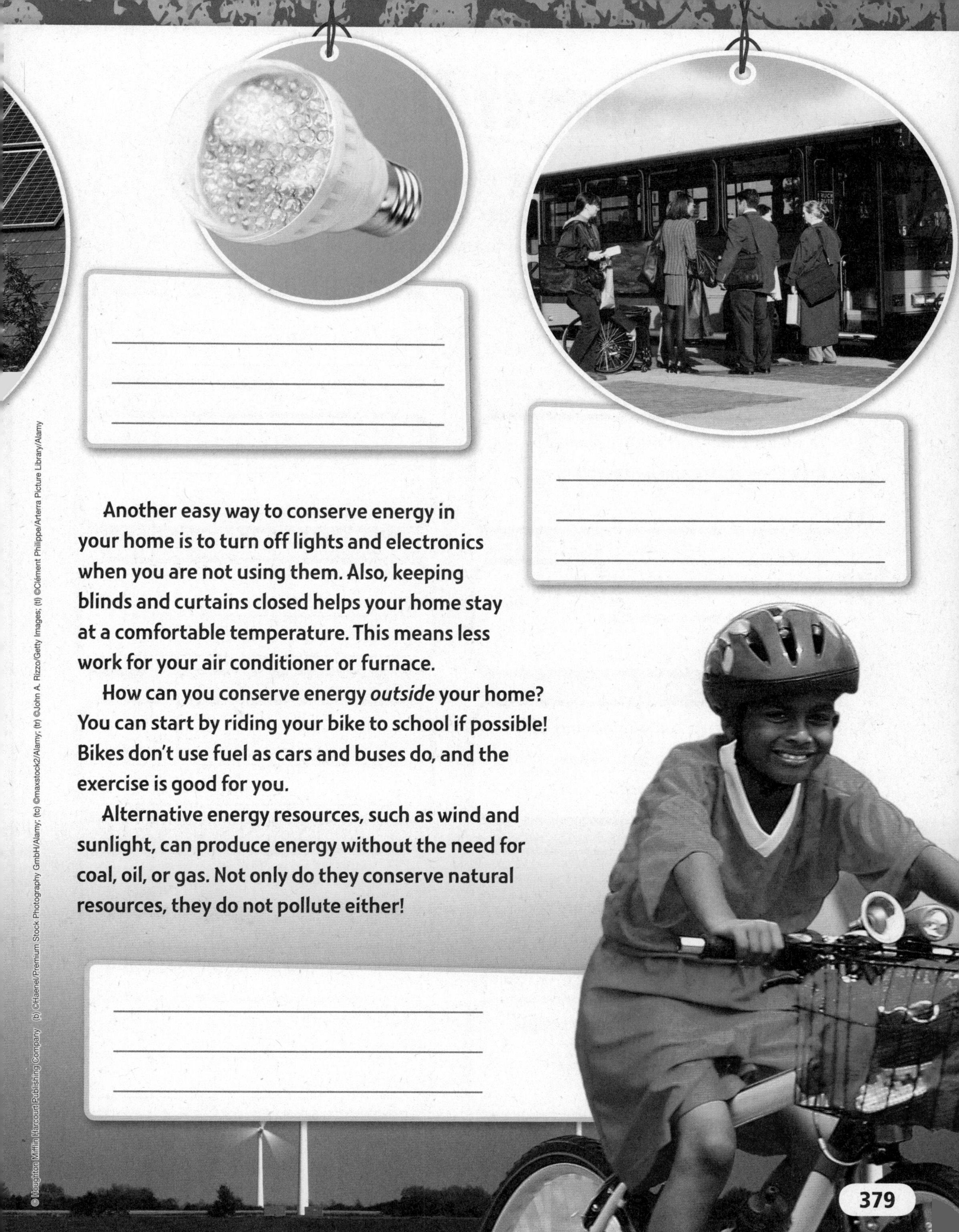

Another easy way to conserve energy in your home is to turn off lights and electronics when you are not using them. Also, keeping blinds and curtains closed helps your home stay at a comfortable temperature. This means less work for your air conditioner or furnace.

How can you conserve energy *outside* your home? You can start by riding your bike to school if possible! Bikes don't use fuel as cars and buses do, and the exercise is good for you.

Alternative energy resources, such as wind and sunlight, can produce energy without the need for coal, oil, or gas. Not only do they conserve natural resources, they do not pollute either!

When you're done, use the answer key to check and revise your work.

**Read the summary statements below. Each one is incorrect. Change the part of the summary in blue to make it correct.**

1. When we conserve resources, we **use more of them**.

   ________________

2. Turning a 2-liter bottle into a planter shows how **waste can be recycled**.

   ________________
   ________________

3. Xeric landscaping uses **nonnative plants that require more water** than other plants.

   ________________
   ________________

4. When farmers use contour farming, they plant **a different crop in the same location every other year**.

   ________________
   ________________

5. To conserve energy resources, **put your computer to "sleep"** when you are not using it.

   ________________
   ________________

6. Water is a renewable resource, **so people can use as much as they want**.

   ________________
   ________________

Answer Key: 1. use less of them 2. waste can be reused 3. native plants that require less water 4. crops in rows that follow the contour of the land 5. turn your computer off 6. but we still need to conserve it

# Brain Check

Lesson 2

Name ______________________________

## Word Play

**1** Unscramble the word to complete each sentence. The letter in the center is the first letter of the word.

______________ When something is _____, it is processed and then used to make something else.

______________ _____ is using natural resources wisely and not wasting them.

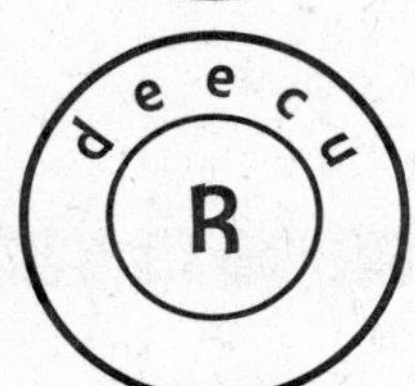


______________ When you _____ waste, you decrease the amount you make.

______________ _____ farming is the planting of crops along the natural curves and slopes of land.

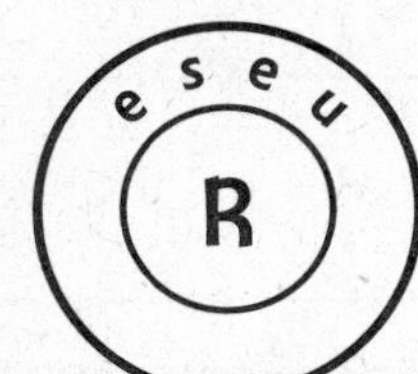


______________ To _____ an item means using it again rather than throwing it away.

# Apply Concepts

2 Many resources are limited. List some informed choices that people can make to conserve, dispose, and recycle different kinds of resources.

3 Draw a room in your home. Label three ways you could conserve energy or water there.

4 Tell what is being conserved in each picture.

Share with your family what you have learned about conservation. Make informed choices about the conservation, disposal, and recycling of materials that you use in your home.

**TEKS** **5.3D** connect grade-level appropriate science concepts with the history of science, science careers, and contribution of scientists **5.7C** identify alternative energy resources such as wind, solar, hydroelectric, geothermal, and biofuels

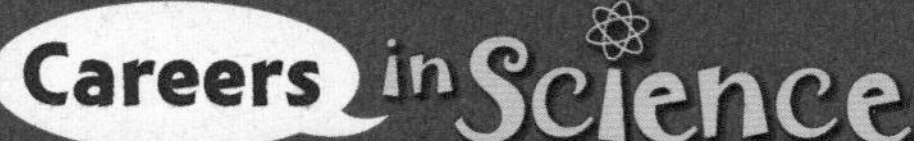

# 10 Things You Should Know About Alternative Energy Engineers

1. Alternative energy engineers reduce our use of fossil fuels.
2. They use renewable resources as energy sources.
3. They convert the sun's energy into heat and electrical energy.
4. They find the best ways to convert the wind's energy into heat and electrical energy.
5. They find ways to use plants such as corn for biofuel.
6. They weigh the pros and cons of each kind of energy.
7. They replace old methods with new technologies that are better for the environment.
8. They share their research results with other scientists.
9. They look for new ideas that have not yet been explored.

10. They try to save Earth's resources, using them wisely.

# Alternative Energy Debate

Electric cars may save money on fuel, but they cost more to buy. Two students are texting the pros and cons of using an electric car. Fill in the reasons for and against alternative energy.

**Great car! Electric cars are a great idea because**

______________________________

______________________________

______________________________

**They're great. One drawback, though, is**

______________________________

______________________________

______________________________

**That's true, but a good thing is**

______________________________

______________________________

______________________________

**Another thing that is a challenge is**

______________________________

______________________________

______________________________

**but the technologies get better every day!**

Inquiry Flipchart page 46

**TEKS** **5.1B** make informed choices in the conservation, disposal, and recycling of materials **5.2C** collect information by detailed observations... **5.3C** draw or develop a model that represents how something works or looks...

Name ______________________________

Essential Question

# How Can We Conserve Resources?

## Set a Purpose

What will you learn from this investigation?

______________________________

______________________________

______________________________

______________________________

## Think About the Procedure

Why do you think starch is added to the pulp mixture?

______________________________

______________________________

______________________________

______________________________

Why is it important to squeeze out the extra water?

______________________________

______________________________

______________________________

______________________________

## Record Your Data

In the space below, describe the physical characteristics of the paper you made.

## Draw Conclusions

Some of the paper you use now has been recycled from old paper. Draw conclusions about why people might choose to make paper from waste material instead of directly from trees.

## Analyze and Extend

1. Just as scientists do, you made a model to see how something might work on a larger scale. Using what you learned, suggest ways recycled paper might be made in a large factory.

2. How does the paper you made compare to the paper you use in school?

3. How does recycling paper help the environment and living things?

4. What are some other ways scrap paper could be recycled?

5. How would you change your paper if you were to make it again?

# Unit 8 Review

Name ______________________

## Vocabulary Review

Use the terms in the box to complete the sentences.

conservation
nonrenewable resource
pollution
recycle
renewable resource
reuse

TEKS 5.1B

1. The process of preserving and protecting an ecosystem or resource is ______________________.

TEKS 5.1B

2. A resource that nature can replace if the resource is used is called a(n) ______________________.

TEKS 5.1B

3. You can paint an old glass bottle and turn it into a vase to ______________________ it.

TEKS 5.9C

4. Any waste product or contamination that harms or dirties an ecosystem and harms organisms is ______________________.

TEKS 5.1B

5. A resource that nature cannot replace once it is used up is called a(n) ______________________.

TEKS 5.1B

6. Reusing the material from a product to make something else after the product has served its original purpose is a way to ______________________ that material and conserve resources.

## Science Concepts

Fill in the letter of the choice that best answers the question.

TEKS 5.7C

7. Where Amar lives, the weather is sunny much of the year. What alternative energy resource could Amar's family use to generate electricity?

   (A) drip irrigation
   (B) wind turbine
   (C) solar panel
   (D) LED bulbs

TEKS 5.7C

8. What is one advantage of using biofuels?

   (A) They conserve soil.
   (B) They are nonrenewable.
   (C) They reduce air pollution.
   (D) They increase energy use.

## Science Concepts

Fill in the letter of the choice that best answers the question.

**TEKS 5.1B, 5.2D**

**9.** You see this symbol on the bottom of a plastic container. What does it tell you about the container?

Ⓐ It cannot be reused or recycled.

Ⓑ It contains recycled materials.

Ⓒ It cannot be reused.

Ⓓ It can be recycled.

**TEKS 5.1B**

**10.** A farmer wants to protect his crops from insects and disease. He also wants to reduce soil erosion. Which soil conservation method should he use?

Ⓐ crop rotation

Ⓑ hydroponics

Ⓒ intercropping

Ⓓ contour farming

**TEKS 5.7C**

**11.** Jonah saw several of these objects in a field while on a trip with his family.

What alternative energy resource does this object use to generate electricity?

Ⓐ biofuel

Ⓑ geothermal energy

Ⓒ hydroelectric energy

Ⓓ wind

**TEKS 5.1B, 5.3A**

**12.** Luisa wants to help her family conserve water. She has made a list of ideas. Which of Luisa's ideas would best help her family save water?

Ⓐ Take baths instead of showers.

Ⓑ Turn off the water while brushing teeth.

Ⓒ Run only small loads in the washing machine.

Ⓓ Run the dishwasher when it is half full.

Name ___________________________

TEKS 5.1B, 5.2D

13. A farmer has used contour plowing to prepare a field before planting a crop in it.

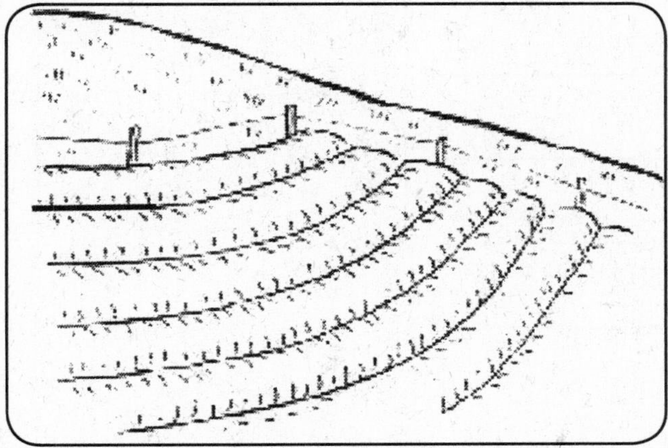

How does this type of plowing help protect soil?

(A) It guards against insects.

(B) It uses very little water.

(C) It prevents disease.

(D) It prevents erosion.

TEKS 5.7C

14. Where would you be most likely to find geothermal energy resources?

(A) in Earth

(B) in moving air

(C) in corn plants

(D) in flowing water

TEKS 5.1B

15. Andrea does the activities shown below every morning.

Which natural resource used in these activities should be conserved because it is nonrenewable?

(A) food

(B) fossil fuels

(C) plants

(D) water

TEKS 5.1B

16. Jake made the poster shown here.

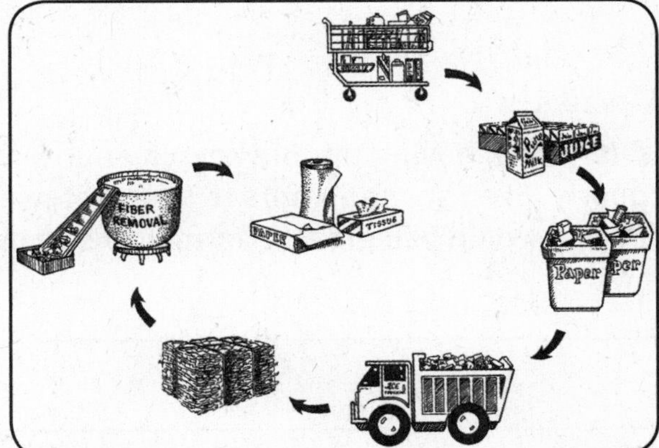


What would be the best title for his poster?

(A) Reusing Paper Reduces Wastes

(B) Dump Trucks Use Fossil Fuels

(C) Recycling Paper Helps Conserve Resources

(D) Grocery Shopping Takes a Lot of Time

## Apply Inquiry and Review the Big Idea

Write the answers to these questions.

TEKS 5.1B, 5.2F

17. Manuel's neighbor put an old tire out with the trash. Manuel found the tire and made the object in the picture. How many of the 3 Rs did Manuel apply? Explain your answer.

TEKS 5.7C

18. Beth is concerned about conserving limited resources and is trying to think of ways her town could decrease their use of fossil fuels. Identify at least four alternative energy resources that could possibly be used in the place of fossil fuels.

TEKS 5.1B; 5.2F

19. A farmer is having trouble keeping nutrients in her soil. As a result, her crops are growing poorly. Even so, she wants to keep her use of chemical fertilizers to a minimum. What advice would you give the farmer as she plans next year's crops? Explain your answer.

TEKS 5.1B

20. A town uses 375 metric tons of aluminum cans each month. It recycles $\frac{4}{10}$ of the aluminum cans it uses each month, but its goal is to recycle $\frac{8}{10}$ of the cans. How many more metric tons of aluminum cans must the town recycle each month to reach its goal?

UNIT 9

# Weather and Climate

## Big Idea

Weather can change, but climate is the pattern of weather an area experiences over a long period of time.

TEKS 5.1A, 5.2A, 5.2F, 5.2G, 5.3A, 5.3D, 5.8A, 5.8B

## I Wonder Why

The desert is hot and dry, but there is a storm on the horizon. How can the desert be dry even when it rains? *Turn the page to find out.*

**Here's why** Deserts may have a hot and dry climate, but the weather in a desert can change. Although it is typically dry in deserts, occasionally, when the conditions are right, it rains. Many desert organisms are ready when the weather changes and the scarce rains arrive.

In this unit, you will explore the Big Idea, the Essential Questions, and the Investigations on the Inquiry Flipchart.

Levels of Inquiry Key ■ DIRECTED ■ GUIDED ■ INDEPENDENT

**Big Idea** Weather can change, but climate is the pattern of weather an area experiences over a long period of time.

## Essential Questions



**Science Notebook**

Before you begin each lesson, be sure to write your thoughts about the Essential Question.

TEKS 5.2D. analyze and interpret information to construct reasonable explanations from... evidence 5.3A analyze, evaluate, and critique scientific explanations by using...logical reasoning, and...examining all sides of scientific evidence of those scientific explanations 5.8B explain how the Sun and the ocean interact in the water cycle

Lesson 1

Essential Question

# How Does Water Move on Earth's Surface?

## Engage Your Brain!

Find the answer to the following question in this lesson and record it here.

The sunlight shines behind the raining cloud. What role does the sun play in the formation of rain?

______________________________

______________________________

______________________________

______________________________

## Active Reading

### Lesson Vocabulary

List each term. As you learn about each one, makes notes in the Interactive Glossary.

______________ ______________

______________ ______________

______________ ______________

### Cause and Effect

Some ideas in this lesson are connected by a cause-and-effect relationship. Why something happens is a cause. What happens as a result of something else is an effect. Active readers look for effects by asking themselves, What happened? They look for causes by asking, Why did it happen?



Inquiry Flipchart p. 47 — Blowing Hot and Cold/Crackling Afternoon

# The Sun and the Sea

Light leaves the sun and travels millions of kilometers through space. What happens when it reaches Earth?

**Active Reading** As you read, draw circles around two things that are being compared.

Solar energy is absorbed, or taken in, by Earth's surface. This energy is then released throughout the day to heat the atmosphere. The **atmosphere** is the mixture of gases, dust, and other small particles that surrounds Earth.

Most of Earth is covered by water. Water heats up and cools down more slowly than land does. Because of this, oceans are like "storage tanks" for heat energy. They hold in heat and slowly release it, helping keep Earth's temperatures stable.

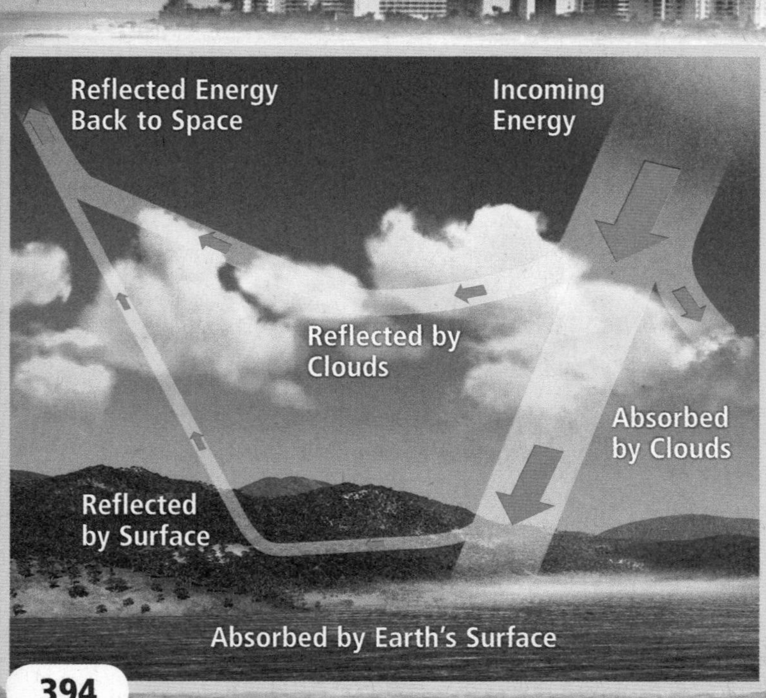


## Sun-Ocean Interaction

The sun is the main source of energy on Earth. Its energy drives many processes, including the movement of water between land, air, and oceans. When the ocean absorbs energy from the sun, its surface heats up. The heated water enters the atmosphere—leaving the salts in the ocean water behind. This water eventually falls back to Earth as rain, snow, or other forms of precipitation.

## Heat Transfer

Ocean currents move heat energy. The sun's energy is more intense near the equator. Ocean currents that start there, such as the Gulf Stream, are warm. These currents keep some coastal areas warmer year-round. Ocean currents that start near the poles are cooler.

Oceans help moderate the weather. They keep the temperatures from being too hot or too cold. Oceans are the main source of the billions of tiny water droplets that make up clouds. These clouds deliver water that was once in the oceans to coastal areas and far inland.

## Heating and Cooling

The different heating and cooling rates of land and water affect daily and seasonal temperatures. Coastal areas are often cooler during the day than inland areas that are the same distance from the equator. How do you think this pattern would change at night?

## Do the Math!

### Interpret a Table

The table shows information about Dallas, TX, which is inland, and Houston, TX, which is near the coast. Use the data to answer the questions below.

| Month | Dallas | | Houston | |
|---|---|---|---|---|
| | Average High (°C) | Average Low (°C) | Average High (°C) | Average Low (°C) |
| January | 12 | 0.4 | 16.4 | 6.1 |
| June | 32.7 | 21.1 | 32.2 | 22.6 |
| November | 19.3 | 7.4 | 22.4 | 11.6 |

1. Analyze the data. What pattern do you observe?

______________________

______________________

______________________

2. Explain why this pattern occurs.

______________________

______________________

______________________

# The Ups and Downs of Water

At any time billions of liters of water pass right in front of your eyes. Don't see it? Neither do scientists. So how do they get to know about water's up and down journey on Earth's surface? Let's find out!

**Active Reading** As you read these two pages, underline three sentences that describe a process we can't directly observe.

Water on Earth's surface is constantly on the go. It moves back and forth between the land, the oceans, and the atmosphere in a cycle. A *cycle* is a series of events or processes that repeat. Some of the processes involved in water's movement are too difficult to observe directly. Sure, we can see clouds and rain, but those are just a part of water's journey.

We use models to study the large-scale movement of water on Earth. Models represent objects, events, or ideas. They help us study things that are too small to see, such as atoms, or events that take place too quickly, too slowly, or on a very large scale. A simple model of water's continuous movement, as shown on these pages, begins with the sun.

## Evaporation

As the sun heats water, its particles move faster and faster. When water gains enough energy, it changes into a gas called *water vapor*. This process is called **evaporation**. Evaporation can occur from surfaces of large bodies of water, such as oceans, lakes, rivers, and streams. It can also occur from small surfaces, like puddles on roads or the water that coats your skin after a swim.

## Condensation

Water vapor rises into the atmosphere, where temperatures are cooler. As it cools, it changes back into liquid water. This process is called **condensation**. Millions of tiny droplets of water come together to form clouds. Clouds that form high in the sky may consist of ice crystals. You can also see condensation on Earth's surface when dewdrops form on grass.

▶ Think about other examples of condensation you see every day. Draw your idea in the space below and explain how your drawing models condensation.

______________________________________

______________________________________

______________________________________

## Precipitation

Water droplets in clouds come together to form larger droplets. Eventually, the droplets become too heavy to remain in the air and fall to Earth as rain. This process is called **precipitation**. Temperature affects the kind of precipitation that forms. In high clouds and during winter, water vapor forms ice crystals, or snow. Rain that falls through freezing air might form hail or sleet or freezing rain.

# What Goes Up, Must Come Down

Did you know that any given time, nearly 13,000 cubic kilometers of water are in the atmosphere? What happens when that water falls to Earth?

**Active Reading** As you read these pages, draw one line under a cause. Draw two lines under the effect.

### Glaciers

Glaciers are large pieces of ice that move very slowly. They are found mainly on mountaintops and at Earth's poles. They can shrink and expand. Sunlight melts and evaporates snow and ice on a glacier's surface.



### Runoff

Gravity causes runoff to flow over Earth's surface. Eventually, it may enter rivers and flow back into the ocean. It can also enter lakes or seep into the ground.



### Groundwater

Groundwater is water that seeps into cracks in the ground and fills up spaces between rock particles. Groundwater near the surface can evaporate within weeks or years. But if it flows deep into the ground, it can take thousands of years to slowly make its way into a river, lake, or ocean.

Luckily, all the water in the atmosphere doesn't fall back to Earth at once. As water falls, some is evaporated back into the atmosphere, where it condenses into clouds. The movement of water between the atmosphere, land, and oceans is called the **water cycle**.

Because oceans are the largest bodies of water, they are the greatest source of evaporated water. They are also the place where most water falls back to Earth.

Several things can happen to precipitation that falls on land. It can be used by plants and evaporate from their leaves in a process called *transpiration*. It also can fall into a lake and then evaporate from the lake's surface. Or it can flow over the ground as **runoff**. Land precipitation can seep into the ground and become *groundwater*. Groundwater in *aquifers*, or layers of rock that store water, is a source of drinking water for many people.

Precipitation that falls as snow on mountaintops or near Earth's poles may form glaciers. This solid water may take a long time to re-enter the water cycle.

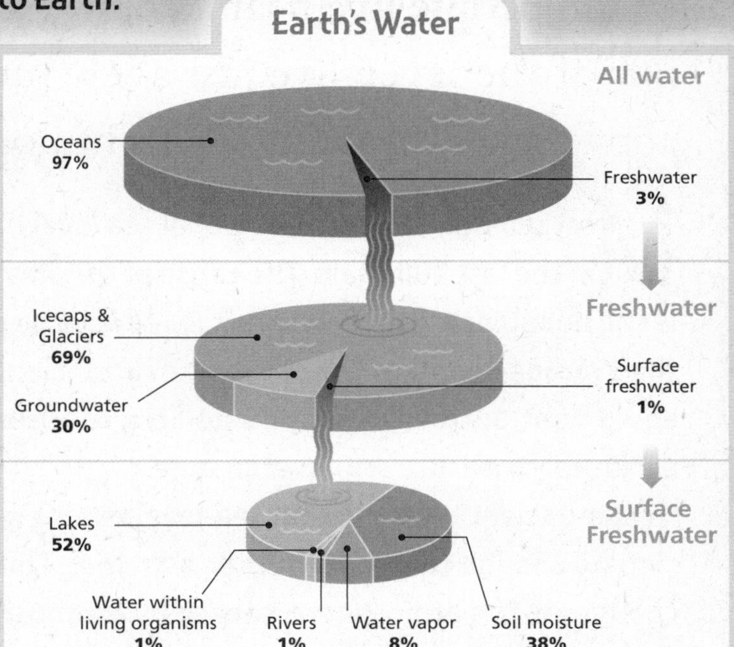


The oceans play a large role in the water cycle. About $\frac{9}{10}$ of the water that evaporates into the atmosphere comes from oceans.

Condensation

Evaporation

▶ Rank glaciers, runoff, and groundwater *1*, *2*, or *3* to indicate which stores water the longest. Rank "1" the place where water evaporates the fastest. Communicate your reasoning orally to your teacher or a classmate.

Why It Matters

# Oceans Rising

Where do you live? Globally, seven out of ten people live near a coast—and three out of the seven live just a few meters above sea level. Why is this important?

Most scientists agree that global sea level has risen in the last 100 years. The cause of this increase is still debated. What are the facts? *Sea level* describes the average height of the ocean's surface. Scientists use equipment, such as ships and satellites, to observe and accurately measure sea-level change.

Some scientists think that sea-level rise is evidence of climate change caused by human activities. They claim that changes to the atmosphere, caused by combustion of fossil fuels, is causing glaciers to melt. As a result, meltwater then flows into the oceans.

Other scientists suggest that sea-level changes are part of a natural cycle. Over millions of years, they note, sea level has risen and fallen several times. During long, cold periods of time known as ice ages, large amounts of water are stored in glaciers. This causes sea level to drop. At the end of ice ages, glaciers melt causing sea level to rise.

Many scientists suggest that a combination of several factors is likely the cause of sea-level rise. They explain that shifting landmasses, sediment buildup at the bottom of the oceans, and human activities all play a role in sea-level rise.

No matter the cause, even a small increase in sea level could cause problems in low-lying coastal cities. These cities could flood during storms. People could lose their homes and wildlife could lose their habitats.

## Changes in Sea Level: 1958–2008

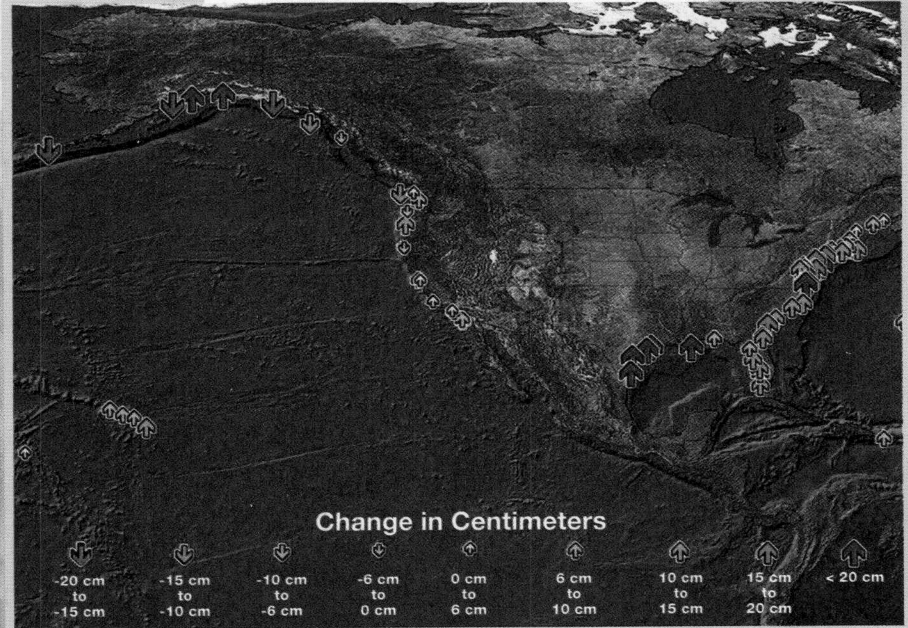


Scientists collect and analyze data from arou[nd] the world to find evide[nce] of changes in sea level. [This] map shows areas in No[rth] America where change[s] have been observed.

Sea level in Galveston Bay, Texas, has risen by 60 cm in the last 100 years. Computer models show that people there could be displaced if this trend continues.

▶ Suppose a classmate examines the information on these pages and concludes: "In less than a year, people living in coastal cities will lose their homes because of sea-level rise caused by their use of fossil fuels." Examine the scientific evidence about sea-level rise on these pages to write a critique of your classmate's explanation.

______________________________________________

______________________________________________

______________________________________________

______________________________________________

______________________________________________

When you're done, use the answer key to check and revise your work.

**The idea web below summarizes the lesson. Complete the web.**

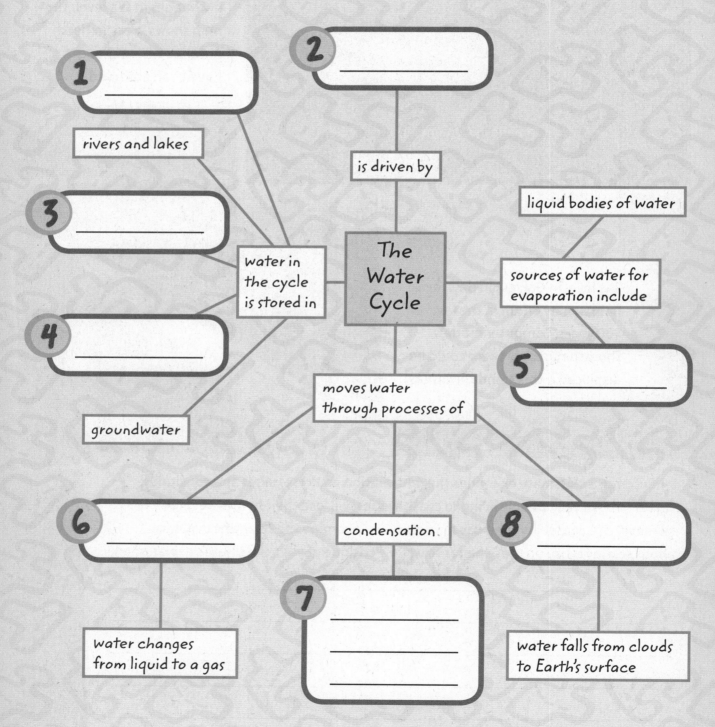

The Water Cycle

water in the cycle is stored in

1 ______________

rivers and lakes

3 ______________

4 ______________

groundwater

is driven by

2 ______________

sources of water for evaporation include

liquid bodies of water

5 ______________

moves water through processes of

6 ______________

water changes from liquid to a gas

condensation

7 ______________ ______________ ______________

8 ______________

water falls from clouds to Earth's surface

Answer Key: 1. Any of the following: oceans, ice caps/glaciers, or atmosphere 2. the sun 3 Any of the following: oceans, ice caps/ glaciers, or atmosphere 4. Any of the following: oceans, ice caps/glaciers, or atmosphere 5. glaciers 6. evaporation 7. water changes from a gas to a liquid 8. precipitation

# Brain Check



Name ________________________________

## Word Play

**1** **Use the words in the lesson to complete the puzzle.**

1. Representation of an object or event
2. Water in a gaseous state
3. Source of most water that evaporates from Earth's surface
4. Snow, sleet, rain, or hail that falls to Earth's surface
5. Mixture of gases, dust, and other small particles that surrounds Earth
6. Water that flows over land
7. Rock layer that contains underground water
8. Shows how water moves between Earth's atmosphere, oceans, and land
9. Huge piece of slow-moving ice
10. Water that seeps into the ground
11. Process by which water changes from a gas to a liquid

1.
2.
3.
4.
5.
6.
7.
8.
9.
10.
11.

**Read down the red squares to answer the riddle below.**

**You don't always need a towel at the pool. Just hang out in the sun and your skin will get dry by _ _ _ _ _ _ _ _ _ _ _.**

# Apply Concepts

2 Explain what makes water's movement on Earth a cycle.

3 Give examples of water in a solid, liquid, and gaseous state in the atmosphere.

4 Draw a model of the path a water particle might take through the water cycle. Use labels and arrows in your drawing. Make sure to include the cycle's energy source.

5 Analyze the data in the table. It is from two cities located the same distance from the equator. Infer which city is near an ocean. Explain your reasoning.

| Average Temperatures (°C) | | |
|---|---|---|
| | City A | City B |
| Summer | 31 | 29 |
| Fall | 18 | 22 |
| Winter | 4 | 13 |
| Spring | 20 | 23 |

Name ______________________



6 Draw an *X* on the map to show a place where most of the sun's energy is absorbed. Circle a place where most of Earth's fresh water is stored. Box a land feature that would quickly return precipitation back to Earth's largest water-storage system.

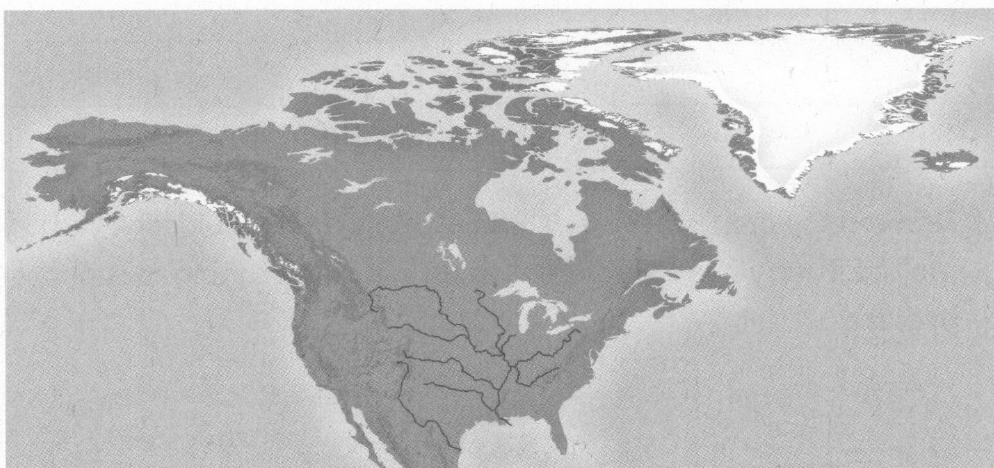

7 Land and water absorb the sun's energy at different rates. Using the setup below, how can you demonstrate this?

______________________

______________________

______________________

8

Scientists have evidence that millions of years ago, all glaciers on Earth's surface melted.

Part A. What can you infer about Earth's atmosphere during this period of time?

______________________________

Part B. How would conditions during this period have affected the water cycle?

______________________________

______________________________

______________________________

Part C. Draw on the map to predict what Earth's surface would look like if glaciers melted. Then write a statement using logical reasoning to support your drawing.

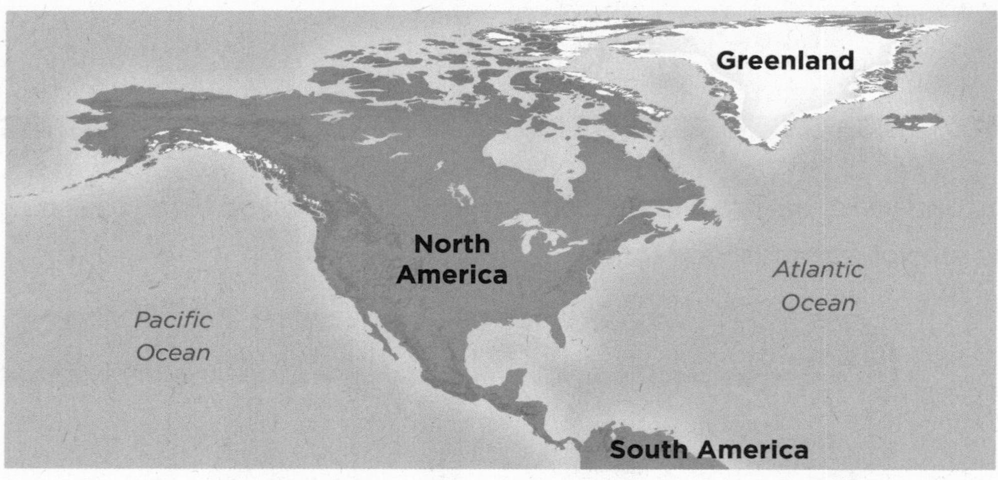


______________________________

______________________________

______________________________

Go outside with a family member on a sunny day. Pour some water on a sidewalk and observe how long it takes to evaporate. Talk about what can happen to the water after it rises into the atmosphere.

**TEKS 5.3D** connect grade-level appropriate science concepts with the history of science, science careers, and contributions of scientists.

# Meet the Stormchasers

## Shirley Murillo

Shirley Murillo studies hurricanes. She flies into the powerful storms on a special aircraft. Murillo works for the National Oceanic and Atmospheric Administration, or NOAA. During flights, she gathers data about hurricanes using special instruments that produce 3-D images of the storm. These tools measure wind speed, wind direction, and pressure. Back in her lab, she uses computers to analyze the information.

Murillo says flying into a hurricane is like riding a roller coaster for 10 hours straight! Her research helps scientists forecast when and where a hurricane may hit, giving people enough time to evacuate.

## Reed Timmer

Reed Timmer is a scientist who chases tornadoes. He photographed his first tornado in 1998, and has witnessed over 330 of the storms. Timmer and his team chase tornadoes in "The Dominator." This armored storm research vehicle uses mobile radar to measure wind speeds in tornadoes. Reed also uses probes to gather data and images inside the violent storms.

Timmer has been inside of a tornado! The data he gathers are used to build structures to withstand severe storms and to create better storm warning systems.

# Meet the Stormchasers

Use the information on the previous page to match the statements in the list to the correct scientist. Write the matching statements in the box labeled with the scientist's name.

## Reed Timmer

## Statements

- Drives in the Dominator
- Develops 3-D images
- Studies tornadoes

- Studies hurricanes
- Uses mobile radar
- Flies in an airplane

## Shirley Murillo

Inquiry Flipchart page 48

**TEKS** **5.3A** in all fields of science...critique scientific explanations by using empirical evidence... **5.3C** draw or develop a model that represents how something works...that cannot be seen **5.8B** explain how the Sun and ocean interact in the water cycle

Name ______________________

Essential Question

# What Happens During the Water Cycle?

## Set a Purpose

**How do models help you study processes such as the water cycle?**

______________________

______________________

______________________

______________________

## Think About the Procedure

**Why did the landform models take up only one-fourth of the containers?**

______________________

______________________

______________________

______________________

**Why did you add salt to the water?**

______________________

______________________

______________________

______________________

**Why did you put the containers on a sunny windowsill?**

______________________

______________________

______________________

______________________

## Record Your Data

**In the space below, write or draw your results.**

| Observations of Models | |
|---|---|
| Model without ocean water | Model with ocean water |
| | |

## Draw Conclusions

How did your models work?

## Analyze and Extend

1. What role do oceans play in the water cycle?

2. Suppose you kept the models under a lamp overnight. What would happen to the models?

3. What is the role of the plastic wrap in the model? What does it represent?

4. What would happen if you left the models uncovered in the sunlight?

5. Draw what would happen if you left the models outdoors in a place with freezing temperatures. Describe your drawing on the lines below.

6. Think of other questions you would like to ask about the water cycle.

**TEKS** **5.2G** construct appropriate simple graphs, tables, maps, and charts using technology including computers to organize, examine, and evaluate information **5.8A** differentiate between weather and climate

Lesson 3

Essential Question

# How do Weather and Climate Differ?

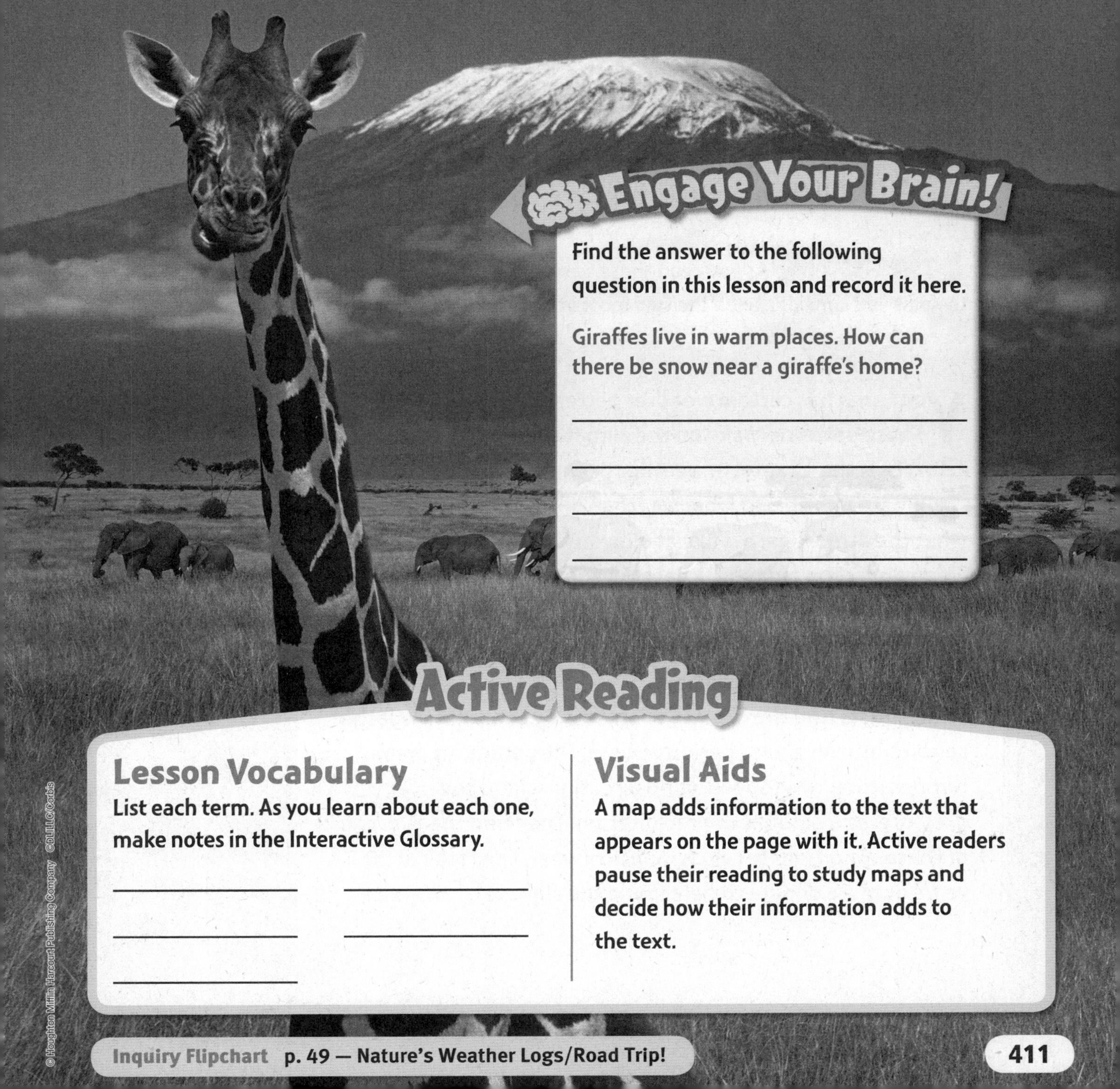

## Engage Your Brain!

Find the answer to the following question in this lesson and record it here.

Giraffes live in warm places. How can there be snow near a giraffe's home?

______________________

______________________

______________________

______________________

## Active Reading

### Lesson Vocabulary

List each term. As you learn about each one, make notes in the Interactive Glossary.

______________ ______________

______________ ______________

______________

### Visual Aids

A map adds information to the text that appears on the page with it. Active readers pause their reading to study maps and decide how their information adds to the text.



Inquiry Flipchart p. 49 — Nature's Weather Logs/Road Trip!

# Climate vs. Weather

During the summer, it might be sunny one day and cloudy the next. But for most places, temperatures in the summer stay warm. The weather changes, but the overall weather pattern stays the same.

**Active Reading** As you read these two pages, draw stars next to what you consider to be the two most important sentences, and be ready to explain why.

Your area has certain weather patterns during the year. These patterns make up the climate where you live. **Climate** is the long-term weather patterns of a place.

Climate is different from weather. **Weather** describes what the atmosphere is like at a given time and place. For example, on average, a desert might get only a few centimeters of rain each year. The desert has a dry climate. But the weather in the desert can be different. It might be rainy one day and dry the next.

Scientists find the climate of an area by averaging weather conditions over a long period of time. They study an area's temperature, wind speed, wind direction, cloud cover, air pressure, and amount of precipitation. They find the average of these conditions for each month or year. They look at 30 years or more of data to determine the climate of an area.

# Do the Math!

## Analyze Data

Use the data in the table to construct a line graph on the computer and attach it to this page. Then compare these graphs to answer the questions below.

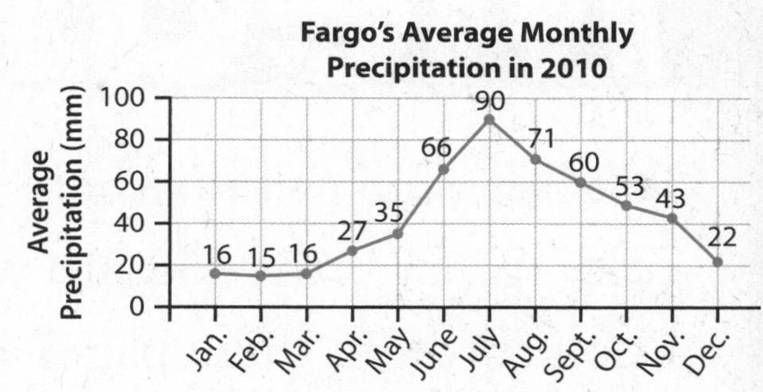


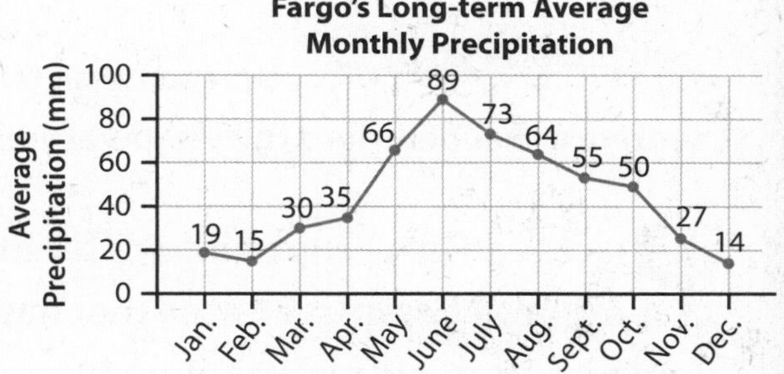


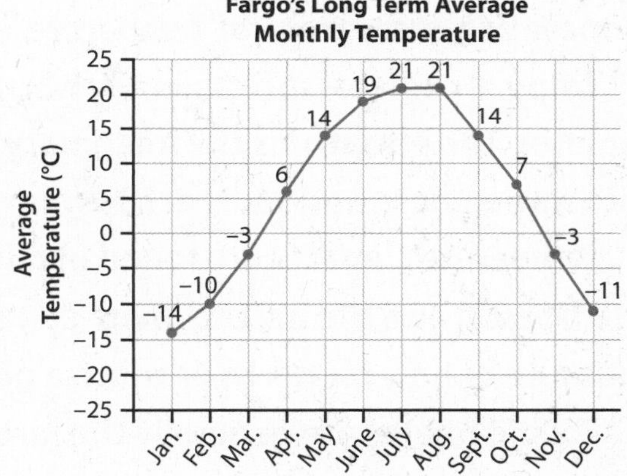


1. During which month in 2010 was Fargo's average precipitation closest to its long-term average? Which month is most different?

_______________

_______________

_______________

2. Examine and evaluate the long-term average monthly temperatures in Fargo and in Houston. What conclusion can you make about climate differences in these two cities?

_______________

_______________

_______________

**Long-term Average Monthly Temperatures for Houston, Texas**

| Month | Average Temp. °C | Month | Average Temp. °C |
|---|---|---|---|
| Jan | 11.0 | July | 28.6 |
| Feb | 13.0 | Aug | 28.5 |
| Mar | 16.8 | Sept | 26.0 |
| Apr | 20.3 | Oct | 21.3 |
| May | 24.3 | Nov | 16.1 |
| June | 27.4 | Dec | 12.1 |

**Attach your computer-constructed graph here.**

# Hot, Cold, and Medium

Is it hot year-round where you live? Or is it cold? What is the climate where you live? Look through these pages and find out!

**Active Reading** As you read these two pages, underline the sentence that describes the temperature in each climate zone.

Places can be grouped into different climate zones. A **climate zone** is an area that has similar average temperatures and precipitation throughout. Three of Earth's climate zones are *tropical, temperate,* and *polar*.

Tropical climates are generally warm. They occur near the equator. The **equator** is the imaginary line that divides Earth into its northern and southern hemispheres, or halves.

Temperate climates are found in middle latitudes, between the tropical and the polar climate zones. **Latitude** is a measure of how far north or south a place is from the equator.

Polar climates are generally the farthest from the equator. They have cold temperatures year-round and low amounts of precipitation.

Temperate climate zones have moderate temperatures and varying precipitation. For most of the year, the temperature ranges from 10 °C to 18 °C. They usually have four distinct seasons. Much of the United States is found in this zone.

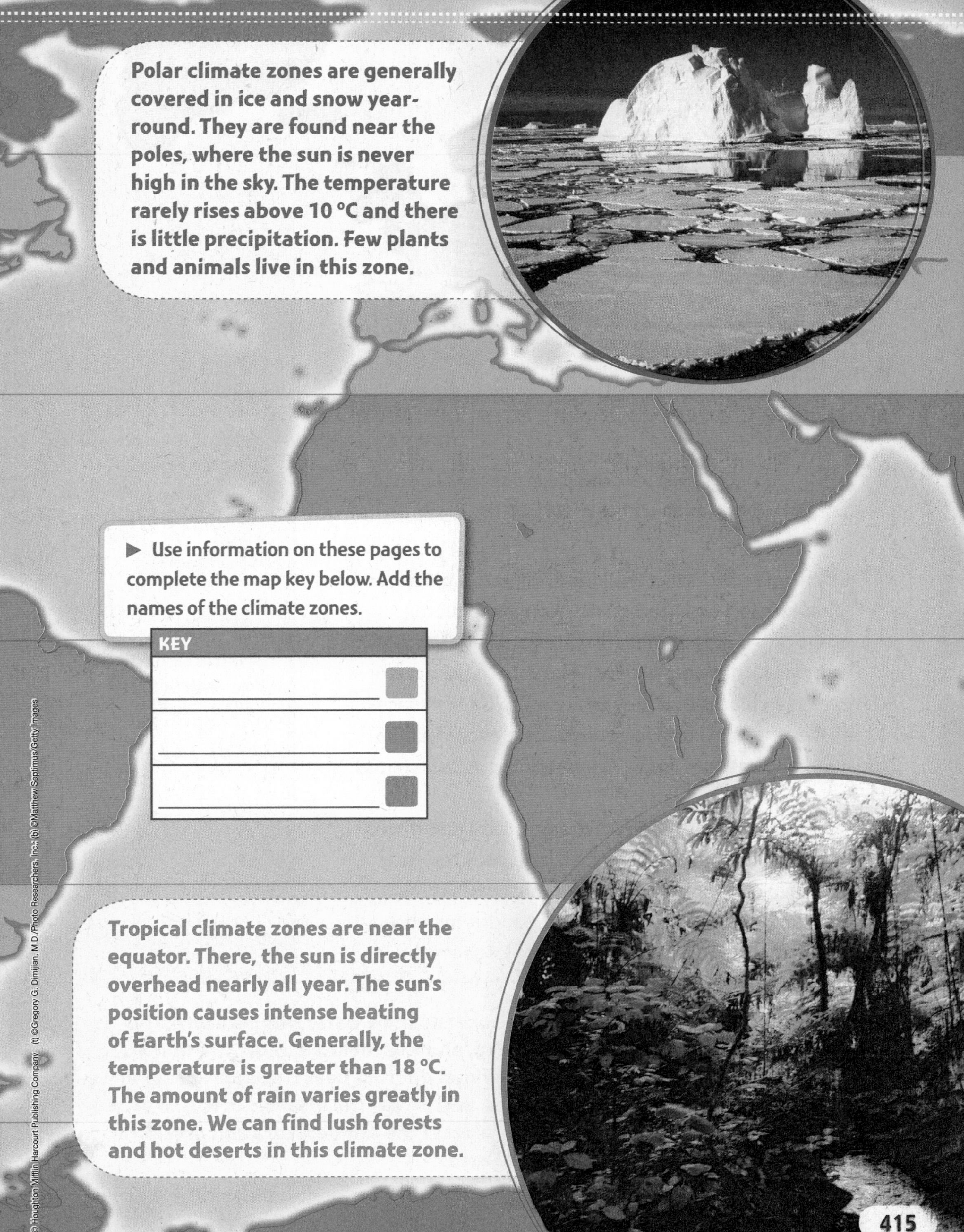
Polar climate zones are generally covered in ice and snow year-round. They are found near the poles, where the sun is never high in the sky. The temperature rarely rises above 10 °C and there is little precipitation. Few plants and animals live in this zone.
▶ Use information on these pages to complete the map key below. Add the names of the climate zones.
KEY
Tropical climate zones are near the equator. There, the sun is directly overhead nearly all year. The sun's position causes intense heating of Earth's surface. Generally, the temperature is greater than 18 °C. The amount of rain varies greatly in this zone. We can find lush forests and hot deserts in this climate zone.

# Why Climates Differ

Why does it rarely snow in Florida? Why isn't Alaska warm year-round? What things make one climate different from another?

**Active Reading** As you read this page, draw one line under a cause. Draw two lines under the effect.

Different factors affect the kind of climate a place has. These factors include distance from the equator, elevation, proximity to bodies of water, and landforms.

Most places that are close to the equator have warmer climates than places that are farther away. But if a place has a high elevation, it will have a cool climate even if it is on the equator. That's why snowy mountaintops can be found in tropical places.

Oceans and large lakes affect climate, too. Water heats up and cools down more slowly than land does. So places near the coast are often cooler in summer and warmer in winter than places far from the ocean. Landforms, such as mountains, can affect the rain pattern of large areas.

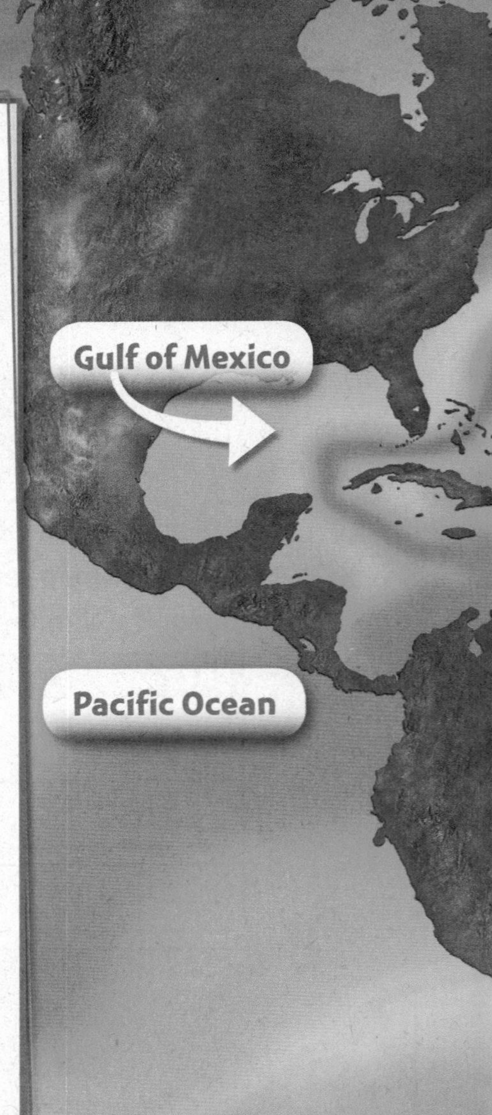


**The different colors on the oceans show water temperature. The warmest water is colored red, and the coolest is blue. The *Gulf Stream* is a warm ocean current. It flows up from near the equator, along the east coast of North America, and across the Atlantic Ocean toward northern Europe. It deeply affects the temperature and precipitation amounts of nearby coastal areas.**

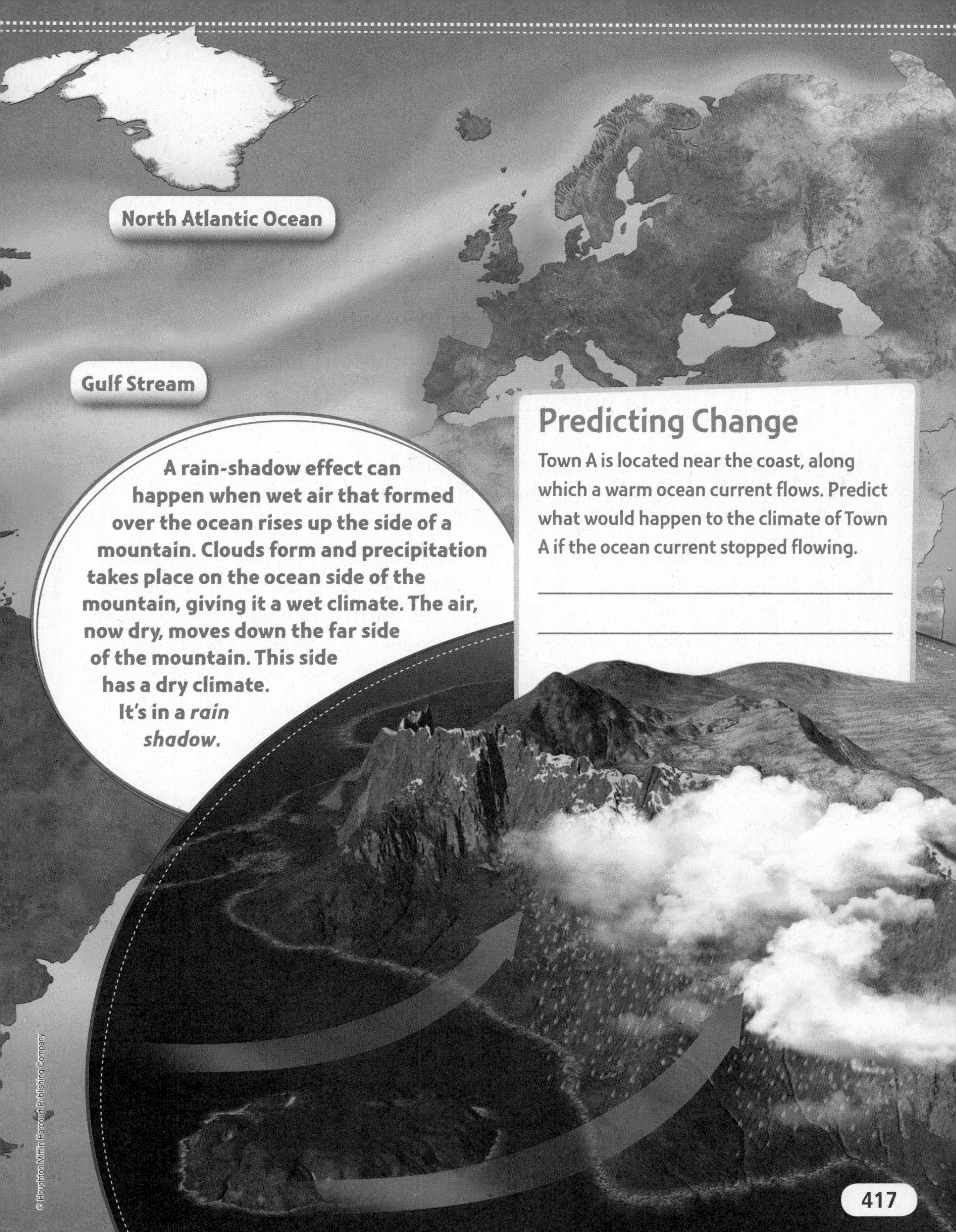


A rain-shadow effect can happen when wet air that formed over the ocean rises up the side of a mountain. Clouds form and precipitation takes place on the ocean side of the mountain, giving it a wet climate. The air, now dry, moves down the far side of the mountain. This side has a dry climate. It's in a *rain shadow*.

## Predicting Change

Town A is located near the coast, along which a warm ocean current flows. Predict what would happen to the climate of Town A if the ocean current stopped flowing.

______________________________

______________________________

# Climate and the Environment

Why do polar bears live in cold places, while elephants live in warm places? How does climate affect the living and nonliving things in a place?

**Active Reading** **As you read this page, find and underline examples of how climate affects living and nonliving things.**

Climate affects where organisms can live. A polar bear has a thick layer of fat that keeps it warm in the polar climate where it lives. Maple trees have broad leaves to capture sunlight during the warm summer months. They shed their leaves during the cold, dry winter to prevent water loss.

Climate also affects the nonliving parts of the environment. Over time, wind-driven waves can reshape a continent's coastline. Rain, wind, and changes in temperature can cause rock to break. The broken bits of rock can mix with dead plant and animal matter to form soil.

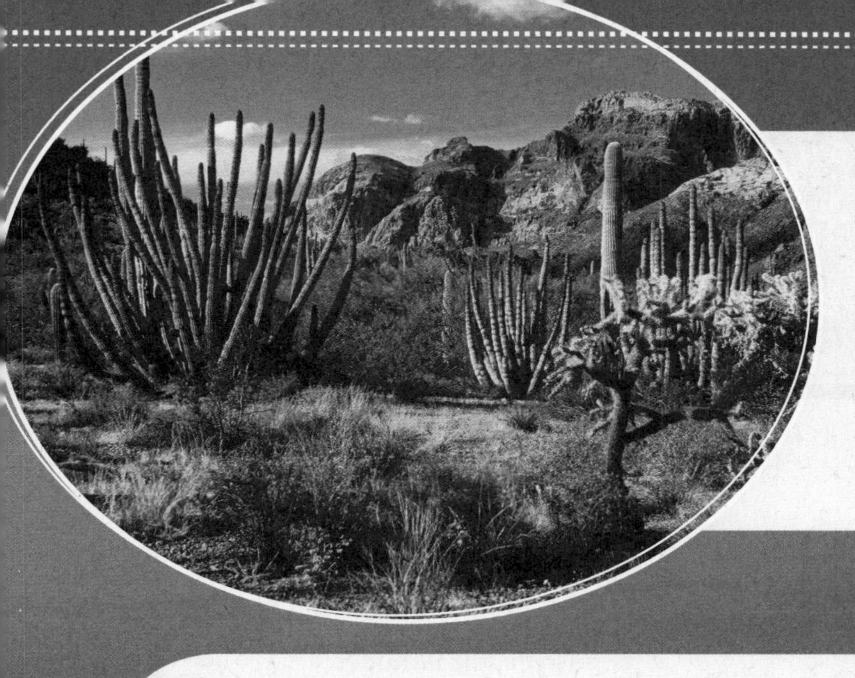

**Desert:** A desert is a dry environment. Temperatures may vary greatly in deserts. It can be very hot during the day and cold at night. Living things in deserts need to be able to survive on little water. Cactuses have a waxy coating that helps them store water.

**Swamp:** Swamps can be covered by fresh water, salt water, or both. Swamps occur in places where the ground cannot soak in all the precipitation or runoff that reaches the area. Temperatures may be very hot in swamps for part of the year. Many types of plants and animals live in swamps.

**Tropical rainforest:** Tropical rainforests are found in warm, wet climates. They receive nearly the same amount of sunlight year-round. Vegetation covers most of the land in tropical rainforests. It provides food and shelter for many animals.

► What effects would a drier climate have in a swamp environment?

______________________________

______________________________

______________________________

______________________________

When you're done, use the answer key to check and revise your work.

**Complete the outline below to summarize the lesson.**

**1**

I. Weather

A. ① ____________________

B. can change from one day to the next

II. Climate

A. ② ____________________

B. determined by the long-term average precipitation and temperature

III. Main climate zones

A. ③ ____________________

1. warm year-round
2. can be wet or dry
3. found near the equator

B. Temperate

1. ④ ____________________
2. different amounts of precipitation
3. found in middle latitudes

C. Polar

1. usually little precipitation
2. ⑤ ____________________
3. found in high latitudes

IV. ⑥ ____________________

A. bodies of water

B. landforms

C. elevation

D. distance from the equator

## Summarize

**Fill in the missing words to tell how scientists determine the climate of a place.**

Climate is different from 7. ________________, which describes what the atmosphere is like at a given time and place. Scientists find the climate of a place by averaging weather conditions over a 8. ________________ period of time.

They study an area's temperature, wind speed, wind direction, cloud cover, air pressure, and amount of 9. ________________.

They find the 10. ________________ of these conditions for each month of the year. They look at 11. ________________ years or more of data to find the climate of a place.

Answer key: 1. what the atmosphere is like at a given place and time 2. the long-term weather patterns of a place 3. Tropical 4. moderate temperatures 5. cold year-round 6. Factors that affect climate 7. weather 8. long 9. precipitation 10. average 11. 30

# Brain Check

Lesson 3

Name ____________________

## Word Play

**1** Use the clues to unscramble the words in the box. Use the word bank if you need help.

| | |
|---|---|
| 1. qaroeut: the imaginary line that divides Earth into the northern and southern hemispheres, or halves | |
| 2. ertmpeate emlciat: has moderate temperatures | |
| 3. taliecm noze: an area with the same kind of climate conditions | |
| 4. dutlatei: distance of a place from the equator | |
| 5. lopricta itleamc: is warm year-round | |
| 6. rewaeth: state of the atmosphere at a certain time and place | |
| 7. ropal atmlcie: is cold year-round | |
| 8. catmile: long-term weather patterns of a place | |

latitude* temperate climate climate zone* polar climate
climate* equator* tropical climate weather*

*Key Lesson Vocabulary

# Apply Concepts

**2** The pictures below show different kinds of clothing you can wear during the year. During what kind of weather would you wear the clothing shown? Write your answers on the lines under the pictures.

_______________ _______________ _______________

**3** Correctly label each statement below with a *C* if it refers to climate and a *W* if it refers to weather.

a. In Antarctica, the average yearly temperature is below freezing. _______

b. Cherrapunji, India, may be the rainiest place on Earth. _______

c. It hasn't rained for two weeks in Macon, Georgia. _______

d. Today's air temperature was the highest this week. _______

**4** In the picture below, add arrows to show how air moves to form a rain shadow. Add labels showing where you would find a dry climate and a wet climate.

Name ___________________________



5 Label the climate zones in the map below.

A ___________________

B ___________________

C ___________________

6 The graph below shows the long-term average monthly temperature of a place. In which climate zone is this place likely to be found? Explain.

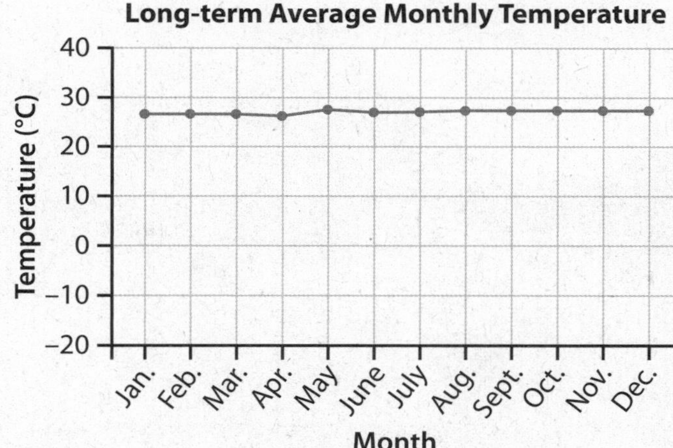


___________________________________________________________

___________________________________________________________

7 Differentiate between climate and weather. Suppose the climate of a rainforest changes. Its temperature is now always near or below freezing, but its precipitation remains high. Draw and describe what this place would look like after a few years.

_______________________________________________

_______________________________________________

_______________________________________________

_______________________________________________

8 The picture shows a landform. Label where the climate will be the coolest and where it will be the warmest on the landform.

Share what you have learned about weather and climate with your family. Find out about how people live in different climates. Work with a family member to make a model of a home in a different climate.

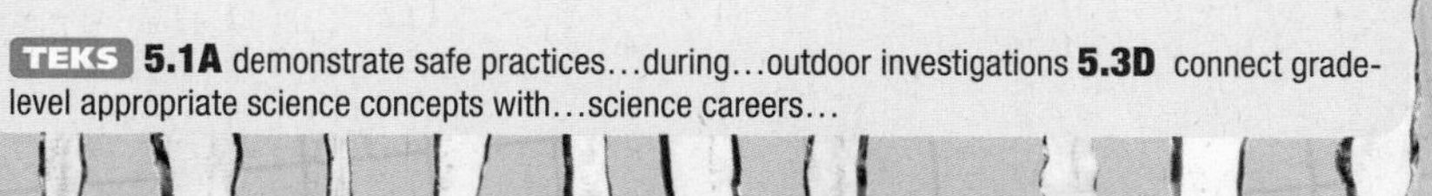

TEKS 5.1A demonstrate safe practices...during...outdoor investigations 5.3D connect grade-level appropriate science concepts with...science careers...


S.T.E.M.

Engineering & Technology

# Extreme Weather Gear

Researchers need special clothing to survive in extreme-weather Arctic environments. Layers that serve different purposes provide protection. But the layers can't be too bulky, or the wearer won't be able to move around easily.

Headwear

Down coat

Mittens/gloves

Down pants

Insulated boots

Boots need to be waterproof, warm, and lightweight. Your feet are far from your heart, so it is harder for warm blood to keep them warm. So gear for hands and feet must be very effective.

This fabric's outer layer keeps out water and wind. Inner layers provide insulation and help keep the body dry.

## Think About It

Keeping warm is important, but so is keeping dry! Clothing that causes a person to sweat can be dangerous. Wet skin can chill quickly. How could extreme-weather clothing be designed to prevent that?

_______________________________________________

_______________________________________________

continued

Dressing to deal with extreme weather conditions applies not only to the cold. The body needs protection in extreme heat as well.

What gear would you wear to protect yourself in the environment below? Draw the gear, and explain what protection it provides.

Suppose you're going to do an outdoor investigation. The weather forecast predicts rain. What would you wear? From what materials should your clothing be made?

## Build On It!

Rise to the engineering design challenge—complete **Design It: Water Catchers** in the Inquiry Flipchart.

# Unit 9 Review

Name ______________________________

## Vocabulary Review

Use the terms in the box to complete the sentences.

| climate |
|---|
| condensation |
| evaporation |
| precipitation |
| water cycle |
| weather |

TEKS 5.8A

1. When describing the atmosphere at a given time and place, you are describing ______________________.

TEKS 5.8B

2. The ______________________ shows how water moves on Earth between the oceans, atmosphere, and land.

TEKS 5.8B

3. The sun's energy causes water to change from a liquid to a gas during the process of ______________________.

TEKS 5.8B

4. During the water cycle, water changes from a gas to a liquid during the process of ______________________.

TEKS 5.8A

5. The average of the weather conditions for an area over a long period of time is called ______________________.

TEKS 5.8B

6. Water that falls from clouds onto Earth's land and into bodies of water is called ______________________.

## Science Concepts

Fill in the letter of the choice that best answers the question.

TEKS 5.3C, 5.8B

7. Theo wants to model the water cycle. What should he use as the source of energy for the water cycle?

   Ⓐ a fan
   Ⓑ a lamp
   Ⓒ a pan of soil
   Ⓓ a spray bottle

TEKS 5.8A

8. A student measures the air temperature and wind speed at her school at noon. Which best describes what she is doing?

   Ⓐ predicting the climate
   Ⓑ forecasting the weather
   Ⓒ observing weather conditions
   Ⓓ determining the climate near school

TEKS 5.2D, 5.8A

9. Darnell read that the central part of Argentina and the central part of the United States have similar climates.

What information provides the best explanation for the climates' similarities?

Ⓐ Both countries are located to the west of the Pacific Ocean.

Ⓑ There are large mountains in the eastern parts of both countries.

Ⓒ The central parts of both countries are about the same distance from the equator.

Ⓓ Both countries are very large compared to other countries.

TEKS 5.8A

10. What two physical factors do scientists use to determine the climate of a place?

Ⓐ types of living things and average temperature

Ⓑ length of seasons and precipitation

Ⓒ distance from ocean and latitude

Ⓓ average temperature and average precipitation

TEKS 5.8B

11. The diagram shows the water cycle.

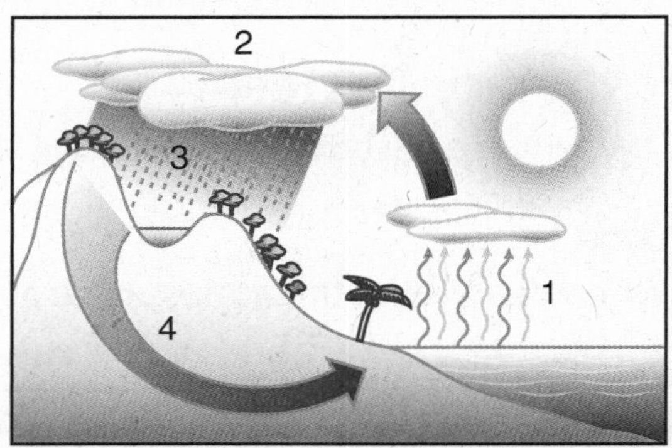


At which point do the sun and the ocean most directly interact in the water cycle?

Ⓐ at point 1 during the process of evaporation

Ⓑ at point 2 during the process of condensation

Ⓒ at point 3 during the process of precipitation

Ⓓ at point 4 during the process of runoff

TEKS 5.2D, 5.8A

12. The table lists some weather conditions at two different locations.

| | Location 1 | Location 2 |
|---|---|---|
| Temperature | 10 °C (50 °F) | 20 °C (68 °F) |
| Precipitation | 3 cm | 2 cm |
| Wind | 3 km/hr west | 8 km/hr east |
| Cloud cover | overcast | mostly cloudy |

Which statement is correct?

Ⓐ Location 1 is experiencing more rain than Location 2.

Ⓑ Both locations are experiencing freezing conditions.

Ⓒ Location 1 is experiencing stronger winds than Location 2.

Ⓓ Both locations have winds blowing from the same direction.

Name ______________________________

**TEKS 5.3A, 5.8B**

**13.** **Ms. Janick's class investigated how the sun and the ocean interact in the water cycle. They placed a glass of water in sunlight for four days. They measured and recorded the level of the water in the glass each day. Which graph shows that the water evaporated over time?**

Ⓐ

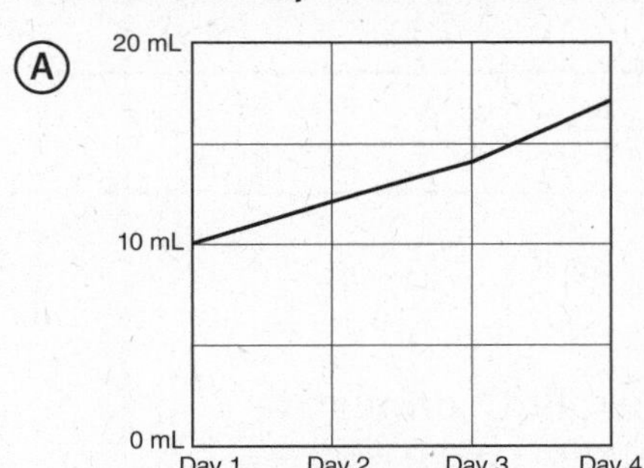


Ⓑ

20 mL
10 mL
0 mL
Day 1
Day 2
Day 3
Day 4

Ⓒ

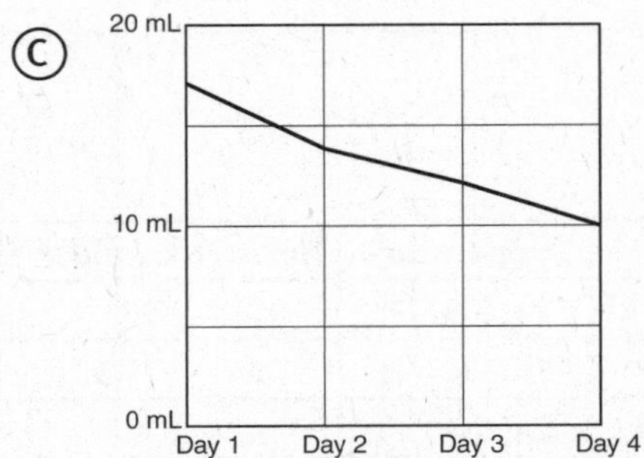


Ⓓ

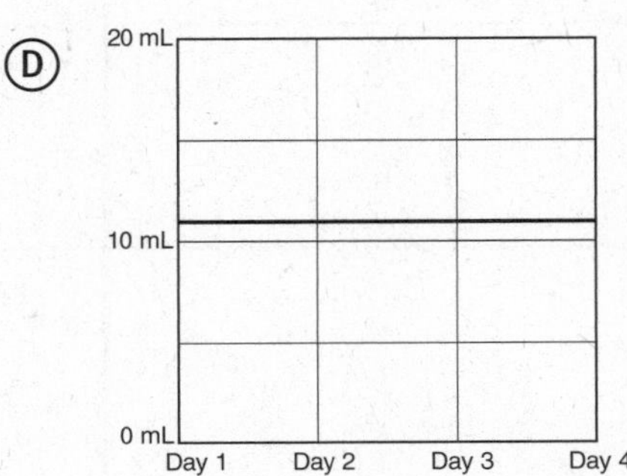


**TEKS 5.8B**

**14.** **Oceans receive fresh water from precipitation, rivers, and runoff. Yet ocean levels do not change very much. Why are ocean levels not greatly affected by the addition of fresh water?**

Ⓐ Water is constantly seeping underground in the ocean.

Ⓑ Water is constantly evaporating from the ocean's surface.

Ⓒ Water is constantly flowing back into rivers from the ocean.

Ⓓ Water is constantly deposited back on land through ocean wave action.

**TEKS 5.8A**

**15.** **Which place is most likely to have cold weather and a cold climate year-round?**

Ⓐ a place at the equator

Ⓑ a place near the equator

Ⓒ a place at a middle latitude

Ⓓ a place far from the equator

# Apply Inquiry and Review the Big Idea

Write the answers to these questions.

TEKS 5.2F, 5.8A

16. A place in a polar climate zone has a day that has very warm weather. How is this possible?

TEKS 5.2B, 5.8B

17. Christina has a glass of water. Michael has a fruit juice drink. Both drinks are at room temperature, and both students add ice to their drinks. Condensation begins to form on the outside of Christina's glass before Michael's. How could they state their observations as a testable hypothesis?

TEKS 5.8A

18. Deanna measured the temperature and relative humidity at her home every afternoon for four days. She recorded the results in the table.

What is the average temperature of the four days in degrees Celsius? Record your answer to the nearest whole number.

| Day | Temperature | Relative humidity (%) |
|---|---|---|
| Monday | 28 °C (82 °F) | 90 |
| Tuesday | 27 °C (81 °F) | 79 |
| Wednesday | 24 °C (75 °F) | 70 |
| Thursday | 28 °C (82 °F) | 69 |

UNIT 10

# Earth, Sun, and Moon System

## Big Idea

The Earth, sun, and moon have distinct characteristics. They form a system in space with recognizable patterns.

**TEKS** 5.2F, 5.3A, 5.3D, 5.8C, 5.8D

## I Wonder Why

The space station glides through space. How is it similiar to an observatory on Earth's surface? *Turn the page to find out.*

**Here's Why** Both the International Space Station and an observatory are used to study space. They, and other kinds of technology, help us to better understand objects in space, including the sun, the moon, and our own planet Earth.

In this unit, you will explore the Big Idea, the Essential Questions, and the investigations on the Inquiry Flipchart.

Levels of Inquiry Key ■ DIRECTED ■ GUIDED ■ INDEPENDENT

**Big Idea** The Earth, sun, and moon have distinct characteristics. They form a system in space with recognizable patterns.

## Essential Questions



**Science Notebook**

Before you begin each lesson, be sure to write your thoughts about the Essential Question.

TEKS **5.8C** demonstrate that Earth rotates on its axis once approximately every 24 hours causing the day/night cycle and the apparent movement of the Sun across the sky **5.8D** identify and compare the physical characteristics of the Sun, Earth, and Moon

Lesson 1

Essential Question

# How Do the Sun, Earth, and Moon Differ?

## Engage Your Brain!

Find the answer to the following question in this lesson and record it here.

The picture shows a solar flare on the sun. How can solar flares affect you on Earth?

______________________________

______________________________

______________________________

______________________________

## Active Reading

### Lesson Vocabulary

List each term. As you learn about each one, make notes in the Interactive Glossary.

______________________________

______________________________

______________________________

______________________________

### Signal Words: Cause and Effect

Signal words show connections between ideas. Words signaling a cause include *because* and *if*. Words signaling an effect include *so* and *thus*. Active readers recall what they read because they are alert to signal words that identify causes and effects.



Inquiry Flipchart p. 51 — Arching Paths/Our Shadowy Moon

# Very Different Orbs

You can't help but notice that the sun and moon are very different from Earth and from each other. What makes them so different? Read on to find out!

**Active Reading** As you read this page, draw boxes around words or phrases that signal comparison, such as *like, unlike, larger,* and *smaller.*

There are millions of kilometers between the sun, moon, and Earth. Yet we feel heat from the sun and see the whitish color of the moon. These are direct evidence that these bodies are different from our planet.

Earth is often called the "blue planet" because most of its surface is covered by water. On the moon's surface, water wouldn't last long. Without a thick atmosphere like Earth's, water on the moon would freeze or be lost to space.

The sun is a star, which is a huge, hot ball of gases that produces its own light. It's about 109 times larger than Earth. Unlike Earth and the moon, the sun does not have a solid surface. Its atmosphere extends out millions of kilometers. From the sun's surface, solar flares explode into space.

The moon is tiny when compared in size to the sun. Unlike Earth, its temperatures are scorching hot during the day and freezing cold at night. Like Earth, it has features such as mountains and flat plains.

## EARTH

Earth is a *planet*, an object that moves around a star, has a nearly round shape, and has cleared its path of most debris. Its characteristics include:

- Diameter: 12,742 km
- Structure: mainly rocky layers, partly liquid core
- Composition: mainly iron, oxygen, silicon, and magnesium
- Atmosphere: mainly nitrogen and oxygen
- Notable features: Lots of liquid water and diverse life forms
- Minimum surface temperature: -88 °C
- Maximum surface temperature: 58 °C

The green hue shows plant life that Earth's waters help support.

## SUN

The sun produces energy deep in its core. This energy makes the sun glow and provides Earth with heat and light.

- Diameter: 1,391,016 km
- Structure: gaseous layers
- Composition: hydrogen and helium
- Atmosphere: hydrogen and helium
- Notable surface features: sunspots, solar flares
- Average surface temperature: 5,500 °C

Solar flares can disrupt energy distribution systems on Earth.

## How Do They Compare?

This circle is a model of Earth. It is 4 cm in diameter. Use a calculator and data on this page to find the diameter for a moon model. Would the moon model fit inside Earth's model? If so, draw it in.

4 cm

_______________________________________

Without water or wind, moon landforms do not change.

## MOON

The moon is visible from Earth because it reflects light from the sun.

- Diameter: 3,475 km
- Structure: rocky layers
- Composition: mainly oxygen, silicon, magnesium, and iron
- Atmosphere: none
- Notable surface features: craters, mountains, plains
- Minimum surface temperature: −233 °C
- Maximum surface temperature: 123 °C

## Beyond the Book

Use the information on these pages to construct a 3-ring Venn diagram to compare the physical characteristics of the sun, Earth, and moon. What makes each object unique?

# The Sun-Earth-Moon System

The moon moves around Earth as Earth moves around the sun. What keeps these objects from flying off in space?

**Active Reading** As you read these two pages, draw boxes around clue words that signal a cause.

What defines the unit of time we call a year? A year is the time it takes for Earth to **revolve**, or go around, the sun. Any object that revolves around another object in space is called a *satellite.* Earth is a satellite of the sun. Because the moon revolves around Earth, it is a satellite of Earth.

The path one space object takes around another is called an **orbit**. It takes Earth about 365 days to complete its orbit around the sun. The moon's orbit is shorter than Earth's. As a result, it takes the moon just 27 days to revolve once around Earth.

The Earth and moon motion around the sun is in part because of gravity. *Gravity* is the force of attraction that exists between all objects. Gravitational attraction between objects depends on two things: the distance between the objects and the masses of the objects.

Sun

**Gravitational Pull** The sun is about 330,000 times more massive than Earth. Its strong gravitational pull keeps all objects near it from flying off into space. Gravity also keeps the moon in its orbit around Earth. Gravitational pull decreases with distance.

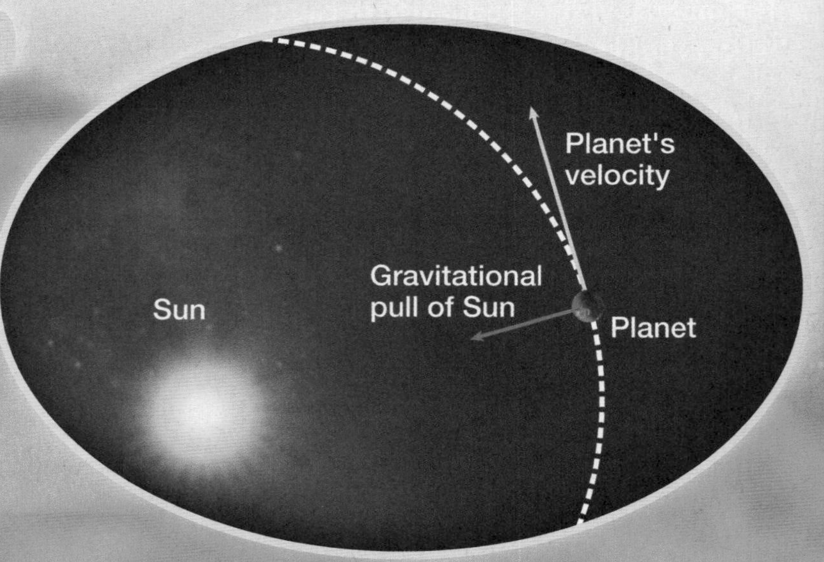

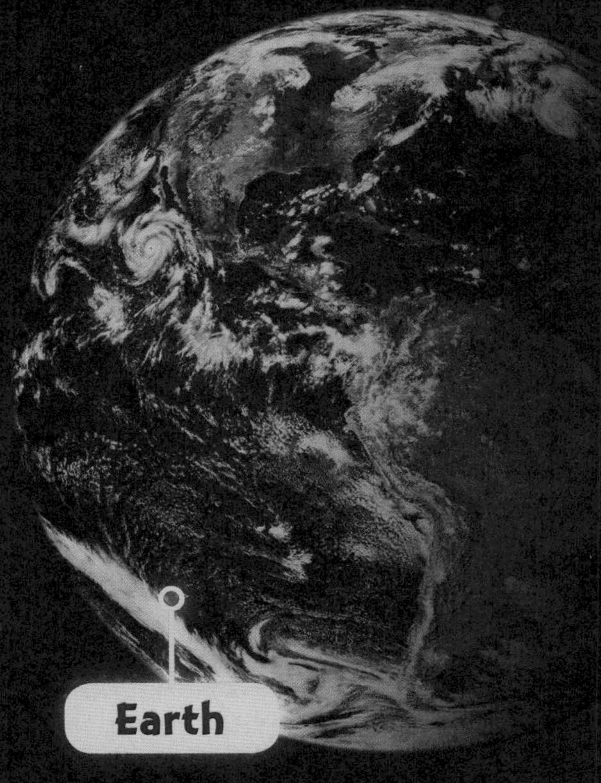


Moon

▶ Scientists have observed that every year the moon gets farther away from Earth. Predict what could happen if the moon gets too far away.

______________________________

______________________________

______________________________

______________________________

**Orbits** Earth revolves around the sun in a counterclockwise orbit. The moon also revolves in a counterclockwise orbit around Earth. Earth's orbit around the sun is nearly circular in shape, with the sun nearly in the center of the circle.

▶ Draw arrows to show how Earth revolves around the sun and the moon around Earth.

Sun

Moon

Earth



Images are not to scale.

# Clear As Day and Night

You've learned that Earth revolves around the sun. What other movement does Earth have?

**Active Reading** As you read these two pages, find and underline the definitions of *rotates* and *axis*.

Each morning, you see the sun appear to rise in the east. At first, the sun is low in the sky. As the day goes on, it seems to move higher, cross the sky, and set in the west.

The sun is not actually moving. Instead, Earth **rotates**, or spins around its axis, once every 24 hours. The **axis** is the imaginary line that goes through Earth from pole to pole. The rotation of Earth around its axis also causes the moon and the stars to appear to move across the sky.

**Evidence of Rotation** You can see evidence of Earth's rotation if you look at the stars at night. The North Star is nearly directly above the North Pole. It does not appear to move as Earth rotates. It's like the hub of a wheel—the stars around it seem to circle around the North Star.

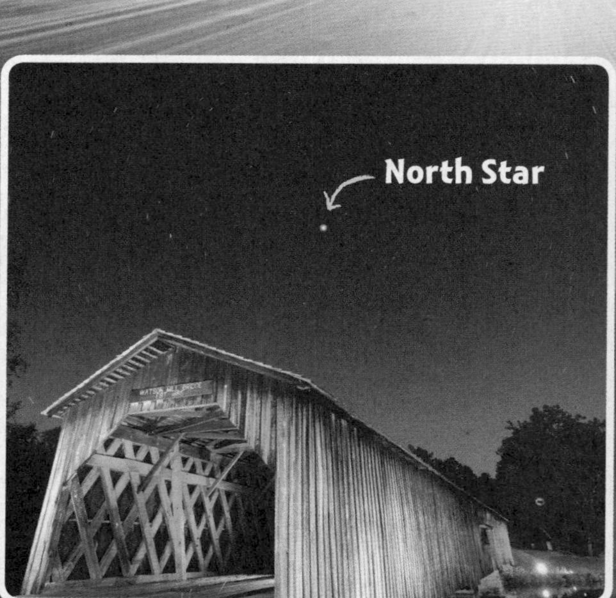


The North Star does not seem to rise, set, or move across the sky.

As Earth rotates, one half of Earth experiences daylight while the other half is in darkness.

**Day/Night Cycle** The rotation of Earth around its axis causes day and night. Look at the diagrams on the right. At 12 a.m., Houston, Texas, faces away from the sun. The people who live there are most likely sleeping. However, Earth is constantly rotating. In the bottom diagram, it is 12 p.m. and Texas is facing the sun. People there may now be outside in the sunshine. While it is day in Texas, it is nighttime on the opposite side of the world.

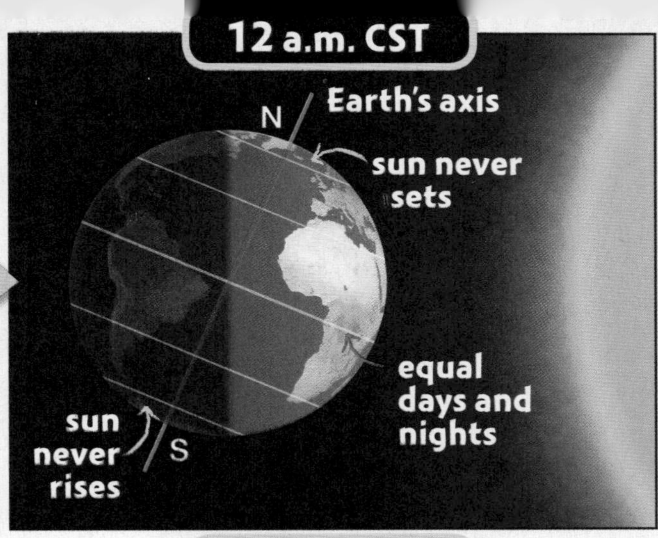


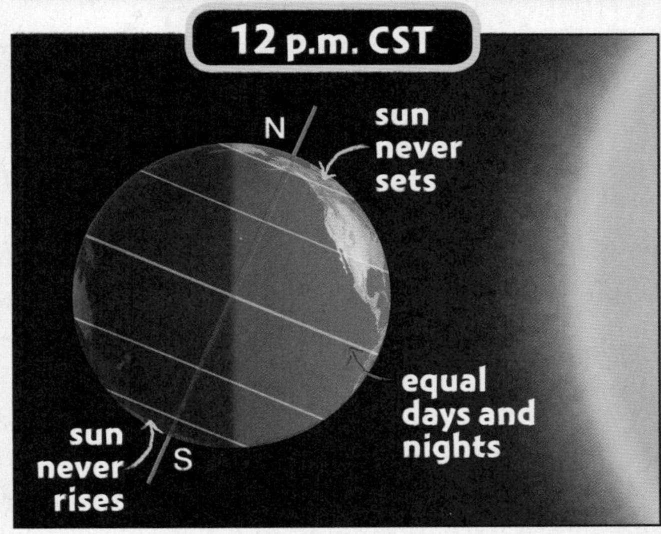

This time-lapse photo shows the circular path stars appear to take around the North Star throughout the night.

## Do the Math!

### Calculate Circumference

Earth takes 24 hours to complete one rotation. It rotates at an average speed of 1,670 km/hour. Calculate Earth's circumference at the equator based on its rotational speed. Show your work below.

# More Earth-Sun Interaction

Earth's rotation around its axis causes night and day. What changes happen on Earth as it also revolves around the sun?

**Active Reading** As you read these two pages, draw a star next to what you think is the most important sentence. Be ready to explain your reasoning.

## Summer Solstice

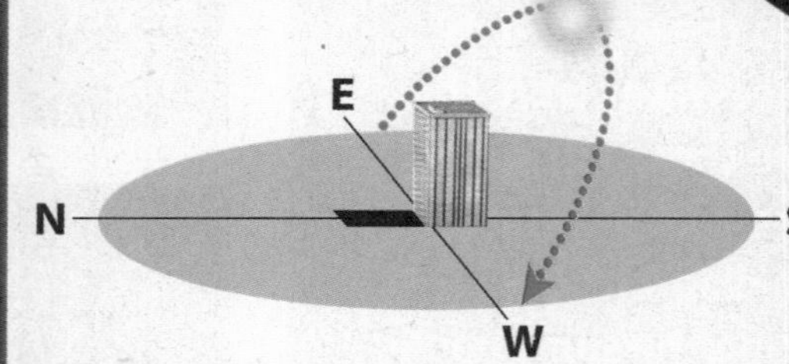


During summer, Earth's axis points toward the sun. The Northern Hemisphere's summer solstice occurs June 20 or 21. It is the longest day of the year and marks the start of the summer season. Summer days are the longest and warmest. The noon sun is high in the sky, causing shadows to be short.

## Fall Equinox

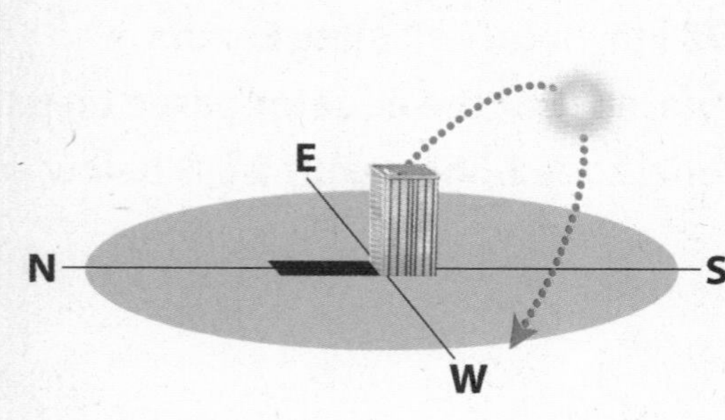


During fall and spring, Earth's axis points neither away nor toward the sun. The fall equinox occurs September 22 or 23 in the Northern Hemisphere. This day marks the start of fall and has equal hours of day and night. In fall, daylight hours grow shorter and the noon sun's height is lower than in summer.



Images are not to scale.

## Earth's Orbit

Look at the diagrams of Earth on these pages. Notice that Earth's axis is not straight up and down. Instead, it is tilted at a 23.5 degree angle. The tilt of Earth's axis as it revolves around the sun causes seasons. *Seasons* are short-term changes in climate. Most places on Earth have four seasons: summer, fall, winter, and spring. Seasons happen because different parts of Earth get different amounts of sunlight throughout the year. This causes changes in temperature and length of day.

### Spring Equinox

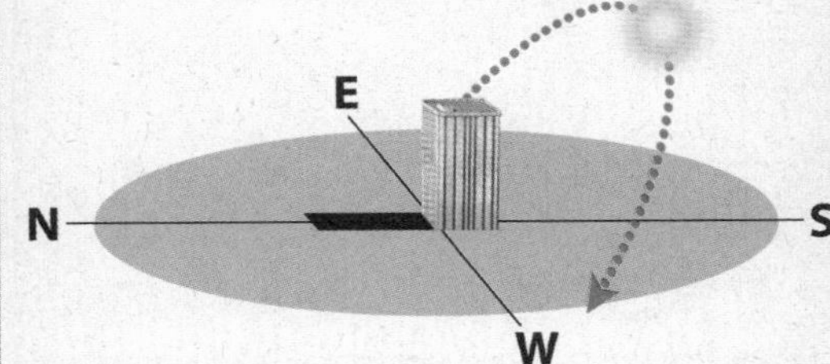


In the Northern Hemisphere, the spring equinox occurs March 20 or 21. In spring, the sun appears higher in the sky than it did in winter, daylight hours grow longer, and temperatures get warmer.

▶ To complete the model, draw the path of the sun as it appears to rise, cross the sky, and set during winter. Then draw the shadow cast by the building.

### Winter Solstice

During winter, Earth's axis points away from the sun. The Northern Hemisphere's winter solstice occurs December 21 or 22. It is the shortest day of the year and marks the start of the winter season. Winter days are the shortest and coldest of the year. The sun is never high in the sky.

E

N S

W

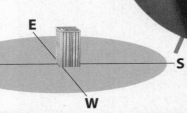

## Why It Matters

# What if Earth Didn't Spin?

How did scientists prove that Earth rotates? What would happen if this rotation stopped?

Great minds such as Sir Isaac Newton and Robert Hooke tried to prove that Earth rotates. In 1679, Newton wrote that objects dropped from a tall tower swerved slightly to the east. Why? By the time they hit the ground, he reasoned, Earth would have already rotated to the east.

For years, scientists tried to find evidence that Newton was correct. Yet the change in a falling object's landing was too small to measure using the technology of the times. Finally, in 1851, a French scientist named Leon Foucault used a pendulum to show that Earth rotates. One of the great questions of science was answered!

**The sun's movement across the sky was once cited as empirical evidence of the sun's revolution around Earth. New technology and additional observation was needed to demonstrate that Earth's rotation was the cause of the sun's apparent motion.**

▶ Explain why finding evidence supporting Newton's hypothesis was difficult. Would an airplane have helped? Explain how.

In 1851, Foucault performed a public demonstration. He used a pendulum that was 60 meters long. Each swing of the pendulum followed a slightly different path, providing evidence that the floor—and Earth beneath it—was moving.

**Earth with No Rotation** Some scientists wonder what would happen if Earth stopped rotating. Computer models show that Earth would be very different. In a spinless Earth, a single day and night cycle would last a whole year. For six months, half of Earth would be in daylight and the other half would be in darkness. The sunlit side of Earth would be very hot!

Earth's magnetic field, produced by its rotation, would disappear. This would allow more solar radiation to reach Earth's surface, causing health problems. Luckily, Earth's rotation shows no signs of stopping!

## Spinless Earth

Part of North America, including the Great Lakes, would be swallowed up by the oceans.

The oceans would move to the poles.

One huge continent would form along the equator.

The ocean floor at the equator becomes a deep valley.

When you're done, use the answer key to check and revise your work.

**Fill in the chart below to show how the sun and moon differ from Earth.**

| Compare sun, Earth, and moon | | |
|---|---|---|
| | Similarities to Earth | Differences from Earth |
| sun | The sun has a(n) 1. ______________ that extends far into space. | The sun produces 3. ________ ________ on its surface that affect communications on Earth. |
| moon | The moon has a(n) 2. ____________ surface and features that include mountains and plains. | Land features on the moon don't 4. ________ ________ because there is no liquid water on the moon's surface. |

## Summarize

**Fill in the missing words about the sun-Earth-moon system.**

Earth 5. ______________ around its axis once every 24 hours. This movement of Earth makes the moon, stars, and 6. ______________ appear to move across the sky. This movement also causes the 7. ______________ and 8. ______________ cycle. Earth 9. ______________ around the sun once every 365 days. The time it takes Earth to go once around the sun is called a 10. ______________. Earth's revolution and the tilt of its axis causes the 11. ______________ to occur. 12. ______________ keeps the moon in its orbit around Earth and Earth in its orbit around the sun.

Answer Key: 1. atmosphere 2. rocky 3. solar flares 4. wear away 5. rotates 6. sun 7. day or night 8. day or night 9. revolves or orbits 10. year 11. seasons 12. Gravity

# Brain Check



Name ___________________________

## Word Play

**1** Use the words in the box to complete the puzzle.

1. has no solid surface and is made up of helium and hydrogen
2. the spinning of Earth around its axis causes this cycle
3. keeps Earth and the moon in orbit around the sun
4. Earth does this around its axis
5. Earth does this around the sun
6. an object in space that moves around the sun, has a round shape, and has cleared its path of most debris
7. the imaginary line that goes through Earth from pole to pole
8. Earth's path around the sun
9. short-term changes in climate caused by Earth's movement around the sun

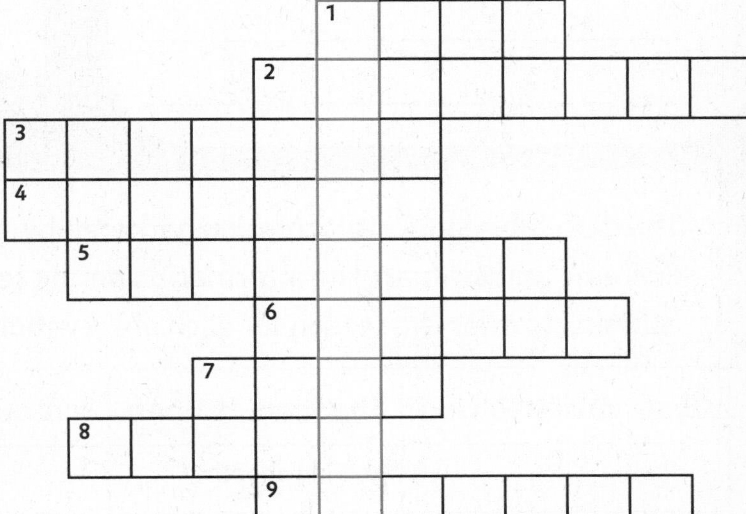


Read the letters going down the column with the red border. Use that word to complete the following riddle.

10. Sally Smith's spaceship goes around and around Earth, so it is a ________________.

| axis* | day/night | gravity | orbit* | planet | revolves* |
|---|---|---|---|---|---|
| rotates* | seasons | star | | | |

* Key Lesson Vocabulary

# Apply Concepts

2 Think about the characteristics of the moon. What would you need to survive there?

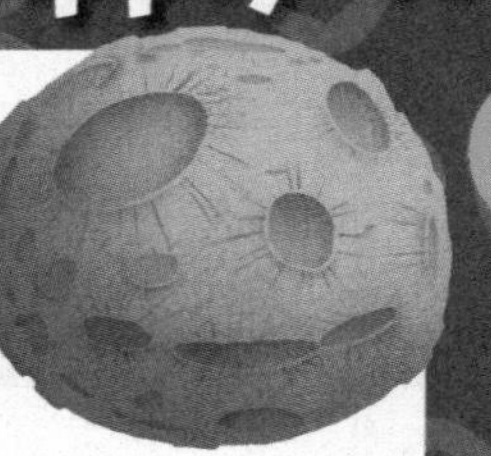

______________________________

______________________________

______________________________

______________________________

3 Suppose east is to the left of the drawing. Draw the apparent path of the winter sun across the sky.

4 The data table shows information gathered by students over a year. Examine and evaluate the information on the second and third columns to infer the season for each observation period.

| Observation Period | Shadows at Noon | Average Temperature | Season |
|---|---|---|---|
| 1 | getting shorter | 18 °C | |
| 2 | shortest | 28 °C | |
| 3 | getting longer | 21 °C | |
| 4 | longest | 7 °C | |

5 Suppose Earth completes one rotation every 12 hours. How would this affect the cycle of day and night?

______________________________

On a sunny day, face north and put a stick in the ground. Observe the shadow cast by the stick. Observe how the shadow changes throughout the day. Explain how these changes are related to Earth's rotation.

# Meet Two Space Explorers

On her first mission, Kalpana Chawla traveled more than six million miles in 15 days!

Kalpana Chawla

As a little girl in India, Kalpana Chawla dreamed about flying airplanes. She came to the United States and studied hard. She soon earned her degree as an aerospace engineer. Kalpana Chawla could fly many kinds of airplanes. Her dreams had come true! But she kept dreaming. She wanted to fly in space. She went to work for NASA and became an astronaut. Soon, Kalpana Chawla became the first Indian-born woman in space!

Claudia Alexander

Claudia Alexander explores outer space, too. But she never leaves Earth! She studies the moons of the planet Jupiter. She was in charge of NASA's *Galileo* mission. The mission sent an unmanned spacecraft to Jupiter. The spacecraft left Earth in 1989. It took six long years to reach Jupiter. Claudia Alexander directed it over 385 million miles! Under her command, *Galileo* was the first spacecraft to take detailed photos of Jupiter and its moons.

*Galileo* space prob

## Two Ways to Study Space

Kalpana Chawla and Claudia Alexander study space in different ways. Write the statements that apply to each scientist in the correct circle.

**Kalpana Chawla**

______________________________
______________________________
______________________________
______________________________
______________________________

- I lead space missions without leaving Earth.
- I traveled on the space shuttle.
- I study the moons of Jupiter.
- I grew up in India and learned to fly many types of airplanes.
- I study objects in space.

The Hubble Space Telescope sends scientists pictures of space from its orbit high above Earth.

**Claudia Alexander**

______________________________
______________________________
______________________________
______________________________
______________________________

Many scientists study space from Earth by using a telescope, such as this one, in an observatory.

Inquiry Flipchart page 52

**TEKS** **5.2F** communicate valid conclusions in...written...form **5.3A** ... analyze, evaluate, and critique scientific explanations...so as to encourage critical thinking... **5.3C** draw...a model that represents how something works...that cannot be seen... **5.8C** demonstrate that Earth rotates...causing the day/night cycle

Name ______________________________

Essential Question

# How Does Earth's Movement Cause Day and Night Cycles?

## Set a Purpose

**What do you think you will learn from this activity?**

______________________________

______________________________

______________________________

______________________________

______________________________

## Think About the Procedure

**What do the lamp and the globe represent in your model?**

______________________________

______________________________

**Write your prediction from Step 5.**

______________________________

______________________________

## Record Your Data

**In the data table below, record your observations and results.**

| | Position of Earth's Axis and Orientation | Observations |
|---|---|---|
| Trial 1 | | |
| Trial 2 | | |

## Draw Conclusions

How would the day/night cycle change if Earth's axis of rotation always pointed toward the sun?

## Analyze and Extend

1. Was your prediction supported? Why or why not?

2. Make an inference. How would life on Earth change if one side of Earth was always facing the sun?

3. Frank concludes that the way time is measured would not change if one side of Earth always faced the sun; a year would still be the same length. Critique this explanation using evidence.

4. Think about how you could use your model to show how Earth's rotation causes the apparent movement of the sun across the sky. Draw and describe your plan in the space below.

5. Think of other questions you would like to ask about the effects of Earth's rotation. Write your questions here.

TEKS 5.3D connect grade-level appropriate science concepts with the history of science, science careers, and contributions of scientists

S.T.E.M.

Engineering & Technology

# Tools in Space

An astronaut often has to use screwdrivers or drills to fix things in space. The astronaut's tools are specially designed for a person wearing bulky gloves and floating in orbit. Hand tools must work in the extreme cold vacuum of space and be tethered so they don't float away. A robotic arm helps the astronaut move around outside. However, the astronaut's most important tool is the space suit that maintains an environment in which the astronaut can breathe.

## Troubleshooting

Find the astronaut's drill. How is it similar to a drill used on Earth? How is it different?

_______________

_______________

_______________

## S.T.E.M.
continued

You are used to doing everything under the pull of Earth's gravity. That's what makes it possible for you feel motions as up, down, and side-to-side. There is no "right side up" in space! It is harder than you might think to work in such an unfamiliar environment.

Turn your book so that the top of this page is closest to you.

---

Hold your pencil near the eraser. Write your name on the line below so that it reads properly when you turn the page right side up again.

What made this task difficult?

---

---

How do engineers account for microgravity when designing the inside of a space station?

---

---

## Build On It!

Rise to the engineering design challenge—complete **Improvise It: How High is That Star?** in the Inquiry Flipchart.

Name ______________________

## Vocabulary Review

Use the terms in the box to complete the sentences.

| axis<br>orbit<br>planet<br>revolve<br>rotate<br>satellite<br>star |
|---|

TEKS 5.8D

1. The path Earth takes around the sun is called a(n)

    ______________________.

TEKS 5.8D

2. The moon revolves around Earth, so it is Earth's

    ______________________.

TEKS 5.8D

3. It takes Earth about 365 days to ______________________ around the sun in a counterclockwise orbit.

TEKS 5.8C, 5.8D

4. Each day, Earth makes one full spin about its

    ______________________.

TEKS 5.8D

5. The sun is a huge ball of hot gases that gives off light, so it

    is a(n) ______________________.

TEKS 5.8D

6. Earth moves around the sun, has a nearly round shape, and has cleared its path of most debris, so it is called a(n)

    ______________________.

TEKS 5.8C

7. It takes Earth 24 hours to ______________________ once around its axis.

# Science Concepts

Fill in the letter of the choice that best answers the question.

TEKS 5.8C

8. What causes the day/night cycle?

Ⓐ Earth's axis

Ⓑ Earth's orbit

Ⓒ Earth's rotation

Ⓓ Earth's revolution

TEKS 5.8C

9. Which of the following is caused by Earth's rotation?

Ⓐ phases of the moon

Ⓑ the rotation of the moon

Ⓒ seasonal changes on Earth

Ⓓ the apparent movement of the sun across the sky

TEKS 5.8D

10. The table compares the diameters of the sun, Earth, and the moon.

| Diameters of Sun, Earth, and Moon | |
|---|---|
| **Object** | **Diameter (km)** |
| Sun | 1,391,016 |
| Earth | 12,742 |
| Moon | 3,475 |

Which best summarizes the data?

Ⓐ Earth is about 8 times bigger than the moon.

Ⓑ The sun is about 109 times bigger than Earth.

Ⓒ The moon is bigger than Earth and the sun combined.

Ⓓ The sun, Earth, and the moon are about the same size.

TEKS 5.2D, 5.8D

11. The diagram shows movements of objects in space.

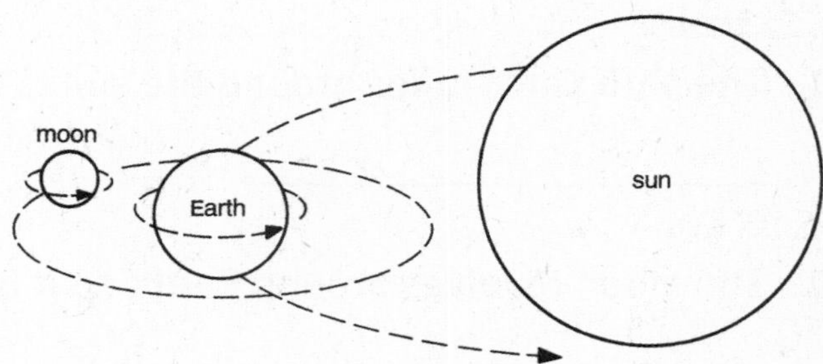


What can you conclude from this diagram?

Ⓐ Earth is a satellite of the moon.

Ⓑ The sun revolves around Earth.

Ⓒ Earth and the moon rotate in different directions.

Ⓓ The moon orbits Earth while Earth orbits the sun.

TEKS 5.3C, 5.8D

12. You want to make a model of the sun, Earth, and the moon. Which objects would best represent the sun, Earth, and the moon?

Ⓐ lamp = sun; basketball = Earth; tennis ball = moon

Ⓑ lamp = moon; basketball = sun; tennis ball = Earth

Ⓒ lamp = Earth; basketball = moon; tennis ball = sun

Ⓓ lamp = moon; basketball = Earth; tennis ball = sun

Name ______________________________

TEKS 5.3A, 5.8C

13. Which of the following is evidence of Earth's rotation?

Ⓐ The stars appear to rotate around the North Star.

Ⓑ The moon appears to change shape each month.

Ⓒ The seasons change throughout the year.

Ⓓ The moon stays in orbit around Earth.

TEKS 5.8D

14. The table shows characteristics of the sun, Earth, and the moon.

| Characteristics of Sun, Earth, and Moon | |
|---|---|
| Sun | gaseous layers, atmosphere made of hydrogen and helium |
| Earth | rocky layers, atmosphere made mainly of nitrogen and oxygen |
| Moon | rocky layers, no atmosphere |

How do the physical characteristics of the sun, Earth, and the moon compare?

Ⓐ Unlike the sun and the moon, Earth is made of gases.

Ⓑ Unlike Earth and the sun, the moon has rocky layers.

Ⓒ Unlike the sun and Earth, the moon has no atmosphere.

Ⓓ Unlike Earth and the moon, the sun's atmosphere contains oxygen.

TEKS 5.8C, 5.8D

15. Look at this diagram of Earth.

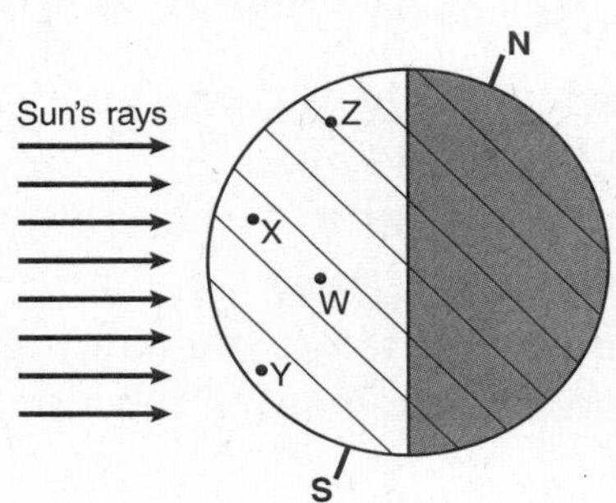


It is 12 p.m. at point X. What will happen in 12 hours at point X?

Ⓐ Point X will be in daylight.

Ⓑ Point X will be in darkness.

Ⓒ Point X will experience summer.

Ⓓ Point X will orbit once around the sun.

TEKS 5.3C, 5.8D

16. The diagram shows a movement of Earth.

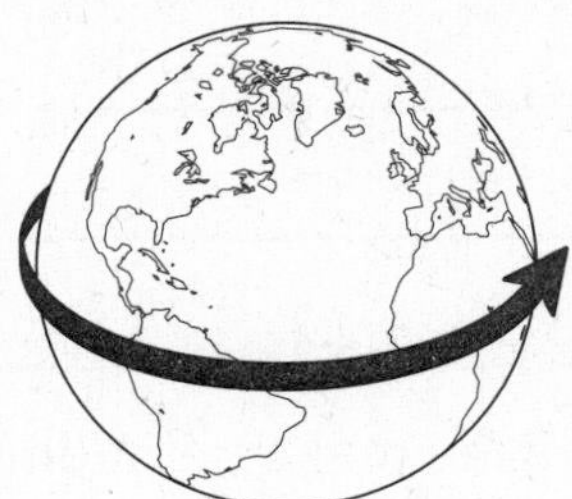

How long does it take Earth to complete this movement one time?

Ⓐ The movement is a phase, so it takes 30 days.

Ⓑ The movement is an orbit, so it takes 27 days.

Ⓒ The movement is rotation, so it takes 24 hours.

Ⓓ The movement is revolution, so it takes 365 days.

# Apply Inquiry and Review the Big Idea

TEKS 5.2F, 5.8C, 5.8D

**17.** The diagram shows the movement of Earth and the moon in space.

Explain what would happen if Earth did not rotate on its axis as it moved around the sun. How would this change the day/night cycle and the apparent movement of the sun across the sky?

_______________

_______________

_______________

_______________

TEKS 5.3C, 5.8C

**18.** Alicia made a model of one effect of Earth's rotation. Her model is shown at right.

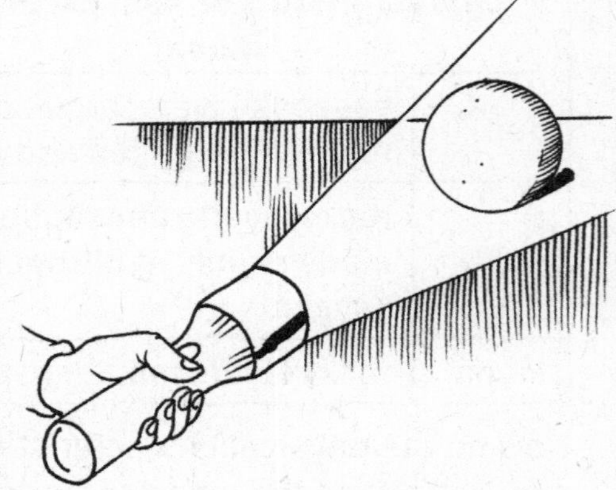

**a.** What effect was she modeling?

_______________

_______________

_______________

**b.** How could she make her model more realistic?

_______________

_______________

_______________

TEKS 5.8D

**19.** Earth's average surface temperature is 14 °C. What is Earth's average surface temperature in degrees Fahrenheit (°F)? Record your answer to the nearest whole. Hint: To convert from °C to °F, multiply by 9, divide by 5, then add 32.

_______________

UNIT 11

# Energy in Ecosystems

## Big Idea

Living things interact in ecosystems. Energy flows from the sun to plants to animals.

TEKS 5.2F, 5.2G, 5.3A, 5.3D, 5.4A, 5.9A, 5.9B, 5.9C, 5.9D

## I Wonder Why

Polar bears and gray whales live in the Arctic. Polar bears eat seals and fish. Why are polar bears eating a whale? *Turn the page to find out.*

**Here's Why** Polar bears mainly hunt seals and fish for food, but they will also scavenge the blubber of dead whales.

In this unit, you will explore the Big Idea, the Essential Questions, and the Investigations on the Inquiry Flipchart.

Levels of Inquiry Key ■ DIRECTED ■ GUIDED ■ INDEPENDENT

**Big Idea** Living things interact in ecosystems. Energy flows from the sun to plants to animals.

## Essential Questions



**Science Notebook**

Before you begin each lesson, be sure to write your thoughts about the Essential Question.

TEKS 5.2G construct appropriate...charts using technology...to organize...information 5.9A observe the way organisms live and survive in their ecosystem by interacting with the living and non-living elements 5.9C predict the effects of changes in ecosystems caused by living organisms, including humans, such as...the building of highways

Lesson 1

Essential Question

# What Is an Ecosystem?

## Engage Your Brain!

Find the answers to the following question in this lesson and record them here.

These three organisms share the same living space. What nonliving elements do they need to live and survive?

_______________

_______________

_______________

_______________

## Active Reading

### Lesson Vocabulary

List the terms. As you learn about each one, make notes in the Interactive Glossary.

_______________ _______________

_______________ _______________

_______________ _______________

### Main Ideas

The main idea of a paragraph is the most important idea. The main idea may be stated in the first sentence, or it may be stated elsewhere. Active readers look for main ideas by asking themselves, What is this section mostly about?



Inquiry Flipchart p. 54 — The Population Puzzle/Compare Climates

# 

What Is an Ecosystem?

A frog that lives in a pond couldn't survive in a desert or on a mountaintop. Could you live in a swamp?

**Active Reading** As you read these two pages, **circle** the biotic parts of environments. Draw a box around abiotic parts.

An organism's **environment** is all the living and nonliving things that surround and affect the organism. You are surrounded by many things that make your environment suitable for you to live in. Would that be true if you lived in a swamp? Environments include biotic parts and abiotic parts. *Biotic* parts are the living elements in an environment: plants, animals, and other organisms. *Abiotic* parts are the nonliving elements. Abiotic parts of an environment include climate, water, soil, light, air, and nutrients.

This swamp environment is made up of nonliving and living elements. The climate, abundance of water, moist air, muddy soils, and shady areas are all abiotic parts that make swamps different from other environments.

White ibis birds, black bears, willow trees, blackberry bushes, pitcher plants, and mosquitoes are all biotic parts of a cypress swamp environment.

The abiotic elements of an environment have an important role. Temperature and amount of water affect which plants and animals can live in a place. An ibis is adapted to living in a warm, wet swamp and cannot survive in a hot, dry desert.

An **ecosystem** includes all the organisms living in a place in addition to their environment. An ecosystem can be huge, such as a large forest or desert. Or it can be small, such as a mud puddle or a single bush. Each ecosystem has its own collection of living and nonliving elements.

## Organize the Swamp

Look at this swamp. Use a computer to construct a chart with examples of the swamp's biotic and abiotic parts.

Attach chart here.

# Populations and Communities

You are part of a group of students in your classroom. There are other classes in your school, too, and other groups of people, such as teachers. Together, you make up your school's community. Other organisms live in communities, too.

**Active Reading** As you read this page, circle two everyday words that have a special meaning in science.

Each ecosystem contains different groups of living things. Observe the picture showing several species of animals sharing water in a savanna ecosystem. A group of organisms of the same species, or kind of living thing, in an ecosystem is called a **population**. For example, a savanna ecosystem may contain a population of zebras as well as populations of gazelles and lions. It also contains populations of grasses and trees.

The different populations that share an ecosystem make up a community. A **community** consists of all the populations that live and interact in an area.

These moray eels are part of a population of eels sharing the same living space. The crack in the rock will hold only so many eels. At a certain point the eels must compete for this living space.

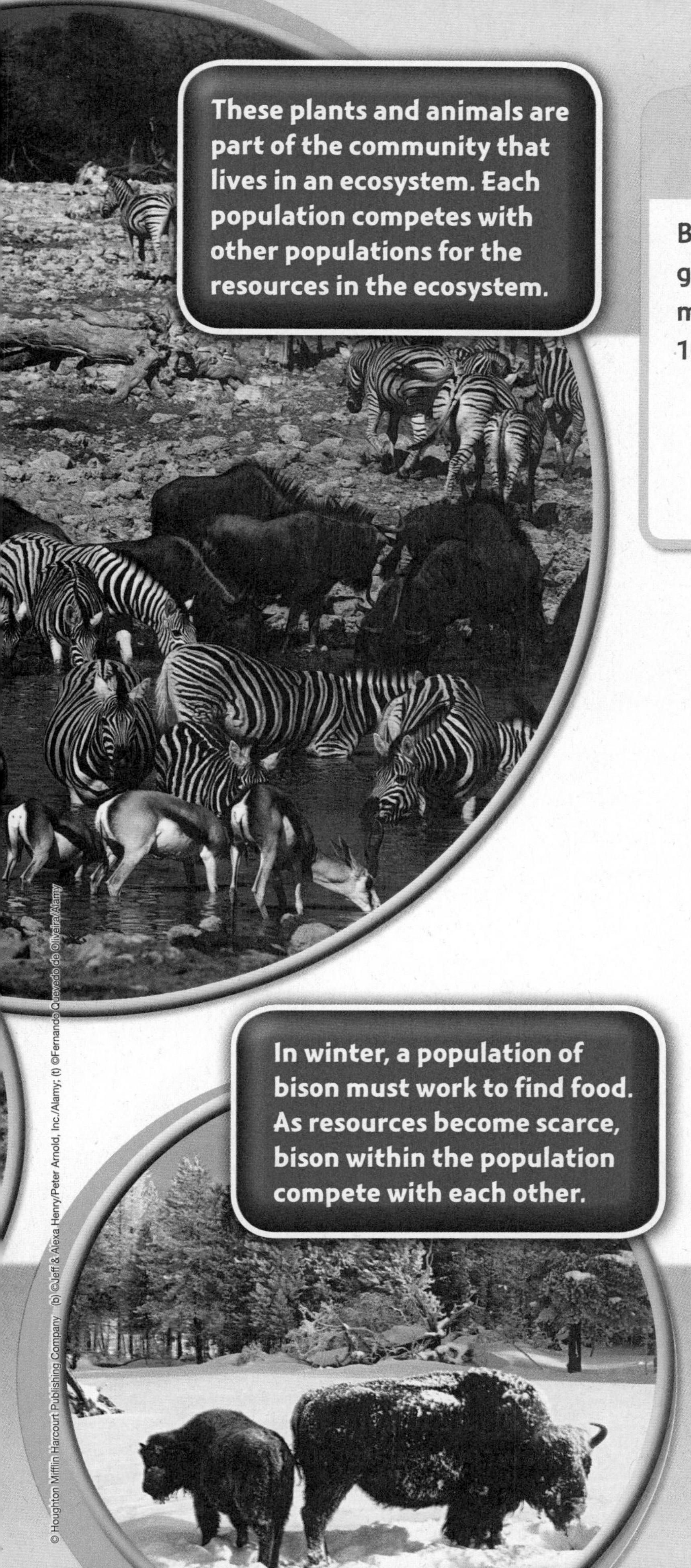

These plants and animals are part of the community that lives in an ecosystem. Each population competes with other populations for the resources in the ecosystem.

In winter, a population of bison must work to find food. As resources become scarce, bison within the population compete with each other.



## Do the Math!

### Calculate Area

Bison graze on grass. It takes 5 acres of grass to feed 2 bison for a season. How much land would be needed to support 100 bison for a season?

Organisms that make up populations live and survive in their ecosystems by interacting with living and nonliving elements. Populations in every ecosystem need food, water, shelter, and space to live. The interaction between populations to meet needs is called *competition*. Populations that compete and obtain enough resources will survive. Those that cannot compete will not survive in the ecosystem. Because there is only enough food, water, shelter, and space to support a certain number of organisms, these resources are called *limiting factors*.

Competition also occurs within populations. The stronger individuals in a population are the ones that get the most food and take the best shelter for themselves. Weaker individuals may not survive.

# Find Your Niche

Maybe you have to share your room, your clothes, or snacks with your family members. Organisms that live in the same ecosystem often compete for available resources.

**Active Reading** As you read these two pages, draw boxes around the clue words or phrases that signal comparison or contrast.

An organism's **habitat** is the place where it lives within an ecosystem. Several populations often live in a single habitat. For example, barred owls and red-shouldered hawks live in habitats with woods, nearby open country, and bodies of water.

An organism's **niche** [NICH] is its complete role, or function, in its ecosystem. A niche is different from a habitat because it includes everything an organism needs to live. An organism's niche includes living and nonliving elements, such as its foods, as well as the climate it thrives in.

The panda has a narrow niche in terms of food. Its diet consists mainly of bamboo, so pandas cannot live in habitats where bamboo does not grow.

Barred owls and red-shouldered hawks share a habitat but have different niches. How is this so?

________________________________________

________________________________________

Every organism has a niche. Having different niches allows organisms to live in the same habitat. When an organism has a very specific way of living, it has a narrow niche. For example, a bird that eats just one type of insect or lives in only one kind of tree has a narrow niche, while an animal that can eat many kinds of food has a broad niche. Organisms with a narrow niche tend to live in specific places, while those with a broad niche often move around large areas.

Populations can share a habitat but not the same niche. Red-shouldered hawks and barred owls, for example, share a habitat, but they have different niches. Hawks hunt by day and owls hunt at night, hunting different prey. If two populations of organisms share a niche, they must compete for resources.

## Nice Niche

Suppose a bird is the only animal in a habitat that eats a certain type of berry. The berries are the bird's only food. Describe how this narrow niche could be both good and bad for the bird.

________________________________________

________________________________________

________________________________________

________________________________________

Sharks have a broad niche in terms of food. They are able to eat many different foods.

# Diversity

Suppose all the shelves in your grocery store held only one kind of food. You couldn't stay healthy for long. Ecosystems need diversity, too.

**Active Reading** As you read these two pages, draw a star next to the most important sentence and be prepared to explain why.

This coral reef is a diverse ecosystem. Many populations live closely together here.

The word *diverse* means "different in kind." *Diversity* is the variety of different species that live in an ecosystem. An ecosystem that is diverse contains a lot of species. Ecosystems without much diversity are inhabited by only a few species.

Why is diversity important? All organisms rely on other organisms for resources. Their relationships are modeled in a large, complex web. The more types of organisms in an ecosystem, the larger the web, and the more resources available.

A rain forest is a diverse ecosystem. The warm temperatures and high rainfall support many different populations.

Why are some ecosystems very diverse while others have only a small number of species? Climate and location affect the amount and types of resources that are available for organisms. Locations of high diversity make a pattern on the map. In general, very diverse ecosystems such as coral reefs and rain forests are found near the equator. The farther away from the equator, the less diverse environments tend to be.

Other things can affect diversity as well. Humans can damage ecosystems and reduce the number of species living in them. Activities such as overhunting may lower the numbers of important species. In some areas, humans have destroyed forests or other environments in order to build highways, cities and other structures. Species in those environments have lost their habitats, and diversity has decreased.

The cold arctic is a less diverse ecosystem. The polar bear is one of a small number of large organisms that can survive there.

## Predict Habitat Change

Describe how you think building a large shopping mall and parking lot might affect the diversity of a forest.

_______________

_______________

_______________

_______________

_______________

Equator

Number of Species per 10,000 km²

- fewer than 100
- 100–200
- 201–500
- 501–1000
- 1001–1500
- 1501–2000
- 2001–3000
- 3001–4000
- 4001–5000
- 5001 or more

Ecosystems that are close to the equator tend to have a lot of diversity. Ecosystems farther from the equator tend to be less diverse.

When you're done, use the answer key to check and revise your work.

**1**

**The words in the ovals describe elements of a desert ecosystem. Draw lines to show whether each part is a *biotic* or *abiotic* element.**

Cactus

Sandy soil

Biotic

Lizard

Rattlesnake

Little water

Sunlight

Abiotic

## Summarize

**2** **Fill in the blanks with words from the word box. Use each word once.**

| | | |
|---|---|---|
| community | ecosystem | environment |
| habitat | niche | population |

An organism's 1. ______________________ includes all the living and nonliving elements that surround and affect the organism. Each different 2. ______________________ is an area made up of biotic and abiotic factors where organisms interact. Within these areas, groups of the same species of organisms, or 3. ______________________, interact with other organisms, forming a large 4. ______________________. The place where an organism normally lives is called its 5. ______________. The way the organism lives there is called its specific 6. ______________.

Answer Key: Biotic: Cactus, Rattlesnake, Lizard; Abiotic: Sunlight, Sandy soil, Little water; 1. environment 2. ecosystem 3. populations 4. community 5. habitat 6. niche

# Brain Check

Name ___________________________

## Word Play

**1** Use the words in the box to complete the puzzle.

**Across**

3. The average weather in an area over time
5. The variety of species in an ecosystem
6. Nonliving

**Down**

1. Living
2. The struggle for resources in an ecosystem
4. The type of factor that determines the size of a population

abiotic
biotic
climate
competition
diversity
limiting

Use the three across words to write a sentence.

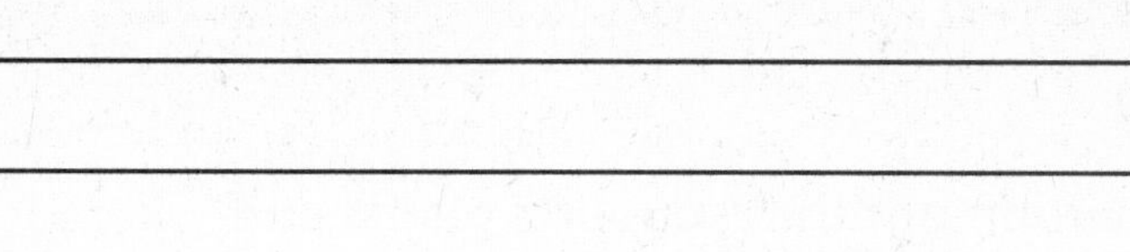

# Apply Concepts

2 Draw an organism and its habitat.

List three abiotic factors that are in your environment right now.

_______________

_______________

_______________

Select an organism in this lesson. Explain how it lives and survives in its ecosystem by interacting with the living and nonliving elements.

_______________________________________________

_______________________________________________

Draw a line from the organism to the ecosystem it would most likely live in.

1. A warm, wet swamp

2. A grassy prairie

3. A snowy arctic ocean area

Your neighborhood is an environment that supports plants and animals. With your family, list as many organisms living in your neighborhood as you can. Compare lists with your classmates.

# Quest for the Serpent Eagle

africa

Jane Juniper is a wildlife surveyor. She is deep in the forest of Madagascar, an island off the coast of Africa, observing birds.

What's that sound? Jane hears a loud, screeching bird call that she never expected to hear. It sounds like... But could it be?

Jane tiptoes quietly through the forest, searching the trees for movement. There!

Jane stands perfectly still. The bird has a dark back and a striped chest. It has yellow eyes, and sharp talons. But it's not supposed to exist!

Jane Juniper has studied all about African birds. It takes her just a moment to be sure. But she is still amazed! With her camera she collects evidence of her find.

Jane Juniper, wildlife surveyor, found a bird that was thought to be extinct—a Madagascar Serpent Eagle!

# Now You Be the Surveyor

Imagine you're a wildlife surveyor. Survey the forest below. Write the kinds of animals you find and the number of each kind.

TEKS 5.9D identify the significance of the carbon dioxide-oxygen cycle to the survival of plants and animals

Essential Question

# What Are Roles of Organisms in Ecosystems?

## Engage Your Brain!

Find the answer to the following question in the lesson and record it here.

Giraffes eat tree leaves to get the energy they need to live and grow. Where do trees get their energy?

______________________

______________________

______________________

______________________

## Active Reading

### Lesson Vocabulary

List the terms. As you learn about each one, make notes in the Interactive Glossary.

______________ ______________

______________ ______________

______________ ______________

### Signal Words: Details

Signal words show connections between ideas. *For example* and *for instance* signal examples of an idea. *Also* and *in fact* signal added facts. Active readers remember what they read because they are alert to signal words that identify examples and facts about a topic.



Inquiry Flipchart p. 55 — True Colors/A "Super" Predator

# Green Machines

You know that animals depend on plants for food. Did you know that animals depend on the oxygen that plants produce, too?

**Active Reading** As you read, underline three things plants need in order to make their own food.

Gases move back and forth between plants and animals in the carbon dioxide–oxygen cycle. This is essential for the survival of plants and animals.

## The Carbon Dioxide–Oxygen Cycle

Plants use carbon dioxide to make the food that most living things need to live.

1. Plants take in carbon dioxide. Plants need carbon dioxide and energy from sunlight to make sugars they use for food. As a byproduct, plants give off oxygen.
2. When animals breathe in they take in oxygen. When animals breathe out, they give off carbon dioxide.
3. Most plants take in some oxygen. Plants use oxygen to process the sugars they make. As plants do so, they give off carbon dioxide.

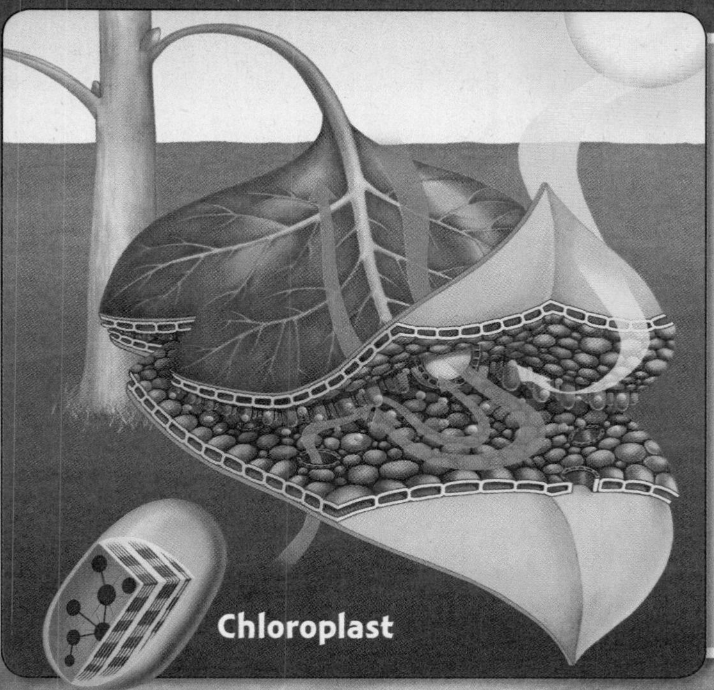


## Photosynthesis

1. Carbon dioxide enters a plant through tiny holes in its leaves.
2. Water from the soil enters the plant through its roots.
3. Chloroplasts inside cells found in leaves and other green parts of the plant capture energy from sunlight.
4. Chlorophyll helps change carbon dioxide, water, and solar energy into sugar and oxygen.

The process by which plants and plantlike organisms make food is **photosynthesis** [foh•toh•SIN•thuh•sis]. Photosynthesis takes place with the help of a green molecule called **chlorophyll** [KLAWR•uh•fil]. Chlorophyll is found in structures within a plant's cell called chloroplasts. During photosynthesis, plants use the energy in sunlight to change water and carbon dioxide into sugars and oxygen. The oxygen is released from tiny holes called stomata on the plants' leaves. All of the oxygen we breathe comes from plants and plantlike organisms.

## The Carbon Dioxide-Oxygen Cycle

Write the missing terms to complete the cycle.

carbon dioxide

give off

used by

_______________

_______________

used by

give off

oxygen

# Eat Your Vegetables!

Have you ever heard these words? You may think that you can live without plants. But even if you skip the spinach, you still depend on plants for food.

**Active Reading** As you read these two pages, circle the clue words or phrases that signal a detail such as an example or an added fact.

All organisms need energy to live and grow. That energy comes from food. **Producers** are organisms that make their own food. Plants are producers. Tiny plantlike organisms called phytoplankton that live in oceans and other bodies of water are also producers.

This hippopotamus is a consumer that eats plants.

Humans are consumers. Most people eat both producers and other consumers.

Squirrels are consumers that eat mostly producers.

Organisms that cannot make their own food are called **consumers**. Consumers eat other living things in order to get the energy they need to live and grow. Some consumers eat only plants. Some eat only animals. Others eat both plants and animals.

No matter what kind of consumer an organism is, it cannot survive without producers. For example, mice and rabbits eat only plants. Hawks eat the mice and rabbits. If there were no plants, then the mice and rabbits would die. The hawks that eat the mice and rabbits would also die. Living things depend on the food made by plants.

## Consumer or Producer?

Write which are producers and consumers.

# You Are What You Eat

Some people eat only foods made from plants. Others eat a mix of meat and plant foods. Just like people, different kinds of consumers eat different types of food.

**Active Reading** As you read this page and the next, underline the definitions of *herbivore, carnivore,* and *omnivore*.

Consumers are classified into three main groups based on what they eat. *Herbivores* eat only producers. Common herbivores are mice, rabbits, and deer. Pandas, koalas, elephants, and most insects, including butterflies, are also herbivores.

Meat-eating consumers are called *carnivores*. When you think of a carnivore, you might think of the lion shown here. But not all carnivores are mammals. Penguins are birds that eat only fish. Ladybugs are beetles that eat other insects.

This snake is a carnivore. It eats other animals for food.

Lions are carnivores that eat other animals such as zebras and antelopes.

Consumers that eat both plants and animals are called *omnivores*. Forest-dwelling box turtles, for example, eat strawberries, blackberries, and mushrooms. The box turtles also eat insects and spiders.

Carnivores and omnivores that hunt and eat other animals are also called *predators*. The animals that predators hunt are called *prey*. The numbers of predators and prey are linked. As a predator population increases, it consumes more and more prey. Eventually the predators consume so much prey that the prey animals become scarce. The predators have trouble finding food. Some predators may move away. Others die. With fewer predators to eat them, prey animals have a chance to increase in number again.

A toucan is an omnivore. It will eat fruit, insects, snakes, and just about anything else it can find.

## Do the Math!

### Interpret a Line Graph

The graph shows the number of lynx and snowshoe hares in an area over time.

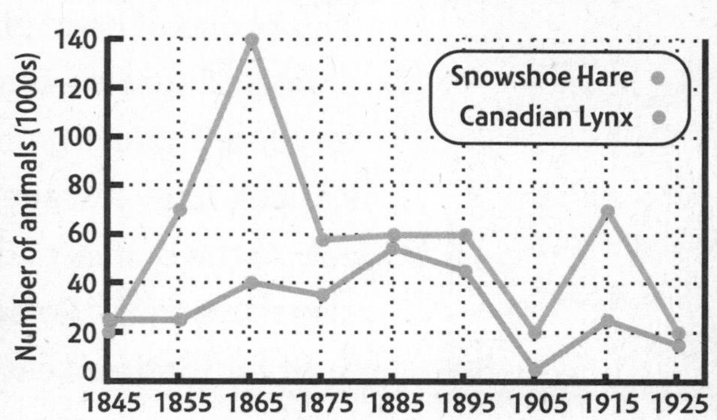


How many hare and lynx were there?

| | in 1865 | in 1905 |
|---|---|---|
| hare | ____________ | ____________ |
| lynx | ____________ | ____________ |

What do you notice about the relationship of predators to prey?

______________________________________

______________________________________

______________________________________

# Break It Down, Clean It Up

Just as garbage collectors remove the garbage people throw away, nature has its own cleanup crew.

**Active Reading** As you read these two pages, underline the main roles of scavengers and decomposers.

Have you ever thought about what happens to the bodies of dead plants and animals? When plants and animals die, some organisms in the environment eat them for food. These organisms are called *scavengers*. Vultures are well-known scavengers. These birds are famous for eating the bodies of dead animals. Some carnivores are also scavengers. Polar bears, sharks, and leopards both hunt for food and eat dead animals that they find. Scavengers play an important role in cleaning up the environment.

Millipedes are scavengers. They eat dead plant matter that they find in the soil.

Crabs scavenge algae, fungi, and decaying matter from the ocean floor.

Many vultures don't have feathers on their heads. This helps them keep clean as they stick their heads inside the bodies of the dead animals they scavenge.

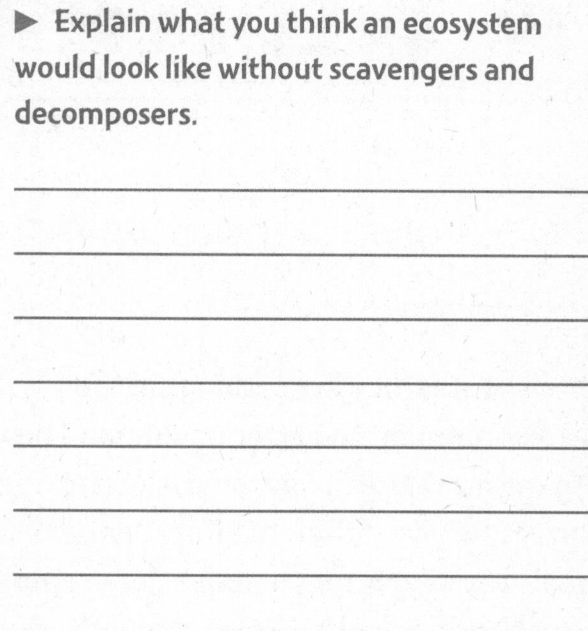

► Explain what you think an ecosystem would look like without scavengers and decomposers.

Scavengers aren't the only living things that clean up dead organisms. **Decomposers** are organisms that break down, or decompose, wastes and the remains of dead organisms. This process returns nutrients to the soil, air, and water. Bacteria are microscopic decomposers that use chemicals called enzymes [EHN•zymz] to break down the last remains of plants and animals and animal wastes. In so doing, they obtain the energy they need to carry out their life processes.

Fungi are decomposers that release enzymes. These enzymes break down dead matter, releasing nutrients that enrich the soil.

Why It Matters

# A Starring Role

Every organism plays an important part in its ecosystem.

Scientists study living things in their environment to better understand how these organisms relate to one another. Some species cannot survive if their habitat changes even in small ways. Tiger salamanders, for example, live in wetlands. Scientists know that if the number of salamanders in a wetland decreases, it is likely a sign that the environment has changed.

Some species, such as the Bengal tiger of South Asia, are in danger of dying out because of habitat loss and illegal hunting. Governments work to protect these species as well as their habitats. When a species' habitat is protected, all the organisms within it are protected, too.

Kelp forests are rich ocean habitats where many fish have their young. Kelp forests are found throughout the world in cold, coastal waters. Protecting these forests helps protect the organisms that depend on them, in the same way that protecting the animals that live in the kelp forests helps protect the forests themselves.

▶ Think of a species that is common in your area. What might happen if this species suddenly disappeared?

_______________

_______________

_______________

_______________

_______________

_______________

Tiger salamander

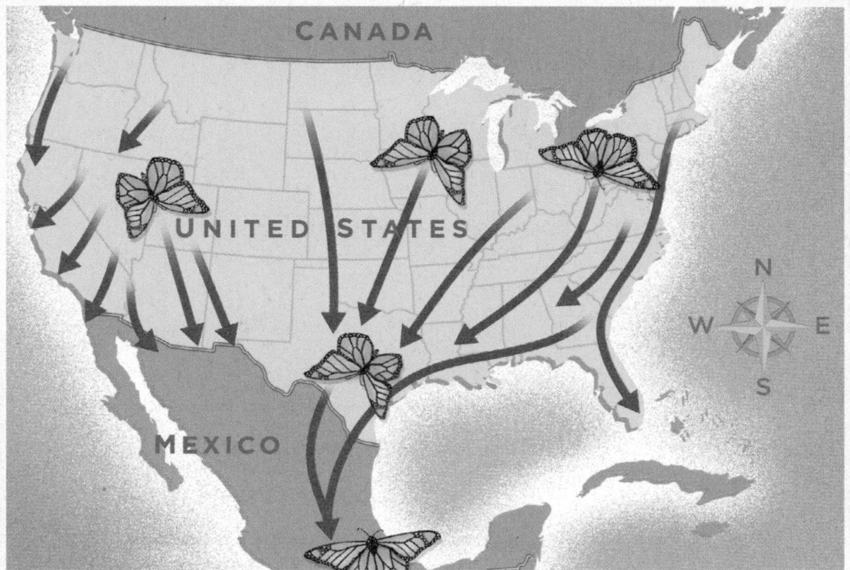


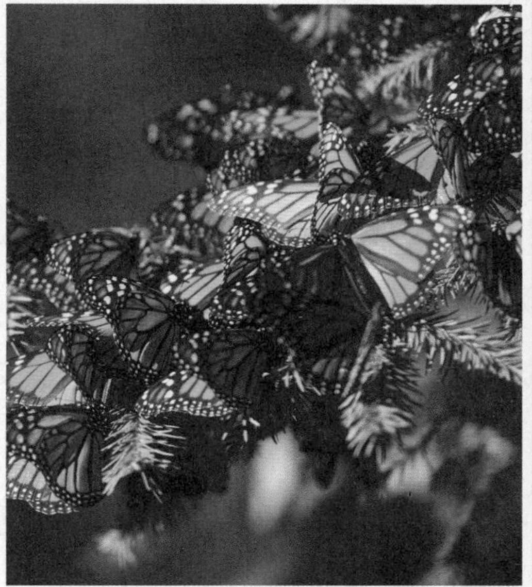

Monarch butterflies migrate south to warm climates for the winter. Over their lifetime, monarchs live in many different ecosystems. Conservationists have worked to protect the areas where these insects live. Doing so also protects other organisms that share the same area with the monarchs.

Sea turtles eat small animals that they find floating in seaweed. Conservationists have focused on protecting sea turtles. That in turn helps protect both their habitats and the organisms that live there.

Sea urchins feed on kelp. If there are too many urchins, they can completely destroy the forest. Sea otters eat sea urchins and help keep kelp beds healthy.

When you're done, use the answer key to check and revise your work.

**Match each picture to its description.**

1

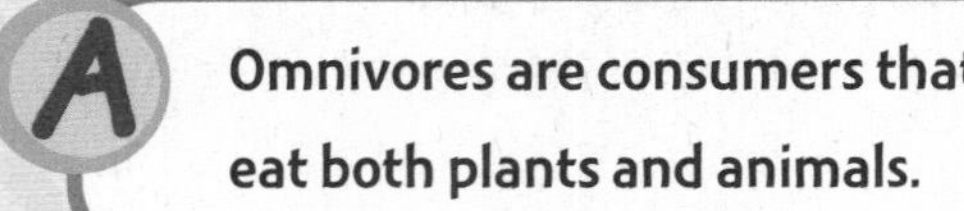

A Omnivores are consumers that eat both plants and animals.

2

B Carnivores and omnivores that hunt and eat other animals are also called predators.

3

C Plants make food through the process of photosynthesis.

## Summarize

The idea web below summarizes the lesson. Complete the web.

Roles of Organisms

A 4. __________________ makes food for itself and other animals.

Carnivores are consumers that 7. __________________ .

Bacteria are 5. __________________ that break down dead matter and wastes.

The number of predators tends to rise when there is a rise in the number of 6. __________________ .



Answer Key: 1. C 2. B 3. A 4. producer 5. decomposers 6. prey 7. eat other animals

# Brain Check

Lesson 2

Name ______________________

## Word Play

**1** Unscramble each group of letters to spell an important term from the lesson. Use the clues to help you.

1. breehivor — — — — — — — — — An animal that eats only producers
2. toradrep — — — — — — — — A living thing that hunts and eats other animals
3. reyp — — — — An animal that is hunted by other animals
4. pocodemser — — — — — — — — — — An organism that breaks down wastes and plant and animal remains and returns their nutrients to the soil
5. evormoni — — — — — — — — An animal that eats plants and other animals
6. vengescra — — — — — — — — — An organism that eats dead plants or animals
7. clyophohlrl — — — — — — — — — — — A green molecule that enables plants to turn water, carbon dioxide, and sunlight into sugars
8. rumcosne — — — — — — — — An organism that cannot make its own food

**Bonus:** List five omnivores.

______________________

______________________

______________________

______________________

______________________

# Apply Concepts

2 Complete the sentences to identify two roles of decomposers in an ecosystem.

a. Decomposers break down the remains of ____________ and the ________ of living organisms.

b. Decomposers return ____________ to the soil.

3 Identify the significance of the carbon dioxide-oxygen cycle to the survival of plants and animals.

____________________

____________________

____________________

____________________

____________________

4 Circle the activity that occurs when plants make sugars for food.

Plants take in oxygen and give off carbon dioxide.

Animals take in oxygen and give off carbon dioxide.

Plants take in carbon dioxide and give off oxygen.

5 Label the consumers and producers.

__________ __________ __________ __________

List all the plants and animals your family eats today in a two-column chart. Don't forget to count the plant materials that make up bread and pasta! Are the members of your family herbivores, carnivores, or omnivores?

Inquiry Flipchart page 56

**TEKS** **5.3A** in all fields of science, analyze, evaluate...scientific explanations by using...observational testing... **5.4A** collect...information using tools, including...materials to support observation of habitats or organisms... **5.9A** observe the way organisms live and survive in their ecosystem by interacting with the living...elements

Name ______________________________

Essential Question

# What Makes Up a Land Ecosystem?

## Set a Purpose

**What do you think you will learn in this activity?**

______________________________

______________________________

______________________________

______________________________

## Think About the Procedure

**Why do you think your sample site should have a variety of plants and soil coverings?**

______________________________

______________________________

______________________________

______________________________

______________________________

**Why did you make sure to accurately measure when marking your sample area?**

______________________________

______________________________

______________________________

______________________________

## Record Your Data

**Use technology to make a chart to organize the different living things found in your sample site and their role in the ecosystem. Attach it below.**

## Draw Conclusions

How did you determine the role that each living thing played?

Compare your results with the results of other groups. Explain any differences or similarities.

## Analyze and Extend

1. What kind of living things did you find in your sample area?

2. Which role in the ecosystem had the greatest amount of living things?

3. In the space below, draw a picture of your sample area. Make sure to include an example of a producer and a consumer that you found living in it.

4. How did organisms survive in their ecosystems by interacting with non-living elements?

5. Think of other questions you would like to ask about how living things interact in the ecosystem.

**TEKS 5.9B** describe how the flow of energy derived from the Sun, used by producers to create their own food, is transferred through a food chain and food web to consumers and decomposers

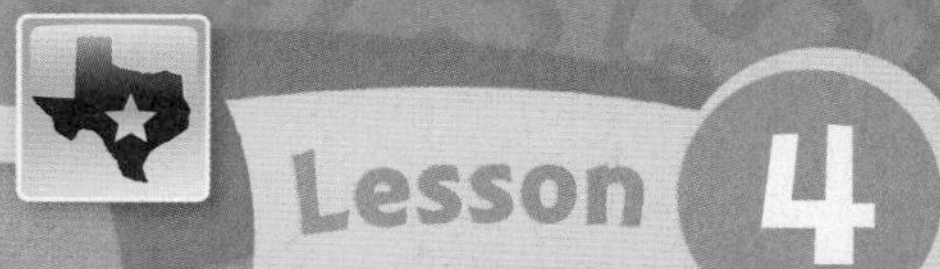


Essential Question

# How Does Energy Move Through Ecosystems?

## Engage Your Brain!

Find the answer to the following question in the lesson and record it here.

There are many kinds of animals at this watering hole. Why aren't they running away from each other?

______________________________

______________________________

______________________________

______________________________

## Active Reading

### Lesson Vocabulary

List the terms. As you learn about each one, make notes in the Interactive Glossary.

______________________________

______________________________

______________________________

### Using Diagrams

Diagrams add information to text that appears on the page with them. Active readers pause their reading to review diagrams and decide how the information in them adds to what is provided in the running text.



Inquiry Flipchart p. 57 — Model a Food Web/Bring It Home

# Food Chains

From producers to consumers to decomposers, the food chain never stops.

**Active Reading** As you read these two pages, underline all the important members of a food chain.

## Tundra Food Chain

The tundra is the coldest, driest ecosystem on Earth. Short summers mean little plant life grows here. Many animals either migrate or hibernate during the long, cold winters.

Reindeer moss uses energy derived from the sun to make sugars. Producers, such as reindeer moss, form the base of tundra food chains.

Caribou are first-level consumers. These herbivores eat reindeer moss and other producers to get energy for their life functions.

Wolves are second-level consumers. They are predators. Animals, such as caribou, are their prey.

The transfer of food energy from one organism to the next in an ecological community is called a **food chain**. Almost every food chain begins when producers capture energy from the sun. Producers use the energy derived from the sun to create chemical energy in sugars, which they use for food. Food not used for life processes is stored in the tissues of the producers and then consumed by herbivores that eat the producers for energy. Herbivores are first-level consumers.

Next in the food chain are carnivores and omnivores, the second-level consumers. Second-level consumers eat herbivores and receive the food energy stored in their bodies. Third-level consumers eat second-level consumers. Scavengers may be second- or third-level consumers, as they eat organisms that have died.

Decomposers are the final link in any food chain. They get energy as they break down the remains of dead plants and animals and return nutrients to the soil.

► Number the pictures to show their position in a food chain.

**Scavengers, such as this Arctic gull, feed on the dead bodies of caribou, wolves, and other animals. Fungi and bacteria do the final cleanup work as they decompose the final remains of tundra organisms.**

# Food Webs

Like a spiderweb held together by many connecting threads, the paths in a food web show the feeding relationships among species in a community.

**Active Reading** As you read, underline the information that helps you understand the food web diagram.

Organisms in food chains don't eat just one type of food. A **food web** shows how food chains overlap. In other words, it shows what eats what. Look at the forest food web on the next page. Both the mouse and the insect eat parts of trees. A snake can eat a mouse, a salamander, or a kinglet. All living things eventually become food for decomposers.

Arrows in the web point in the direction that energy moves. Find the acorns and the mouse. Which way does the arrow point? From the acorns to the mouse. As shown by this example, energy derived from the sun is used by producers to create their own food, and the energy is transferred through the food web to consumers and decomposers.

Just as in food chains, decomposers are the final link in a food web. Common decomposers are fungi and bacteria. They get their energy when breaking down the remains of dead plants and animals.

Predators limit the number of animals in a food web. If snakes were removed from this forest food web, the number of mice would increase. More mice mean that more plants would be eaten. Eventually, the mice might run out of food and begin to die off. This would affect the living things that eat mice. As you can see, all of the organisms in a food web are interdependent.

▶ In the forest food web, trace two overlapping food chains that include the snake. Make the path of each food chain a different color.

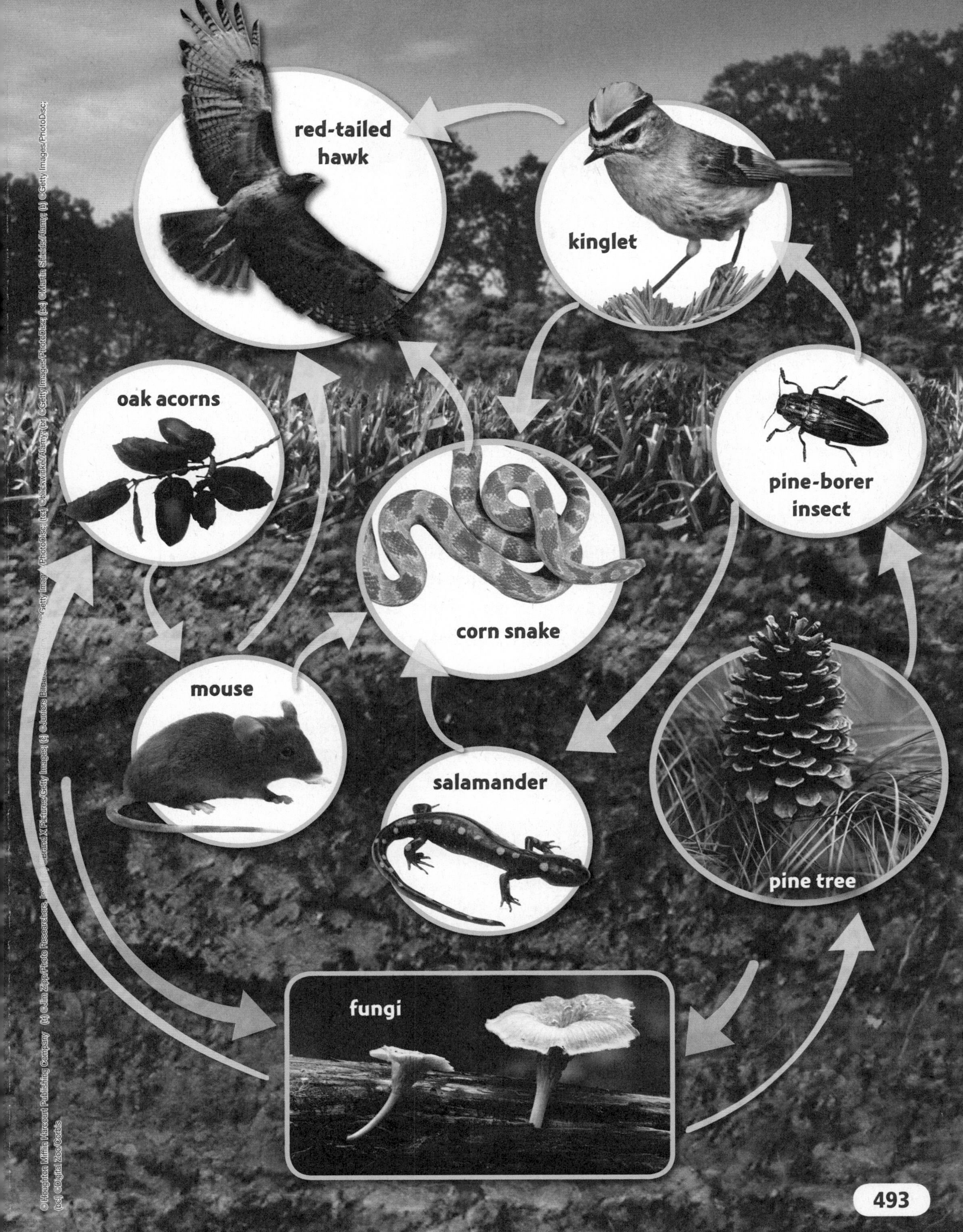
red-tailed hawk
kinglet
oak acorns
pine-borer insect
corn snake
mouse
salamander
pine tree
fungi

# At the Top

It takes a lot of grass to support a hawk at the top of a food chain. Although hawks don't eat grass, the energy they use comes from the grass at the bottom.

**Active Reading** As you read, circle the lesson vocabulary each time it is used.

An **energy pyramid** shows how much energy passes from one organism to another up a food chain. The organisms in a layer of the pyramid eat those in a lower layer. Because it takes many producers to support a smaller number of consumers, producers who get their energy from the sun are the most numerous group.

Third-level consumers like the leopard seal, a predator at the top of this energy pyramid, have the least amount of energy available to them. That is why their population is small.

Second-level consumers, such as octopuses and salmon, feed on first-level consumers below them in the pyramid. Because less energy is available to them, they are fewer.

Krill, clams, and herring are first-level consumers. They consume phytoplankton. Some first-level consumers eat millions of tiny phytoplankton every day.

Producers called phytoplankton are the base of this ocean energy pyramid.

# Do the Math!

## Calculate Units

At each level of an energy pyramid, 90% of the energy received from the lower level is used for life processes. Only 10% is available to be passed upward.

If the grasses have 100 units of energy, how much can be passed to the grasshoppers?

_______________

Why do the snakes only get 1 unit of energy?

_______________

_______________

**BONUS** How much energy is available to the owls that eat the snakes? Show your work.

_______________

Environmental changes can affect energy flow in an energy pyramid. Suppose the number of salmon is reduced because of overfishing. Seals that eat the salmon may go hungry. They may even starve. Without salmon to eat them, the krill population could increase at a rapid rate. Such a large number of krill could then eat up its own food source as well as that of other species. One change in the flow of energy through an ecosystem affects every species in the ecosystem. Whatever happens at one level affects the energy available in the rest of the pyramid.

**When you're done, use the answer key to check and revise your work.**

**Fill in the missing words to summarize the main ideas of the lesson.**

**Energy Moves Through Ecosystems**

### Food Chains

The first organisms in a food chain are

1. ____________________.

Herbivores are the

2. ______________-level consumers, and

3. ____________________

and 4. ______________ are the second- and third-level consumers.

5. ____________________

are the final organisms in all food chains. They recycle materials by breaking down plant and animal remains, thereby returning nutrients to the environment.

### Food Webs

A food web shows how food chains

6. ____________________.

Arrows show the direction of

7. ____________________

transfer through the web.

### Energy Pyramids

Most of the energy in an ecosystem is present in the

8. ____________________.

At each level, organisms use

9. ______________ percent

of the available energy for life processes. Only

10. ______________

percent of the energy is passed from one level to the next level above.

Answer Key: 1. producers 2. first 3. carnivores 4. omnivores 5. Decomposers 6. overlap 7. energy 8. producers 9. 90 10. 10

# Brain Check

Lesson 4

Name ______________________

## Word Play

**1** Unscramble the terms. The first letter of each term is in the center of the target. Use the definitions to help you.

1. d b o w e o F ______________________ A diagram that shows overlapping food chains (2 words)

2. 

______________________ Plants and some plantlike microorganisms

3. 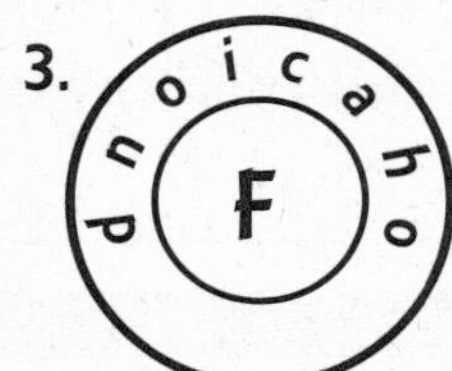

______________________ A single path that shows how food energy moves from one organism to the next in an ecosystem (2 words)

4. 

______________________ Animals that eat plants and animals

5. 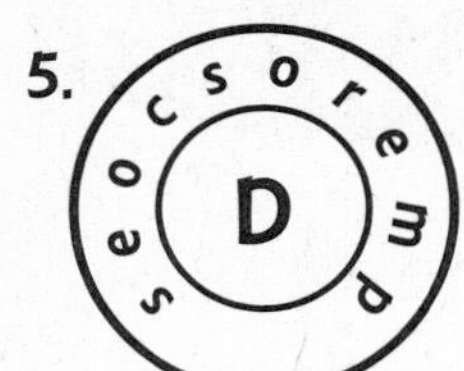

______________________ Organisms that break down the nutrient remains of dead things

6. 

______________________ A diagram that shows how energy is used, stored, and passed on in each level of a food chain (2 words)

# Apply Concepts

**2** This food chain is scrambled. Rewrite the links in order of energy flow.

hawk → bacteria → corn → mouse

__________ → __________ → __________ → __________

**3** Complete the facts about the energy pyramid below.

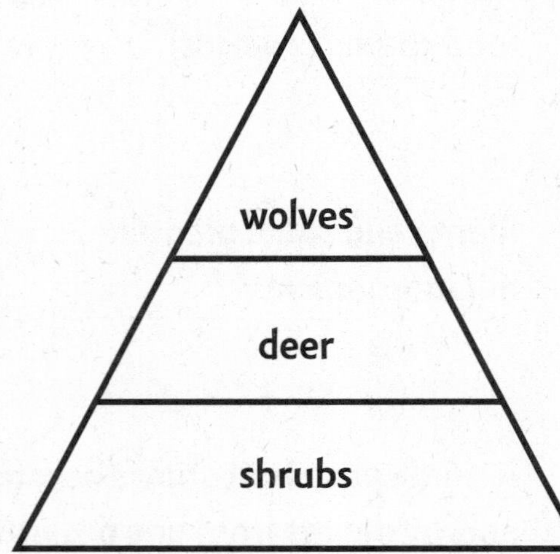


a. The shrubs use ________ percent of their energy and pass on ________ percent to the deer that eat them.

b. Which organisms get the least amount of energy?

______________________________

c. Which organisms must be the most plentiful to support this food chain?

______________________________

**4** Many food chains used energy derived from the sun to produce the food in this sandwich. The cheese came from milk from a cow that ate grass. Fill in the other chains.

sun ______________________________ → you

sun ______________________________ → you

sun ______________________________ → you

Name ______________________



5 Label the role of each organism. Some have more than one role. Use these terms: *producer, herbivore, carnivore, first-level consumer, second-level consumer, decomposer*.

______ ______ ______ ______

______ ______ ______ ______

6 Describe how the flow of energy that is derived from the sun, and used by producers to create their own food, is transferred through food chains and food webs.

______________________________________________

______________________________________________

______________________________________________

______________________________________________

______________________________________________

______________________________________________

______________________________________________

______________________________________________

______________________________________________

______________________________________________

**7**

Draw arrows to show what the hawk would eat.

Give the correct order of the flow of energy derived from the sun for one food chain in this food web.

______________________________________________

______________________________________________

Explain what might happen if the grass in this food web were to disappear.

______________________________________________

______________________________________________

______________________________________________

______________________________________________

**Take It Home!**

At your next meal, make a game with your family to identify the food chains that led to the different foods you are eating. What is the longest chain? The shortest chain?

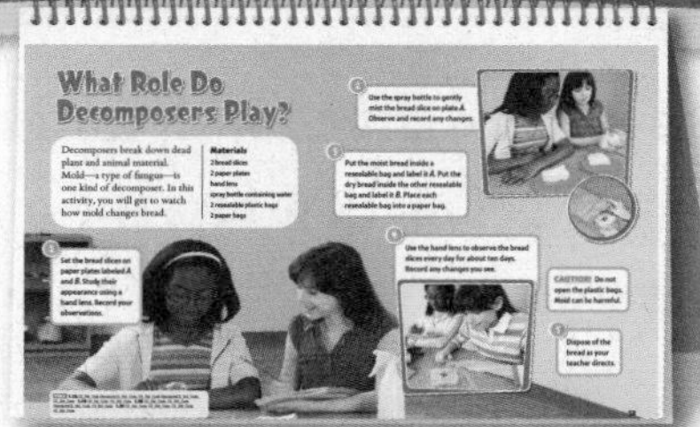

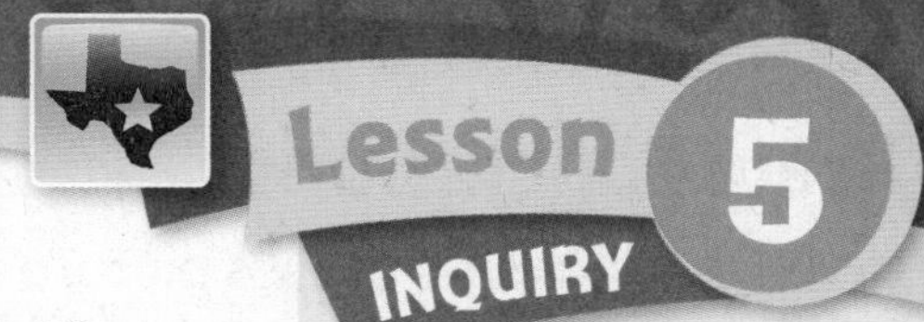


Inquiry Flipchart page 58

**TEKS** **5.2F** communicate valid conclusions in both written and verbal forms **5.9B** describe how the flow of energy derived from the sun, used by producers to create their own food, is transferred through a food chain and food web to consumers and decomposers

Name ______________________________

Essential Question

# What Role Do Decomposers Play?

## Set a Purpose

How do you think decomposers change materials?

______________________________

______________________________

______________________________

______________________________

Write a statement summarizing how you think mold changes the food it grows on.

______________________________

______________________________

______________________________

______________________________

## Think About the Procedure

What are different observations you can make about the appearance of the bread?

______________________________

______________________________

______________________________

Why do we spray one of the bread slices with water and not the other?

______________________________

______________________________

______________________________

## Record Your Data

In the space below, make a chart in which you record your observations.

## Draw Conclusions

In the space below, draw a picture of the appearance of breads *A* and *B* during the last day of your investigation.

Did your observations indicate that mold is a decomposer? Explain.

## Analyze and Extend

1. How did the mold change the bread?

2. Where do you think mold gets its energy from?

3. Did spraying the bread with water have any effect on how fast the mold grew? Explain.

4. What do you think would happen to the bread if you continued to let the mold grow on it?

5. Use your observations to describe the role of decomposers in the environment.

6. Think of other questions you would like to ask about decomposers.

**TEKS 5.9C** predict the effects of changes in ecosystems caused by living organisms, including humans, such as the overpopulation of grazers or the building of highways

Lesson 6

Essential Question

# How Do Environmental Changes Affect Organisms?

## Engage Your Brain!

Find the answer to the following question in this lesson and record it here.

A forest fire can change a landscape in a matter of minutes! Trees are burned, and animals run for shelter. How could a forest fire be a good thing?

_______________

_______________

_______________

## Active Reading

### Lesson Vocabulary

List the terms. As you learn about each one, make notes in the Interactive Glossary.

_______________

_______________

### Compare and Contrast

Many ideas in this lesson are connected because they explain comparisons and contrasts—how things are alike and different. Active readers stay focused on comparisons and contrasts when they ask themselves, How are these things alike? How are they different?



Inquiry Flipchart p. 59 — Hunting for Beans/Compost in a Bag

# Change Comes Naturally

All environments change over time. Some changes happen slowly, while others occur quickly.

**Active Reading** As you read these two pages, draw a box around events that change the environment rapidly. Draw a circle around events that change the environment slowly.

Over hundreds of thousands of years, mountains weather and erode. Rivers cut canyons into rock and change course through valleys and plains. Gradual changes like these affect the organisms that live in environments.

Weather patterns change over time as well. Like changes to the land, *climate changes* affect organisms. Throughout Earth's history, the average temperature has gone up and down many times.

An ice age happens when Earth's temperatures are colder than normal for a very long time. Large areas of land are covered with ice for thousands of years. During warmer climate cycles, ice melts and uncovers land.

During the last ice age, ice nearly 4 km thick covered much of North America. Because the ice held so much frozen water, the level of the oceans dropped and coastlines changed.

PACIFIC OCEAN

ATLANTIC OCEAN

Volcanic eruptions can quickly change the environment. Centuries of forest growth and the wildlife that live in it can be destroyed within hours.

Earth is now in a warming cycle. Many scientists predict that this warming trend will continue and believe it is in part linked to human activities. It is unclear how warming might affect the planet as a whole. As some areas become warmer, the organisms that inhabit those areas will move, adapt to the change, or disappear.

Many things can happen to change environments quickly as well. Heavy storms can cause floods that wash away land. Mudslides can destroy years of plant growth in minutes. Volcanic eruptions can be destructive, but they can also form entirely new land that will eventually be inhabited by plants and animals and become an ecosystem.

## Do the Math!

### Interpret a Graph

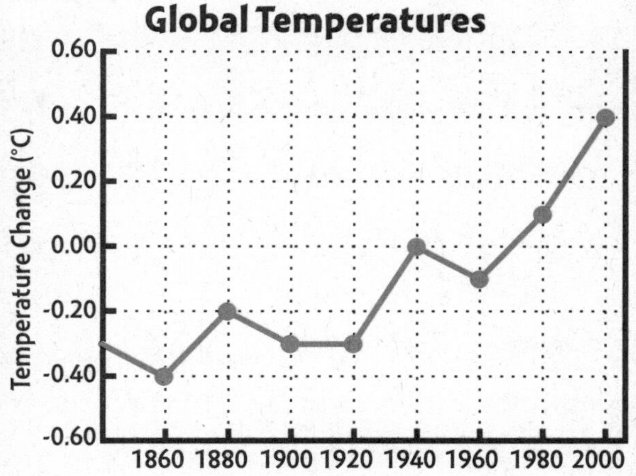


**The graph shows average temperatures on Earth over time. Use the graph to describe temperature trends between 1900 and 2000.**

_______________

_______________

_______________

_______________

A *drought* occurs when little rain falls. Without water, plants and animals will disappear.

# Next, Please!

Ecosystems change all the time, but the changes are often so slow that they are hard to notice.

**Active Reading** As you read these two pages, write numbers next to appropriate sentences to show the order of events.

The picture below shows how bare rock can change into an ecosystem filled with living things. The gradual change of organisms in an ecosystem is called **succession**. *Primary succession* begins on bare rock, such as after a volcano erupts. Dust settles in cracks in the rocks. The first organisms to colonize are called pioneer species. Lichens are common pioneers. They break down the rock as they grow, producing soil. When they die, their litter decays, adding nutrients to the soil.

As soil develops, plants can begin to grow. Mosses flourish, and they help produce more soil. The soil becomes thicker, and bigger plants take hold. Eventually, trees grow. A mature, stable community establishes itself.

It can take hundreds of years for a stable community to establish itself. Where water is plentiful, succession can happen more quickly. Even mature, stable communities continue to change.

*Secondary succession* occurs where an ecosystem has been disturbed, but soil is still present. Areas burned by forest fires undergo secondary succession. Secondary succession occurs more quickly than primary succession. The existing soil usually contains seeds and roots that sprout and grow after the fire is over. The first plants to grow tend to be hardy shrubs and grasses. Gradually, larger plants colonize the burned area. Animals also return. Eventually a stable ecological community re-establishes itself.

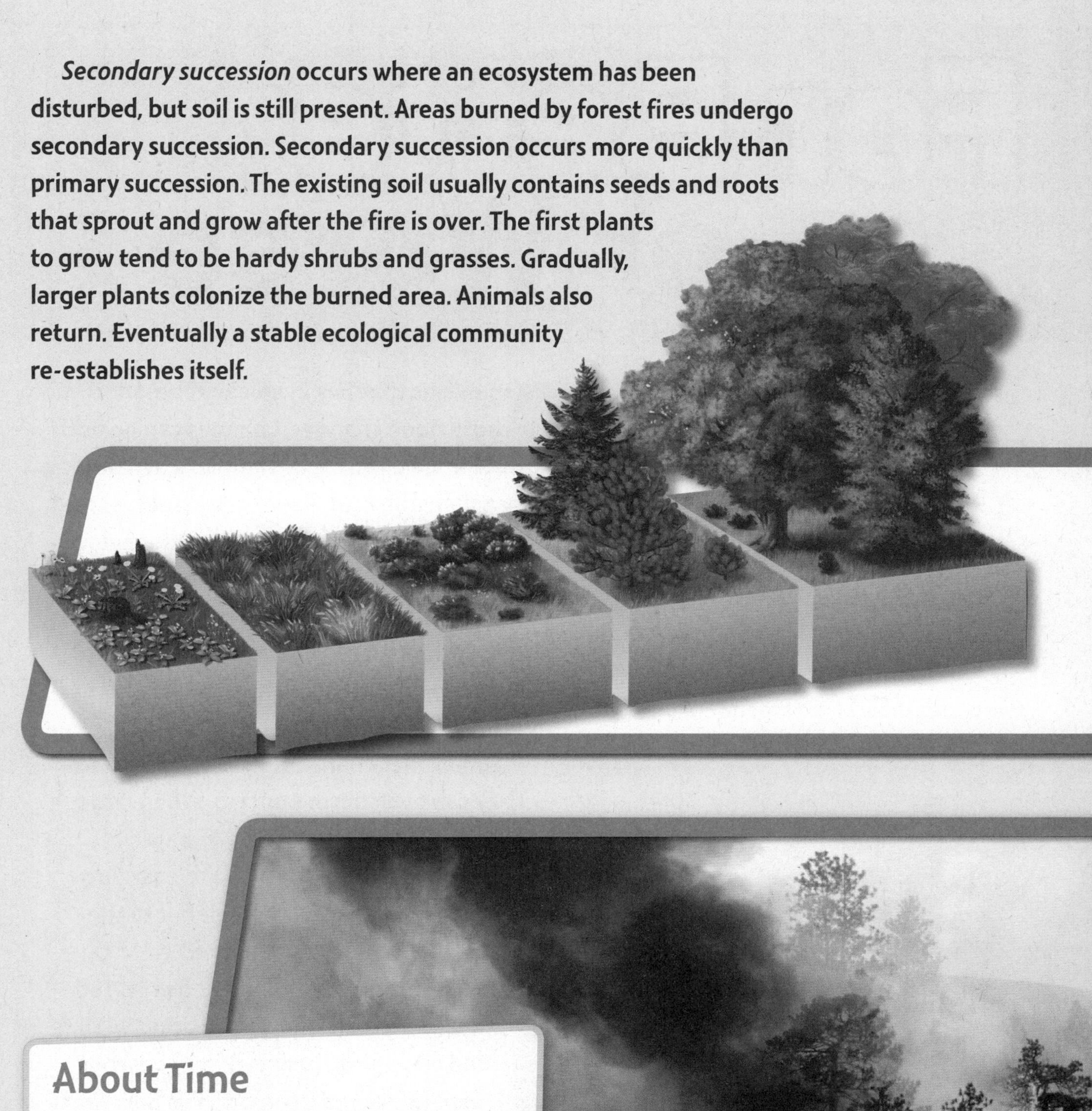

## About Time

An area with no plants or animals returns to a grassy plain within a year. What kind of succession has occurred? Explain your answer.

______________________________

______________________________

______________________________

# For Better or Worse

Living things change the places where they live. Is this a good thing or a bad thing? It depends on your point of view!

**Active Reading** As you read these two pages, draw boxes around clue words that signal examples.

Organisms that live in an environment can cause huge changes. Changes can be both harmful and helpful. For example, when beavers make a dam, they cut down many trees—trees that provide food and shelter for other living things. In addition, the dam slows the flow of water, which affects animals that rely on faster-flowing water to live. On the other hand, the dams produce wetlands, which provide homes for other organisms.

Sometimes changes harm an ecosystem. They can even harm humans. When large numbers of algae in bodies of water reproduce rapidly, the algae release large amounts of harmful chemicals into the water and cause oxygen levels to drop. The resulting condition is known as red tide, which can kill fish and other wildlife and can poison people. When beaches experience red tides, officials post signs warning people to stay out of the water.

The algae that make up a red tide release harmful chemicals and use up oxygen that fish need to breathe.

Beavers change their environment by building dams across streams. The dams cause flowing water to back up and form ponds. These changes create environments where new plants and animals can establish themselves.

## Contrast

Describe a way that the activities of beavers can be helpful to an ecosystem. Then describe one way in which their activities can be harmful.

| Helpful | Harmful |
|---|---|
| ______________________ | ______________________ |
| ______________________ | ______________________ |
| ______________________ | ______________________ |

Goats, sheep, and other grazing animals remove grass and other plants from an environment. When too many animals graze in an area, they eat grass faster than it can grow back.

# Invasive Species

You may have seen a movie where space aliens invaded Earth. Invasions happen on Earth every day! Here's what happens when a new species moves into an environment.

Populations of native harvester ants have been destroyed as invasive fire ants moved into harvester ant habitats and successfully competed with them for resources.

**Active Reading** As you read these two pages, draw boxes around clue words or phrases that signal a main idea.

Sometimes the population of a species grows quickly after it is introduced into a new environment. This type of organism is called an *invasive species.* Invasive species take food and space away from *native species*, the organisms already living in an ecosystem. The factors that limit the growth of native species, such as predators, pests, and diseases, do not affect invasive species. The two species compete for resources. If no other species in the ecosystem can use the invasive species for food, only the environment's physical properties, such as climate, may limit its expansion. The native species least able to compete with the invasive species will be most vulnerable.

Zebra mussels are invasive to North America. They were accidentally carried into the Great Lakes in the hulls of ocean-going ships. Zebra mussels now grow in such large populations that they totally cover surfaces, block water outlets, and clog pipes in the lakes they have invaded.

The brown anole [uh•NOH•lee] is an invasive species of lizard brought into the Southeast, where populations of green anoles were common. Brown anoles quickly began to populate the region, competing for food with green anoles. Fewer predators ate brown anoles, so the population of native green anoles decreased.

Plants can be invasive, too. Japanese honeysuckle grows quickly. It covers the ground with thick tangles of vines and leaves. A full-grown honeysuckle uses large amounts of water and blocks sunlight, preventing native plants from growing. Originally planted in gardens, Japanese honeysuckle spread beyond the gardens where it had been planted when birds and the wind carried its seeds into the natural environment.

Native green anole populations are threatened by the invasive brown anoles.

## Predict the Outcome

Predict the effect of the changes in an ecosystem if someone chose to plant Japanese honeysuckle in a garden.

_______________________________________________

_______________________________________________

_______________________________________________

_______________________________________________

_______________________________________________

# Humans Change the Environment

Humans are not outside of the environment, and we have a large impact on our ecosystems. The effects of humans on the environment can be both harmful and beneficial.

**Active Reading** As you read these two pages, draw brackets around sentences that describe ways in which people harm the environment. Underline sentences that describe ways people help the environment.

Human activities can harm an ecosystem. For example, people mine coal to produce energy for homes and businesses. Open-pit mining, as shown here, kills all the plants living in the area where the mine is dug. Animals that depend on the plants for food must move.

Highways can also disrupt ecosystems. Land must be cleared of plants and animals before a highway can be built. Often hills get leveled and valleys get filled in, blocking streams. Communities of plants and animals that lived in the ecosystem can no longer survive.

Humans produce a large amount of waste that is disposed of as trash. Most trash ends up in landfills. If landfills are not built properly, wastes can pollute soil and water. *Pollution* is the contamination of air, water, or soil by substances harmful to organisms.

Not all changes caused by humans are harmful. People work to protect their environment and to protect organisms from harm as a result of ecosystem change. Protecting ecosystems and the organisms living in them is called *conservation.*

People try to restore habitats and repair damaged ecosystems by replanting trees and cleaning up pollution. People also remove invasive plants and animals so native organisms can survive.

In addition, people try to help organisms affected by natural disasters. People care for animals injured or orphaned by these disasters.

## Predict the Outcome

In the space below, predict the effects of changes in ecosystems that will occur when humans help the environment.

___

___

___

Why It Matters

# Gone!

Some living things change when their environment changes. Some living things move to new places. Others do not survive.

Millions of years ago, Earth was covered with giant reptiles. Now most of those reptiles are extinct. **Extinction** happens when all the members of a certain species die. Giant reptiles, such as the *Tyrannosaurus rex* shown here, lived in a time in which Earth was warm. Over time, the environment cooled, and many of the reptiles could not survive.

Golden toads were once numerous in a part of the mountainous tropical forest of Costa Rica. Scientists think a period of drought that dried up the pools where the toads laid their eggs and where tadpoles matured caused a rapid population decline. The drought also allowed a fungus that harmed the toads to spread. Golden toads have not been seen since 1989 and are thought to be extinct.

The Tasmanian wolf lived in Australia and New Guinea. Ranchers believed the wolves killed sheep and cattle, but this was never proven. The Tasmanian wolf was hunted to extinction by the 1930s.

The dodo bird lived on an island in the Indian Ocean. Around 1600, people arrived on the island. They hunted the birds for food. They cut down the island's forests to make room for houses. Invasive species, such as cats and pigs brought by people, destroyed the dodo birds' nests. Within 80 years, dodo birds were extinct.

## Time Traveler

If you could go back to the island of the dodo birds in 1600, what advice could you give to help conserve dodo birds?

_______________________________________________

_______________________________________________

_______________________________________________

_______________________________________________

_______________________________________________

Today, people work to conserve habitats and protect organisms from extinction. Even so, many organisms are in danger of becoming extinct. As these organisms' environments continue to change, some will adapt, some will move, and some will not survive.

When you're done, use the answer key to check and revise your work.

**Read the summary statements below. Each one is incorrect. Rewrite the part of the summary in blue so it is correct.**

**1**

1. Pollution is all the living and nonliving things that affect an organism's life.

______________________________

2. A natural event that causes the environment to change slowly is an earthquake.

______________________________

3. People can help conserve habitats by mining, building landfills, and cutting down forests.

______________________________

______________________________

4. Protecting ecosystems is an example of extinction. ______________

**2** **The idea web below summarizes the lesson. Complete the web. Start with number 5.**

A gradual buildup of organisms in an environment that consists of bare rock is called 7. ______________ succession.

A gradual buildup of organisms in an environment that has soil is called 8. ______________ succession.

An environment can change 5. ______________ or 6. ______________.

A(n) 9. ______________ is any nonnative plant or animal that takes over an environment.

An environment can be changed suddenly by a natural event such as a 10. ______________ ______________.

Answer Key: 1. any harmful substance that gets into the environment 2. ice age 3. replanting forests, cleaning up garbage, and removing invasive plants and animals 4. conservation 5. quickly 6. slowly 7. primary 8. secondary 9. invasive species 10. flood, earthquake, or volcano eruption

Brain Check



Name ______________________

# Word Play

**1** Use the clues to unscramble the words below.

1. iavinvse _ _ _ _ _ _ _ _: A nonnative animal that moves into a new place
2. ecnntavosroi _ _ _ _ _ _ _ _ _ _ _ _: Protecting ecosystems and the organisms living in them
3. nlpituloo _ _ _ _ _ _ _ _ _: Litter on the ground or harmful chemicals in the water
4. tgurhdo _ _ _ _ _ _ _: Occurs when no rain falls for a long period of time
5. consisuces _ _ _ _ _ _ _ _ _ _: The gradual change and buildup of organisms in an environment
6. galea _ _ _ _ _: Organism that causes red tide when present in large numbers
7. vebera _ _ _ _ _ _: Can be helpful or harmful, depending on point of view
8. lonea _ _ _ _ _: Brown lizard that has invaded some areas of Florida
9. vmetneonrin _ _ _ _ _ _ _ _ _ _ _: Everything around an organism, such as other organisms, air, water, and land
10. txoniecnit _ _ _ _ _ _ _ _ _ _: Happened to dodo birds and Tasmanian wolves
11. navoolc _ _ _ _ _ _ _: Can cause long-term environmental change by blowing dust and gases into the sky

Bonus: What kind of dinosaur accidentally smashes everything in its path?

______________ ________

# Apply Concepts

**2** Label each picture as a change caused by people, animals, or a natural event.

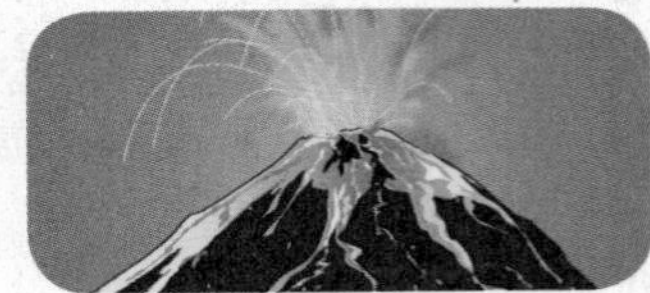
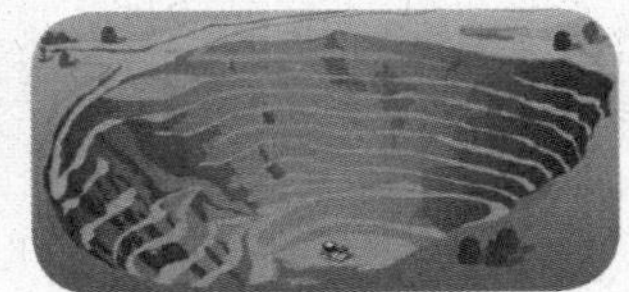

**3** Name four invasive species and describe their effect on ecosystems.

**4** Draw one circle around animals that became extinct because of natural events. Draw two circles around animals that became extinct because of human activities.

Name ___________________________



5 In the first box below, draw a landscape that includes a river. In the second box, draw how the same landscape might look after a flood. Include captions explaining how the environment changed.

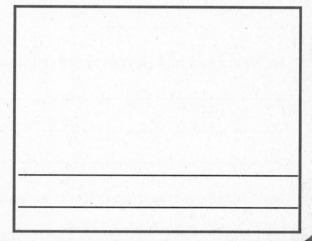

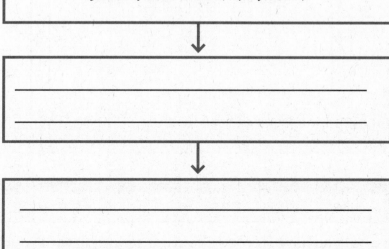

6 Fill in the graphic organizer below to describe how beavers change the environment. The first box is already completed.

Beavers build a dam in a stream.

↓

___________________________

___________________________

↓

___________________________

___________________________

Explain how people could try to solve each environmental problem listed below and predict the outcomes of their solutions.

7 Coal mining can harm habitats and cause pollution.

8 Building a new highway destroys habitats and can lead to soil erosion.

9 Waste from garbage in landfills can enter the ground and pollute soil and water.

10 Imagine that an orange tree frog eats only a certain type of small blue fly. A giant red fly starts moving into the tree frog's ecosystem. The red fly eats all the blue fly's food. In the space below, draw a flow chart that shows what might happen to the frog.

Bonus: How might orange frogs change because of the red fly?

Take It Home!

Share what you have learned about conservation with your family. Come up with at least four ways to help conserve resources at home. Carry out your family's plan, and report the results to the class.

TEKS 5.4A collect, record, and analyze information using tools, including...materials to support observations of habitats or organisms such as terrariums and aquariums

International Space Station

S.T.E.M.

Engineering & Technology

# How It Works:

## Life in a Box

How are an aquarium, a terrarium, and the International Space Station similar? In each contained space, habitats and organisms can be observed, and different parts of the environment must be controlled to make it possible for organisms to live there. Some of these parts include light, heat, water, and oxygen.

Terrarium

Aquarium

## Troubleshooting

An aquarium is usually outfitted with a filter, a pump, a heater, an aerator (to add oxygen to the water), and a light. Choose one of these devices, and tell what might happen to the living things in the aquarium if it failed and explain why.

_______________________________________________

_______________________________________________

continued

Artificial environments must have all of the things that the organisms living inside them need.

Draw an organism in an artificial environment. Explain how the environment is designed to supply what the organism needs.

Research Biosphere 2. What is it?

What was one problem people living in such a closed system would have?

How could they solve it?

Biosphere 2

# Build On It!

Rise to the engineering design challenge—complete **Design It: Mobile Ecosystems Lab** in the Inquiry Flipchart.

# Unit 11 Review

Name ___________________________

## Vocabulary Review

Use the terms in the box to complete the sentences.

| |
|---|
| community |
| consumers |
| food chain |
| habitat |
| photosynthesis |
| population |
| producers |
| succession |

TEKS 5.9A, 5.9B

1. Organisms that do not make their own food are called

   ____________________.

TEKS 5.9A

2. A scientist would look at a group of rabbits that live in a meadow and call them a(n) ____________________.

TEKS 5.9A, 5.9B

3. Organisms that make their own food are called

   ____________________.

TEKS 5.9A

4. A scientist who is describing the place where an organism lives is defining the organism's ____________________.

TEKS 5.9B

5. The transfer of food energy from a producer to consumers is called a(n) ____________________.

TEKS 5.9A, 5.9B

6. Plants make their own food through a process known as

   ____________________.

TEKS 5.9A

7. The gradual change of organisms in an ecosystem that follows an event, such as a volcanic eruption, is called

   ____________________.

TEKS 5.9A

8. A group of plants and animals that live in the same area and interact with each other is called

   a(n) ____________________.

## Science Concepts

**Fill in the letter of the choice that best answers the question.**

**TEKS 5.9B**

**9. The picture below shows organisms that live in a land ecosystem.**

**1.**

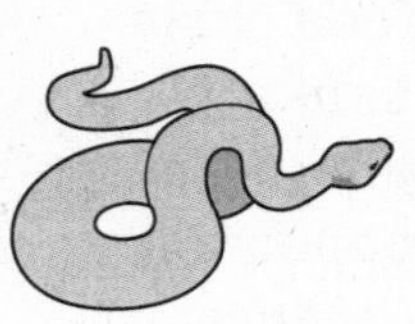

**2.**

**3.**

**4.**

**Which organism is the producer?**

Ⓐ organism 1 Ⓒ organism 3

Ⓑ organism 2 Ⓓ organism 4

**TEKS 5.9A**

**10. The organisms that live around a pond interact with biotic and abiotic factors. Which of the following is a biotic factor of the pond environment?**

Ⓐ muddy soil

Ⓑ cattail plants

Ⓒ slowly flowing water

Ⓓ warm temperature

**TEKS 5.9B**

**11. What is the role of algae in an ocean food web?**

Ⓐ producers

Ⓑ decomposers

Ⓒ first-level consumers

Ⓓ second-level consumers

**TEKS 5.9B**

**12. This diagram shows the movement of energy through an ecosystem.**

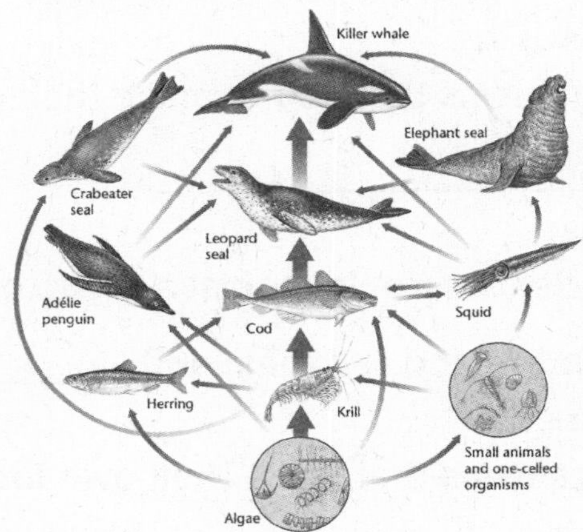


**Which statement is the best description of how energy derived from the sun flows through this food web?**

Ⓐ consumer → producer → decomposer

Ⓑ producer → decomposer → consumer

Ⓒ producer → consumer → decomposer

Ⓓ decomposer → producer → consumer

**TEKS 5.9B**

**13. Which is the initial source of energy in most ecosystems?**

Ⓐ sunlight

Ⓑ decomposers

Ⓒ nutrients in soil

Ⓓ oxygen in the air

**TEKS 5.9A, 5.9B**

**14. Pablo has a hamburger and a salad for lunch. Which term describes Pablo?**

Ⓐ producer Ⓒ herbivore

Ⓑ scavenger Ⓓ omnivore

Name ______________________________

TEKS 5.9A, 5.9D

15. Plants and animals are interdependent. Plants rely on animals to produce carbon dioxide. What do plants produce that animals need to survive?

Ⓐ food and oxygen

Ⓑ sunshine and rain

Ⓒ carbon dioxide and food

Ⓓ herbivores and carnivores

TEKS 5.9B, 5.9C

16. An ecosystem includes this food chain.

pine seed → mouse → snake → hawk

What would happen if all the mice died from a disease?

Ⓐ The snakes would eat pine seeds instead of mice.

Ⓑ The producers would stop making food.

Ⓒ The population of snakes would increase.

Ⓓ The population of snakes would decrease.

TEKS 5.9A, 5.9C

17. Sometimes a species that is introduced to an area grows quickly and crowds out organisms that were already living there. What is this introduced species called?

Ⓐ native species

Ⓑ protected species

Ⓒ invasive species

Ⓓ beneficial species

TEKS 5.9C

18. A new shopping center was built on a vacant lot. The table shows the numbers of plants before and after construction.

| Plants | Before | After |
|---|---|---|
| flowers | 500 | 1,000 |
| grass | 1,000 | 0 |
| shrubs | 260 | 50 |
| trees | 26 | 3 |

Based on these data, which is true?

Ⓐ Humans did not change the environment.

Ⓑ There were fewer total plants before the shopping center was built.

Ⓒ There were more kinds of plants before the shopping center was built.

Ⓓ There were more kinds of plants after the shopping center was built.

TEKS 5.9A

19. A tree has fungi growing on one side. What are fungi, and what are these organisms doing?

Ⓐ Fungi are producers. They are making their own food.

Ⓑ Fungi are scavengers. They are eating the dead parts of the tree.

Ⓒ Fungi are producers. They are providing the tree with food.

Ⓓ Fungi are decomposers. They are decomposing a part of the tree.

# Apply Inquiry and Review the Big Idea

Write the answers to these questions.

TEKS 5.9B

20. This diagram shows various organisms that live in the same ecosystem.

Describe a food-chain relationship between the four organisms shown.

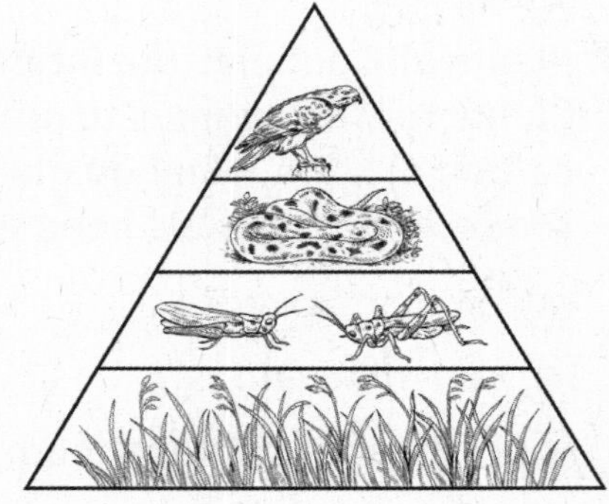

TEKS 5.9D

21. This diagram shows the carbon dioxide–oxygen cycle.

Explain the cycle, the gases involved, how they are used, and how the cycle is significant to the survival of other organisms.

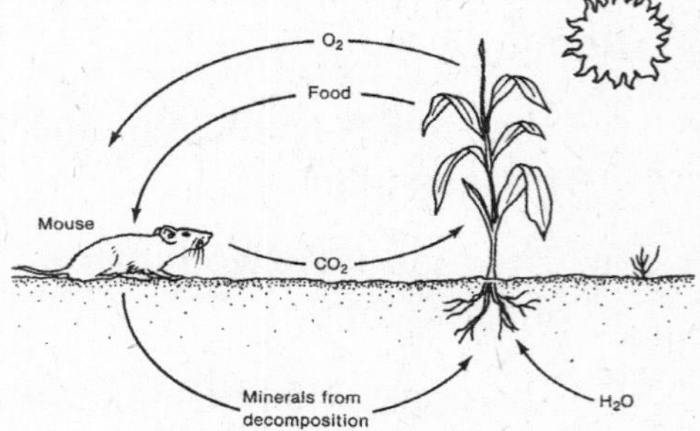


a. Plants in sunlight:

b. Animals at any time:

TEKS 5.9C

22. The table shows the number of deer and wolves in an area over time.

What was the average deer population from 1800–1875?

**Population of Deer and Wolves: 1800–1875**

| | Deer | Wolves |
|---|---|---|
| 1800 | 1,216 | 53 |
| 1825 | 1,309 | 59 |
| 1850 | 1,017 | 52 |
| 1875 | 814 | 44 |

UNIT 12

# Heredity and Adaptations

## Big Idea

All living things have characteristics that can be passed on to their offspring.

TEKS 5.3A, 5.3C, 5.3D, 5.9A, 5.10A, 5.10B, 5.10C



## I Wonder Why

It's got spines like a porcupine. It has a long, sticky tongue like an anteater. And it lays eggs! What is this strange-looking animal? I wonder why scientists would classify it as a mammal? *Turn the page to find out.*

**Here's why** Scientists classify the echidna as a mammal, even though it lays eggs. Most mammals give birth to live young. When the echidna's eggs hatch, the young are tiny. They are no bigger than a lima bean!

In this unit, you will explore the Big Idea, Essential Questions, and Investigations on the Inquiry Flipchart.

Levels of Inquiry Key ■ DIRECTED ■ GUIDED ■ INDEPENDENT

**Big Idea** All living things have observable characteristics that can be passed on to their offspring.

## Essential Questions



**Science Notebook**

Before you begin each lesson, be sure to write your thoughts about the Essential Question.

TEKS 5.10A compare the structures and functions of different species that help them live and survive, such as hooves on prairie animals or webbed feet in aquatic animals 5.10B differentiate between inherited traits of plants and animals such as spines on a cactus or shape of a beak and learned behaviors

Lesson 1

Essential Question

# What Are Physical and Behavioral Adaptations?

## Engage Your Brain!

Find the answer to the following question in this lesson and record it here.

Watch out! Don't get bitten by that... caterpillar? What type of adaptation does this caterpillar have?

______________________________

______________________________

______________________________

## Active Reading

### Lesson Vocabulary

List the terms. As you learn about each one, make notes in the Interactive Glossary.

______________________________

______________________________

### Signal Words: Details

This lesson gives details about how living things are suited to where they live. Signal words link main topics to added details. *For example* and *for instance* are often used as signal words. Active readers look for signal words that link a topic to its details.



Inquiry Flipchart p. 61 — Gobbling Up Your Greens/Animal Adaptations

# Adaptations

Living things have many similarities. They also have many interesting differences.

**Active Reading** As you read this page, underline the definition of *adaptation*.

Deserts are home to many kinds of snakes. This is because snakes have characteristics that help them survive in a desert. For example, snakes have tough, scaly skin that keeps them from drying out.

A characteristic that helps a living thing survive is called an **adaptation**. Suppose an animal is born with a new characteristic. If this characteristic helps the animal survive, the animal is likely to reproduce and pass on the characteristic to its young. As long as the animal's habitat doesn't change, the young that have this characteristic are also likely to survive and reproduce. Over time, the adaptation becomes more common in the population. In this way, populations of plants and animals become adapted to their habitats.

**These hares live in very different habitats. Because of this, they have different adaptations.**

**An arctic hare lives in a cold habitat. It has thick fur to keep it warm and small ears that prevent heat from being lost.**

**A jackrabbit lives in a hot habitat. Jackrabbits have large ears that help keep their blood cool.**

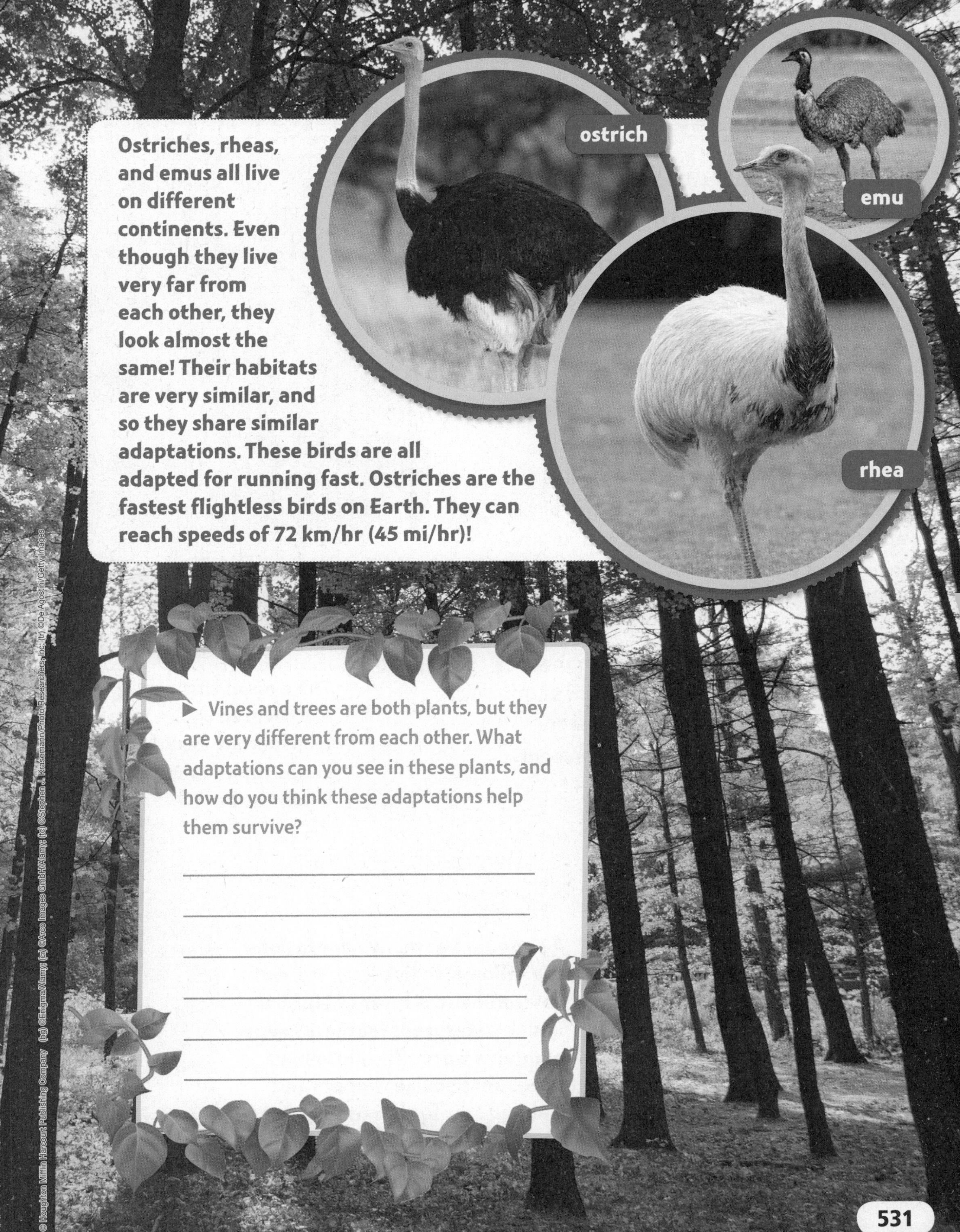


Ostriches, rheas, and emus all live on different continents. Even though they live very far from each other, they look almost the same! Their habitats are very similar, and so they share similar adaptations. These birds are all adapted for running fast. Ostriches are the fastest flightless birds on Earth. They can reach speeds of 72 km/hr (45 mi/hr)!

► Vines and trees are both plants, but they are very different from each other. What adaptations can you see in these plants, and how do you think these adaptations help them survive?

_______________________________________________

_______________________________________________

_______________________________________________

_______________________________________________

_______________________________________________

_______________________________________________

# Form and Function

Why can penguins live in the Antarctic while most other birds can't? They have a layer of blubber to keep them warm!

**Active Reading** As you read these two pages, underline the words and phrases that describe animal and plant adaptations.

Some adaptations are differences in the bodies of organisms. These are called physical adaptations. Organisms have physical adaptations that help them live and survive in different environments. When a plant or animal has a characteristic that enables it to survive in a way that other plants or animals cannot, the organism with the adaptation has an advantage. Consider how some of the organisms shown on these two pages are better able to survive in their environments than organisms that do not have these adaptations.

The eyes of this bird are covered with a thin, transparent eyelid that keeps the eye moist when the bird flies.

A penguin has many adaptations that allow it to live in an icy, wet environment. A layer of blubber under waterproof feathers keeps penguins warm. They also have wings shaped like flippers and webbed feet for swimming.

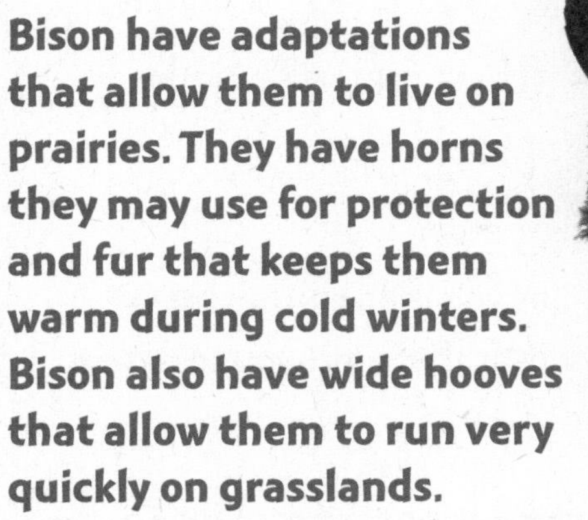

**Bison have adaptations that allow them to live on prairies. They have horns they may use for protection and fur that keeps them warm during cold winters. Bison also have wide hooves that allow them to run very quickly on grasslands.**

**The sharp spines of a cactus are actually modified leaves. The spines have a small surface area that minimizes water loss. The cactus shown has a thick stem that holds water, which is another important adaptation in a dry desert environment.**

▶ Choose an animal or a plant. Write a description of the environment in which the animal or plant live. Then describe the adaptations that help the animal or plant to live in that specific environment.

________________________________________

________________________________________

________________________________________

________________________________________

________________________________________

________________________________________

________________________________________

# Eat or Be Eaten

Whether blending in or standing out, physical adaptations help organisms survive.

**Active Reading** As you read the next two pages, circle signal words that alert you to details about the main idea.

Some physical adaptations protect living things from being eaten. For example, roses have sharp thorns that help keep their stems from being eaten. Other physical adaptations help to keep an animal hidden. This type of adaptation is called *camouflage* [KAM•uh•flazh]. When green lizards hide in green grass, they are camouflaged.

Animals that hunt, such as eagles, have adaptations that help them catch food. Eagles have very good eyesight. They also have sharp claws on their feet, which they use to capture their food.

Many plants have adaptations that help spread their seeds. Some seeds can be carried by the wind. Other seeds are inside berries. When the berries are eaten, the seeds are carried to a new location.

Can you see the owl in this picture? The owl is camouflaged to look like bark.

The bright color of this rose attracts pollinators, but the thorns keep plant-eating animals away.

# Catching Flies

**Bright coloring on an animal is often a warning that the animal is dangerous. Many animals know that paper wasps, like the one shown below, have a painful sting. The black and yellow hoverfly doesn't have a stinger. It is completely harmless. But because the hoverfly looks like a wasp, animals will think twice before trying to eat it. This adaptation is called *mimicry*.**

▶ Draw a line from the chameleon's tongue to the insect it would most likely eat.

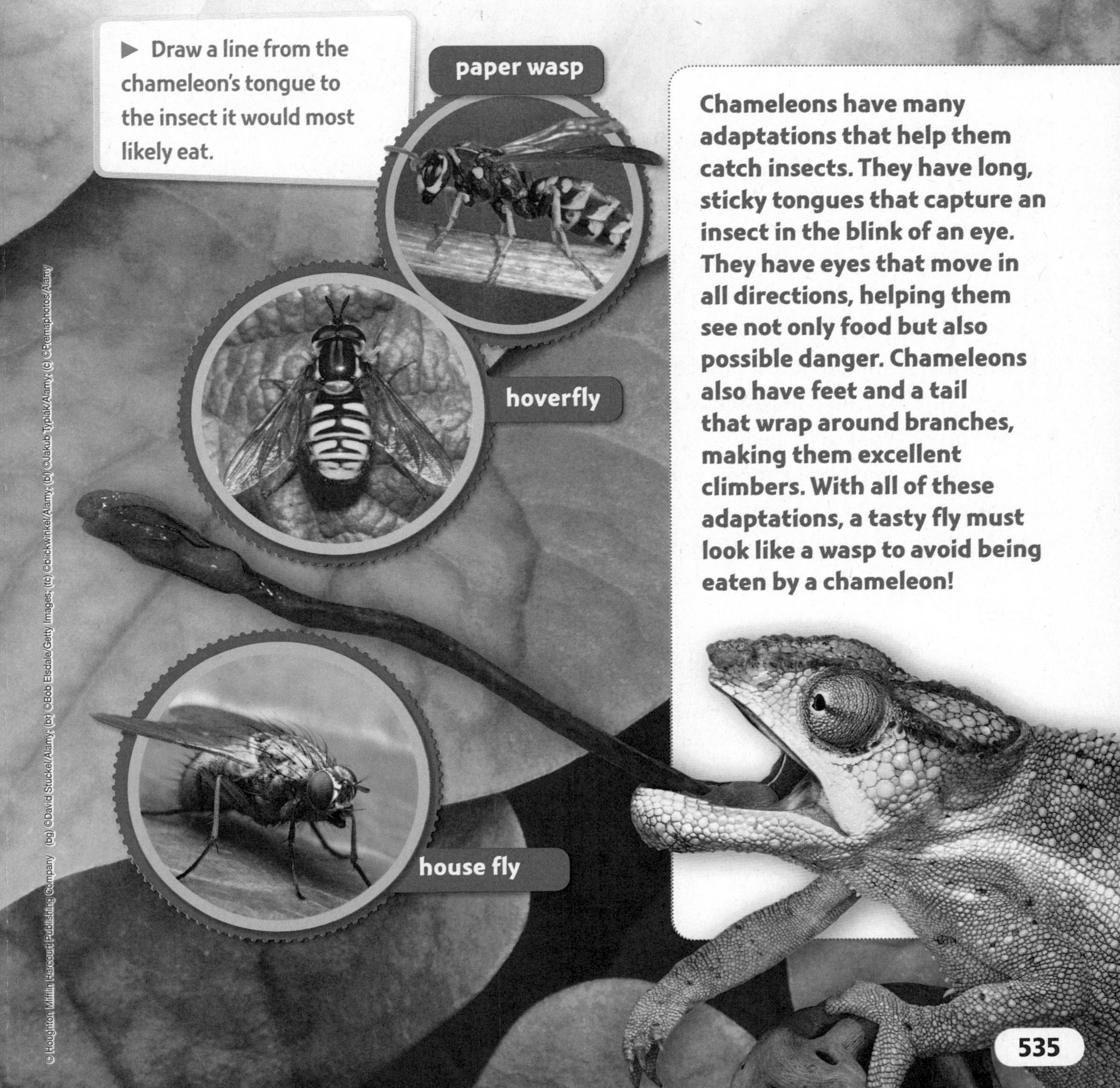


**Chameleons have many adaptations that help them catch insects. They have long, sticky tongues that capture an insect in the blink of an eye. They have eyes that move in all directions, helping them see not only food but also possible danger. Chameleons also have feet and a tail that wrap around branches, making them excellent climbers. With all of these adaptations, a tasty fly must look like a wasp to avoid being eaten by a chameleon!**

# On Your Best Behavior

The way living things act is called behavior. Some behaviors are adaptations that help animals survive.

**Active Reading** As you read the paragraph below, circle examples of instinctive behavior and underline examples of learned behavior.

Some things that animals do seem to come naturally. Babies do not have to be taught how to cry. Spiders are not taught how to spin webs. Behaviors that animals know how to do without being taught are called **instincts**. Animals have to learn other types of behaviors. For example, a lion cub is not born knowing how to hunt. It learns to hunt by watching its mother. Raccoons learn to wash food by watching other raccoons.

Some bats are *nocturnal*. This means they are active at night and sleep during the day. This allows bats to hunt insects that are active only at night.

Many animals have behaviors that help protect them from predators. When an octopus is frightened, it releases ink into the water. If the octopus is being attacked, the animal attacking it will not be able to see, and the octopus can escape.

**Each year, millions of snow geese migrate south in autumn and north in spring.**

Some animals move to different locations at certain times of the year to find food, reproduce, or escape very cold weather. This instinctive behavior is called *migration*. Many birds, butterflies, and some bats migrate long distances.

Some animals hibernate. *Hibernation* is a long period of inactivity that is like sleeping. But hibernation is not the same as sleeping. When an animal hibernates, its body processes slow down and it stays inactive for months. Can you imagine taking a three-month nap?

The way that animals act toward other animals of the same type is called *social behavior.* Honeybees have very complex social behavior. They communicate using movements called the "waggle dance." A bee that finds food will return to the hive and do a waggle dance. The pattern of the dance gives other bees a lot of information! The dance communicates which way to go, how far away the food is, how much food there is, and even what kind of food it is!

## Do the Math!

### Interpret Data in a Bar Graph

Ground squirrels hibernate. They must eat a lot during the spring, summer, and fall to store up enough energy to survive hibernation. Study the graph below.

**Ground Squirrel Body Mass**

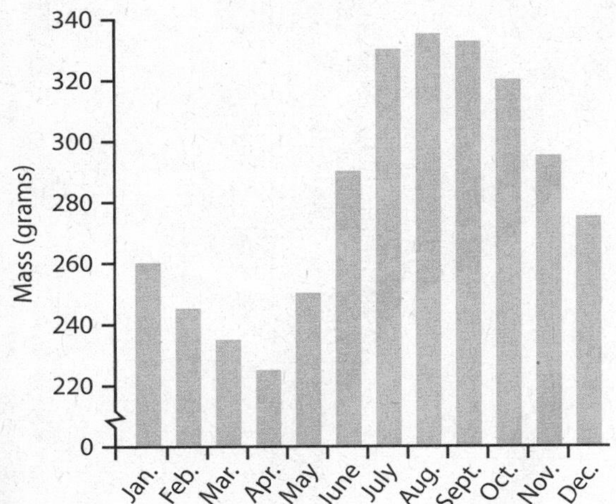

About how much mass does a ground squirrel have in March?

____________________________

During which month do ground squirrels start to hibernate? How do you know?

____________________________

____________________________

# The Circle of Life

All living things grow and develop. The way that living things develop can be an adaptation.

**Active Reading** Circle two different examples of organisms whose life cycles keep adults and young from competing for food.

Living things go through stages of growth and development called a *life cycle*. A living thing's life cycle is related to its habitat. Because of this, differences in life cycles are a type of adaptation.

Most frogs are adapted to live near water. A frog's life cycle starts when its eggs are laid in water. When the eggs hatch, tadpoles emerge. Tadpoles live in water until they grow legs and lungs. At this point, they are frogs and ready to live on land. In places where water dries quickly, tadpoles develop more quickly. This variation in frog life cycles helps tadpoles survive.

Tadpoles and frogs live in different places, and eat different foods. This is another kind of adaptation. Frogs and tadpoles don't compete with each other for food, allowing for more frogs to survive. Many other organisms have similar adaptations. For example, caterpillars eat plant leaves and most butterflies sip nectar from flowers.

adult luna moth

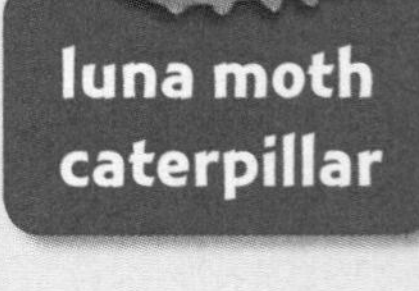
luna moth caterpillar

salmon eggs

Adult salmon live in the ocean, which is a dangerous place for young salmon. Adults migrate from the ocean to shallow rivers to lay eggs. More young salmon are able to survive in rivers.

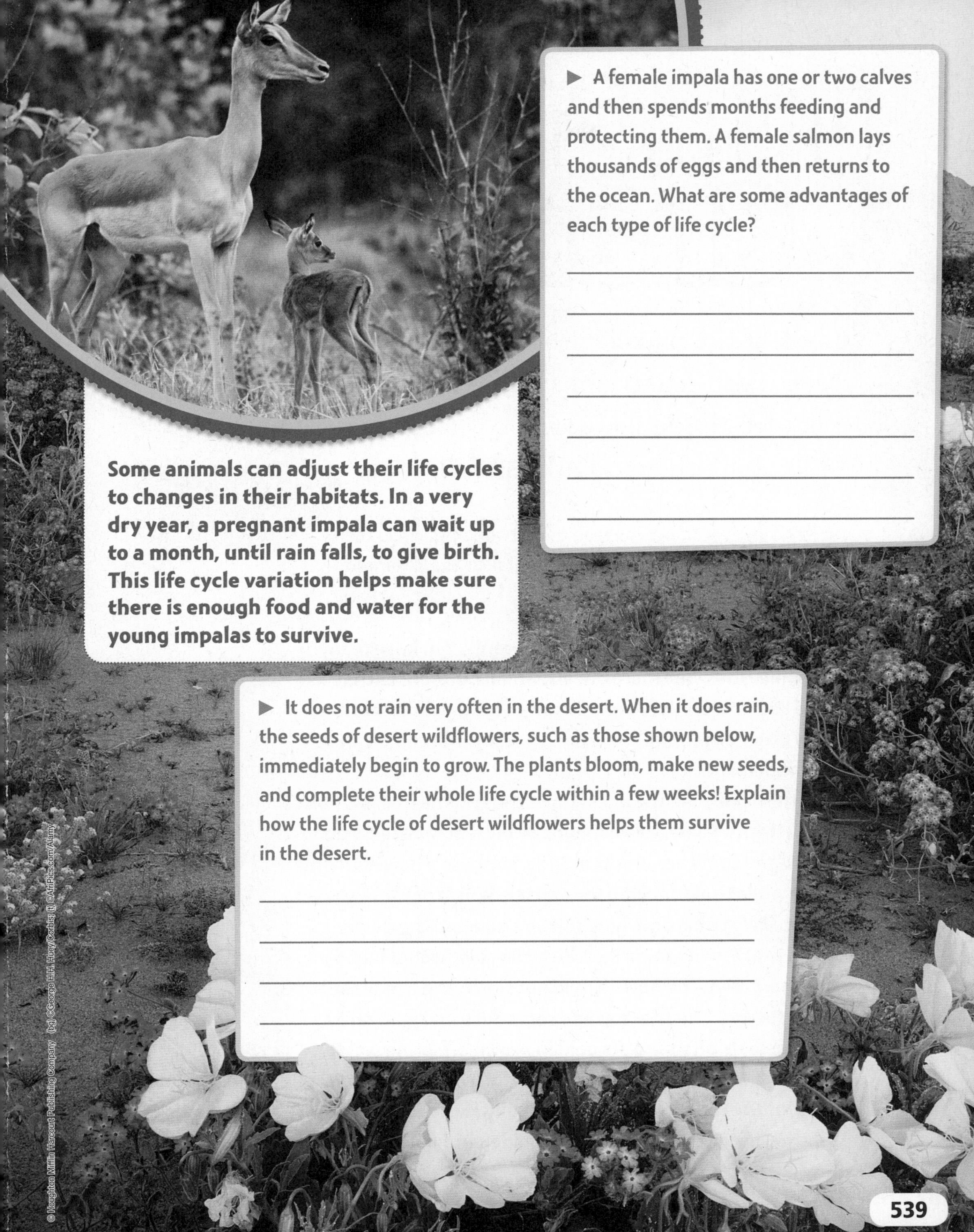

▶ A female impala has one or two calves and then spends months feeding and protecting them. A female salmon lays thousands of eggs and then returns to the ocean. What are some advantages of each type of life cycle?

_______________________________________________

_______________________________________________

_______________________________________________

_______________________________________________

_______________________________________________

_______________________________________________

_______________________________________________

**Some animals can adjust their life cycles to changes in their habitats. In a very dry year, a pregnant impala can wait up to a month, until rain falls, to give birth. This life cycle variation helps make sure there is enough food and water for the young impalas to survive.**

▶ It does not rain very often in the desert. When it does rain, the seeds of desert wildflowers, such as those shown below, immediately begin to grow. The plants bloom, make new seeds, and complete their whole life cycle within a few weeks! Explain how the life cycle of desert wildflowers helps them survive in the desert.

_______________________________________________

_______________________________________________

_______________________________________________

_______________________________________________

# Living Things Change

Look at the snakes slithering on this page. Each snake looks different, but they are all the same kind of snake. Why don't they look the same?

**Active Reading** As you read these two pages, circle the clue word or phrase that signals a detail such as an example or an added fact.

You don't look exactly like your parents. You have many similarities, but there are also small differences that make you unique. Every organism is slightly different from every other organism. Sometimes these differences can be very important.

Corn snakes, like the ones shown here, come in many colors and patterns. Some are very light colored, some are golden brown, and some are bright orange. Suppose a hawk is flying over a wheat field, looking for a snack. Which of these snakes is least likely to become lunch? If you guessed the golden brown snake, you are correct. Why? Its color would blend in with the wheat. The hawk would not see it, and the snake would survive. The snake would reproduce and pass on its coloring to its offspring. Its golden brown offspring would have a better chance of surviving in the wheat field and would also produce more offspring. Eventually, most of the snakes living in the wheat field would be golden brown.

Sometimes living things change because their environment changes. For example, bacteria have changed as a result of their changing environment. Since the discovery of antibiotics, people have learned how to kill bacteria. The first antibiotic, penicillin, saved many lives by killing bacteria that cause disease.

But in a very large population of bacteria, a few are not affected by penicillin. These bacteria survive and multiply. Over time, they produce large populations of bacteria that are not affected by penicillin.

Researchers have had to find new antibiotics to kill these bacteria. But, again, some bacteria are not killed. These bacteria continue to multiply.

While different types of antibiotics have been developed, bacteria have become resistant to many of them. Now there are bacteria that are resistant to almost all known types of antibiotics. These bacteria are extremely difficult to kill.

## Do the Math!

### Find Median and Mean

| Length of Corn Snakes | |
|---|---|
| Snake 1 | 3.5 m |
| Snake 2 | 5.5 m |
| Snake 3 | 4.6 m |
| Snake 4 | 5.1 m |
| Snake 5 | 4.8 m |
| Snake 6 | 3.9 m |
| Snake 7 | 5.3 m |

Adult corn snakes vary not only in color, but also in length. The table shows the lengths of several adult corn snakes. Study the data, and then answer the questions.

1. The median is the middle number of a data set when the numbers are placed in numerical order. Find the median of the data set. ______
2. The mean is the average of a data set. Find the mean of the data set. ______

Antibiotics in soaps and cleaners kill many bacteria. However, when not all of the bacteria are killed, the ones that survive multiply. Little by little, bacteria are becoming resistant to antibacterial soap and cleaners.

When you're done, use the answer key to check and revise your work.

**The outline below is a summary of the lesson. Complete the outline.**

## Summarize

I. Instincts: A behavior that a living thing does without being taught to do.

A. Example: ______________________________

______________________________

B. Example: ______________________________

______________________________

II. Adaptations: A characteristic that helps a living thing survive is called an adaptation. Kinds of adaptations include:

A. Physical Adaptations

1. Example: ______________________________

______________________________

2. Example: ______________________________

______________________________

B. Behavioral Adaptations

1. Example: ______________________________

______________________________

2. Example: ______________________________

______________________________

C. Life Cycle Adaptations

1. Example: ______________________________

______________________________

2. Example: ______________________________

______________________________

Answer Key: Your answers may vary. Sample answers: I.A. spiders spin webs I.B. babies cry II.A.1. camouflage II.A.2. thorns that keep plant-eating animals away II.B.1. migration II.B.2. hibernation II.C.1. controlling when offspring are born II.C.2. having young that don't eat the same food as adults

Name ____________________

## Word Play

1 Use words from the lesson to complete the puzzle.

### Across

1. What type of adaptation helps a living thing hide in its environment?
6. An animal that is active at night is described as being ________________.
7. Stages that living things go through as they develop are called life ________________.

### Down

2. An example of ________________ is birds flying south in winter.
3. What are characteristics that help an animal survive?
4. What behavior causes an animal to be inactive for a long period of time?
5. A behavior that an animal doesn't need to learn is a(n) ________________.

# Apply Concepts

**2** Draw a picture of a cactus. Next to the cactus, draw a plant that is found in a non-desert environment. Label three adaptations and their functions that help the cactus plant live and survive in a desert.

**3** Circle the camouflaged animal.

**4** In winter, ground squirrels retreat into burrows and do not come out until spring. Circle the term that best describes this behavior.

Communication    Hibernation
Migration    Nocturnal hunting

**5** A narrow-mouthed frog's eggs hatch directly into tiny frogs. The environment where narrow-mouthed frogs live is very dry. How is this adaptation helpful?

______________________________

______________________________

______________________________

______________________________

Go for a walk through your neighborhood or a local park with your family. Look at different plants and animals, and point out different adaptations that the plants or animals have.

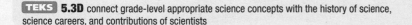

# Meet the Animal Activists

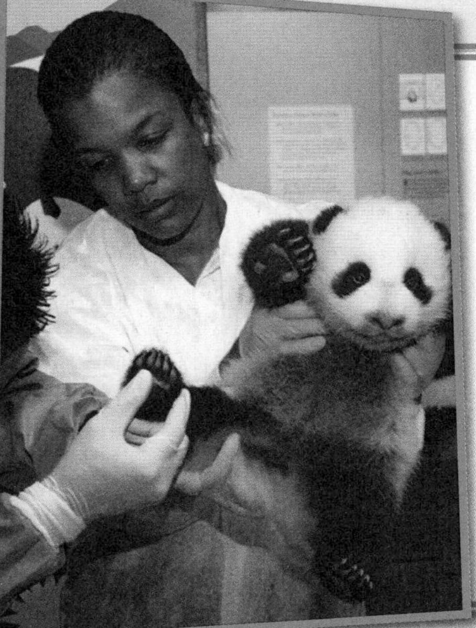

## Lisa Stevens

Lisa Stevens is a zoologist. She has worked with animals for most of her life. Stevens manages the giant-panda exhibit at the National Zoo in Washington, D.C. As part of her job, she teaches people about this endangered species. When the panda cub Tai Shan was born at the National Zoo, Stevens took care of him. There are only 1,600 giant pandas living in the wild today. About 250 live in zoos around the world.

## Raman Sukumar

Raman Sukumar grew up in India, where he loved studying nature. His grandmother called him *vanavasi*, an Indian name for "forest dweller." He has studied Asian elephants in the wild for more than 30 years. Sukumar wants to find a solution to the problem caused by people and elephants using the same land. He has taught many people why it is important to preserve the habitats of this endangered species.

# SAVE THE TAMARINS!

Golden lion tamarins are an endangered species. Read the story about the golden lion tamarin. Draw the missing pictures to complete the story.

Golden lion tamarins live in the rainforests of Brazil.

Logging and building have broken up the tamarins' habitat into small areas cut off from each other.

There are few golden lion tamarins left. There is little food and no place to roam.

**Solution:** People can set aside land as the tamarins' habitat.

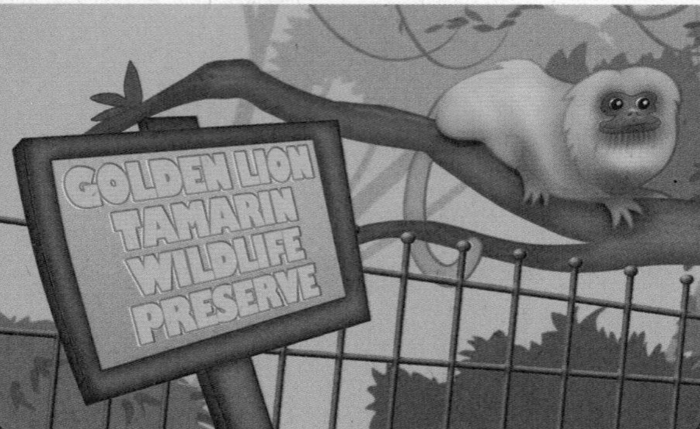


Over time, the number of tamarins increases. They will have the food they need to live.

**TEKS 5.10A** compare the structures and functions of different species that help them live and survive… **5.10C** describe the differences between complete and incomplete metamorphosis of insects

Lesson 2

Essential Question

# How Do Animals Grow and Reproduce?

## Engage Your Brain!

Find the answers to the following questions in the lesson and record them here.

How are these organisms similar? How are they different?

____________________

____________________

____________________

____________________

## Active Reading

### Lesson Vocabulary

List the terms. As you learn about each one, make notes in the Interactive Glossary.

____________________

____________________

____________________

### Main Idea and Details

Detail sentences give information about a topic. The information may be examples, features, characteristics, or facts. Active readers stay focused on the topic when they ask, What fact or information does this sentence add to the topic?

**Inquiry Flipchart** p. 62 — How Can You Model Metamorphosis? / How Do They Change?

# The More You GROW

Animals grow and change throughout their life cycles. How is your growth like that of the big cats on this page?

**Active Reading** As you read these two pages, draw two lines under a main idea.

One Cell

Two Cells

Four Cells

Eight Cells

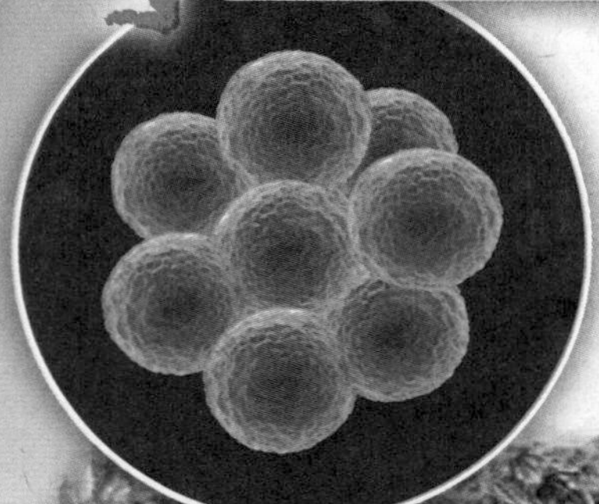

Look at the animals on these pages. What similarities and differences do you see? The cheetahs look different from—but have many things in common with—humans. Both cheetahs and humans are mammals. Most mammals develop inside their mothers' bodies, and have hair on their bodies. Most mammals also look a lot like their parents, and do not change much during their lives. A mammal typically begins its **life cycle**, or the stages an animal goes through during its life, in the same way. In fact, all animals begin life as a single cell—a fertilized egg.

All animals start life as a single cell. This fertilized egg divides, and one cell becomes two. Then, the two cells divide into four cells, the four cells into eight cells, and so on.

As an animal grows, its cells divide and become specialized to do different jobs. For example, a bone cell has a different job than a liver cell. A brain cell has a different job than a skin cell. After cells specialize, they make nearly exact copies of themselves each time they divide. Why do you think this is important?

You can sometimes see evidence of cell division. For example, you can observe young animals growing larger. Yet even when animals are full-grown, you can still see evidence of cell division in hair and nail growth. Other times, evidence of cell division is hidden. It takes place inside the body, where tissues and organs are built, maintained, and repaired. The new cells that form when a cell divides allow this to happen.

Humans babies look very different from older children and adults, but they have most of the same features. Like other animals, they grow from a single cell.

This cub began as a single cell growing and dividing inside its mother's body, but it was born fully formed. Its body cells will continue to divide as it grows.

## Do the Math!
### Interpret a Table

Fill in the table to calculate how many cells will be present after 3 and 6 cell divisions.

| Division | Number of Cells |
|---|---|
| 1 | 2 |
| 2 | 4 |
| 3 | |
| 4 | 16 |
| 5 | 32 |
| 6 | |

# EGGScellent on Land and in Water

All animals develop from a single cell, but not all animals develop in their mothers' bodies. How do birds and fish develop?

**Active Reading** As you read these two pages, underline the phrases that give details, such as an example or an added fact.

Some animals do not develop within their mother's bodies. Instead, they grow and develop in eggs. In fact, the single cell they grow from, and in, is the egg! Birds and most fish develop in eggs.

As with other animals, a fertilized egg divides. Eventually, new cells that are specialized form. When the young animal is developed enough to allow it to live outside of its egg, it hatches. Animals that hatch from eggs may look like smaller versions of the parent, but this is not always the case. The young of some kinds of animals, like certain birds, may need their parents' care. Other animals are independent from the moment they hatch.

**Day 1**

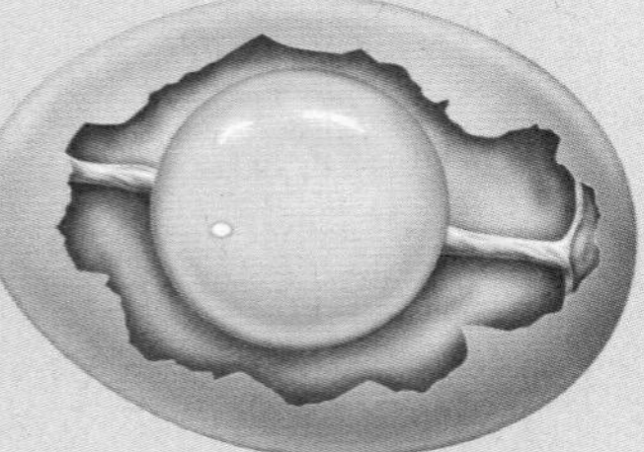

On day 1 of development, there is nothing in the egg that looks like a bird at all! The tiny chick is beginning to develop as just a small spot in the yellow yolk.

**Day 7**

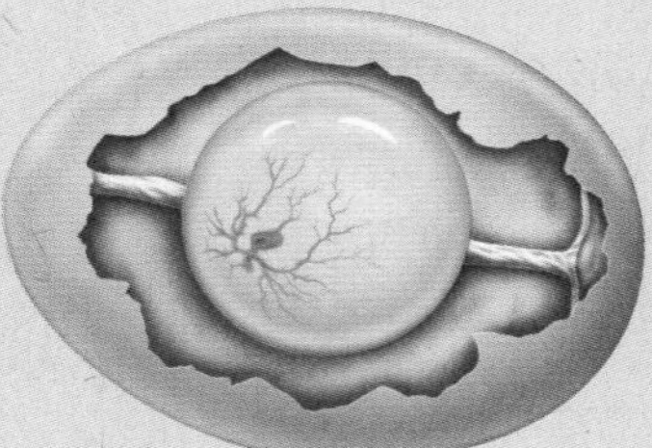

By the seventh day, the tiny chick growing in the yolk has gotten bigger, but it still doesn't look like a chicken.

**Day 14**

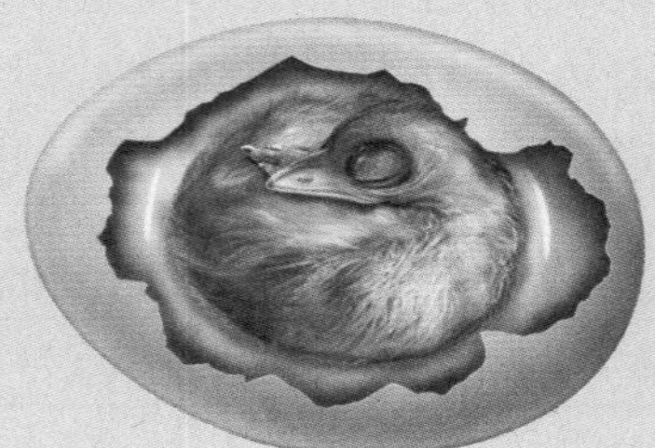

After 14 days, the chick is still growing in the yolk, and you can see its head, body, beak, wings, and legs. Some feathers may be visible.

Egg

Embryo

Larva

Fry

Adult

Like other animals, the life of a fish begins with one cell. As the cell divides, it will begin to look more and more like a fish. Eventually, the tiny fish will hatch into its larval stage. Like a developing chicken, the larval fish gets food from the egg's yolk that is still attached to its body. Once the yolk sac is used up, the fish are called fry. They will continue to grow and change until they resemble small adult fish. They are now called juveniles. Finally, the fish will grow into fully developed adults.

Like birds, most fish do not develop in their mothers' bodies. Most fish lay eggs. Inside the eggs, fish develop until they are ready to hatch. These photos show the changes a single cell undergoes as it develops into a fish. Once hatched, young fish are usually not cared for by their parents.

Day 21

A short time after it hatches, the chick can fend for itself. Many other kinds of birds, however, are helpless and need a parent's care.

## Compare and Contrast

How is the development of a fish like the development of a chicken? How does their development differ?

_______________________________________

_______________________________________

_______________________________________

_______________________________________

_______________________________________

# We're Not So Similar

Chameleon

Snake

Most reptiles and amphibians hatch from eggs. How do their life cycles differ?

**Active Reading** As you read these two pages, draw boxes around the clue words that signal things are being compared.

Both reptiles and amphibians hatch from eggs. They may look similar when they are adults, but they usually look very different while they are young. Look at the chameleon on this page. How is it like the salamander on the next page? How is it different? One difference that is hard to see is that chameleons are reptiles and salamanders are amphibians.

## Reptiles

Reptiles include animals such as lizards, snakes, turtles, gharials, and crocodiles. They have scaly skin to keep from drying out. Like birds, most reptiles hatch from eggs. A reptile's egg differs from a bird egg, though. It usually has a tough, leathery shell to protect the growing reptile. Like birds, most young reptiles usually look like smaller versions of their parents. Most young reptiles do not need their parents' care.

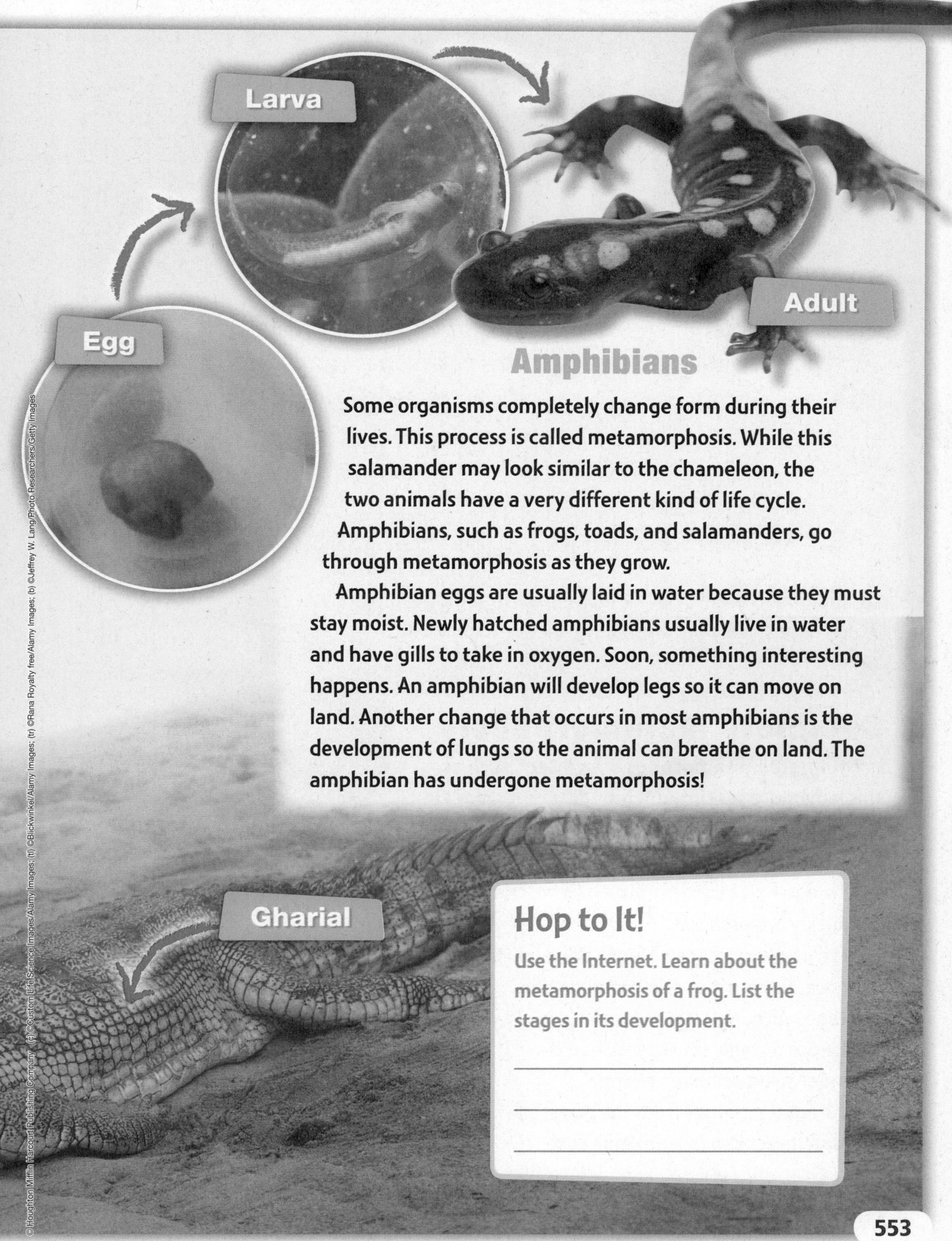


## Amphibians

Some organisms completely change form during their lives. This process is called metamorphosis. While this salamander may look similar to the chameleon, the two animals have a very different kind of life cycle. Amphibians, such as frogs, toads, and salamanders, go through metamorphosis as they grow.

Amphibian eggs are usually laid in water because they must stay moist. Newly hatched amphibians usually live in water and have gills to take in oxygen. Soon, something interesting happens. An amphibian will develop legs so it can move on land. Another change that occurs in most amphibians is the development of lungs so the animal can breathe on land. The amphibian has undergone metamorphosis!

### Hop to It!

Use the Internet. Learn about the metamorphosis of a frog. List the stages in its development.

______________________

______________________

______________________

# It's Time for a Change

Some animals don't just get larger as they grow. An animal may change so much that at different stages it doesn't even look like the same organism!

**Active Reading** As you read these two pages, draw boxes around the clue words that signal things are being compared.

Amphibians aren't the only organisms that may completely change as they grow. In fact, insects are the most common animals that undergo metamorphosis.

## Complete Metamorphosis

In **complete metamorphosis**, an insect, such as this ladybug, goes through four different stages in its life cycle.

1. The insect begins life as an egg.
2. The egg hatches to produce a *larva*. The larva eats and quickly grows in size.
3. A larva develops into a *pupa*. Because the pupa does not move, this is often called the "resting stage." Although it is not moving in the pupa stage, the insect's body is undergoing dramatic change.
4. The adult emerges from the pupa. The adult insect can fly and reproduce.

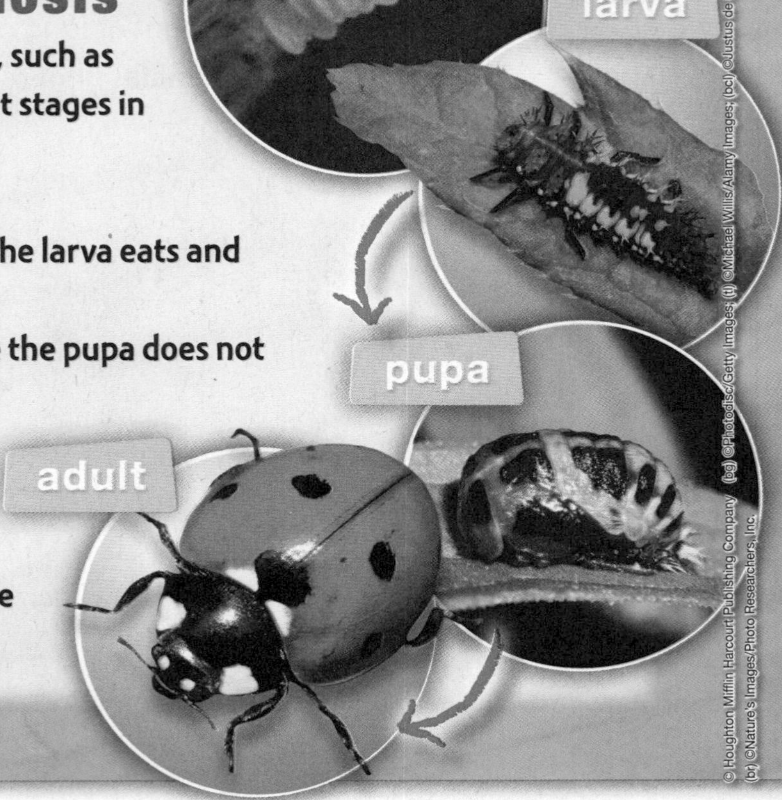

# Incomplete Metamorphosis

Another type of metamorphosis that occurs in some insects is incomplete metamorphosis. **Incomplete metamorphosis** has three stages: the egg, the *nymph*, and the adult. The nymph stage looks like a smaller version of the adult, but a nymph cannot fly or reproduce. As the nymph grows, it *molts*, or sheds its hard outer shell. The nymph molts several times until it finally becomes an adult.

The cicada goes through incomplete metamorphosis. A small nymph emerges from the egg. The nymph grows and molts until it becomes a mature adult.

## Insect Life Cycles

You see an insect egg lying on a leaf. Which stage is next? Name or describe the stage you would expect to see come out from the egg if the insect undergoes

a. an incomplete metamorphosis:

______________________________

b. a complete metamorphosis:

______________________________

When you're done, use the answer key to check and revise your work.

## Summarize

**Fill in the missing words to explain how animals develop.**

All animals start life as a single cell, a(n) 1.________ ________. Most 2.________ develop inside their mothers' bodies. These animals drink their mothers' milk. 3.________ are feathered animals that develop inside eggs. When they hatch, they are helpless and need care from their parents. Other animals develop in eggs, too. Land animals with leathery eggs are called 4.________. With their scaly skin, they look like small versions of adults, and need no care once they hatch. In contrast, most 5.________ develop in eggs laid in water. When they hatch, they look very different from adults. They go through a process called 6.________, during which they develop adult features.

**Fill in the boxes with the missing stages for insect metamorphosis.**

Incomplete metamorphosis

Egg → 7.________ → Adult

Complete metamorphosis

Egg → 8.________ → 9.________ → Adult



Answer Key: 1. fertilized egg 2. mammals 3. Birds 4. reptiles 5. amphibians 6. metamorphosis 7. nymph 8. larva 9. pupa

# Brain Check



Name ____________________

## Word Play

**1** Draw lines to match the definition to a word or phrase and then to the photo.

| Definition | Word/Phrase | Photo |
|---|---|---|
| The second phase of incomplete metamorphosis | fertilized egg |  |
| Animals with scaly skin that hatch looking like small adults and need no care from parents | adult | 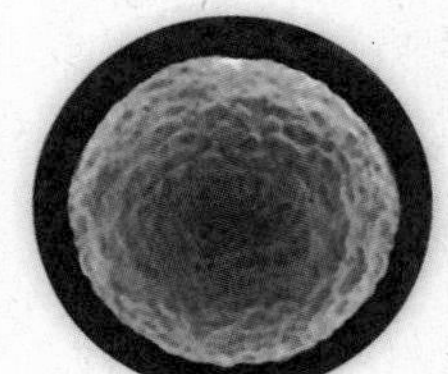 |
| The last stage of an amphibian's life cycle at the end of metamorphosis | pupa |  |
| "Resting stage" of complete metamorphosis | reptile |  |
| How all animals begin their life cycle | nymph | 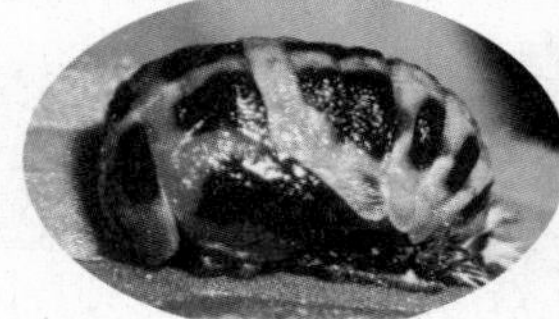 |

# Apply Concepts

**2** Write a number below each picture to show the correct order of the ladybug life cycle.

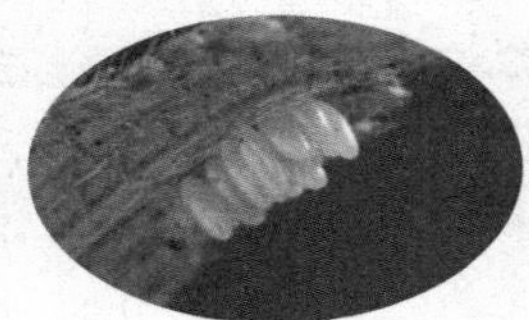
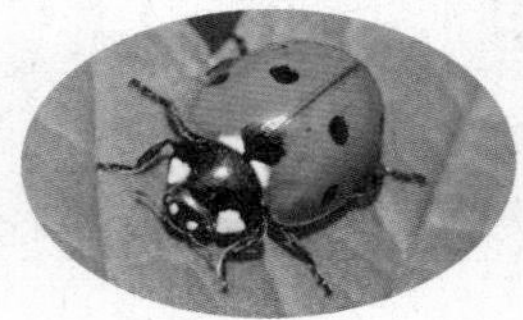

______ ______ ______ ______

**3** Circle the animals that usually lay eggs.

**4** Differentiate between complete and incomplete metamorphosis of insects.

______________________________

______________________________

______________________________

______________________________

Make a deck of cards showing the animals discussed in this lesson. Work with a family member and pick cards from the deck. Explain to your family member if the animal lays eggs or gives live birth to its young.

TEKS **5.3A** in all fields of science, analyze, evaluate, and critique scientific explanations... examining all sides of scientific...explanations...to encourage critical thinking... **5.3D** connect grade-level appropriate science concepts with the history of science...contributions of scientists **5.10B** differentiate between inherited traits of plants and animals...and learned behaviors...

**Essential Question**

# How Are Traits Passed from Parents to Offspring?

## Engage Your Brain!

**Find the answers to the following question in the lesson and record it here.**

Organisms usually inherit physical traits from their parents. What are some of the inherited traits that this snow leopard displays?

______________________________

______________________________

______________________________

______________________________

## Active Reading

### Lesson Vocabulary

**List the terms. As you learn about each one, make notes in the Interactive Glossary.**

______________ ______________

______________ ______________

______________ ______________

### Signal Words: Details

**Signal words show connections between ideas. *For example, for instance,* and *such as* signal examples of an idea. *Also* and *in fact* signal added facts. Active readers remember what they read because they are alert to signal words that identify examples and facts about a topic.**



Inquiry Flipchart p. 63 — That's Inherited! / Behave Yourself!

# You Got It Where?

Siblings often look similar, but why do you think this brother and sister look so much alike?

**Active Reading** As you read these two pages, underline the sentences that include examples of a main idea.

Typically, members of the same family look alike. This is because most characteristics can be passed from parents to their young. These characteristics, called **inherited traits**, include physical features as well as some behaviors. In humans, inherited traits include hair color, eye color, freckles, hair texture, and dimples. Other animals have inherited traits, too. These include fur color, eye color, and fur texture. Like humans and other animals, plants have inherited traits. Traits in plants may include flower color, seed shape, and leaf shape.

You're probably wondering how traits are passed from parents to their young. Recall that all living things begin life as a cell. All the information for inherited traits can be found in this one cell.

### Plants

**What are some inherited traits that you see in this tree? Height, bark texture, flower color, and type of fruit were each coded for by genes that this tree inherited from its parents.**

Not all inherited traits are physical characteristics that can be seen. Some inherited traits affect behavior. For example, are you right-handed or left-handed? Scientists believe that which hand you use is a behavioral trait that you inherited. Another inherited trait is how you cross your arms over your chest. Try it now! Which arm is on top? You got this trait from your parents.

Human behavioral traits usually do not affect your survival. Yet in other organisms, traits may make the difference between life and death.

## How Are They Different?

Look at the trees and cats on these pages. Differentiate between the inherited traits of plants and animals. List three traits that are only found in plants and three traits that are only found in animals.

_______________

_______________

_______________

_______________

_______________

## Animals

**These kittens have some traits in common, but are not exactly alike. This is because each kitten gets a different combination of genes from its parents.**

DNA

## Chromosomes

**This is a chromosome, which is found in living things. It consists of a pair of long, thin molecules, called DNA, that has sections called genes. Genes carry the information for the inherited traits in a living thing.**

# How Do We Know?

We know that inherited traits are coded for by genes in parents' cells. But how did scientists discover this?

**Active Reading** As you read these two pages, circle the clue words or phrases that signal a detail such as an example or an added fact.

People have always observed that traits are passed to offspring. But for years, scientists did not understand how traits were passed on. From 1856 to 1863, an Austrian monk, Gregor Mendel, did a series of experiments using pea plants. His results shed light on how traits are inherited. He noted the traits of parent plants and then carefully observed the traits that appeared in the offspring.

## Punnett Square

Mendel used a Punnett square to predict offspring traits. In pea plants, green seedpods are dominant. Yellow seedpods are recessive. Dominant traits are designated by a capital letter, in this case a *G*, while recessive traits are designated by the same letter, but in lowercase.

Here, both parents have one dominant factor and one recessive factor. The parents' factors are shown along the top and side of the square. To predict the traits of the offspring, look at the letters that are on the top and side of each of the smaller boxes. How many offspring have yellow seedpods?

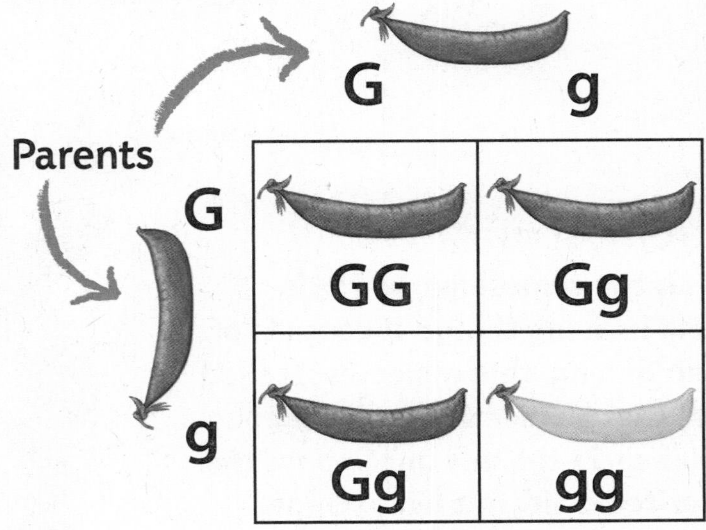

Mendel found that each plant characteristic was controlled by a factor that was passed on from each parent. Some factors code for **dominant traits**. Dominant traits appear in offspring even if only one parent contributes the factor for it. For example, purple flower color is a dominant trait in pea plants. If one parent only has factors for purple flowers and one parent has white flowers, the offspring will all have purple flowers. Mendel found that some factors code for **recessive traits**. Recessive traits appear only when both parents contribute the same factor for the trait. For example, both parents of a pea plant with white flowers contribute factors for white flowers, a recessive trait.

## Do the Math!

### Interpret a Table

In mice, black fur color is dominant. The black mouse has one dominant factor and one recessive factor. This light brown mouse has two recessive factors. Fill in the Punnett square to predict the fur color of their offspring. What fraction of the baby mice could have black fur?

| | B | b |
|---|---|---|
| b | | |
| b | | |

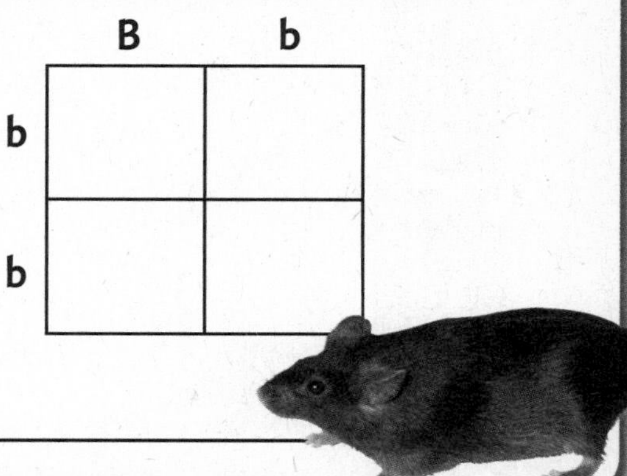

________________________

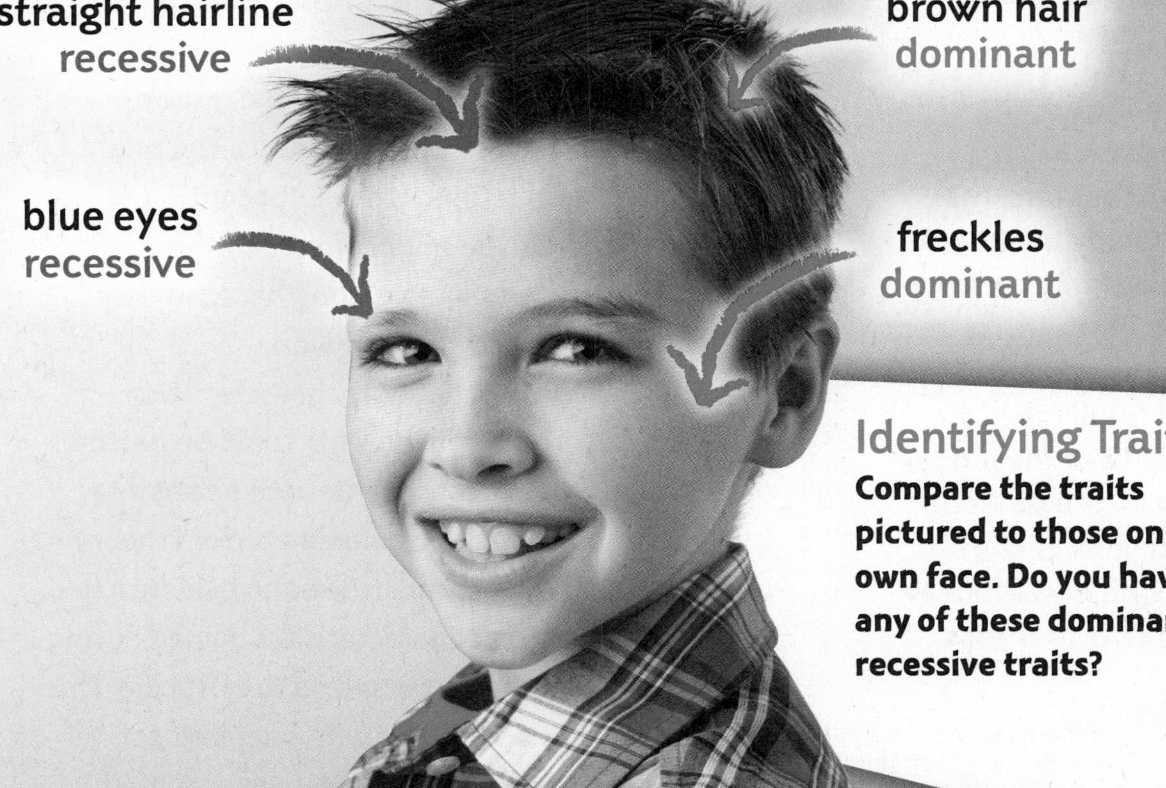


### Identifying Traits

**Compare the traits pictured to those on your own face. Do you have any of these dominant or recessive traits?**

# New Ideas on Inheritance

Scientists' theories are supported, but hypotheses that aren't supported can still be helpful.

In the eighteenth century, some scientists had observed that the children of blacksmiths had strong, muscular bodies, like their fathers. These scientists hypothesized that blacksmiths became strong and muscular as a result of a lifetime of hard work, and that they would pass this trait to their children.

As you read about blacksmiths and giraffes, you might see flaws in this hypothesis. You might wonder why giraffes' necks have not continued to grow longer. Or you might wonder if the blacksmiths' children grew strong because they helped their fathers with their work.

Mendel theorized that only characteristics that were inherited from parents could be passed on to offspring. His experiments with pea plants caused some scientists to question the old theory of inheritance. They found little or no evidence to support the idea that characteristics gained during a parent's lifetime were passed on to offspring. This earlier hypothesis lost favor with scientists for many years after Mendel's theory was accepted.

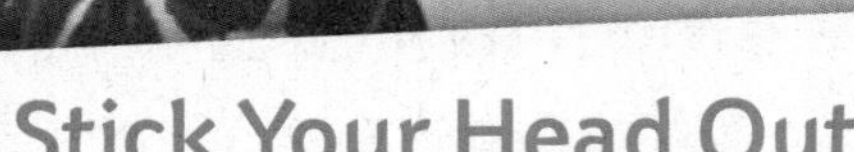

## Stick Your Head Out

**One scientist in the eighteenth century thought that ancient giraffes had short necks. He argued that during a giraffe's lifetime, its neck stretched longer to reach leaves on tall trees. He believed that the longer neck was then passed on to its young, so each generation had a longer neck than its parents.**

## In the Lab

**New technologies allow scientists to gather new kinds of evidence and develop a better understanding of inheritance.**

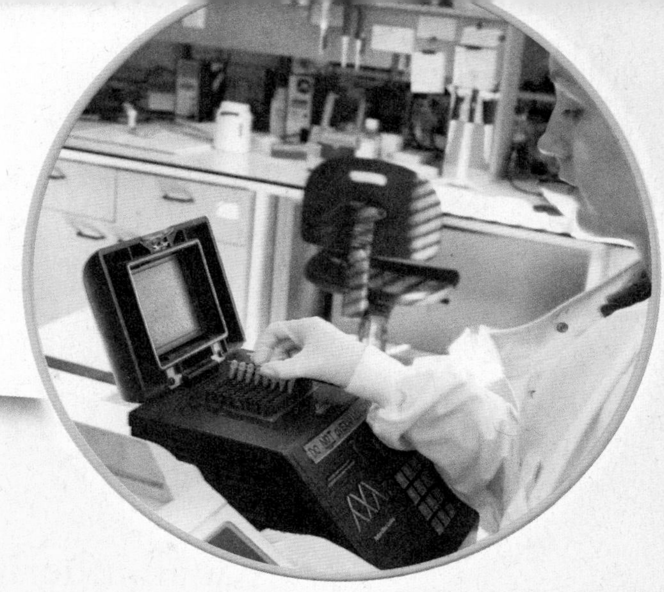

Because technology has improved over the years, scientists have recently been able to study new aspects of the theory of inheritance. Scientists have found that some factors in the environment may cause changes to genes that could be inherited by offspring. For example, there is evidence that some chemicals may change genes in some kinds of cells. When these cells divide, the original cell can pass its changed genes to the new cells. Now that scientists know that genes may change during an organism's life, they are working to discover if, how, and when these changes are passed to offspring.

▶ There are often many sides to a scientific argument. Analyze, evaluate, and critique both ways that scientists explained how traits are inherited. How have the different arguments made scientists think in new ways?

______________________________

______________________________

______________________________

______________________________

______________________________

______________________________

## Family Ties

**While the early hypothesis about blacksmiths and their children was not correct, family members often do resemble one another.**

# You Can Do What?

Not all inherited traits are physical traits. Some are behaviors. What behaviors were you born with?

**Active Reading** As you read these two pages, draw a box around a sentence that gives an example of an innate behavior in humans.

You've learned that some inherited traits are physical. But also recall that some inherited traits are behavioral. These behavioral traits can help people meet important needs. For example, human babies cry when they are hungry. They sleep when they are tired. Babies are born with these **innate behaviors**, or behaviors that do not need to be taught. Not all innate behaviors help you meet important needs. For example, the ability to curl your tongue is an innate behavior that some people have. It may be fun to do, but it is not necessary for survival.

The innate behaviors of many organisms are often necessary for survival. For example, fish are born able to swim. Chickens peck the ground for food. These behaviors are important to these organisms because, without them, they would die. They are not behaviors learned from other animals, but instead are shared by all members of a species.

## Salmon

**Salmon hatch in freshwater rivers but eventually swim to the ocean. When it's time for them to reproduce, salmon innately know to return to the same river where they hatched.**

## Peacock Spider

**To attract a mate, this peacock spider has the innate behavior of fanning out its colorful abdomen and waving its legs.**

## Birds

**Birds innately know to build nests, but some species of birds learn how to make better nests each time they build one.**

## Toward the Light

**Some scientists consider gravitropism, or plant growth according to gravity, and phototropism, which is plant growth toward light, to be behaviors.**

## You Do What?

What innate behaviors were you born with? List three behaviors humans are born with the ability to do.

_______________________________________

_______________________________________

_______________________________________

## Dogs

**Animals within a species may have slightly different innate behaviors. Herding is an innate behavior among border collies. What innate behaviors do other dog breeds have?**

# Who Taught You That?

You weren't born knowing how to ride a bicycle. You had to learn. What other behaviors have you learned?

**Active Reading** As you read these two pages, underline clue words that signal an added fact.

Not all behaviors are innate. Some behaviors are **learned behaviors**. Most mammals have many behaviors that they need to learn during their lifetimes. For example, kittens must learn to walk. While not all learned behaviors are important for survival, many, such as learning to hunt for food, are.

Sometimes, innate behaviors are modified by learned behaviors. For example, human babies are born with the instinct to cry. Over time, though, babies learn to change the sounds of their cries. A baby's hunger cry is different than the cry it makes when hurt. It may also cry one way when it's bedtime, and another when it's time to wake up.

## Honeybees

**Honeybees have the instinct to gather nectar, but they learn the locations of flowers from other members of their hive.**

## Whales

**A baby orca is born with the instinct to breathe. But first it must learn to rise to the water's surface to get air.**

Animals, such as dogs, can be taught tricks for fun, but animals can also be trained to help people. These trained animals are called service animals. Service animals can be dogs, but they can also include capuchin monkeys, miniature horses and donkeys, and even parrots. Service animals can help those who are vision-impaired or hearing-impaired. Some of these animals learn to retrieve objects, or pull wagons or wheelchairs. What all of these animals have in common is that they learn behaviors that help people overcome limitations.

## Service Animals

**This miniature pony helps her vision-impaired owner travel throughout the day.**

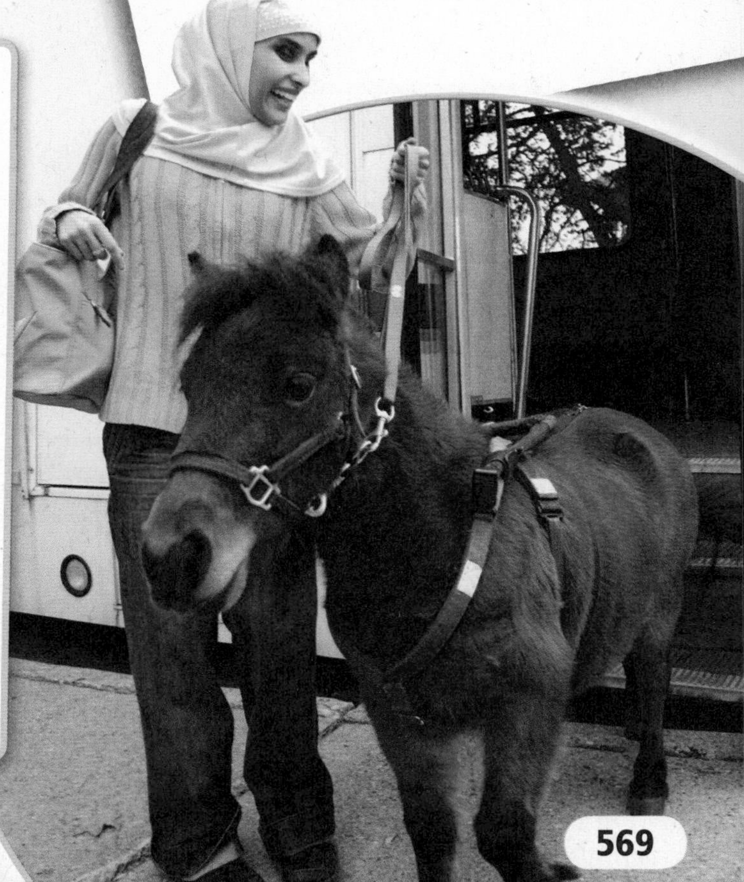

## Differentiate Behaviors

List your own innate and learned behaviors.

| Innate Behaviors | Learned Behaviors |
|---|---|
| | |

When you're done, use the answer key to check and revise your work.

## Summarize

**Fill in the missing words to describe inherited traits.**

Animals are born with 1. ________________ , or characteristics, that were passed on from their parents. These characteristics can be physical, but they can also be 2. ________________. The Austrian monk, 3. ________________, did a series of experiments in pea plants that shed light on how traits were inherited. He did this by observing the traits of the parent plants and then he 4. ________________ traits that appeared in the controlled offspring. He learned that there were two kinds of traits in many inherited characteristics, 5. ________________ traits and 6. ________________ traits.

**Fill in the graphic organizer below with examples of innate behaviors and learned behaviors.**

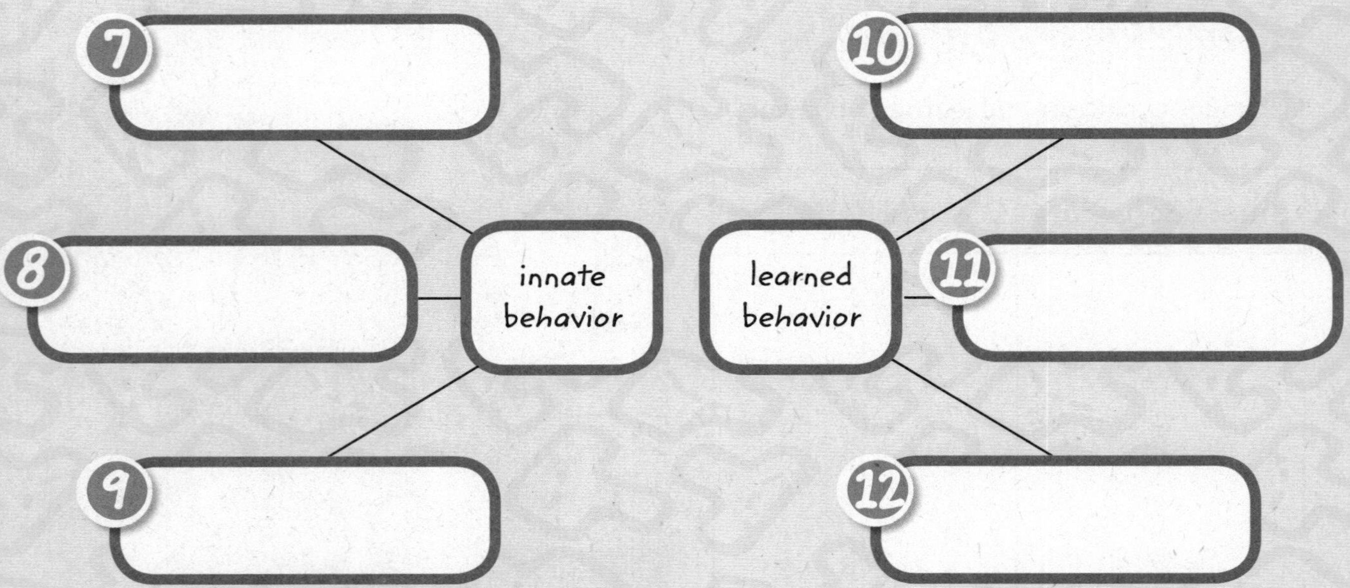


Answer Key: 1. inherited traits 2. behavioral 3. Gregor Mendel 4. observed 5. dominant 6. recessive 7, 8, and 9: Answers may vary; baby crying, nest building, chickens pecking 10, 11, and 12: Answers may vary; dogs doing tricks, bike riding, kittens walking

Name ______________________________

## Word Play

1 Use the hints to unscramble the words below.

Hint: Characteristics passed from parents to offspring

hneiidter sritta ______________________

Hint: Tiny part of a chromosome that codes for just one trait

nege ______________________

Hint: One version of a gene for a trait, such as flower color

cfatro ______________________

Hint: A characteristic that appears only when the offspring receives a factor from both parents

sseeecvir ritta ______________________

Hint: An instinct, or behavior an animal is born with

tannei aoivrheb ______________________

Hint: A characteristic that appears when the offspring receives a factor from one or both parents

tnnaomid aitrt ______________________

Hint: A behavior an animal is not born with, such as a child riding a bicycle

deearnl boviareh ______________________

# Apply Concepts

**2** In mice, the factor for black fur is dominant (B). The factor for brown fur is recessive (b). Use the Punnett square to predict what fraction of offspring will be black.

| | B | B |
|---|---|---|
| b | | |
| b | | |

______________________________

______________________________

______________________________

**3** Differentiate behaviors as innate, learned, or both innate and learned.

| Behavior | Innate, Learned, or Both Innate and Learned |
|---|---|
| Salmon swimming upstream | |
| Bird building a nest | |
| Child riding a bicycle | |

**4** What are three inherited traits of plants?

______________________________________________________________

______________________________________________________________

**5** Describe what you expect will happen if the flowerpot is not righted. Explain your answer.

______________________________________________

______________________________________________

______________________________________________

**Take It Home!**

Research other dominant and recessive traits on the Internet and make a poster. Share your findings with a family member.

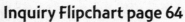

Inquiry Flipchart page 64

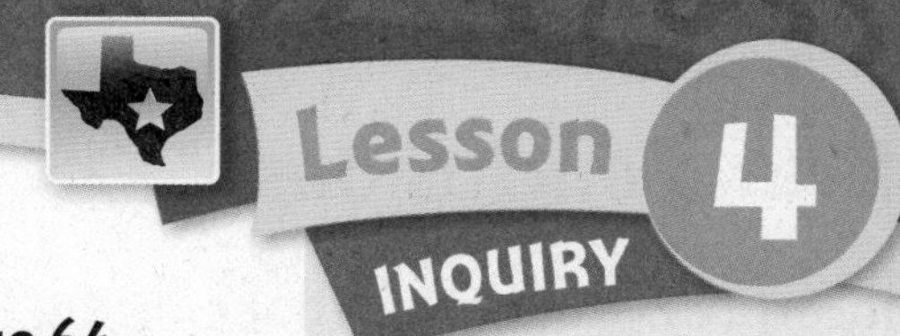


**TEKS 5.3C** draw or develop a model that represents how something works or looks that cannot be seen **5.10B** differentiate between inherited traits of plants and animals such as spines on a cactus or shape of a beak and learned behaviors such as an animal learning tricks or a child riding a bicycle

Name ______________________________

Essential Question

# How Can We Model Inherited Traits?

## Set a Purpose

What will you learn from this investigation?

______________________________

______________________________

______________________________

______________________________

## State Your Hypothesis

Write your hypothesis or testable statement.

______________________________

______________________________

______________________________

______________________________

## Think About the Procedure

Why are there two envelopes containing factors for each characteristic?

______________________________

______________________________

What information does this give you about how traits are passed from parents to offspring?

______________________________

______________________________

Why do you think you had to pick so many factors?

______________________________

______________________________

## Record Your Data

Record the factors you selected and the resulting traits in the table below.

| Envelope | Combined Factors | Trait |
|---|---|---|
| Ear shape | | |
| Color | | |
| Tail | | |
| Height | | |

## Draw Conclusions

Interpret your data. What can you conclude about how traits are passed from parents to offspring?

Compare your results with the results of other groups. Explain any differences or similarities.

## Analyze and Extend

1. Scientists use models to better understand scientific processes. How did building a model of the offspring help you better understand the way traits are passed from parents to their offspring?

2. How could you modify this investigation to differentiate between the inherited traits of plants and animals?

3. In the space below, draw a picture of your model.

4. Think of other questions you would like to ask about how traits can be inherited.

**TEKS** **5.3D** connect grade-level appropriate science concepts with the history of science, science careers, and contributions of scientists **5.9A** observe the way organisms live and survive in their ecosystems by interacting with the living and non-living elements

S.T.E.M.

Engineering & Technology

# How It Works:

## Tracking Wildlife

**Tracking animals helps scientists learn the animals' patterns of movement. Researchers fit animals with a variety of devices that send back information. Mammals often wear tracking collars. Toads can wear tracking belts. Fish can swallow tiny devices that work inside their bodies!**

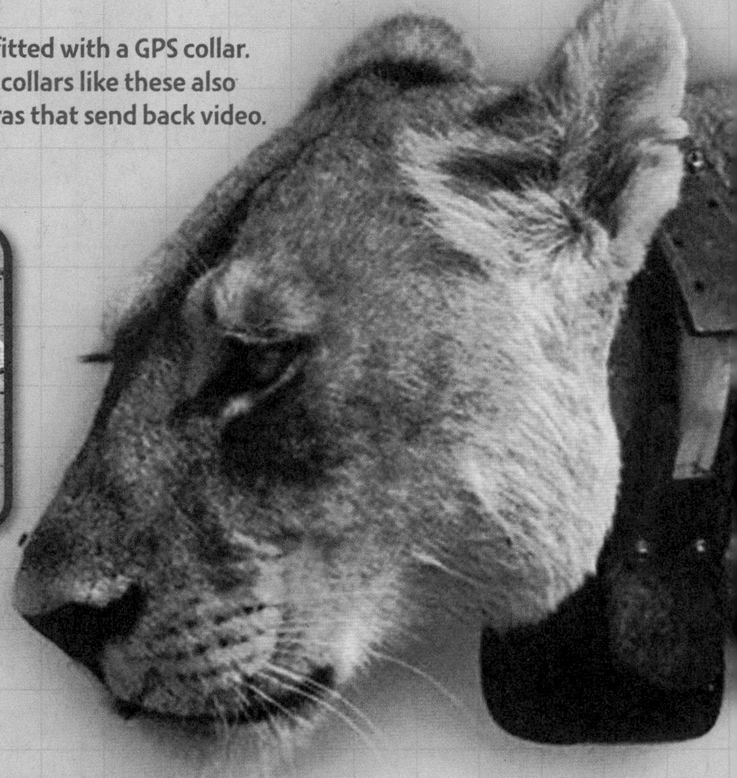

This lion is fitted with a GPS collar. Sometimes collars like these also have cameras that send back video.

Tracking devices are attached to marine animals with glue or suction cups. The devices send signals to GPS satellites, enabling scientists to locate and track the animals over time.

## Troubleshooting

**Describe how an animal's body, its movement, and its environment determine the design of a tracking device.**

______________________________________________

______________________________________________

continued

Animal tracking devices help scientists observe the way organisms live and survive in their ecosystem by interacting with the living and non-living elements.

Choose an animal. Draw a diagram of how a tracking device might be attached to the animal. Explain how the device is attached and what information it captures.

Research an animal species that has been studied using a tracking device. Which kind of device was used? What kind of data did it gather, and what did scientists learn about the species?

## Build On It!

Rise to the engineering design challenge—complete **Make a Process: Mimicking an Adaptation** in the Inquiry Flipchart.

# Unit 12 Review

Name ______________________

## Vocabulary Review

Use the terms in the box to complete the sentences.

adaptation
complete metamorphosis
gene
incomplete metamorphosis
inherited trait
innate behavior
learned behavior
life cycle

1. The different processes that an animal, such as an insect, goes through as it grows and reproduces is called its ______________________.

TEKS 5.10B

2. A characteristic, such as flower color, that is passed from parents to offspring is a(n) ______________________.

TEKS 5.10C

3. An insect that goes through three stages during its life cycle experiences ______________________.

TEKS 5.10B

4. An inherited trait, such as a baby crying, is an example of a(n) ______________________.

TEKS 5.10B

5. A behavior that needs to be taught is called a(n) ______________________.

TEKS 5.10C

6. An insect that goes through four stages during its life cycle experiences ______________________.

TEKS 5.10A

7. Any characteristic that helps an organism live and survive is considered to be a(n) ______________________.

TEKS 5.10B

8. The part of a chromosome that contains information for specific inherited traits is a(n) ______________________.

## Science Concepts

Fill in the letter of the choice that best answers the question.

**TEKS 5.10A**

**9. The coloring of the rough green snake allows it to blend in with its background. What type of adaptation is the rough green snake's color?**

Ⓐ behavioral adaptation

Ⓑ life-cycle adaptation

Ⓒ physical adaptation

Ⓓ reproductive adaptation

**TEKS 5.10A, 5.10B**

**10. Jason is learning about the life cycle of frogs. During which stage in the life cycle of a frog is it best able to survive on land?**

Ⓑ

Ⓒ

Ⓓ

**TEKS 5.10A**

**11. The diagram shows a polar bear in its natural habitat.**

**Which of the following helps the polar bear live and survive in its habitat?**

Ⓐ thick fur
Ⓑ long tail
Ⓒ large ears
Ⓓ wide hooves

**TEKS 5.3D**

**12. Which scientist is known for his work on dominant and recessive traits?**

Ⓐ Albert Einstein

Ⓑ Gregor Mendel

Ⓒ Isaac Newton

Ⓓ Marie Curie

**TEKS 5.10B**

**13. Which statement about the behavior of living things is true?**

Ⓐ Only plants have innate behaviors.

Ⓑ Only animals have innate behaviors.

Ⓒ Only animals have learned behaviors.

Ⓓ Both plants and animals have learned behaviors.

Name ______________________________

TEKS 5.10C

**14. Vanessa is observing an organism undergoing metamorphosis. Which stage must she observe in order to conclude that the organism undergoes incomplete metamorphosis?**

Ⓐ adult

Ⓑ larva

Ⓒ nymph

Ⓓ pupa

TEKS 5.10A, 5.10B

**15. The diagram below shows how an antlion gets food.**

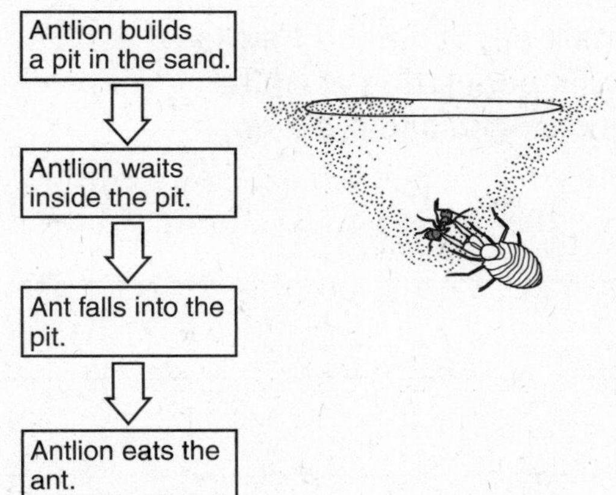


**What does the diagram suggest about the antlion?**

Ⓐ The antlion uses mimicry to catch prey.

Ⓑ The antlion is not adapted to its environment.

Ⓒ The antlion lives on a diet of both plants and animals.

Ⓓ The antlion uses a behavioral adaptation to catch prey.

TEKS 5.10C

**16. The diagram below shows the life cycle of a butterfly.**

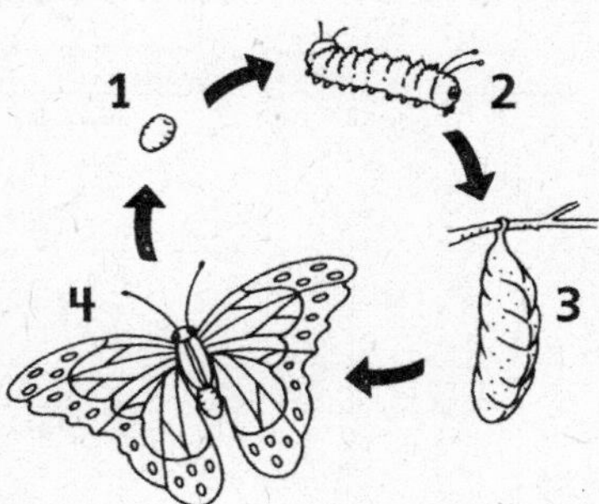


**What can you conclude from this diagram?**

Ⓐ A butterfly does not undergo metamorphosis.

Ⓑ A butterfly undergoes complete metamorphosis.

Ⓒ A butterfly undergoes incomplete metamorphosis.

Ⓓ A butterfly undergoes both complete and incomplete metamorphosis.

TEKS 5.10A

**17. The picture shows an example of an adaptation that helps an insect survive and live in its environment.**

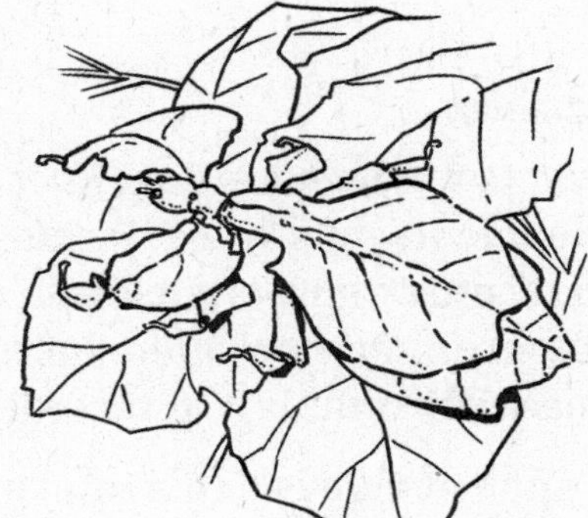

**How would you classify this adaptation?**

Ⓐ camouflage

Ⓑ metamorphosis

Ⓒ life cycle

Ⓓ recessive trait

# Apply Inquiry and Review the Big Idea

Write the answers to these questions.

**TEKS 5.3C, 5.10A**

**18.** The table shows different bird adaptations.

Use the table to draw a model bird that is adapted to swimming and eating fish.

**Beak and Feet Adaptations**

| Type of beak | Adapted for | Type of foot | Adapted for |
|---|---|---|---|
| | eating seeds | | perching |
| | eating insects | | wading |
| | probing for food | | preying |
| | preying on animals | | swimming |
| | straining food from water | | climbing |
| | eating fish | | |

**TEKS 5.2F, 5.10A**

**19.** A population of white rabbits lives in a snowy mountain environment. Hawks that fly high in the air hunt the rabbits. Predict how the population of white rabbits might change if the climate on the mountain changed and it did not snow for a long period of time. Explain your prediction.

______________________________

______________________________

______________________________

**TEKS 5.2D, 5.3C, 5.10B**

**20.** Tommy wants to teach his dog, Rocco, how to catch a treat in its mouth. He decides he wants to keep a record of how often Rocco catches the treats he tosses and how often Rocco misses. Tommy makes this table and records his data.

Over the span of 4 days and a total of 80 tosses, what was the average number of treats that Rocco caught each day? Round your answer to the nearest whole.

**Rocco's Catching Rates**

| | Catches | Misses |
|---|---|---|
| Day 1 | 4 | 16 |
| Day 2 | 8 | 12 |
| Day 3 | 13 | 7 |
| Day 4 | 16 | 4 |

______________________________

# Interactive Glossary

As you learn about each term, add notes, drawings, or sentences in the extra space. This will help you remember what the terms mean. Here are some examples.

**Fungi** [FUHN•jeye] A kingdom of organisms that have a nucleus and get nutrients by decomposing other organisms

A mushroom is from the kingdom Fungi.

**physical change** [FIZ•i•kuhl CHAYNJ] Change in the size, shape, or state of matter with no new substance being formed

When I cut paper, the paper has a physical change.

## Glossary Pronunciation Key

With every glossary term, there is also a phonetic respelling. A phonetic respelling writes the word the way it sounds, which can help you pronounce new or unfamiliar words. Use this key to help you understand the respellings.

| Sound | As in | Phonetic Respelling | Sound | As in | Phonetic Respelling |
|---|---|---|---|---|---|
| a | bat | (BAT) | oh | over | (OH•ver) |
| ah | lock | (LAHK) | oo | pool | (POOL) |
| air | rare | (RAIR) | ow | out | (OWT) |
| ar | argue | (AR•gyoo) | oy | foil | (FOYL) |
| aw | law | (LAW) | s | cell | (SEL) |
| ay | face | (FAYS) | | sit | (SIT) |
| ch | chapel | (CHAP•uhl) | sh | sheep | (SHEEP) |
| e | test | (TEST) | th | that | (THAT) |
| | metric | (MEH•trik) | | thin | (THIN) |
| ee | eat | (EET) | u | pull | (PUL) |
| | feet | (FEET) | uh | medal | (MED•uhl) |
| | ski | (SKEE) | | talent | (TAL•uhnt) |
| er | paper | (PAY•per) | | pencil | (PEN•suhl) |
| | fern | (FERN) | | onion | (UHN•yuhn) |
| eye | idea | (eye•DEE•uh) | | playful | (PLAY•fuhl) |
| i | bit | (BIT) | | dull | (DUHL) |
| ing | going | (GOH•ing) | y | yes | (YES) |
| k | card | (KARD) | | ripe | (RYP) |
| | kite | (KYT) | z | bags | (BAGZ) |
| ngk | bank | (BANGK) | zh | treasure | (TREZH•er) |

## A

**accurate** [AK•yuh•ruht] In measurements, very close to the actual size or value (p. 49)

**adaptation** [ad•uhp•TAY•shuhn] A trait or characteristic that helps an organism survive (p. 530)

**atmosphere** [AT•muh•sfeer] The mixture of gases that surround Earth (p. 394)

**axis** [AK•sis] The imaginary line around which Earth rotates (p. 438)

## B

**balance** [BAL•uhns] A tool used to measure the amount of matter in an object, which is the object's mass (p. 46)

**balanced forces** [BAL•uhnst FAWRS•iz] Forces that cancel each other out because they are equal in size and opposite in direction (p. 154)

**bioengineering** [by•oh•en•juh•NEHR•ing] The application of the engineering design process to living things (p. 92)

**biofuel** [BY•oh•FYOO•uhl] A fuel produced by biological materials, such as wood (p. 361)

**biotechnology** [by•oh•TEK•nahl•uh•jee] A product of technology used to benefit organisms and the environment (p. 93)

**circuit** [SER•kuht] A path along which electric charges can flow (p. 228)

## C

**cast** [KAST] A model of an organism, formed when sediment fills a mold and hardens (p. 319)

**chemical energy** [KEM•ih•kuhl EN•er•jee] Energy that can be released by a chemical reaction (p. 189)

**chlorophyll** [KLAWR•uh•fil] A green pigment in plants that allows a plant cell to use light to make food (p. 475)

**climate** [KLY•muht] The pattern of weather an area experiences over a long period of time (p. 412)

**climate zone** [KLY•muht ZOHN] An area that has similar average temperatures and precipitation throughout (p. 414)

**community** [kuh•MYOO•ni•tee] A group of organisms that live in the same area and interact with each other (p. 462)

**complete metamorphosis** [kuhm•PLEET met•uh•MAWR•fuh•sis] A complex change that most insects undergo that includes larva and pupa stages (p. 554)

**consumer** [kuhn•SOOM•er] A living thing that cannot make its own food and must eat other living things (p. 477)

**condensation** [kahn•duhn•SAY•shuhn] The process by which a gas changes into a liquid (p. 397)

**control** [kuhn•TROHL] The experimental setup to which you will compare all other setups (p. 29)

**conductor** [kuhn•DUK•ter] A material that lets heat or electricity travel through it easily (p. 226)

**criteria** [kry•TEER•ee•uh] The standards for measuring success (p. 72)

**conservation** [kahn•ser•VAY•shuhn] The process of preserving and protecting an ecosystem or a resource (p. 372)

## D

**decomposer** [dee•kuhm•POH•ser] A living thing that gets energy by breaking down dead organisms and animal wastes into simpler substances (p. 481)

**deposition** [dep•uh•ZISH•uhn] The dropping or settling of eroded materials (p. 306)

**dominant trait** [DAHM•ih•nuhnt TRAYT] A trait that appears if an organism has one factor for that trait (p. 563)

## E

**ecosystem** [EE•koh•sis•tuhm] A community of organisms and the environment in which they live (p. 461)

**electric current** [ee•LEK•trik KER•uhnt] The flow of electric charges along a path (p. 218)

**electrical energy** [ee•LEK•tri•kuhl EN•er•jee] Energy that comes from electric current (p. 187)

**electromagnetic spectrum** [ee•lek•troh•mag•NET•ik SPEK•truhm] All energy waves that travel at the speed of light in a vacuum, including radio, infrared, visible, ultraviolet, x-rays, and gamma rays (p. 271)

**energy** [EN•er•jee] The ability to cause changes in matter (p. 180)

**energy pyramid** [EN•er•jee PIR•uh•mid] A diagram that shows how much energy is passed from one organism to the next at each level in a food chain (p. 494)

**engineering** [en•juh•NEER•ing] The use of science and math for practical uses, such as the design of structures, machines, and systems (p. 67)

**evaporation** [ee•VAP•uh•ray•shuhn] The process by which a liquid changes into a gas (p. 396)

**environment** [en•VY•ruhn•muhnt] All the living and nonliving things that surround and affect an organism (p. 460)

**evidence** [EV•uh•duhns] Information collected during a scientific investigation (p. 6)

**equator** [ee•KWAY•ter] An imaginary line around Earth, equally distant from the North and South Poles (p. 414)

**experiment** [ek•SPAIR•uh•muhnt] An investigation in which all the conditions are controlled to test a hypothesis (p. 23, 28)

**erosion** [i•ROH•zhuhn] The process of moving sediment from one place to another (p. 304)

**extinction** [ek•STINGK•shuhn] A plant or an animal species that is no longer living or existing (p. 514)

## F

**food chain** [FOOD CHAYN] The transfer of food energy between organisms in an ecosystem (p. 491)

**food web** [FOOD WEB] A group of food chains that overlap (p. 492)

**force** [FAWRS] A push or pull, which may cause a change in an object's motion (p. 150)

**fossil** [FAHS•uhl] The remains or traces of a plant or an animal that lived long ago (p. 319)

**fossil fuel** [FAHS•uhl FYOO•uhl] Fuel, such as coal, oil, and natural gas, formed from the remains of once-living things (p. 320)

**frequency** [FREE•kwuhn•see] A measure of the number of waves that pass a point in a second (p. 252)

**friction** [FRIK•shuhn] A force that acts between two touching objects and that opposes motion (p. 153)

## G

**gas** [GAS] The state of matter in which a substance does not have a definite shape or volume (p. 112)

**genes** [JEENZ] The part of cells that controls or influences inherited traits such as hair color and eye color (p. 561)

**geothermal energy** [jee•oh•THER•muhl EN•er•jee] A type of energy produced naturally beneath Earth's surface (p. 360)

**gravity** [GRAV•ih•tee] The force of attraction between objects, such as the attraction between Earth and objects on it (p. 152)

## H

**habitat** [HAB•i•tat] The place where an organism lives and can find everything it needs to survive (p. 464)

**heat** [HEET] The energy that moves between objects of different temperatures (p. 200)

**hydroelectric energy** [hy•droh•ee•LEK•trik EN•er•jee] Energy produced by using the mechanical energy of falling water (p. 360)

## I

**incomplete metamorphosis** [in•kuhm•PLEET met•uh•MAWR•fuh•sis] Developmental change in some insects in which a nymph hatches from an egg and gradually develops into an adult (p. 555)

**index fossil** [IN•deks FAHS•uhl] A fossil of a type of organism that lived in many places during a relatively short time span (p. 333)

**inherited traits** [in•HAIR•it•ed TRAYTS] Characteristics passed from parents to their offspring (p. 560)

**innate behavior** [in•ATE bee•HAYV•yer] A behavior an organism is born with (p. 566)

**instincts** [IN•stinkts] Behaviors that an organism inherits and knows how to do without being taught (p. 536)

**insulator** [IN•suh•layt•er] A material that does not let heat or electricity move through it easily. (p. 226)

**investigation** [in•ves•tuh•GAY•shuhn] A procedure carried out to carefully observe, study, or test something in order to learn more about it (p. 4)

## K

**kinetic energy** [ki•NET•ik EN•er•jee] The energy an object has because of motion (p. 182)

## L

**latitude** [LAT•ih•tood] A measure of how far north or south a place is from the equator (p. 414)

**learned behavior** [LERND bee•HAYV•yer] A behavior that an animal doesn't begin life with, but develops as a result of experience or by observing other animals (p. 568)

**life cycle** [LYF SY•kuhl] The stages that a living thing passes through as it grows and changes (p. 548)

**light** [LYT] A form of energy that can travel through space and lies partly within the visible range (p. 268)

**liquid** [LIK•wid] The state of matter in which a substance has a definite volume but no definite shape (p. 112)

## M

**mass extinction** [MAS ek•STINGK•shuhn] A period in which a large number of species become extinct (p. 338)

**matter** [MAT•er] Anything that has mass and takes up space (p. 108)

**mechanical energy** [muh•KAN•ih•kuhl EN•er•jee] The total potential and kinetic energy of an object (p. 188)

**microscopic** [my•kruh•SKAHP•ik] Too small to be seen without using a microscope (p. 43)

**mixture** [MIKS•cher] A combination of two or more different substances in which the substances keep their identities (p. 127)

**mold** [MOHLD] An impression of an organism, formed when sediment hardens around the organism (p. 319)

## N

**natural resource** [NACH•er•uhl REE•sawrs] Anything from nature that people can use (p. 356)

**niche** [NICH] The role a plant or an animal plays in its habitat (p. 464)

**nonrenewable resource** [nahn•ri•NOO•uh•buhl ree•sawrs] A resource that, once used, cannot be replaced in a reasonable amount of time (p. 357)

## O

**opaque** [oh•PAYK] Not allowing light to pass through (p. 278)

**opinion** [uh•PIN•yuhn] A personal belief or judgment based on what a person thinks or feels, but not necessarily based on evidence (p. 9)

**orbit** [AWR•bit] The path of one object in space around another object (p. 436)

## P

**parallel circuit** [PAIR•uh•lel SER•kit] An electric circuit that has more than one path for the electric charges to follow (p. 231)

**photosynthesis** [foh•toh•SIN•thuh•sis] The process that plants use to make their own food (p. 475)

**pitch** [PICH] The highness or lowness of a sound (p. 252)

**pollution** [puh•LOO•shuhn] Any waste product or contamination that harms or dirties an ecosystem and harms organisms (p. 363)

**population** [pahp•yuh•LAY•shuhn] All the organisms of the same kind that live together in an ecosystem (p. 462)

**potential energy** [poh•TEN•shuhl EN•er•jee] Energy that an object has because of its position or its condition (p. 182)

**precipitation** [pree•sip•uh•TAY•shuhn] Water that falls from clouds to Earth's surface (p. 397)

**prism** [PRIZ•uhm] A transparent object that bends and separates white light into the colors of the rainbow (p. 283)

**producer** [pruh•DOOS•er] A living thing, such as a plant, that can make its own food (p. 476)

**prototype** [PROH•tuh•typ] The original or test model on which a product is based (p. 70)

## R

**recessive trait** [ree•SES•iv TRAYt] A trait that appears only if an organism has two factors for that trait (p. 563)

**reflection** [RI•flehk•shuhn] The bouncing of light waves when they encounter an obstacle (p. 280)

**refraction** [RI•frak•shuhn] The bending of light waves as they pass from one material to another (p. 282)

**relative density** [RE•la•tiv DEN•suh•tee] It determines whether one substance will sink or float in another substance (p. 111)

**renewable resource** [ri•NOO•uh•buhl REE•sawrs] A resource that can be replaced within a reasonable amount of time (p. 356)

**revolve** [ri•VAWLV] To go around, or orbit, another object (p. 436)

**rotate** [ROH•tayt] To spin on an axis (p. 438)

**runoff** [RUHN•awf] Water that does not soak into the ground and instead flows across Earth's surface (p. 399)

## S

**science** [SY•uhns] The study of the natural world through observation and investigation (p. 5)

**scientific methods** [sy•uhn•TIF•ik METH•uhds] The different ways that scientists perform investigations and collect reliable data (p. 22)

**sedimentary rock** [sed•uh•MEN•tuh•ree RAHK] A type of rock that forms when layers of sediment are pressed together (p. 308)

**series circuit** [SIR•eez SER•kit] An electric circuit in which the electrical charges have only one path to follow (p. 230)

**solid** [SAHL•id] The state of matter in which a substance has a definite shape and a definite volume (p. 113)

**solubility** [sawl•yoo•BIL•i•tee] The ability of a substance to dissolve in another substance (p. 115)

**solution** [suh•LOO•shuhn] A mixture that has the same composition throughout because all its parts are mixed evenly (p. 128)

**spring scale** [SPRING SKAYL] A tool used to measure force (p. 47)

**static electricity** [STAT•ik ee•lek•TRIS•uh•tee] The buildup of electric charges on an object (p. 215)

**succession** [suhk•SESH•uhn] A gradual change of the kinds of organisms in an ecosystem (p. 506)

## T

**technology** [tek•NAHL•uh•jee] The use of science knowledge to solve practical problems (p. 68)

**temperature** [TEM•per•uh•cher] The measure of the average energy of motion of particles of matter, which we feel as how hot or cold something is (pp. 110, 199)

**thermal energy** [THUR•muhl EN•er•jee] The total amount of kinetic energy of the particles in a substance (p. 198)

**translucent** [trahns•LOO•suhnt] Allows only some light to pass through (p. 279)

**transparent** [trahns•PAIR•uhnt] Allows light to pass through (p. 279)

## U

**unbalanced forces** [uhn•BAL•uhnst FAWRS•iz] Forces that cause a change in an object's motion because they don't cancel each other out (p. 154)

## V

**variable** [VAIR•ee•uh•buhl] Any condition that can be changed in an experiment (p. 29)

**volume** [VAHL•yoom] The amount of space something takes up (p. 108)

**volume** [VAHL•yoom] The loudness of a sound (p. 252)

## W

**water cycle** [WAW•ter SY•kuhl] The process in which water continuously moves from Earth's surface into the atmosphere and back again (p. 399)

**wave** [WAYV] A disturbance that carries energy, such as sound or light, through matter or space (p. 250)

**weather** [WETH•er] The condition of the atmosphere at a certain place and time (p. 412)

**weathering** [WETH•er•ing] The breaking down of rocks on Earth's surface into smaller pieces (p. 300)

# Index

**Note:** Page numbers in **boldface** type show where terms are highlighted and defined.

## A

## B

D

U

X

Y

Z